ENGLISH RENAISSANCE
THEATRE HISTORY
a reference guide

A
Reference
Guide
to
Literature

James L. Harner
Editor

ENGLISH RENAISSANCE THEATRE HISTORY

a reference guide

DAVID STEVENS

G.K.HALL&CO.

70 LINCOLN STREET, BOSTON, MASS.

Library of Congress Cataloging in Publication Data

Stevens, David, 1947-
  English Renaissance theatre history.

  Includes index.
  1.   Theater--England--History--16th century--Bibliog-
raphy.   2.   Theater--England--History--17th century--
Bibliography.   I.   Title.
Z2014.D7S78   [PN2589]   016.792'0942   82-2965
ISBN 0-8161-8361-9   AACR2

This publication is printed on permanent/durable acid-free paper
MANUFACTURED IN THE UNITED STATES OF AMERICA

Contents

The Author   vi

Preface   vii

Acknowledgments   ix

Introduction   xi

Abbreviations   xv

English Renaissance Theatre History   1

Index   319

The Author

David Stevens is associate professor of theatre and chairman of the Department of Theatre and Dance at Oakland University. His articles and reviews have appeared in Theatre Journal, Extrapolation, The Scope of the Fantastic, Survey of Science Fiction Literature, and Choice. He has delivered papers at the annual meetings of the American Theatre Association, the Speech Communication Association, and the Popular Culture Association. In 1972 he was awarded a Woodrow Wilson Fellowship while completing the Ph.D. at Bowling Green University; more recently, he participated in a National Endowment for the Humanities Summer Seminar at the University of Iowa in 1981.

Preface

This reference guide provides an annotated, chronological list of the
scholarship from 1664 through 1979 on Elizabethan theatrical history.
My intention was to compile a comprehensive guide, with brief annotations to aid the researcher in determining whether a specific item
might be helpful. I quickly discovered that the enumerative bibliographer is far more dependent than I had thought on the works of his
or her predecessors. Consequently, the term "comprehensive" must be
applied with caution. I began with existing bibliographies (silently
correcting their errors as I expect to be corrected), adding all other
scholarship that I could find. I was, however, dependent upon
indexes for many of my additions--I could not page through each volume
of every journal that might have a relevant item in it. Therefore,
it is probably safe to assume that I have missed some, especially
short notes that are frequently not indexed. While I have found many
of·these brief notes (especially in the Times Literary Supplement and
Notes and Queries), I look forward to filling in the gaps at some
future time. For now, I am reasonably sure that I have not missed
many major items.

Since the field the guide covers is theatre history, I have
eliminated almost all items whose scope is purely literary. The
exceptions are those whose titles might lead a reader to believe they
deal with the theatrical, and those that were listed in one or more
of the bibliographies usually consulted for theatrical history, particularly volume I of the New Cambridge Bibliography of English
Literature. I have also arbitrarily excluded almost all editions of
Shakespeare (even though many contain basic discussions of the
Elizabethan stage), as well as almost all general histories of the
theatre.

I have chosen a chronological organization simply because my
other alternative--a topical organization--would have yielded too
many cross-references, since many of these items would fit under two
or more categories. As a partial remedy I offer the Index, which
includes both authors and subjects, with frequent cross-references to
the Index in the text. (The note "See Index . . ." in an annotation
refers to the Index in the present volume, not that in the work cited.)

The annotations are in all but two or three cases my own; the only exceptions are quotations from English abstracts of foreign-language articles, always credited. I have attempted to be descriptive rather than evaluative in my comments, although at times my biases may be apparent. I have also severely limited my comments, with the result that at times I devote more space to a brief article than to a major book. The amount of space taken up by an annotation should not be read as an indication of comparative value; my intention is to provide a guide to purpose, scope, and method so that the scholar can decide if seeing an item might be valuable.

Many of the American and Canadian dissertations listed were annotated from authors' abstracts published in <u>Dissertation Abstracts</u> and <u>Dissertation Abstracts International</u>. Those dissertations for which abstracts were not so available were annotated from the complete dissertation or from photocopies of selected pages from the library of the degree-granting institution. In one case the author graciously provided me with photocopies from his Australian dissertation.

An asterisk (*) preceding an entry number indicates that I have not personally seen the item. For each such entry I have provided my source for the reference.

Acknowledgments

One of the greatest joys of completing a project such as this one lies in the contemplation of all those who provided substantial assistance. While this list is necessarily incomplete (if for no other reason than the fact that so many librarians do their yeoman's work anonymously), I owe a large debt to each of the individuals and groups named below. To all, my profound thanks.

- The Oakland University Research Committee, who provided two small grants for the purchase of materials and a Faculty Research Fellowship for the summer of 1980. Without this material assistance, this Reference Guide would have ended somewhere around 1910.

- The Interlibrary Loan Department of the Oakland University Library, especially Mary Wright before her departure and Linda Guyotte, who cheerfully processed literally hundreds of requests for obscure, foreign, or sometimes handwritten items. Their success rate was remarkable.

- Tamara McIntyre, Beth Grafe, and Kathy Bradley, present and former Oakland University students, who provided valuable translation services for many items in French and German.

- Professor Jane Eberwein, my colleague in English at Oakland University, who interrupted a vacation to gather material for me in the Cornell University Library.

- The staffs of the Reference Deparment and the Rare Books Room of the University of Michigan Library, where I lived for what seemed months at a time.

- Professor Adeline Hirschfeld-Medalia, my colleague in Communication Arts and Director of the Theatre Arts Program at Oakland University, who helped arrange my teaching schedule for two years to provide the maximum amount of time for research and writing.

- Professor James L. Harner, friend and colleague, mentor and editor, who was willing to take a chance, and who has provided

Acknowledgments

advice and encouragement every step of the way.

- Professor Carol D. Stevens, my colleague, friend, and spouse, who alone knows the extent to which this work is hers as well as mine.

To all of you, and to all the others who have helped in this project, thanks, thanks, and ever thanks. What virtues it may have are due to your assistance; its vices, of course, are mine own.

Introduction

The English theatre during the reigns of Elizabeth I, James I, and Charles I (1558-1642) developed from its humble medieval origins into one of the finest flowerings of the player's art that the world has yet seen. William Shakespeare, of course, stands head and shoulders above the rest of the theatre artists of the period, but this was also the time of great actors such as Richard Burbage and Edward Alleyn, the influential designer and architect Inigo Jones, and other great playwrights such as Ben Jonson and Christopher Marlowe. Standing in the shadow of these giants were many theatre artists who would themselves have been considered among the best of their age had they lived at any other time--actor Nathan Field, playwrights John Fletcher and James Shirley, to name but a few. But because there are so few written records, only a half-dozen or so murky drawings, and a few tantalizingly vague eyewitness accounts, we actually know very little about one of the greatest periods of theatrical history. What we do know we owe to the efforts of the theatre historians whose work is the subject of this volume.

What is a theatre historian? He or she is a scholar whose particular interest is the description and explanation of the art form of <u>the theatre</u> as it has existed in the past and developed into the present.[1] I say <u>the theatre</u> very specifically as opposed to <u>the drama</u>, because the two are not synonymous. Drama is a separate art form, a variety of literature. Theatre is concerned with the physical aspects of play production: the playhouses, actors and acting, costumes, stage lighting, music, and so on. Theatre history is also concerned with what might be termed the sociological and political aspects of production: the nature of the audience and the actor-audience relationship, government control, debates about propriety and decorum. Economics, too, interests the theatre historian: how productions are financed is often a crucial question.

As is the case with other historians, the discovery and interpretation of evidence is crucial to the theatre historian's task. Objectivity is the ideal, and the ultimate goal is the determination of the historical facts. Unfortunately, in this as in other areas of human endeavor, "historical facts" are elusive creatures, apparently changing as our society (and hence our point of view) changes. Perhaps the best that can be hoped for is an interpretation of whatever evidence may be unearthed consonant with our current view of history and our best effort at objectivity.

This is at least part of the reason, I think, that scholarship in the field of Elizabethan theatre history (as this field is conventionally called, despite the fact that part of it is Jacobean and Caroline rather than Elizabethan) is cyclical. Herbert Berry has discussed this cycles,[2] dividing the scholarship to date into three periods, breaking at the publication dates of the two major reference works in the field: Chambers's The Elizabethan Stage (1923.2), and Bentley's final volumes of The Jacobean and Caroline Stage (1968.2). Berry sees the earliest period as dominated by the Germans and focusing on the alternation theory; the middle period as dominated by J. C. Adams and focusing on the debate on the inner stage; and the present period as focusing on single-playhouse studies and what we consider to be tight control of acceptable evidence. The evidence has not changed (or at least, not very much); what we make of it (our vision of "the historical facts") has.

Within Berry's useful framework, I would like to distinguish a few of the more than 1600 works that follow as landmarks of the history of the Elizabethan theatre history.

Heading the list would be Edmund Malone, the first important Elizabethan theatre historian. In his seminal Historical Account of the Rise and Progress of the English Stage (1790.1) and Boswell's later edition of it (1823.1), Malone revealed the fruits of his labors among the many documents he discovered. Some of these documents have since been lost, and we have only Malone's transcriptions to go on. All theatre historians working in this field owe a major debt to this pioneering scholar.

The nineteenth century was virtually dominated by two giants in the field: James Orchard Halliwell-Phillipps and John Payne Collier. Both worked extensively with documents, producing many important works of interpretation. Unfortunately, some of the documents that Collier "discovered" were in fact his forgeries, creating a controversy that echoes into our own time. Nonetheless, we would do the man's memory a disservice if we did not acknowledge his many important contributions.

Perhaps the single most important discovery in the history of the field was made in 1888 by Karl Theodor Gaedertz. In the University of Utrecht library Gaedertz found a copy of a contemporary sketch of the Swan Playhouse--the now famous and widely reproduced DeWitt/VanBuchell drawing. From that day to this, no historian can afford to ignore the Swan drawing. It may be rejected, it may be accepted as flawed, or it may be accepted as it stands, but it must be considered. Our current understanding of the physical features of the playhouse stages of the period owes a great deal to this single sketch.

Another important document that much of our present knowledge of the Elizabethan theatre is based on was published by W. W. Greg in 1904, 1907, and 1908: Philip Henslowe's diary and account books. Henslowe was an entrepeneur, investor, and theatre owner, and his meticulous accounts are an invaluable resource. Collier had earlier published an edition, but Greg's stood as a landmark in the field for many years.

Probably the most diligent document-finder the field has known, Charles William Wallace, was active from about 1905 to about 1915. Wallace combed the Public Record Office with his wife during those years, trumpeting each new discovery (especially about Shakespeare) in the popular press. The Wallaces engaged in spirited competition with another, less well-known, document searcher, Mrs. Charlotte Carmichael Stopes, who published alternate interpretations of many of the same documents.

Mrs. Stopes was involved in the two major controversies in the field during the second decade of the twentieth century, over the authenticity of the seventeenth-century Revels Accounts, and over the site of the Globe Playhouse. The debates were fascinating, if somewhat repetitive, and both can be followed through the years with the use of the Index to this reference guide.

The scholar whose name appears most frequently in these pages is W. J. Lawrence. It has been said that wherever the theatre historian ventures, he will find the footprints of this man. Certainly this is the case in the field of Elizabethan theatre history. His many articles and collections must be consulted by the contemporary scholar, and frequently we find that, even after fifty years, we can add nothing to Lawrence's conclusions. His lack of an academic appointment or a private income forced him to write for popular consumption, but popularization did not diminish the quality of his scholarship.

Joseph Quincy Adams published two remarkable books in 1917, Shakespearean Playhouses and The Dramatic Records of Sir Henry Herbert, Master of the Revels. The former was concerned exclusively with the exteriors and locations of the various playhouses, and is still valuable, and the latter is indispensable for tracing the repertories and production patterns of the various playhouses and companies in the latter part of the period.

As previously mentioned, E. K. Chambers's The Elizabethan Stage stands preeminent among the early studies. While somewhat in need of revision in light of more than fifty years of subsequent scholarship, it still ranks as one of the two most valuable works yet produced in the field. Leslie Hotson attempted the same task for a later period in his <u>Commonwealth and Restoration Stage</u> (1928), and many of the documents he prints concern the earlier time.

A slim volume that received little critical attention at the time was published by George F. Reynolds in 1940. <u>The Staging of Elizabethan Plays at the Red Bull Theatre, 1605-1625</u>, however, has since become one of the most influential works in the field. Almost all studies of staging since use some variation on the method that Reynolds pioneered.

John Cranford Adams made a much greater immediate impact with his <u>The Globe Playhouse: Its Design and Equipment</u> in 1942. Unlike Reynolds's, however, Adams's theories have been in constant decline since the middle fifties. To this day, however, it is Adams's reconstruction of the Globe that most people think of in connection with the Elizabethan theatre. Despite being discredited by two generations of scholarship, it remains perhaps the most influential single work yet produced.

Hotson, J. C. Adams, and Reynolds all first entered the field through their work on doctoral dissertations. In 1941 G. E. Bentley published a revised and expanded version of his dissertation that has developed into one of the two most important works in the field. <u>The Jacobean and Caroline Stage</u>, continued in 1956 and 1968, ranks with Chambers's great work as part of the backbone of all Elizabethan theatre history studies.

As we come closer to our own time it is more difficult to pick out the landmarks, probably because we are too close to them yet. Certainly among the most important recent scholars in the field I would list Richard Hosley, C. Walter Hodges, Glynne Wickham, Herbert Berry, John Orrell, T. J. King, and David Bergeron. And there are so many others who could easily be added to such a list. Rather than try to be comprehensive and offend anyone, I invite readers to examine the scholarship and decide for themselves its value.

Notes

1. Oscar J. Brockett, "Research in Theatre History," <u>Educational Theatre Journal</u> 19, no. 2A (June 1967):267-75.

2. Herbert Berry, "Americans in the Playhouses," <u>Shakespeare Studies</u> 9 (1976):31-44.

Abbreviations

ADDT	American Dissertations in Drama and Theatre
AnRS	Annual Report of Studies (Kyoto, Japan)
Archiv	Archiv für das Studium der Neueren Sprachen und Literaturen
ArchivL	Archiv für Litteraturgeschichte
ArchR	Architectural Review
ArtJ	Art Journal
BLR	Bodleian Library Record
BMg	Burlington Magazine
BNYPL	Bulletin of the New York Public Library
CE	College English
Century	Century Monthly Magazine
CHEL	Cambridge History of English Literature
CM	Current Musicology
ColQ	Colorado Quarterly
CompD	Comparative Drama
ContempR	Contemporary Review
CUS	Colorado University Studies
DEAL	Dissertations in English and American Literature

Abbreviations

DuV	Dichtung und Volkstum
EA	Etudes Anglaises: Grande-Bretagne, Etats-Unis
E&S	Essays and Studies (London)
EHR	English Historical Review
EIE	English Institute Essays
ELH	ELH [formerly Journal of English Literary History]
ELR	English Literary Renaissance
ES	English Studies: A Journal of English Language and Literature
ESRS	Emporia State Research Studies (Kansas)
EStudien	Englische Studien
ETJ	Educational Theatre Journal
FortR	Fortnightly Review
GMg	Gentlemen's Magazine
GRM	Germanisch-Romanische Monatsschrift
GuildMisc	Guildhall Miscellany
Harper's	Harper's Monthly Magazine
HLB	Harvard Library Bulletin
HLQ	Huntington Library Quarterly
ISLL	Illinois Studies in Language and Literature
JBArA	Journal of the British Archaeological Association
JDSG	Jahrbuch der Deutschen Shakespeare-Gesellschaft
JDSh	Jahrbuch der Deutschen Shakespeare-Gessellschaft West (Heidelberg)

Abbreviations

JEGP	Journal of English and Germanic Philology
JHI	Journal of the History of Ideas
JMRS	Journal of Medieval and Renaissance Studies
JRIBA	Journal of the Royal Institute of British Architects
JWCI	Journal of the Warburg and Courtland Institutes
L&LT	Life and Letters Today
Lippincott's	Lippincott's Monthly Magazine
LQHR	London Quarterly and Holborn Review
M&L	Music and Letters
MLN	MLN [formerly Modern Language Notes]
MLQ	Modern Language Quarterly
MLR	Modern Language Review
MP	Modern Philology: A Journal Devoted to Research in Medieval and Modern Literature
MSC	Malone Society Collections
MuK	Maske und Kothurn: Internationale Beiträge zur Theaterwissenschaft
MusAnt	Musical Antiquary
MusQ	Musical Quarterly
N&Q	Notes and Queries
N&QSD	Notes and Queries for Somerset and Dorset
NCBEL	New Cambridge Bibliography of English Literature
Neophil	Neophilologus (Netherlands)
NS	Die Neueren Sprachen
NTM	New Theatre Magazine

Abbreviations

NYCROJ	North Yorkshire County Record Office Journal
NYRB	New York Review of Books
ORRD	Opportunities for Research in Renaissance Drama [later RORD]
PAPS	Proceedings of the American Philosophical Society
PBA	Proceedings of the British Academy
PMLA	PMLA: Publications of the Modern Language Association
PMPA	Publications of the Missouri Philological Association
PMusA	Proceedings of the Musical Association
PP	Philologica Pragensia
PQ	Philological Quarterly
PRMA	Proceedings of the Royal Musical Association
PRPSG	Proceedings of the Royal Philosophical Society of Glasgow
QJS	Quarterly Journal of Speech
QQ	Queen's Quarterly
QR	Quarterly Review
REEDN	Records of Early English Drama Newsletter
RenD	Renaissance Drama
RenN	Renaissance News
RenP	Renaissance Papers
RES	Review of English Studies: A Quarterly Journal of English Literature and the English Language
RHT	Revue d'Histoire du Théâtre

Abbreviations

RLC	Revue de Littérature Comparée
RORD	Research Opportunities in Renaissance Drama
RTh	Revue Théatral
SAQ	South Atlantic Quarterly
SCJ	Sixteenth Century Journal
Scribner's	Scribner's Monthly Magazine
SCSML	Smith College Studies in Modern Language
SEL	Studies in English Literature, 1500-1900
SFQ	Southern Folklore Quarterly
ShAB	Shakespeare Association Bulletin
ShFQ	Shakespeare Fellowship Quarterly
ShN	Shakespeare Newsletter
ShS	Shakespeare Survey: An Annual Survey of Shakespearian Study and Production
ShSP	Shakespeare Society Papers
ShSt	Shakespeare Studies
ShStage	Shakespeare Stage
ShStudies	Shakespeare Studies (Tokyo)
SIMG	Sammelbände der Internationalen Musik-Gesellschaft
SMC	Studies in Medieval Culture
SMNN	Selborne Magazine and Nature Notes
SP	Studies in Philology
SpMon	Speech Monographs
SQ	Shakespeare Quarterly
SR	Sewanee Review

SRO	Shakespearean Research and Opportunities: The Report of the MLA Conference
TDR	The Drama Review [formerly Tulane Drama Review]
ThArts	Theatre Arts Monthly
ThR	Theatre Research International
ThS	Theatre Survey: The American Journal of Theatre History
ThW	Theatre Workshop
TJ	Theatre Journal [formerly ETJ]
TLS	Times Literary Supplement (London)
TN	Theatre Notebook: A Journal of the History and Technique of the British Theatre
TQ	Texas Quarterly
TR	Texas Review
TrLeLPS	Transactions of the Leicester Literary and Philosophical Society
TrLMArchS	Transactions of the London and Middlesex Archaeological Society
TrNShS	Transactions of the New Shakspere Society
TrRHS	Transactions of the Royal Historical Society
TrRSL	Transactions of the Royal Society of Literature
TrWASAL	Transactions of the Wisconsin Academy of Science, Art, and Literature
TSL	Tennessee Studies in Literature
TSLL	Texas Studies in Literature and Language: A Journal of the Humanities
UNS	University of Nebraska Studies

Abbreviations

UR	Universal Review
WRUB	Bulletin of Western Reserve University
YR	Yale Review: A National Quarterly
ZDP	Zeitschrift für Deutsche Philologie
ZFEU	Zeitschrift für Französichen und Englischen Unterricht

English Renaissance Theatre History

1664

1 FLECKNOE, RICHARD. "A Short Discourse of the English Stage."
   In Love's Kingdom. London: Printed by R. Wood, sigs.
   G4^r - G8^r.
      The earliest extant attempt at a history of the Eliza-
   bethan stage. Flecknoe notes companies using inns, praises
   Burbage and Field for their acting ability, and lists
   Shakespeare, Jonson, and Fletcher as the best playwrights.
   He refers to the stages as "simple," with old tapestry and
   rushes. Reprinted: 1909.11; 1957.7; 1963.3; 1972.33;
   1973.5.

1699

1 WRIGHT, JAMES. Historia Histrionica: An Historical Account
   of the English Stage. London: printed by G. Groom, for
   W. Hawes, 36 pp.
      Set up as "A Dialogue of Plays and Players," this is
   the second attempt at a history and the first important one.
   Wright emphasizes the medieval origins in discussing both
   acting and playhouses. Much of the information presented
   has since been verified from historical records. See
   1845.1. Reprinted: 1872.2; 1874.3; 1876.2; 1972.33.

1788

1 NICHOLS, JOHN. The Progresses and Public Processions of Queen
   Elizabeth. Vols. 1 and 2. London: J. Nichols, 1230 pp.
      Comprehensive compilation of works presented during the
   Queen's progresses and on other occasions. For vol. 3, see
   1805.1. Reprinted: 1823.1.

<u>1790</u>

1 MALONE, EDMOND, ed. "An Historical Account of the Rise and
    Progress of the English Stage, and of the Economy and
    Usages of Our Ancient Theatres." In <u>Plays and Poems of</u>
    <u>William Shakespeare</u>. Vol. 1, pt. 2. London: J.
    Rivington & Sons, 294 pp.
        The earliest scholarly history; based on documentary
    sources, some of which have since been lost. Although
    Malone carries his history to roughly 1740, he concentrates
    on the pre-Restoration stage. <u>See</u> 1842.1. Reprinted:
    1790.2; 1794.1; 1799.2; 1800.1; 1813.4; 1821.1; 1839.1;
    1901.3.

2 _____. <u>An Historical Account of the Rise and Progress of the</u>
    <u>English Stage, and of the Economy and Usages of Our Ancient</u>
    <u>Theatres</u>. London: H. Baldwin, 294 pp.
        Reprint of 1790.1.

<u>1794</u>

1 MALONE, EDMOND, ed. "Historical Account of the Rise and
    Progress of the English Stage; of the Economy and Usages
    of Our Ancient Theatres; and of the Original Actors in
    Shakespeare's Plays." In <u>Plays and Poems of William</u>
    <u>Shakespeare</u>. Vol. 2. Dublin: Exshaw, 346 pp.
        A reprint of 1790.1, with an additional section on the
    actors of the Chamberlain's/King's Men.

<u>1797</u>

1 CHALMERS, GEORGE. "Of the History of the Stage." In <u>An</u>
    <u>Apology for the Believers in the Shakspeare Papers, Which</u>
    <u>Were Exhibited in Norfolk-Street</u>. London: Thomas Egerton,
    pp. 339-471.
        An attempt at a comprehensive history of the stage in
    England, chiefly composed of additions and corrections to
    1790.1. Chalmers begins his treatment of the Elizabethan
    period with a discussion of the boy companies, then goes
    on to the adult companies, government regulation, the
    playhouses, and the actors. Reprinted: 1799.1; 1813.4;
    1821.1.

1798

1 ELLIS, HENRY. The History and Antiquities of the Parish of
St. Leonard Shoreditch and Liberty of Norton Folgate in
the Suburbs of London. London: J. Nichols, pp. 208-12.
  The relevant section includes information about the
Theatre and the Curtain, both of which were built in
Shoreditch, and on actors and playwrights associated with
the parish. Lists entries related to the Curtain in the
parish register from 1580 to 1639.

1799

1 CHALMERS, GEORGE. "Of the History of the Stage." In A Sup-
plemental Apology for the Believers in the Shakespeare
Papers: Being a Reply to Mr. Malone's Answer, Which Was
Early Announced, but Never Published. London: Thomas
Egerton, pp. 147-92.
  Reprint of 1797.1.

2 MALONE, EDMOND, ed. "An Historical Account of the Rise and
Progress of the English Stage, and of the Economy and
Usages of Our Ancient Theatres." In The Plays of William
Shakespeare. Vol. 3. Basil: J. J. Tourneisen, 430 pp.
  Reprint of 1790.1.

1800

1 MALONE, EDMOND. An Historical Account of the Rise and Progress
of the English Stage, and of the Economy and Usages of the
Ancient Theatres in England. Basil: J. J. Tourneisen,
423 pp.
  Reprint of 1790.1.

1805

1 NICHOLS, JOHN. The Progresses and Public Processions of Queen
Elizabeth. Vol. 3. London: J. Nichols, 682 pp.
  Continuation of 1788.1. Reprinted: 1823.1.

1813

1 HASLEWOOD, JOSEPH [Eu. Hood]. "Of the London Theatres. No.
I." GMg 83, pt. 2 (August):121-23.

1813

       Presents information on the Fortune, from the contract
and other contemporary sources. This is the first of a
series on theatres of the period. See also 1813.2; 1813.3;
1814.1. Reprinted: 1837.1.

2   ___. "Of the London Theatres, No. II." GMg 83, pt. 2
    (September):217-8.
       Examines the Whitefriars, supposedly pulled down in
1580, and the Salisbury Court. Part of a series. See also
1813.1; 1813.3; 1814.1. Reprinted: 1837.1.

3   ___. "Of the London Theatres. No. IV." GMg 83, pt. 2
    (November):437.
       Brief discussion of the Rose, the Hope, and the Swan.
Part of a series; see also 1813.1; 1813.2; 1814.1.
Reprinted: 1837.1.

4 MALONE, EDMUND. "An Historical Account of the English Stage."
    In Works of William Shakespeare. Vol. 3. Edited by Samuel
    Johnson and George Steevens. New York: D. Appleton & Co.,
    541 pp.
       Reprint of 1790.1, with additions related to the
Henslowe papers and Chalmers (1797.1). See also 1821.1.

<u>1814</u>

1 HASLEWOOD, JOSEPH [Eu. Hood]. "Of the London Theatres. No.
    VI." GMg 84, pt. 1 (April):337-39.
       Discusses Paul's Boys and their playhouse. Part of a
series; see also 1813.1-3. Reprinted: 1837.1.

<u>1821</u>

1 MALONE, EDMOND. "Mr. Malone's Historical Account of the Rise
    and Progress of the English Stage, and of the Economy and
    Usages of Our Ancient Theatres." In The Plays and Poems
    of William Shakespeare. Vol. 1. Edited by James Boswell
    the younger. London: F. C. and J. Rivington, 522 pp.
    [Boswell's Malone.]
       Reprint of 1790.1, with additions from 1813.1, includ-
ing Chalmers (1797.1) and a new appendix by Malone.

1823

1 NICHOLS, JOHN. The Progresses and Public Processions of Queen
   Elizabeth. 3 vols. London: J. Nichols, 1912 pp.
      Reprint of 1788.1 and 1805.1.

1825

1 WILKINSON, ROBERT. Londina Illustrata. Vol. 2, Theatrum
   Illustrata: Graphic and Historic Memorials of Ancient
   Playhouses, Modern Theatres, and Other Places of Amusement
   in the Cities and Suburbs of London and Westminster.
   London: R. Wilkinson, plates 165-73.
      Contains reproductions of nine engravings and woodcuts
   showing London theatres, including the baiting houses,
   the Globe and the Rose (transposed), two other views of the
   Globe, the Swan (the Antwerp view), the Red Bull, and the
   second Fortune. Wilkinson provides brief descriptions.

1826

*1 BRAYLEY, EDWARD WEDLAKE. Historical and Descriptive Accounts
   of the Theatres of London. Illustrated by Daniel Havell.
   London: J. Taylor, 92 pp.
      Cited in NUC Pre-1956 Imprints 73:310. Reprinted:
   1833.1.

1828

1 NICHOLS, JOHN. The Progresses, Processions, and Magnificent
   Festivities of King James the First, his Royal Consort,
   Family and Court. 4 vols. London: J. B. Nichols, 2552 pp.
      Comprehensive compilation of "poetical panegyrics; des-
   criptions of various solemnities and festivities; or
   dramatic performances" including forty masques and ten
   civic pageants, arranged chronologically.

1831

1 COLLIER, J[OHN] PAYNE. The History of English Dramatic
   Poetry to the Time of Shakespeare; and Annals of the Stage
   to the Restoration. 3 vols. London: J. Murray, 1450 pp.
      An ambitious early work, preceded only by Malone
   (1790.1). The first volume begins with the "Annals of the

1831

Stage," a lengthy recitation of documentary evidence
related to play production. This is completed in the
second volume, which also begins "The History of Dramatic
Poetry." The third volume completes this section and also
contains "An Account of the Old Theatres of London,"
"Details Connected with the Performance of Plays," and an
index. See 1844.5; 1861.1; and 1886.4. See also the
much revised second edition, 1879.2.

1833

1 BRAYLEY, EDWARD WEDLAKE. Historical and Descriptive Accounts
of the Theatres of London. Illustrated by Daniel Havell.
London: J. Yates, 92 pp.
The first chapter mentions the Phoenix in passing as
preparation for a discussion of Restoration playhouses.
Reprint of 1826.1.

1836

1 KEMPE, ALFRED JOHN, ed. The Losely Manuscripts. London:
J. Murray, pp. 15-117.
An edition of the well-known manuscripts containing a
good deal of documentary evidence concerning the Elizabethan theatre. The relevant section contains a brief
discussion of the career of Sir Thomas Carwarden, Master of
the Revels, and various documents related to his office.

1837

1 HASLEWOOD, JOSEPH. "Account of the Old London Theatres." In
Roxburghe Revels, and Other Related Papers. Edited by
James Maidment. Edinburgh: Roxburghe Club, pp. 85-128.
Reprint of 1813.1-3; 1814.1.

2 NICHOLS, JOHN GOUGH. London Pageants. London: J. B. Nichols
& Son, 125 pp.
Contains accounts of fifty-five royal processions and
entertainments in London from 1236 to 1831 and a bibliog-
raphical list of Lord Mayor's Pageants from 1585 to 1831.
The accounts are taken from contemporary writers. See
Index, under Lord Mayor's Pageants, Royal Processions, and
Royal Progresses, for other references.

1839

1 MALONE, EDMOND. "An Historical Account of the English Stage."
   In Historical and Explanatory Notes with Various Readings
   Illustrative of the Works of W. Shakspeare. Paris:
   Baudry's European Library, pp. liii-lxxxiv.
       Reprint of 1790.1, with additions from 1813.1 and
   1821.1.

1841

1 COLLIER, J[OHN] PAYNE. Memoirs of Edward Alleyn, Founder of
   Dulwich College: Including Some New Particulars Respecting
   Shakespeare, Ben Jonson, Massinger, Marston, Dekker, &c.
   London: Shakespeare Society, 219 pp.
       A biography of the important actor, based on manuscripts
   held at Dulwich College. Included in an appendix is
   Alleyn's part for Orlando Furioso, one of the most important extant documents from this period. Collier cites
   documents freely, and many are in Alleyn's own hand.
   Henslowe's relationship with Alleyn and the founding of
   the College are fully detailed. Eight pages of notes and
   corrections, from other documents seen later, follow the
   text, as does an appendix including Alleyn's father's will,
   the part of Orlando, two legal documents, and the agreement
   for the building of the College. See Index, under Alleyn,
   for additional references. See 1843.1.

1842

1 CUNNINGHAM, PETER, ed. Extracts from the Accounts of the
   Revels at Court in the Reigns of Queen Elizabeth and King
   James I. London: Shakespeare Society, 228 pp.
       Contains a lengthy introduction by the editor describ-
   ing the circumstances of his discovery of these documents,
   of interest for what it tells us about nineteenth-century
   antiquarians as well as about the subject itself.
   Cunningham claims to correct several errors of Malone
   (1790.1). He provides an index of plays mentioned,
   although a more complete index would be helpful. These
   documents were later the subject of a continuing controversy over their genuineness. See Index under Revels
   Accounts.

1843

1 COLLIER, J[OHN] PAYNE, ed. <u>The Alleyn Papers: A Collection</u>
   <u>of Original Documents Illustrative of the Life and Times</u>
   <u>of Edward Alleyn</u>. London: Shakespeare Society, 110 pp.
       Additions to the earlier biography of Alleyn (1841.1),
   based on additional documents held by Halliwell-Phillipps.
   The introduction contains Collier's discussion of the
   documents, which form the bulk of the volume. Collier here
   concentrates on Alleyn's acquisition of wealth and accumu-
   lation of property. He also prints the actor's will. <u>See</u>
   Index, under Alleyn, for additional references.

2 FAIRHOLT, FREDERICH W[ILLIAM]. <u>Lord Mayor's Pageants: Being</u>
   <u>Collections Towards a History of These Annual Celebrations</u>.
   Percy Society, no. 10, pt. 1. London: Percy Society,
   178 pp.
       A history of the Lord Mayor's Pageants from 1236 to 1841.
   Fairholt describes the pageants for each year, based on
   contemporary records, and prints a selection in a companion
   volume.

1844

1 BRUCE, JOHN. "Who Was 'Will, My Lord of Leycester's Jesting
   Player'?" <u>ShSP</u> 1:88-95.
       The phrase alluded to in the title occurs in a letter of
   Sir Philip Sidney. Bruce narrows the possibilities to
   three, and concludes that Will Kempe was a likelier
   candidate than either William Shakespeare or Will Johnson.
   He then speculates that Leicester's Men (including
   Shakespeare) may have accompanied Sidney to the Low
   Countries in 1585. <u>See</u> <u>also</u> 1958.13; 1959.13.

2 DRAMATICUS [pseud.]. "On the Profits of Old Actors." ShSP
   1:21-23.
       A brief note citing corroborative evidence for the
   profitability of acting around 1600.

3 HALLIWELL[-PHILLIPPS], JAMES ORCHARD. <u>Tarleton's Jests, and</u>
   <u>News Out of Purgatory: With Notes, and Some Account of</u>
   <u>the Life of Tarleton</u>. London: Shakespeare Society, 182 pp.
       Essentially an edition of the two works, with a brief
   biography of the famous clown of Shakespeare's company.
   <u>See</u> Index, under Tarlton, for additional references.

4 HERBERT, J. F. "Additions to The Alleyn Papers." ShSP
   1:16-20.
   Contains four minor items, including a note signed by
   dramatist Robert Daborne; an agreement with a tailor signed
   by William Rowley, Joseph Taylor, and Robert Pallant;
   verses in the form of an acrostic by John Day; and a
   charitable appeal in prose, also by Day. The originals at
   the time were in the possession of the author, having been
   collected by his father and grandfather.

5 TOMLINS, THOMAS EDLYNE. "Origins of the Curtain Theatre, and
   Mistakes Regarding It." ShSP 1:29-35.
   Repudiates Collier's conjecture (in 1831.1) that the
   Curtain Playhouse drew its name from the similarly named
   land on which it stood (which may have been part of the
   fortifications of London) by publishing the documents
   Collier cited but did not print.

1845

1 CUNNINGHAM, PETER. "Did General Harrison Kill 'Dick
   Robinson' the Player?" ShSP 2:11-13.
   Confirms the suggestion (in 1699.1) that actor Richard
   Robinson was killed by General Harrison at the taking of
   Basing House by citing a previously unknown tract on the
   Great Rebellion held in the British Library.

2 _____. "Plays Acted at Court, Anno 1613 (from the Accounts
   of Lord Harrington, Treasurer of the Chamber to James I)."
   ShSP 2:123-26.
   The first printing of Joseph Haslewood's notes on the
   Treasurer's Account, as well as a brief history of the
   source from which they were derived.

3 FAIRHOLT, FREDERICK WILLIAM. The Civic Garland: A Collection
   of Songs from the London Pageants. Percy Society, no. 12.
   London: Percy Society, 134 pp.
   The subtitle explains the contents. Fairholt provides a
   lengthy introduction discussing his sources and a headnote
   for each of the twenty-eight songs included. Selections
   range from mid-sixteenth century to 1702.

4 HENSLOWE, PHILIP. The Diary of Philip Henslowe from 1591 to
   1609. Edited by John Payne Collier. London: Shakespeare
   Society, 290 pp.
   The first complete printing of the diary, but superseded
   by the editions of Greg (1904.7; 1907.15; 1908.11), Foakes

and Rickert (1961.13), and the facsimile (1977.8). Collier
provides copious annotations and the inventories in an
appendix. See also Malone's transcription of part of the
diary in 1790.1.

1846

1 COLLIER, J[OHN] PAYNE. Memoirs of the Principal Actors in the
   Plays of Shakespeare. London: Shakespeare Society, 296 pp.
      Brief biographies of the actors listed as principal
   players in the First Folio, with the exception of Shakespeare
   himself. They vary in length and detail, depending, of
   course, on what Collier knew of the actor. Thus, Richard
   Burbage is given fifty-six pages while Samuel Crosse rates
   two. Collier cites relevant documents fully. See Index
   under Actors and under names of individuals; and see
   especially Chambers (1923.2), Nungezer (1929.12), and
   Bentley (1941.1).

2 RIMBAULT, EDWARD F[RANCIS]. Who Was "Jack Wilson" the Singer
   of Shakespeare's Stage? London: John Russell Smith, 16 pp.
      Attempts to identify the Jack Wilson who played Balthazar
   in Much Ado about Nothing and composed music to several of
   Shakespeare's songs with Dr. John Wilson, who became Oxford
   Professor of Music in 1644.

1847

1 REARDON, JAMES PURCELL. "An Unknown Tract by Philip Stubbes,
   the Enemy of Theatrical Performances in 1583." ShSP
   3:15-21.
      A brief antitheatrical tract by the author of The Anato-
   my of Abuses, discovered by Reardon.

2 TOMLINS, THOMAS EDLYNE. "A New Document Regarding the Authority of the Master of the Revels Over Play-Makers, Plays,
   and Players, in 1581." ShSP 3:1-6.
      Text of the document giving Edmund Tylney extraordinary
   powers to command the services of any playwright or actor
   he saw fit and to imprison any who refuse. Tylney was also
   given the right to require any company to present any of
   their plays to him at any time.

3 TYSON, WILLIAM. "Heming's Players at Bristol in the Reign of
   Henry VIII." ShSP 3:13-14.
      A brief note disclosing discovery of a five-shilling

payment to "Mr. henings players" in Bristol in 1544. Tyson
speculates that this might have been the father of John
Heminge, first editor of Shakespeare.

1848

1 CUNNINGHAM, PETER; PLANCHE, J[AMES] R[OBINSON]; and COLLIER,
   J[OHN] PAYNE. Inigo Jones: A Life; Remarks on Some of his
   Sketches for Masques and Dramas; and Five Court Masques.
   London: Shakespeare Society, 148 pp.
        The earliest biography of Jones to cite records exten-
   sively, particularly with regard to the expenses of the
   masques for James I. The authors include a detailed
   examination of Jones's quarrel with Jonson, as well as a
   discussion of their collaboration. The volume places more
   emphasis on the architecture than the theatre work in
   discussing Jones's career, but the designs for the masques
   are discussed in the second essay. Five documents and
   fifteen costume sketches are included in an appendix. See
   Index, under Jones, for more references; and see especially
   1973.10 and 1973.21.

2 MACHYN, HENRY. The Diary of Henry Machyn, Citizen and
   Merchant-Taylor of London, from A.D. 1550 to A.D. 1563.
   Edited by John Gough Nichols. Camden Society Publications,
   no. 42. London: Camden Society, 464 pp.
        Contains first-hand descriptions of the Lord Mayor's
   Pageants of 1553-57 and 1561-62, and of a variety of
   interludes and plays. Frequently cited by Collier in
   1879.2.

1849

1 COLLIER, J[OHN] PAYNE. "Original History of 'The Theatre,' in
   Shoreditch, and Connexion of the Burbadge Family with It."
   ShSP 4:63-70.
        Discusses details of the lease of the grounds on which
   James Burbage built the Theatre in Shoreditch. Collier
   assumes that the statement that the Burbages and others
   tore down the building and carried the timber away to
   build another playhouse cannot be true, since he dates the
   first Globe at 1594 or 1595 rather than 1599. See Index,
   under Burbage, James, and under Theatre Playhouse; see also
   Stopes, Charlotte Carmichael, and Wallace, Charles William,
   for additional references.

1849

2 _____. "Richard Field (the Printer of Shakespeare's Venus and
Adonis and Lucrece), Nathaniel Field, Anthony Munday, and
Henry Chettle." ShSP 4:36-40.
Discloses details about the apprenticeship bindings of
actors Field, Munday, and Chettle, all of which were broken.

3 CUNNINGHAM, PETER. "Sir George Buc and the Office of the
Revels." ShSP 4:143-44.
A brief note including a letter from Sir George Buc,
ca. 1610, dealing with his loss of a house and his request
for help from the Earl of Salisbury.

4 _____. "The Whitefriars Theatre, the Salisbury Court Theatre,
and the Duke's Theatre in Dorset Gardens." ShSP 4:89-109.
Consists primarily of five sixteenth-century documents
related to theatrical affairs at these three playhouses.
Included are the Indenture on 15 July 1629 of the Earl of
Dorset; Heton's Instructions for his Patent and Draught of
the same; Bird's "Instructions Touching Salisbury Court
Playhouse, 14 Septem., 1639," made on behalf of William
Beeston; and Tyrrill, Wyndham, and Archer's deposition
against Beeston, 1667.

5 DRAMATICUS [pseud.]. "The Players Who Acted in The Shoemaker's
Holiday, 1600, a Comedy by Thomas Dekker and Robert Wilson."
ShSP 4:110-22.
The anonymous author's anonymous friend provided him with
a copy of the play with Wilson's name accompanying Dekker's
at the end of an epistle to the reader, and the same copy
has the names of the actors of the principal roles written
in as they enter.

6 FORMAN, SIMON. The Autobiography and Personal Diary of Dr.
Simon Forman the Celebrated Astrologer, from A.D. 1552 to
A.D. 1602, from the Unpublished Manuscripts in the
Ashmolean Museum, Oxford. Edited by James Orchard
Halliwell [-Phillipps]. London: privately printed, 32 pp.
Does not include Forman's eyewitness accounts of four
of Shakespeare plays. See 1876.1.

7 HALLIWELL[-PHILLIPPS], J[AMES] O[RCHARD]. "Dispute Between
the Earl of Worcester's Players and the Corporation of
Leicester in 1586: From the Records of that City." ShSP
4:145-46.
Records of an attempt in 1586 by the city fathers of
Leicester to bribe Lord Worcester's Players into not
performing in their community and the subsequent quarrel
that developed.

8 REARDON, JAMES PURCELL. "Two Specimens of the Poetry of
     Philip Stubbes, Author of The Anatomy of Abuses, 1583, and
     the Enemy of Theatrical Performances, Unknown to Bibliog-
     raphers." ShSP 4:71-88.
        Two brief prose tracts, in the style of the Anatomy, and
     two pieces in rhymed couplets, all opposing the theatre and
     discovered by Reardon.

9 TOMLINS, T[HOMAS] EDLYNE. "Three New Privy Seals for Players
     in the Time of Shakespeare." ShSP 4:41-49.
        The privy seals for the Prince's Men, 1607; Queen Anne's
     Men, 1610; and the Duke of York's Men (later Charles I) are
     here printed for the first time.

                              1854

1 L., H. "'Retainers to Seven Shares and a Half.'" N&Q 9 (4
     March):199.
        Questions the meaning of the quotation from Crashaw.
     The editor responds with a brief description of the sharing
     system, with references to a variety of primary sources and
     to Collier (1831.1).

                              1855

1 KELLY, WILLIAM. Royal Progresses to Leicester. London:
     Leicester Mercury, 15 pp.
        Text of a paper read to the Leicester Literary and
     Philosophical Society on 29 January 1855. Includes accounts
     of visits by Elizabeth in 1575, 1576, and 1585; and by
     James I in 1612, 1614, and 1616; as well as by various
     members of the royal family in 1604, 1608, and 1612. Kelly
     includes various details of finance and spectacle, taken
     from historical records.

                              1857

1 SMITH, WILLIAM HENRY. Bacon and Shakespeare: An Inquiry
     Touching Players, Playhouses, and Play-Writers in the Days
     of Elizabeth. London: John Russell Smith, pp. 48-78.
        The relevant section examines players and playhouses
     briefly. Smith covers no new ground, but presents Collier
     (1831.1) and Malone (1790.1) as the ultimate authorities.

                              13

1858

1 HALL, S[AMUEL] C[ARTER], and HALL, Mrs. S[AMUEL] C[ARTER].
    "The Book of the Thames, from Its Rise to Its Fall. Part
    XXI." ArtJ, n.s. 4 (September):277-80.
       In part describes the Paris Garden, or Swan, and the
    Globe, with illustrations. Of little historical value.
    Reprinted: 1859.1; 1867.1; 1869.1; 1877.1.

1859

1 HALL, S[AMUEL] C[ARTER], and HALL, Mrs. S[AMUEL] C[ARTER].
    The Book of the Thames, from Its Rise to Its Fall. London:
    A. Hall, Virtue, & Col.
       Includes 1858.1.

1860

1 WRIGHT, GEORGE R. "The English Stage in the Year 1638."
    JBArA 16 (December):275-76.
       Discusses the list of plays acted "before the King and
    queene this year of our Lord, 1638." Wright mistakes the
    Cockpit-in-Court for Beeston's Cockpit (or Phoenix) Play-
    house in Drury Lane. He prints a facsimile of the
    document. Revised: 1887.13.

1861

1 INGLEBY, CLEMENT MANSFIELD. A Complete View of the Shakespeare
    Controversy. London: Nattali & Bond, 350 pp.
       Examines the question of Collier's alleged forgeries in
    detail, concluding that he indeed forged portions of at
    least seven documents used in 1831.1.

1865

1 KELLY, WILLIAM, ed. Notices Illustrative of the Drama and
    Other Popular Amusements Chiefly in the Sixteenth and
    Seventeenth Centuries Incidentally Illustrating Shakespeare
    and his Contemporaries; Extracted from the Chamberlain's
    Accounts and Other Manuscripts of the Borough of Leicester.
    London: John Russell Smith, 310 pp.
       The first 184 pages consist of a detailed introduction,
    which serves to focus for the reader the wealth of

1869

documentary material contained in the rest of the volume.
Prints extracts from documents from 1467 to 1749 illustrating the variety of popular entertainments available in
Leicester during those years. Most important for present
purposes is the section dealing with visits of the London
companies.

2 RYE, WILLIAM BRENCHLEY. England as Seen by Foreigners in the
   Days of Elizabeth and James the First: Comprising Translations of the Journals of the Two Dukes of Wartemberg in
   1592 and 1610, Both Illustrative of Shakespeare; With
   Extracts from the Travels of Foreign Princes and Others.
   London: J. R. Smith, 300 pp.
      Seventeen translations from five languages, from 1558
   to 1617, with three or four scattered theatrical references.

1867

1 HALL, S[AMUEL] C[ARTER], and HALL, Mrs. S[AMUEL] C[ARTER]. The
   Book of the Thames, from Its Rise to Its Fall. London:
   Alfred W. Bennett.
      Includes 1858.1.

1868

1 MANNINGHAM, JOHN. Diary of John Manningham, of the Middle
   Temple, and of Bradbourne, Kent, Barrister-at-Law, 1602-
   1603. Edited by John Bruce. Westminster: Camden Society,
   188 pp.
      An edition of the diary, which contains an eyewitness
   account of the Middle Temple production of Twelfth Night
   (p. 18) and a bawdy anecdote about Shakespeare and Richard
   Burbage (p. 39).

1869

1 HALL, S[AMUEL] C[ARTER], and HALL, Mrs. S[AMUEL] C[ARTER]. The
   Book of the Thames, from Its Rise to Its Fall. London and
   New York: Cassell, Petter, & Galpin.
      Includes 1858.1.

2 HAZLITT, W[ILLIAM] C[AREW], ed. English Drama and Stage Under
   the Tudor and Stuart Princes, 1543-1664. London: Roxburghe
   Library, 289 pp.
      Compilation of thirty-two documents and thirteen

1869

treatises dealing with stage history in the period.
Extremely valuable, although largely superseded by
subsequent reprintings such as the various Malone Society
Collections and the 1972 "Theatrum Redivivum" series of
Johnson Reprint Corporation.

1870

1 ANON. "The Globe and Blackfriars Theatres." N&Q 42 (20
   August):166.
   Announces (erroneously) that it is now certain that
   Shakespeare was never a proprietor at either playhouse,
   referring the reader to Halliwell-Phillipps's announcement
   of the discovery of documents (see 1874.2).

2 BRENDON, HEN[RY] S. "Early London Theatres." N&Q 42 (10
   December):515.
   Suggests on the authority of a contemporary letter that
   the Fortune burnt in December 1621.

3 HALLIWELL-PHILLIPPS, J[AMES] O[RCHARD], ed. A Collection of
   Ancient Documents Respecting the Office of Master of the
   Revels, and Other Papers Relating to the Early English
   Theatre, from the Original Manuscripts Formerly in the
   Haslewood Collection. London: T. Richards, 100 pp.
   Contains documents from the time of Henry VIII to the
   time of Charles II, with most drawn from the later period.
   Included in the collection are several documents tracing
   the history of the office. This is a valuable source book.

4 RANKIN, GEORGE. "Early London Theatres." N&Q 42 (8 October):
   306.
   Discusses the legend of the Devil joining in a dance at
   the Fortune, eventually burning the building down.

5 T., S. W. "Early London Theatres." N&Q 42 (10 September):216.
   Requests information on the supposed seventeen theatres
   in London 1570-1629. The editor responds with the names
   of thirteen and refers to various inns as other possibilities.

1872

1 RIMBAULT, EDWARD FRANCIS. The Old Cheque Book, or Book of
   Remembrance, of the Chapel Royal from 1561 to 1744. London:
   Camden Society, 250 pp.

1874

An edition of the manuscript documents of the Chapel
Royal. While of some importance in the history of music,
and while the Children of the Chapel were an important
acting company, this work sheds little light on their
theatre work.

2 WRIGHT, JAMES. Historia Histrionica: An Historical Account
    of the English Stage. Edited by [Edward] W[illiam] Ashbee.
    London: Mr. Ashbee's Occasional Fac-Simile Reprints, 32 pp.
       Reprint of 1699.1.

1873

1 KINGSLEY, CHARLES. "Plays and Puritans." In Plays and
    Puritans, and Other Historical Essays. London: Macmillan,
    pp. 1-80.
       Essentially an attack on pre-civil war morality as
    expressed in the plays of the period. Reprinted: 1889.5.

1874

1 ELLIS, GEORGE. "'The Private House in Drury Lane.'" N&Q 49
    (27 June):508.
       Questions the meaning of "private" on title pages. See
    1875.1 for a response.

2 HALLIWELL-PHILLIPPS, J[AMES] O[RCHARD]. Illustrations of the
    Life of Shakespeare. Pt. 1. London: Longmans, Green,
    128 pp.
       Contains a variety of documents, including the Fortune
    contract, various licenses to playwrights, and papers
    related to shares in the Globe and Blackfriars in an
    appendix. There is also an intriguing correspondence with
    the honorary President of the New Shakspere Society
    concerning unflattering references to some of Halliwell-
    Phillipps's work.

3 WRIGHT, JAMES. Historia Histrionica: A Dialogue of Plays and
    Players. In A Select Collection of Old English Plays. 4th
    ed. Vol. 3. Edited by W[illiam] C[arew] Hazlitt and
    Robert Dodsley. London: Reeves & Turner, pp. 399-431.
       Reprint of 1699.1.

1875

1 WYLIE, CHARLES. "'The Private House in Drury Lane.'" N&Q 50
(11 July):35–36.
Responds to 1874.1, referring Ellis to Collier (1831.1)
and Malone (1821.1). Wylie suggests (following Collier)
that "private" refers to the possibility of locking the
boxes.

1876

1 FORMAN, SIMON. "Dr. Forman's Book of Plays, or Notes in 1611
on Shakspere's Richard II, Winter's Tale, Cymbeline, and
Macbeth, from the Writer's Own Manuscript, Ashmole 208,
Article X. With the Lord Treasurer's Payments for the
Acting of 6 of Shakspere's Plays in 1613." TrNShS 6:413–20.
Prints Forman's eyewitness accounts of the four plays
and the record of the Lord Treasurer's payments.

2 WRIGHT, JAMES. Historia Histrionica. In A Select Collection
of Old English Plays. 4th ed. Vol. 15. Edited by
W[illiam] C[arew] Hazlitt and Robert Dodsley. London:
Reeves & Turner, 399–431.
Reprint of 1699.1.

1877

1 BLANCH, WILLIAM HARNETT. Dulwich College and Edward Alleyn.
London: E. Wallen, pp. 55–75.
The relevant section contains a brief biography of the
actor/philanthropist, with little of theatrical interest
and no new information. See 1841.1; 1843.1; see also
Index under Alleyn.

2 HALL, S[AMUEL] C[ARTER] and HALL, Mrs. S[AMUEL] C[ARTER]. The
Book of the Thames, from Its Rise to Its Fall. 2d ed.
London: A. Hall, Virtue & Co.
Includes 1858.1.

1878

1 BAKER, H[ENRY] BARTON. Our Old Actors. Vol. 1. London: R.
Bentley & Sons, pp. 3–32.
The relevant section is the first two chapters, "Bur-
badge and his Contemporaries" and "The Original Actors of

Shakespeare's Plays." Baker discusses Pavy, Tarlton, Burbage, Kempe, Sly, Armin, Lowin, Field, Taylor, and Alleyn, as well as the persecution of the players after the closing of the theatres. The style is rather anecdotal. Reprinted: 1879.1; revised, 1881.1.

2 OVERALL, WILLIAM HENRY, and C., H., eds. Analytical Index to the Series of Records Known as the Remembrancia: Archives of the City of London, A.D. 1579-1664. London: E. J. Francis & Co., pp. 350-57.
     The relevant section deals with "Plays and Players" and lists and abstracts twenty-five documents held in the Town Clerk's Record Room.

3 RENDLE, WILLIAM. "The Bankside, Southwark, and the Globe." In Harrison's Description of England in Shakespeare's Youth, pt. 2. Edited by Frederick J. Furnivall. London: New Shakspere Society, pp. 12-18.
     A brief discussion that puts Harrison's description in perspective for the reader.

4 _____. Old Southwark and Its People. London: W. Drewett, 333 pp.
     The only items of theatrical interest concern the residence of various minor players in the area and their disputes.

1879

1 BAKER, HENRY BARTON. English Actors From Shakespeare to Macready. Vol. 1. New York: H. Holt & Co., 3-32.
     Reprint of 1878.1.

2 COLLIER, J[OHN] PAYNE. The History of English Dramatic Poetry to the Time of Shakespeare: And Annals of the Stage to the Restoration. 2d ed. 3 vols. London: George Bell & Sons, 1540 pp.
     Second edition, much revised and expanded, of 1831.1. The basic structure of the volumes remains unchanged. The most important section is the first, the Annals of the Stage, wherein the documentary evidence is presented. See, however, 1861.1, for indications of Collier forgeries. This work was important in its time, but has since been superseded by (at least) Chambers (1923.2) and Bentley (1941.1; 1956.4; 1968.2). One example of misinformation contained in the preface to the new edition is that Richard Burbage's father is definitely established as Edmond Burbage, a Bedfordshire farmer. See 1886.4.

1880

1 TITTMAN, JULIUS. <u>Die Schauspiele der englischen Komödianten</u>
   <u>in Deutschland</u>. Leipzig: F. A. Brockhaus, 264 pp.
      Essentially an edition of seven plays in German per-
   formed by English players in Germany during the sixteenth
   century, with a lengthy introduction touching on theatrical
   matters.

1881

1 BAKER, H[ENRY] BARTON. <u>Our Old Actors</u>. London: R. Bentley &
   Sons, pp. 1-12.
      Revised and corrected version of 1878.1. Baker elimi-
   nates many of the anecdotes of the previous volume. The
   relevant section is the Prologue, "From the Earliest Times
   to the Commonwealth." Baker briefly discusses Tarlton,
   Burbage, Kempe, Field, Taylor, and Alleyn, as well as the
   persecution of the players during the Interregnum.

2 FLEAY, F[REDERICK] G[ARD]. "On the Actor Lists, 1578-1642."
   TrRHS 9:44-81.
      Examines twelve complete cast lists, three plots of
   nonextant plays with complete casts, and more than six
   dozen lists of various companies within the indicated dates.
   Fleay arranges the actors' names into eight tables for
   comparison and discussion.

3 HALLIWELL-PHILLIPPS, J[AMES] O[RCHARD]. <u>Outlines of the Life</u>
   <u>of Shakespeare</u>. Brighton: privately printed, 192 pp.
      An initial biographical effort of little theatrical
   value, but later greatly expanded. <u>See</u> the subsequent
   editions: 1882.3; 1884.2; 1885.5; 1886.3; 1887.3; 1889.4;
   1890.2; 1891.2; 1898.1; 1907.12.

4 WARNER, GEORGE FREDERIC. <u>Catalogue of the Manuscripts and</u>
   <u>Muniments of Alleyn's College of God's Gift at Dulwich</u>.
   London: Longman's, Green, & Co., 388 pp.
      In two parts, the first describing manuscripts 1-18 and
   the second the muniments, along with an appendix describing
   manuscripts 19-36, about which Warner did not initially
   know. The most important from a theatrical point of view
   are MS 1, containing Alleyn's theatrical papers; MS 2,
   containing his papers on the Bear Garden; MS 7, the diary
   and account book of Philip Henslowe; MS 8, Alleyn's
   memorandum book; and MS 9, Alleyn's diary and account book.
   Muniments 1-72 (Section 1) are documents concerned with the
   Bear Garden. <u>See</u> the facsimiles, 1977.8.

<u>1882</u>

1 FLEAY, F[REDERICK] G[ARD]. "On the History of the Theatres
   in London from Their First Opening in 1576 to Their Closing
   in 1642." TrRHS 10:114-33.
       A paper read before the Royal Historical Society, pre-
   senting a brief sketch of the changes in the companies and
   playhouses during the period. Fleay also attempts to
   assign playwrights to each theatre and company. This,
   along with 1881.2, was a preliminary work for his more
   important and complete 1890.1.

2 FURNIVALL, F[REDERICK] J. "The End of Shakspere's Playhouse."
   Academy 22 (28 October):314-15.
       A brief note transcribing manuscript additions to a copy
   of the 1631 edition of Stow's Survey, with information about
   the demolition of the Globe, the Blackfriars, the Fortune,
   the Hope, the Phoenix, and the Salisbury Court.

3 HALLIWELL-PHILLIPPS, J[AMES] O[RCHARD]. Outlines of the Life
   of Shakespeare. 2d ed. London: Longmans, Green & Co.,
   703 pp.
       Second edition of 1881.3, greatly expanded, with informa-
   tion of theatrical interest throughout.

4 NICHOLSON, BRINSLEY. "Kemp and the Play of Hamlet--Yorick and
   Tarlton--a Short Chapter in Dramatic History." TrNShS
   8:57-66.
       A paper read at a meeting of the Society, 12 March 1880.
   Nicholson argues that Kempe's quarrel with the company and
   the lack of a ready replacement for him shaped the play in
   part.

<u>1883</u>

1 ALBRECHT, ALEXANDER. Das englische Kindertheater. Halle:
   Waisenhauses, 56 pp.
       Published version of a doctoral dissertation at
   Friedrichs-Universität, Halle-Wittenberg. Albrecht examines
   the children's theatres of the church and the court as well
   as the development of the public boys' companies. He
   clarifies modes of performance and profiles individual
   actors, concluding with the repertories for the three
   companies.

2 HALLIWELL-PHILLIPPS, J[AMES] O[RCHARD]. Outlines of the Life
   of Shakespeare. 3d ed. London: Longmans, Green, 736 pp.

1883

Third edition of 1881.3, expanded, with information of theatrical interest throughout.

1884

1 FLEAY, F[REDERICK] G[ARD]. "Shakespeare and Puritanism." Anglia 7:223-31.
    Discusses references to Puritanism and Puritans in the plays rather than Puritan opposition to Shakespeare and the theatre.

2 HALLIWELL-PHILLIPPS, J[AMES] O[RCHARD]. Outlines of the Life of Shakespeare. 4th ed. London: Longmans, Green, 480 pp.
    Fourth edition of 1881.3, expanded, with information of theatrical interest throughout.

3 HALLIWELL-PHILLIPPS, JAMES ORCHARD. Two Old Theatres: Views of the Globe and Bear Garden. Brighton: privately printed, 3 pp.
    A reprint of a portion of the Visscher view of London, with the two buildings.

4 MEISSNER, JOHANNES. "Die englische Komödianten in Oesterreich." JDSG 19:113-54.
    Chronicles English actors performing in Austria in the sixteenth and seventeenth centuries, based on various city records. See also 1884.5 for a more complete treatment.

5 _____. Die englischen Komoedianten zur Zeit Shakespeares in Oesterreich. Beiträge zur deutschen Literatur und des gestigen Lebens in Oesterreich, no. 4. Vienna: Carl Konegen, 188 pp.
    Traces performances by English touring players in Austria in the late sixteenth and early seventeenth centuries, touching on performances in the Netherlands and Germany. Meissner bases his discussion on documentary sources, most frequently the account books of the towns. He also prints an edition of the manuscript play Der Jud von Venedig.

1885

1 GREENSTREET, JAMES. "Documents Relating to the Players at the Red Bull, Clerkenwell, and the Cockpit in Drury Lane in the Time of James I." TrNShS 10, pt. 3, no. 22:489-512.

Discusses and prints documents related to various court cases in the early seventeenth century. Queen Anne's Men played at both playhouses for a time, and there was some complicated litigation over the management of the group. See 1885.2-4.

2 _____. "Drury Lane Theatre in the Reign of James I." Athenaeum, 21 February, p. 258.
Prints the bill of complaint and its answer from a Chancery suit of 1623, bearing on the Red Bull and Cockpit companies, the late manager Thomas Greene, and his widow, Susan Browne Greene Baskervile. Continued in 1885.3-4; see 1885.1.

3 _____. "Drury Lane Theatre in the Reign of James I." Athenaeum, 29 August, p. 282.
Continuation of 1885.2. Greenstreet prints the will of Thomas Greene, manager of the Red Bull company, with particulars of that playhouse, along with the deposition of Henry Herbert, Master of the Revels, in the Baskervile proceedings against the Cockpit company. Continued in 1885.4; see 1885.1.

4 GREENSTREET, J[AMES]. "The Red Bull Playhouse in the Reign of James I." Athenaeum, 28 November, pp. 709-10.
Two documents from Woodford v. Holland, a Court of Requests suit, with commentary. The bill of complaint, unfortunately not yet discovered, would probably provide much information about the early history of the Red Bull. Concludes 1885.2-3; see 1885.1.

5 HALLIWELL-PHILLIPPS, J[AMES] O[RCHARD]. Outlines of the Life of Shakespeare. 5th ed. London: Longmans, Green, 640 pp.
Fifth edition of 1881.3, expanded, with information of theatrical interest throughout.

6 ORDISH, T. FAIRMAN. "London Theatres, No. 1: The Theatre and Curtain." Antiquary 11 (March):89-97.
Reviews the state of scholarship in Malone, Collier, Halliwell-Phillipps, and Fleay, supplemented with documentary evidence. See also 1885.7-11; 1886.4-8; 1887.5-7.

7 _____. "London Theatres, No. II: The Globe and Lesser Bankside Playhouses, Part I." Antiquary 11 (May):212-18.
As a prologue to his discussion of the Globe, Ordish sketches the history of Henslowe's Rose, with reference to the diary. See also 1885.6, 8-11; 1886.4-8; 1887.5-7.

1885

8 _____. "London Theatres, No. II: The Globe and Lesser Bankside Playhouses, Part II." Antiquary 11 (June):243-49.
    Continues 1885.7 with a discussion of the Hope, also
known as the Bear Garden. See also 1885.9-11; 1886.4-8;
1887.5-7.

9 _____. "London Theatres, No. II: The Globe and Lesser Bankside Playhouses, Part III." Antiquary 12 (August):41-49.
    Continues 1885.6-8 with a discussion of the Globe.
Ordish accepts Rendle's site south of Maid Lane and relies
on the Fortune contract for information as to its construction. Here, as elsewhere, he essentially repeats the
conclusions of Malone, Collier, Halliwell-Phillipps, Fleay,
and others. See also 1885.10-11; 1886.4-8; 1887.5-7.

10 _____. "London Theatres, No. II: The Globe and Lesser Bankside Playhouses, Part IV." Antiquary 12 (November):192-98.
    Discusses the "internal economy, arrangements, and
aspect of the playhouse," including time of performance,
composition and behavior of audience, and staging and acting
conventions. See also 1885.6-9, 11; 1886.4-8; 1887.5-7.

11 _____. "London Theatres: The Globe and Lesser Bankside Playhouses (Concluded)." Antiquary 12 (December):245-48.
    Discusses what is known about the Swan (three years
before the discovery of the DeWitt/VanBuchell sketch).
Ordish concentrates on the competition between the Swan and
the Theatre, and the confusion over the names of the playhouses. See also 1885.6-10; 1886.4-8.

12 RENDLE, W[ILLIAM]. "The Globe Playhouse." Walford's Antiquarian Magazine and Bibliographer 8 (November):209-16.
    The fourth and final article in a series; see also
1885.13-15. Rendle cites the "epigrammatic sayings of
contemporaries" to write his "brief but real picture of
the Globe." In other words, he presents the contemporary
reputation of the playhouse.

13 _____. "The Playhouses at Bankside in the Time of Shakespeare,
Part I." [Walford's] Antiquarian Magazine and Bibliographer
7 (May):207-12.
    The first of a series on the public playhouses south of
the Thames; see also 1885.12, 14, 15. Rendle here, as
elsewhere, is rather anecdotal, taking the reader on an
imaginary tour of the area. He stops first at the Swan,
reciting some twenty references to that playhouse from
1594 to 1630.

14 _____. "The Playhouses at Bankside in the Time of Shakespeare, Part II." [Walford's] Antiquarian Magazine and Bibliographer 7 (June):274-79.
   Sequel to 1885.13; see also 1885.15, 12. Here Rendle discusses the conditions of the area surrounding the Swan. He concentrates on Holland's Leaguer, a bawdy house.

15 _____. "The Playhouses at Bankside in the Time of Shakespeare, Part III." Walford's Antiquarian Magazine and Bibliographer 8 (August):55-62.
   The third of a series; see also 1885.12-14. Here Rendle discusses the old Bear Garden; the Hope, or new Bear Garden; and the Rose.

1886

1 COHN, ALBERT. "Englische Komödianten in Köln (1592-1656)." JDSG 21:245-76.
   Drawing on city records, Cohn chronicles the performances of English touring companies in Cologne.

2 GREENSTREET, JAMES. "The Blackfriars Playhouse: Its Antecedents." Athenaeum, 7 January, p. 25.
   A document from a Chancery suit of Queen Mary's time, related to the Master of the Revels and his use of the Blackfriars property, with commentary. Continued in 1888.5.

3 HALLIWELL-PHILLIPPS, J[AMES] O[RCHARD]. Outlines of the Life of Shakespeare. 6th ed. 2 vols. London: Longmans, Green, 784 pp.
   Sixth edition of 1881.3, expanded, with information of theatrical interest throughout.

4 ORDISH, T. FAIRMAN. "London Theatres, No. III: The Blackfriars Playhouse." Antiquary 14 (July):22-27.
   Discusses Burbage's second Blackfriars, the first being unknown at the time. Here Ordish is primarily concerned with the use of the playhouse by the boy companies before 1608, and with the errors of Collier in 1831.1 and 1879.2. Continued in 1886.5-6; see also the rest of the series: 1885.6-11; 1886.7-8; 1887.5-7.

5 _____. "London Theatres, No. III: The Blackfriars Playhouse (Continued)." Antiquary 14 (August):55-58.
   Continuation of 1886.5. Ordish here examines the opposition to the King's Men at this playhouse. Continued in 1886.7; see also the rest of the series: 1885.6-11; 1886.7-8; 1887.5-7.

1886

6 _____. "London Theatres, No. III: The Blackfriars Playhouse
(Continued)." Antiquary 14 (September):108-13.
    Continuation of 1886.4, 5. Discusses the shares and
finance of the King's Men at the Blackfriars, as well as
the music which accompanied performances. See also the
rest of the series: 1885.6-11; 1886.7-8; 1887.5-7.

7 _____. "London Theatres, IV: The Fortune Playhouse."
Antiquary 14 (November):205-11.
    Concentrates on Alleyn's career and finances, especially
as connected with the Fortune. See also the rest of the
series: 1885.6-11; 1886.4-6, 8; 1887.5-7.

8 _____. "London Theatres, No. V: The Red Bull." Antiquary
14 (December):236-41.
    Discusses what is known of the Red Bull, primarily from
the work of Greenstreet (1885.1-4) and Collier (1879.2).
See the rest of the series: 1885.6-11; 1886.4-7; and
1887.5-7; see also Ordish's book (1894.4) on the subject,
for which these served as the basis.

9 TRAUTMANN, KARL. "Englische Komoedianten in Nürnberg bis zum
Schlusse des Dreissigjähr Krieges (1593-1648)." ArchivL
14 (Spring):113-36.
    Chronicles the performances of English actors in
Nuremberg during the years indicated, based on documentary
sources held in that city.

10 VATKE, TH[EODOR]. "Das Theater und das London Publikum in
Shakespeares Zeit." JDSG 21:226-44.
    Examines the relationship between the audience and the
theatre in Shakespeare's time. Vatke traces audience
behavior and dress through references in plays, prologues,
inductions, and pamphlets, as well as the growing opposition among the Puritans.

1887

1 ANON. "A Middlesex Sessions Record Touching James Burbage's
'Theater.'" Athenaeum, 12 February, pp. 233-34.
    A brief note citing a court record which illuminates the
relationship between Burbage and Braynes.

2 CRÜGER, JOHANNES. "Englische Komoedianten in Strassburg im
Elsass." ArchivL 15 (Spring):113-25.
    Chronicles the visits of English players to Strassburg,
1596-1657, based on official city records of payment.

3　HALLIWELL-PHILLIPS, J[AMES] O[RCHARD]. Outlines of the Life
　　of Shakespeare. 7th ed. 2 vols. London: Longmans,
　　Green, 848 pp.
　　　　Seventh edition of 1881.3, expanded, with information of
　　theatrical interest throughout.

4　_____. The Visits of Shakespeare's Company of Actors to the
　　Provincial Cities and Towns of England, Illustrated
　　by Extracts Gathered from Corporate Records. Brighton:
　　privately printed, 48 pp.
　　　　A variety of provincial notices of the Chamberlain's/
　　King's Men, arranged alphabetically by town from Barnstaple
　　to Worcester. Fifteen entries in all are included, with
　　the greatest amount of information in the last. This, the
　　earliest work on its subject, has been superseded by various
　　Malone Society Collections and Records of Early English
　　Drama. See Index under Provincial Tours.

5　ORDISH, T. FAIRMAN. "London Theatres, VI: Cockpit, Drury
　　Lane." Antiquary 15 (March):93-97.
　　　　Discusses the destruction of the playhouse by the London
　　apprentices in 1617, the renaming of the theatre as the
　　Phoenix, and several changes of company between 1617 and
　　1642. See the rest of the series: 1885.6-11; 1886.4-8;
　　1887.6-7.

6　_____. "London Theatres, VII: Whitefriars: Salisbury
　　Court." Antiquary 15 (June):262-65.
　　　　Examines the evidence for the existence of an early
　　Whitefriars Playhouse, which Ordish dismisses as "a crude
　　stage," in preparation for a more detailed discussion (in
　　1887.7) of the Salisbury Court. See also the rest of the
　　series: 1885.6-11; 1886.4-8; 1887.5.

7　_____. "London Theatres, VII: Whitefriars: Salisbury
　　Court." Antiquary 16 (December):244-47.
　　　　In the last article in his series, composed of 1885.6-11,
　　1886.4-8, and 1887.5-7, Ordish discusses what is known of
　　the last playhouse of the period, the Salisbury Court. He
　　takes his information primarily from Collier (1831.1;
　　1879.2) and Fleay (1882.1). See also his book (1894.4)
　　based on this series.

8　RENDLE, WILLIAM. "Paris Garden and Christ Church, Blackfriars."
　　N&Q 75 (26 March):241-43.
　　　　In essence a review of an 1881 private publication, The
　　Manor of Old Paris Garden by Joseph Meymott. Rendle
　　concludes that the dates are often inaccurate in the

1887

Elizabethan/Jacobean section of the book, but there is much of value. Despite the title and Rendle's other work in theatre history, there is nothing here of theatrical interest. Continued in 1887.9-10.

9 _____. "Paris Garden and Christ Church, Blackfriars." N&Q 75 (30 April):343.
Continues 1887.8; concluded in 1887.10.

10 _____. "Paris Garden and Christ Church, Blackfriars." N&Q 75 (4 June):442-44.
Concludes 1887.8-9.

11 TRAUTMANN, KARL. "Englische Komoedianten in Stuttgart (1600, 1609, 1613-14) und Tübingen (1597)." ArchivL 15 (Spring): 211-16.
Discusses the visits of English actors to the two cities in the years indicated, based on city records of payment.

12 _____. "Englische Komoedianten in Ulm (1602." ArchivL 15 (Spring):216-17.
A brief note of a visit of Robert Browne's company.

13 WRIGHT, GEORGE R. "On a Manuscript List of Plays of the Year 1638." In Archaeologic and Historic Fragments. London: Whiting & Co., pp. 1-24.
Revision of 1860.1, with the same basic confusion of the Cockpit (Phoenix) in Drury Lane for the Cockpit-in-Court.

1888

1 ARCHER, WILLIAM. "A Sixteenth Century Playhouse." UR 1 (June): 281-88.
Discusses Gaedertz's discovery of the Swan drawing (see 1888.4), prints it, and speculates on what it tells us. Archer follows Gaedertz in believing that curtains could be drawn between the pillars to form a large inner stage. He concludes with a comparison of the Swan drawing with the Wits frontispiece.

2 BOLTE, JOHANNES. "Englische Komödianten in Dänemark und Schweden." JDSG 23:99-108.
Chronicles the performances of touring English players in Denmark and Sweden in the sixteenth and seventeenth centuries, based on government documents recording payments.

3 FIRTH, C[HARLES] H[ARDING]. "The Suppression of the Drama
   During the Protectorate and Commonwealth." N&Q 78 (18
   August):122-23.
      Cites four newspapers of the 1650s to show that private
   performances were frequently given during the Interregnum.

4 GAEDERTZ, KARL THEODOR. Zur Kenntis der altenglischen Bühne,
   nebst andern Beiträgen zur Shakespeare-Litteratur. Bremen:
   C. E. Müller, pp. 1-18.
      Includes DeWitt's description of the Swan and VanBuchell's
   copy of his sketch, discovered by Gaedertz in the Utrecht
   University Library. He believed, however, that curtains
   were hung up between the posts to divide the platform into
   outer and inner stages. This is certainly among the most
   important discoveries in the field.

5 GREENSTREET, JAMES. "The Blackfriars Playhouse: Its Antecedents." Athenaeum, 7 January, pp. 25-26.
      Continuation of 1886.2. Greenstreet prints a Privy Seal
   Signet Bill from 1561 authorizing tennis-playing in the
   neighborhood of Blackfriars, along with the actual license,
   with commentary. He attempts to show something of the
   history of the area's connection with entertainment
   enterprises. Continued in 1888.6-7; 1889.3.

6 _____. "The Blackfriars Theatre in the Time of Shakespeare,
   I." Athenaeum, 7 April, pp. 445-46.
      Abstracts of five documents related to the 1612 Chancery
   case, Kirkham v. Painton. Continued in 1888.7; 1889.3.

7 _____. "The Blackfriars Theatre in the Time of Shakespeare,
   II." Athenaeum, 21 April, p. 509.
      Continuation of 1888.6. Abstracts of two additional
   documents from the same case. Concluded in 1889.3.

8 _____. "The Whitefriars Theatre in the Time of Shakespeare."
   TrNShS 13, pt. 3:269-84.
      Text of a paper read before the Society, 9 November 1888.
   Greenstreet discusses the Chancery suit of 1609 concerning
   the management of Whitefriars, and he prints the documents
   of the case.

9 LOWE, ROBERT W. A Bibliographical Account of English Theatrical Literature from the Earliest Times to the Present Day.
   London: John C. Nimms, 384 pp.
      The earliest attempt at a bibliography of theatrical
   literature. The alphabetical subject listing of books dealing with the theatre as opposed to the drama contains items

relevant to this period throughout. See also 1970.1, and
Index under Bibliographies.

10 RENDLE, WILLIAM. "The Swan Playhouse, Bankside, circa 1596."
N&Q 78 (22 September):221-22.
    Discusses Gaedertz's discovery and publication of the
Swan drawing (1888.4).

11 _____, and NEWMAN, PHILIP P. The Inns of Old Southwark and
Their Associations. London: Longmans, Green, 437 pp.
    Includes references to the Boar's Head, the Rose, the
Globe, the Newington Butts, and various inns associated with
the playhouses. These are brief mentions, however, in a
sort of "walking tour of the area" format. Not of major
importance.

12 WHEATLEY, HENRY B. "On a Contemporary Drawing of the Interior
of the Swan Theatre, 1596." TrNShS 12, pt. 2:213-25.
    A paper read before the Society, 9 November 1888.
Wheatley reports on Gaedertz's discovery and printing of the
Swan drawing (see 1888.4), questioning the capacity (given
by DeWitt as 3000) and commenting on the composition of the
building and its arrangements.

1889

1 BAKER, H[ENRY] BARTON. The London Stage: Its History and
Traditions from 1576 to 1888. Vol. 1. London: W. H. Allen
& Co., pp. 1-31.
    The relevant section is the first chapter, "The Eliza-
bethan Stage." Baker briefly discusses the Theatre, the
Curtain, the Swan, the Hope, the Globe, the Newington
Butts, the Blackfriars, the Fortune, the Red Bull, the
Cockpit (or Phoenix), the Whitefriars, and the Salisbury
Court playhouses; actors, including Burbage and Alleyn;
audiences; music; finance; and government regulation. This
is a popular work, based on secondary sources. See 1904.2
for a revision.

2 CREIZENACH, W[ILHELM MICHAEL ANTON]. Die Schauspiele der
englischen Komödianten. Deutsche National-Literatur, no.
23. Berlin and Stuttgart: W. Spemann, 352 pp.
    An essentially literary study of the drama of the English
actors in Germany, but with information of theatrical
interest throughout.

3 GREENSTREET, JAMES. "Blackfriars Theatre in the Time of
    Shakespeare." Athenaeum, 10 August, pp. 203-4.
        Concludes 1888.5-7. Extracts from the Star Chamber suit
    alluded to in the Chancery suit abstracted earlier.

4 HALLIWELL-PHILLIPPS, J[AMES] O[RCHARD]. Outlines of the Life
    of Shakespeare. 8th ed. 2 vols. London: Longmans, Green,
    896 pp.
        Eighth edition of 1881.3, expanded, with information of
    theatrical interest throughout.

5 KINGSLEY, CHARLES. "Plays and Puritans." In Plays and Puritans,
    and Other Historical Essays. 2d. ed. London: Macmillan,
    pp. 1-83.
        Second edition of 1873.1.

6 SIMPSON, WILLIAM SPARROW. Gleanings from Old S. Paul's.
    London: Elliot Stock, pp. 101-18.
        The relevant section is Chapter Six, "Plays Acted by
    the Children of Paul's." Simpson lists thirty-five plays
    performed by the children, mostly based on title-page
    claims or the work of Halliwell-Phillipps. He does not
    examine acting or physical staging. Not of major theatrical
    importance.

7 YOUNG, WILLIAM. The History of Dulwich College; With a Life
    of Edward Alleyn. Vol. 2. Edinburgh: Morrison & Gibb,
    pp. 1-265.
        The first three chapters of volume two concern the life
    of Alleyn, his diary, and the Fortune Playhouse. Young is
    more careful in his use of records than was Collier in
    1841.1, and is able to correct the biography in many details.
    The diary is printed complete, with a facsimile of three
    pages. The brief chapter on the Fortune is primarily a
    compilation of all the material in the Dulwich manuscripts
    and muniments that deal with that playhouse. See also
    the facsimile of the Henslowe papers (1977.8) and the
    catalogue of the papers (1881.4).

1890

1 FLEAY, FREDERICK GARD. A Chronicle History of the London
    Stage, 1559-1642. London: Reeves & Turner, 424 pp.
        Divides the period into seven parts, breaking at 1586,
    1593, 1603, 1613, 1636, and 1642. One chapter is devoted
    to each section, examining court performances, companies,
    playhouses, playwrights, and general stage history for the

years in question. Fleay presents information chronologically, with sources listed, and he uses many tables to
organize the data. A dozen subject indexes round out the
volume. This is the most important work between Collier on
the one hand (1879.2) and Adams (1917.3) and Chambers
(1923.2) on the other.

2 HALLIWELL-PHILLIPPS, J[AMES] O[RCHARD]. Outlines of the Life
    of Shakespeare. 9th ed. 2 vols. London and New York:
    Longmans, Green, 1084 pp.
       Ninth edition of 1881.3, expanded, with information of
    theatrical interest throughout.

3 RENDLE, WILLIAM. "Philip Henslowe." Genealogist, n.s. 4, no.
    3:149-59.
       A brief biography of the financier and theatre manager,
    concentrating on the Henslowe v. Henslowe suit in Chancery,
    the documents of which are held in the Public Record Office.

                              1891

1 CARGILL, ALEXANDER. "Shakespeare as an Actor." Scribner's 9
    (May):613-35.
       A brief biography, concentrating on theatrical matters.
    Reprinted: 1916.4.

2 PAGET, A[LFRED] H[ENRY]. The Elizabethan Playhouses. London:
    G. Gibbons, 14 pp.
       Reprint of 1891.3.

3 _____. "The Elizabethan Play-Houses." TrLeLPS (January):237-
    50.
       A paper read before the Leicester Literary and Philo-
    sophical Society in 1890. Paget briefly reviews the state
    of knowledge of the Elizabethan theatre (drawn primarily
    from Halliwell-Phillipps and Collier) and goes on to examine
    the discovery space. He postulates a recessed alcove under
    the required balcony, closed by curtains and used for
    discoveries. Remarkably moderate for its time. Reprinted:
    1891.2.

                              1892

1 HIPIWELL, DANIEL. "Prices of Admission to Theatres, Temp.
    Elizabeth." N&Q 85 (21 May):412.
       Records two references to "two penny rooms." See 1892.3
    for a response.

1894

2 JUNIUS, PHILIP. "Diary of the Journey of Philip Junius Duke
   of Stettin-Pomerania Through England in the Year 1602."
   Edited by Gottfried von Bülow and Wilfred Powell. TrRHS,
   n.s. 6:1-67.
        A facing-page translation of the diary, including accounts
   of performances the Duke attended.

3 NICHOLSON, BR[INSLEY]. "Prices of Admission to Theatres, Temp.
   Elizabeth." N&Q 85 (18 June):499.
        Responds to 1892.1, pointing out the commonness of the
   term and its parallel to the gallery.

4 STOPES, CHARLOTTE CARMICHAEL. "William Hunnis." JDSG 27:200-
   217.
        A brief biography and list of publications of the play-
   wright and Master of the Queen's Chapel. See also 1900.3
   and especially 1910.19.

1893

1 ARCHER, THOMAS. The Highway of Letters and Its Echoes of
   Famous Footsteps. London: Cassell; New York: Randolph,
   pp. 189-220.
        The relevant section examines "Dramatists, Plays and
   Players." While the Elizabethan period is touched on, this
   is not of great theatrical importance.

2 BOLTE, JOHANNES. Die Singspiele der englischen Komödianten
   und ihrer Nachfolger in Deutschland, Holland und
   Skandinavien. Theatergeschichte Forschungen, no. 7.
   Hamburg and Leipzig: Leopold Voss, 194 pp.
        Discusses the origins and characteristics of the
   English plays with music performed on the continent during
   the sixteenth and seventeenth centuries. The Angel-like
   Roland (1596) is the most important, and Bolte prints both
   text and music.

1894

1 CALMOUR, ALFRED CECIL. Fact and Fiction about Shakespeare,
   with Some Account of the Playhouses, Players, and Playwrights of His Period. Stratford-upon-Avon: George Boyden,
   112 pp.
        A slight volume intended for the general reader and
   riddled with errors of fact and interpretation. Of little
   interest to the theatre historian.

1894

2 ORDISH, T. FAIRMAN. Early London Theatres--In the Fields.
   London: Elliot Stock, 298 pp.
      Histories of the Theatre, the Curtain, the amphitheatres,
   Newington Butts, the Rose, the Bear Garden, the Hope, the
   Paris Garden, and the Swan. The Globe is excluded since
   Ordish proposes to examine it in a separate volume; the
   same is true of the city theatres. Neither projected
   volume ever appeared. Staging is not considered. This is
   the most comprehensive survey of its time, roughly equiva-
   lent to Fleay (1890.1), but was superseded by Adams (1917.3).
   Ordish based his book on his earlier series of articles:
   1885.6-11; 1886.4-8; and 1887.5-7. Reprinted: 1899.2;
   1971.13.

                         1895

1 BOLTE, JOHANNES. Das Danziger Theater im 16. und 17.
   Jahrhundert. Hamburg and Leipzig: Leopold Voss, 296 pp.
      Essentially a chronicle history, citing documentary
   evidence on a year-by-year basis. Of interest because of
   the English actors who performed in Danzig before the
   Restoration. Bolte includes in an appendix a German version
   of a Marston play performed by one such group. See also
   1979.19.

2 PENNIMAN, JOSIAH HARMAR. "The War of the Theatres." Ph.D.
   dissertation, University of Pennsylvania, 168 pp.
      Published: 1897.2.

                         1897

1 LOGEMAN, H. "Johannes de Witt's Visit to the Swan Theatre."
   Anglia 19:117-34.
      Suggests that the play depicted in the Swan drawing is
   Twelfth Night, and tries to show that the date of the play
   and the date of DeWitt's visit may have coincided. See
   also 1951.7.

2 PENNIMAN, JOSIAH H[ARMAR]. The War of the Theatres. Publications of the University of Pennsylvania Series in Philology,
   Literature, and Archaelogy, vol. 4, no. 3. Boston: Ginn &
   Co., 168 pp.
      Published version of 1895.2. Penniman examines the
   quarrels of Marston and Dekker with Jonson, which found
   expression in fifteen satirical plays. Despite the title
   this study is almost completely literary in approach and
   consequently of only passing theatrical interest.

1898

1 HALLIWELL-PHILLIPPS, J[AMES] O[RCHARD]. Outlines of the Life of Shakespeare. 10th ed. 2 vols. London: Longmans, Green, 848 pp.
   Tenth edition of 1881.3, expanded, with information of theatrical interest throughout.

1899

1 BINZ, GUSTAV. "Londoner Theater und Schauspiele im Jahre 1599." Anglia 22:456-64.
   Discusses Thomas Platter's observations. See also 1929. 13; 1937.9; 1956.29.

2 ORDISH, THOMAS FAIRMAN. Early London Theatres in the Fields. London: E. Stock, 298 pp.
   Reprint of 1894.2.

1900

1 BOLTE, JOHANNES. "Englische Komödianten in Munster und Ulm." JDSG 36:273-75.
   Using municipal records, Bolte chronicles five performances, from 1601 to 1647, of English touring players in the two cities.

2 GREG, W[ALTER] W[ILSON]. "Webster's White Devil." MLQ 3 (December):112-40.
   Though primarily a literary study, of interest because of Greg's discussion of the alternation theory, called here "dramatic enjambement," in the second part of the essay. Reprinted: 1966.7.

3 STOPES, CHARLOTTE CARMICHAEL. "William Hunnis, the Dramatist." Athenaeum, 31 March, pp. 410-12.
   A brief recitation of the achievements of the Master of the Chapel Royal, focusing on the plays performed for the Queen. See 1910.8 for a more detailed treatment.

1901

1 DOBELL, BERTRAM. "Newly Discovered Documents of the Elizabethan and Jacobean Periods, II: Letters of George Chapman and Ben Jonson." Athenaeum, 30 March, pp. 403-4.

1901

Three letters of Chapman and excerpts from seven of
Jonson, relating to their quarrel over Eastward Ho, part of
the War of the Theatres. See also 1897.2; 1923.7.

2 MAAS, HERMAN. Die Kindertruppen: Ein Kapitel aus der
Geschichte der englischen Theatergesellschaften in dem
Zeitraume von 1559 bis 1642. Bremen: Grube & Dathe, 35 pp.
Published version of a Gottingen Ph.D. dissertation.
This is one chapter of a projected longer work. Maas out-
lines the activities and repertories of the children's
companies during the reigns of Elizabeth, James, and Charles.
Most sources are secondary. See also his more comprehensive
treatment, 1907.16, as well as Index under Children's
Companies.

3 MALONE, EDMOND. "An Historical Account of the English Stage."
In Complete Works of Shakespeare. New York: P. F. Collier
& Son, 522 pp.
Reprints 1790.1, with additions from 1813.1 and 1821.1.

4 MANTZIUS, KARL. Skuespilkunstens Historie. Vol. 3. Engelske
Theaterforhold i Shakespearetiden. Copenhagen: F. Hegel
& Son, 236 pp.
The English Renaissance volume of Mantzius's comprehen-
sive history of theatre. See 1904.9 for an English
translation. Reprinted: 1937.6.

1902

1 ANON. "A London Theatre Temp. Queen Elizabeth." Builder 82
(10 May):468-69.
Describes an exhibition held in the Hall of Clifford's
Inn of maps, views, and models of sixteenth- and
seventeenth-century London and models of playhouses of
Shakespeare's time. The author describes the model of the
Globe, based on the Swan drawing and the Fortune contract,
in detail.

2 BROTANEK, RUDOLPH. Die englischen Maskenspiele. Wiener
Beiträge zur englischen Philologie, no. 15. Vienna and
Leipzig: W. Braumüller, 371 pp.
By the sixteenth century, disguises as a dramatic form
were enjoyed by courtly audiences and peasants alike. In
the seventeenth century, disguises on stage were seldom a
performance in themselves but rather enhancements to a
speech, song, instrumental music, or dance. France exerted
a strong influence on the development of the English masque.

Brotanek concludes with a chronological register and bibliography of masques.

3 DURAND, W[ALTER] Y[ALE]. "Notes on Richard Edwards." JEGP 4
    (July):348-69.
       Argues that Damon and Pythias was performed at Whitehall
    on Christmas, 1564; and that the lost Palaemon and Arcyte
    was not Shakespeare's source for Two Noble Kinsmen.

4 GRABAU, CARL. "Zur englischen Bühne um 1600." JDSG 38:230-36.
       Examines stage directions in The Cuck-Queanes and
    Cuckolds Errant and The Faery Pastorall or Forrest of Elues,
    two manuscript plays not printed until the nineteenth
    century. Grabau finds evidence for three doors, each
    representing a different location throughout, indicated by
    signs. Further, there is an indication that the playhouse
    at St. Paul's may not have had a trap.

5 LAWRENCE, W[ILLIAM] J[OHN]. "History of a Peculiar Stage Cur-
    tain." GMg 293 (July):53-59.
       Traces the history of the front curtain, noting its use
    in Jonson's Masque of Blackness (1605) and in Charles I's
    royal entry into Edinburgh in 1633. Reprinted: 1912.15.

6 MEYER, C. F. "Englische Komödianten am Hofe des Herzog Philip
    Julius [sic] von Pommern-Wolgast." JDSG 38:196-211.
       Examines the visits of touring English players to the
    court of Archduke Philip Junius in the first quarter of the
    seventeenth century. See also 1892.2.

7 SCHELLING, FELIX E. "The Elizabethan Theatre." Lippincott's
    69 (March):309-23.
       A general discussion for a popular audience, with
    illustrations. Schelling first establishes the political
    and geographical backgrounds and then examines the public
    playhouses, most notably the Globe.

1903

1 CREIZENACH, WILHELM MICHAEL ANTON. Geschichte des neueren
    Dramas. Vols. 2 and 3. Halle: S. M. Niemaeyer.
       See English translation, 1916.5. Second edition, 1923.4.

2 HALE, EDWARD EVERETT, Jr. "The Influence of Theatrical
    Conditions on Shakespeare." MP 1 (June):171-92.
       Attempts to examine the conditions under which
    Shakespeare wrote as an aid to understanding the plays.

Hale stresses the "rhetorical" nature of performances, the
absence of a front curtain, the use of the upper stage for
separate scenes, the use of costumes and properties, the
habit of improvisation on the part of the clowns, and the
need for imagination on the part of the audience.

3 HERZ, EMIL. Englische Schauspieler und englisches Schauspiel
zur Zeit Shakespeares in Deutschland. Theatergeschichtliche
Forschungen, no. 18. Hamburg and Leipzig: L. Voss, 143 pp.
Published version of a Bonn Ph.D. dissertation. Each of
the first ten chapters treats an English company touring
in Germany. The second section then discusses the repertory
of these companies in detail, concentrating on Shakespeare's
plays as presented in Germany.

4 LAWRENCE, WILLIAM J[OHN]. "A Forgotten Stage Conventionality."
Anglia 26 (June):447-60.
Argues that the English proscenium doors with balconies
above, in use during the Restoration and eighteenth century,
were derived from the stage doors of the Elizabethan period
and used for the same purposes. Reprinted: 1912.15.

5 LAWRENCE, W[ILLIAM] J[OHN]. "The Mounting of the Stuart
Masques." English Illustrated Magazine, n.s. 30 (November):
174-81.
Examines recently discovered designs for masques by
Inigo Jones and the texts of The Triumph of Peace and The
Temple of Love. Reprinted: 1912.15.

6 _____. "Some Characteristics of the Elizabethan-Stuart Stage."
EStudien 32:36-51.
Discusses the absence of the front curtain and its
implications, and the use of the traverse. Lawrence also
argues against accepting the Swan drawing because it is
"hearsay evidence," undated, self-contradictory, and shows
no upper and lower traverses.

7 SYMMES, HAROLD S. Les débuts de la critique dramatique en
Angleterre jusqu'à la mort de Shakespeare. Paris: Ernest
Leroux, 218 pp.
Published version of a University of Paris Ph.D. dissertation. Symmes discusses three stages in the early development of dramatic criticism in England: the early
Puritan attacks, the beginning of the development of
classical ideals, and the more sophisticated use of classical ideals in the Restoration. When compared with France
and Italy, according to Symmes, England's critics lagged far
behind, holding to medieval values until well into the
seventeenth century.

8   THOMPSON, ELBERT NEVIUS SEBRING. "The Controversy between the
    Puritans and the Stage." Ph.D. dissertation, Yale Univer-
    sity, 275 pp.
        Published: 1903.9.

9   THOMPSON, ELBERT N[EVIUS] S[EBRING]. The Controversy between
    the Puritans and the Stage. Yale Studies in English, no.
    20. New York: H. Holt & Co., 275 pp.
        Published version of 1903.8. Thompson divides his work
    into two parts, the Puritan attack on the stage (17 chap-
    ters) and the dramatists' reply to the Puritans (3 chap-
    ters). The detailed accounts of various treatises are
    especially clear. Of most interest to the theatre historian
    are Chapter Four on the Gosson-Lodge debate, Chapter Ten on
    legislation covering the stage, and all of Part Two.

10 WOOLF, ARTHUR H. Shakespeare and the Old Southwark Playhouses.
    London: privately printed, 19 pp.
        Text of a lecture delivered at the Southwark town hall on
    23 April 1903. Woolf simply presents the main facts concern-
    ing Shakespeare's connection with the area and its play-
    houses. He discusses the Rose (placing Shakespeare there
    for the initial performance of Henry VI and Titus) and the
    Globe (stating that it was built from the timbers of the
    demolished Curtain, rather than the Theatre) in some detail.
    Similar minor errors of fact are scattered throughout.

1904

1   ADAMS, JOHN CHESTER. "The Predecessors of the XVII Century
    Court Masque in England." Ph.D. dissertation, Yale
    University, pp. 106-66.
        The relevant section discusses masking during Elizabeth's
    reign. Adams distinguishes between "masking entertain-
    ments" and true masques with speeches and scenery, concen-
    trating on the latter. The masques performed outside the
    Elizabethan court are the true predecessors of the
    seventeenth-century court masques, with the Masque of
    Proteus as the most significant.

2   BAKER, H[ENRY] BARTON. History of the London Stage and Its
    Famous Players (1576-1903). London: G. Routledge & Sons;
    New York: E. P. Dutton & Co., pp. 3-29.
        Revision of 1889.1. The relevant section is Chapter One
    of Part One, covering the period 1576-1642. Since Baker
    attempts to discuss all the playhouses in twenty-seven
    pages, the work is necessarily general, and it is riddled

1904

with such common misstatements as "the Globe was a hexagonal building."

3 BANG[-KAUP], W[ILLY]. "Zur Bühne Shakespeares." JDSG 40:223-25.
    Responds to Brodmeier (1904.5), suggesting a slightly different arrangement for the curtains to the rear stage. See 1904.8.

4 BRANDL, A[LOIS]. "Englische Komödianten in Frankfurt a. M." JDSG 40:229-30.
    A brief note citing Moryson's description of a play he saw in Frankfurt.

5 BRODMEIER, CECIL. Die Shakespeare-Bühne nach den alten Büchenweisungen. Weimar: A. Haschke, 121 pp.
    Published version of a Jena Ph.D. dissertation. Brodmeier reconstructs a typical Elizabethan public playhouse from stage directions in a wide variety of plays. He locates the curtains between the pillars, and places a trap, two doorways, and a spacious upper stage in this "hinterbühne." He also discusses the use of properties and music. This is one of the clearest statements of the alternation theory. See 1904.3; 1904.8.

6 FURNIVALL, F[REDERICK] J. "The Fortune Theatre in 1649." N&Q 109 (30 January):85.
    Cites a 1649 Chancery suit showing that the Fortune was held by Edward Alleyn's College of God's Gift in Dulwich, and leased one to Lisle. Lisle wanted to convert the playhouse to some other use, but the College refused.

7 HENSLOWE, PHILIP. Henslowe's Diary. P. 1, Text. Edited by Walter Wilson Greg. London: A. H. Bullen, 240 pp.
    For many years the standard edition of the most important extant document from the Elizabethan playhouses. In the Introduction Greg describes the manuscript and its contents, discusses Collier's forgeries (see 1845.3), and gives his general plan for the projected three volumes. This one contains only the diary and notes; see 1908.11 for Greg's commentary and 1907.15 for other Henslowe papers. See also 1961.13 for another edition and 1977.8 for the facsimile of the diary and papers.

8 KELLER, WOLFGANG. "Nochmals zur Bühne Shakespeares." JDSG 40:225-27.
    Responds to Brodmeier (1904.5) and Bang (1904.3), suggesting an alternative arrangement of curtains, with one

set dividing the front stage from the rear stage and a
second set at the back of the rear stage between the two
doors.

9 MANTZIUS, KARL. A History of Theatrical Art in Ancient and
   Modern Times. Vol. 3, The Shakespearean Period in England.
   Translated by Louise von Cassel. London: Duckworth & Co.,
   250 pp.
      Translation of 1901.4. The three major sections of this
   popular treatise examine the theatres, general theatrical
   conditions, and acting. Mantzius discusses the Theatre, the
   Globe, the Fortune, the Curtain, the Blackfriars, the Rose,
   Newington Butts, the Red Bull, the Swan, the Phoenix, and
   the Salisbury Court playhouses, as well as such miscellaneous topics as hours of performance, expenses, and play-
   bills. The section on acting treats Tarlton, Kempe, Burbage,
   Alleyn, and Field. Reprinted: 1937.6.

10 SCHELLING, FELIX E. "'An Aery of Children, Little Eyases.'" In
   The Queen's Progress and Other Elizabethan Sketches.
   London: T. W. Laurie, pp. 103-28.
      Examines the boy actors, concentrating on court and legal
   records concerning them and the plays which they presented.

11 ____. "Plays in the Making." In The Queen's Progress and
   Other Elizabethan Sketches. London: T. W. Laurie, pp.
   149-70.
      Examines Henslowe's management practices as revealed in
   the diary, concentrating on the "thraldom" of the playwrights (notably Dekker) who worked for him.

1905

1 DURAND, W[ALTER] Y[ALE]. "Palaemon and Arcyte, Progne, Marcus
   Geminus, and the Theatre in Which They Were Acted as
   Described by John Bereblock (1566)." PMLA 20 (September):
   502-28.
      Essentially a translation of relevant sections of
   Bereblock's Latin account, with commentary. Durand describes
   the preparations made for production as paralleling the
   preparations made at an innyard. Particularly interesting
   is his argument that "every main feature of the early
   playhouse can be traced to the conditions either of the
   hall or the innyard."

2 LAWRENCE, W[ILLIAM] J[OHN]. "A Forgotten Restoration Playhouse." EStudien 35 (Spring):279-89.

Using records of a French actor who visited London in
1661 and Pepys's diary, Lawrence suggests that the Phoenix
in Drury Lane was rebuilt, fitted with scenes, and
operated during the Restoration.

3   MÖNKEMEYER, PAUL. Prolegomena zu einer Darstellung der
englischen Volksbühne zur Elisabeth- und Stuart-Zeit nach
den alten Büchen-Anweisungen. Hanover and Leipzig:
Hahnische Buchandlung, 94 pp.
Published version of a Gottingen Ph.D. dissertation.
The three chapters of this "Prologue to an Examination of
the Elizabethan and Stuart Public Theatre Through the Old
Stage Directions" examine staging before 1576, the choice
of materials for the study, and the stage directions in
selected plays. Since this is but a prologue, Mönkemeyer
reaches no conclusions.

4   MURRAY, JOHN TUCKER. "English Dramatic Companies in the Towns
Outside of London, 1550-1600." MP 2 (April):539-59.
Attempts an account of the customs of the touring
companies--their methods of performance, relations to town
authorities, amounts paid, and so on. Murray identifies
three types of company (London, Nobleman's, Town) and
follows them through typical activities. See also 1910.15;
1920.30.

5   REYNOLDS, GEORGE FULLMER. "Some Principles of Elizabethan
Staging." Ph.D. dissertation, University of Chicago, 63 pp.
Published in two parts: 1905.6-7; also 1905.8.

6   REYNOLDS, GEORGE F[ULLMER]. "Some Principles of Elizabethan
Staging, Part I." MP 2 (April):581-614.
First part of published version of 1905.5; continued in
1905.7. Also published in monograph form: 1905.8.

7   _____. "Some Principles of Elizabethan Staging, Part II." MP
3 (June):69-97.
Continuation of 1905.6; published version of 1905.5.
Also published in monograph form: 1905.8.

8   _____. Some Principles of Elizabethan Staging. Chicago:
University of Chicago Press, 63 pp.
Published version of 1905.5; also published as 1905.6-7.
Reynolds examines the alternation theory and finds it
wanting, then develops a theory of simultaneity similar to
medieval practice. The theory is based on the passages in
plays of the period that render alternation unlikely or
impossible. Other items touched on are the scene boards

indicating location, the existence of three stage doors at
least in some theatres, and the availability of a curtained
alcove for discoveries. For later contributions to the
field, see Index under Reynolds.

9 STOPES, CHARLOTTE CARMICHAEL. "Mary's Chapel Royal and Her
Coronation Play." Athenaeum, 9 September, pp. 346-47.
Examines the membership of Queen Mary's Chapel Royal and
the events of her coronation, including the play presented;
speculates on its content and authorship.

1906

1 CHAMBERS, E[DMUND] K. "Court Performances before Queen
Elizabeth." MLR 2 (October):1-13.
Lists previously unknown court performances, from the
Declared Accounts of the Treasurer of the Chamber, in
effect abstracts of the Original Accounts, which unfortunately have several missing years. For each entry Chambers
shows the date, the company, and the payees, which leads to
a number of deductions concerning companies and actors.

2 _____. Notes on the History of the Revels Office Under the
Tudors. London: A. H. Bullen, 80 pp.
A brief history based on available documentary evidence.
Chambers begins with the late fifteenth century, with most
of the material belonging to Elizabeth's reign.

3 CORBIN, JOHN. "Shakespeare and the Plastic Stage." Atlantic
Monthly 97, no. 3 (March):369-83.
A discussion of Elizabethan staging methods for the
general reader, attempting to correct the "bare stage and
a blanket" impression. Corbin focuses on the use of
properties (citing Henslowe's diary for corroboration) and
the holdover of medieval conventions.

4 GRABO, CARL H. "The Stage for Which Shakespeare Wrote, I:
The Mystery Plays." Chautauquan 44 (September):98-106.
Despite the main title, this deals exclusively with
medieval drama as background for the rest of the series.
See also 1906.5-7; 1907.10-11.

5 _____. "The Stage for Which Shakespeare Wrote, II: The
Ancestry of the English Theater." Chautauquan 44 (October):
211-19.
Discusses the Cornish rounds and the Tudor inns, as
additional background for the series. See also 1905.6-7;
1907.10-11.

1906

6 _____. "The Stage for Which Shakespeare Wrote, III: Theatres
of Elizabeth's London." Chautauquan 44 (November):354-66.
    Continuation of 1905.4-5. Discusses the various play-
houses, placing considerable importance on the Fortune
contract and the Swan drawing. Grabo stresses the lack of
a curtain in the modern sense and the rapid flow of action.
Continued in 1906.7; 1907.10-11.

7 _____. "The Stage for Which Shakespeare Wrote, IV: The Stage
Properties and Costumes." Chautauquan 45 (December):79-89.
    Continuation of 1906.4-6. Grabo discusses the use of
props and costumes, beginning with an examination of the
stage doors and location signs (citing Reynolds, 1905.8) and
continuing with the prop lists and costume notes from
Henslowe's diary. He concludes that "stage properties and
costumes were . . . as elaborate and accurate as circumstances would permit." Continued in 1907.10-11.

8 PLOMER, HENRY R. "Fortune Playhouse." N&Q 114 (11 August):
107.
    Cites an advertisement in a London newspaper from 1660/61,
which offers the Fortune Playhouse and its adjoining ground
for the building of tenements and a street.

9 RAVN, V[ILHELM] C[ARL]. "English Instrumentalists at the
Danish Court in the Time of Shakespeare." SIMG 7:550-63.
    Examines a small group of English "instrumentalists" who
also, apparently, presented dances and interludes in Denmark
during 1579-1586. Ravn also discusses Leicester's Men,
including Will Kempe.

10 WALLACE, CHARLES WILLIAM. "Old Blackfriars Theatre: Fresh
Discovery of Documents." Times (London), 12 September, p.
6.
    Letter to the editor announcing discovery of four law-
suits bearing on the Blackfriars and offering some conclusions drawn from them. Wallace's arguments are developed
more fully in 1908.18, the published version of his dissertation (1906.11).

11 _____. "The Children of the Chapel at Blackfriars, 1597-1603."
Ph.D. dissertation, Freiburg University, 207 pp.
    Published: 1908.18.

1907

*1   ARCHER, WILLIAM. "The Fortune Theatre, 1600." <u>Tribune</u>
(London) 12 October.
Cited in <u>NCBEL</u> 1, col. 1385. Abstract of 1908.2.

2   BOAS, FREDERICK S. " A 'Defence of Oxford Plays and Players.'"
<u>FortR</u> 88 (August):309–19.
Discusses a previously unknown defense of the academic
stage by playwright William Gager, from 1592, directed to
John Rainolds. Gager answers Rainolds's attack point for
point. See also 1916.17–18; 1974.3.

3   CHAMBERS, E[DMUND] K. "The Elizabethan Lords Chamberlain."
<u>MSC</u> 1, pt. 1:31–42.
Traces the succession of Lords Chamberlain from 1558 to
1603. Chambers includes brief biographies of William
Howard, Thomas Ratliffe, Henry Carey, and William Brooke,
as well as brief notes on the various companies connected
with the Chamberlain's office.

4   _____. "The Stage of the Globe." In <u>The Works of Shakespeare</u>.
Vol. 10. Edited by A. H. Bullen. Stratford: Shakespeare
Head Press, 351–62.
After a lengthy preamble setting forth the problems of
reconstruction, Chambers describes the Globe on the model
of the Fortune contract, "eighty feet square without and
fifty-five feet square within." The description of the
stage follows Brodmeier (1904.5), with three divisions of
the stage (inner, outer, upper) and scenes alternating
among them. Chambers believes, however, that there were no
stage posts at the Globe. His inner stage is smaller than
Brodmeier's, and more in line with Reynolds's "alcove"
(1905.8).

5   _____, and GREG, W[ALTER] W[ILSON], eds. "Dramatic Records
from the City of London: The Remembrancia." <u>MSC</u> 1, pt.
1:43–100.
A selection of letters and other documents from the
Remembrancia preserved in the Office of the Town Clerk in
the City of London. See also 1878.2; 1956.35.

6   CLARK, ANDREW. "Maldon Records and the Drama." <u>N&Q</u> 115 (9
March):181–83.
Examines the archives of the borough of Maldon, Essex,
for information on dramatic production from 1447 to 1635;
lists all recorded payments for theatrical purposes. See
also 1909.10. Continued in 1907.7–9.

1907

7 _____. "Maldon Records and the Drama." N&Q 115 (4 May):342–
43.
Continues 1907.6; continued in 1907.8–9.

8 _____. "Maldon Records and the Drama." N&Q 115 (1 June):422–
23.
Continues 1907.6–7; concluded in 1907.9.

9 _____. "Maldon Records and the Drama." N&Q 116 (20 July):
43–44.
Concludes 1907.6–8; see also 1909.10.

10 GRABO, CARL H. "The Stage for Which Shakespeare Wrote, V:
The Staging of Macbeth and Romeo and Juliet." Chautauquan
45 (January):206–18.
Continuation of 1906.4–7. Grabo here discusses the two
plays in terms of stage directions for each scene. Concluded
in 1907.11.

11 _____. "The Stage for Which Shakespeare Wrote, VI: Some
Effects of Elizabethan Stage Conditions upon Shakespeare's
Method." Chautauquan 45 (February):331–43.
Concludes the series consisting of 1906.4–7 and 1907.10.
The time of performances, the nature of the acting, and the
modification or shaping of dramatic structure are Grabo's
topics. In all, this series is balanced in its approach and
deserving of a wider reputation than it has in the field.

12 HALLIWELL-PHILLIPPS, J[AMES] O[RCHARD]. Outlines of the Life
of Shakespeare. 11th ed. 2 vols. London: Longmans,
Green, 946 pp.
Eleventh edition of 1881.3, expanded, with information
of theatrical interest throughout.

13 HARRIS, CHARLES. "English Actors in Germany in the Sixteenth
and Seventeenth Centuries." WRUB, n.s. 10, no. 6
(November):136–63.
A general discussion, summarizing the state of research
in the field. See Index under Actors--English on Continent.

14 _____. "The English Comedians in Germany before the Thirty
Years War: The Financial Side." PMLA 22, no. 3:446–64.
Analyzes playgoing expenses recorded in Moryson's
Itinerary in order to estimate the income of a touring
English company around 1600. Harris puts the average
income at around £55, a quite substantial sum at the time.

15 HENSLOW, PHILIP. Henslowe Papers: Being Documents Supplemen-
    tary to Henslowe's Diary. Edited by Walter W[ilson] Greg.
    London: A. H. Bullen, 187 pp.
        Contains abstracts of selected documents relating to the
    theatres and the Bear Garden, to the drama and stage, and
    to bearbaiting; Edward Alleyn's memorandum book; and
    miscellaneous notes and papers. Three appendixes contain
    a list of documents not at Dulwich, dramatic plots, and
    Alleyn's part in Orlando Furioso. See also 1977.8.

16 MAAS, HERMAN. Aussere Geschichte der englischen Theatertruppen
    in dem Zeitraum von 1559 bis 1642. Materialien zur Kunde
    des älteren englischen Dramas, no. 19, edited by Willy
    Bang[-Kaup.] Louvain: A. Uystpruyst, 283 pp.
        A comprehensive examination of the acting companies of
    the period. Seven chapters treat the adult groups and
    five the children's, with chronological coverage. This is
    primarily a compilation of documentary sources rather than
    an interpretive history. At the time of publication this
    work stood as the most important in its field, but it has
    since been superseded by Murray (1910.15), Chambers
    (1923.2), and Bentley (1941.1).

17 PERCY, EUSTACE. The Privy Council under the Tudors. Oxford:
    B. Blackwell, 74 pp.
        The Stanhope Essay, 1907. While this is an excellent
    historical analysis of a most important political body,
    there is nothing here of theatrical interest. Included
    because of listing in NCBEL 1, col. 1383.

18 REYNOLDS, GEORGE F[ULLMER]. "'Trees' on the Stage of
    Shakespeare." MP 5 (October):153-68.
        Examines the use of forest and tree settings to illus-
    trate Elizabethan staging methods. Reynolds argues here
    that such settings existed, included real trees, and were
    used to suggest solitude and desolation. He bases his
    conclusions on textual references and Simon Forman's
    descriptions of four plays he saw. Essentially this is an
    argument for simultaneous staging in the public theatres.

19 STOPES, CHARLOTTE CARMICHAEL. "Elizabethan Stage Scenery."
    FortR 87 (June):1107-17.
        Attempts first to account for differences in staging
    styles by comparing what she calls "the national spirit" of
    the Elizabethan period and her own time, then to counter
    the modern notion of scenery with the Elizabethan usage of
    properties and hangings.

1907

20 WEGENER, RICHARD. Die Büchneneinrichtung des Shakespeareschen
    Theaters nach den zeitgenössischen Dramen. Halle: Max
    Niemeyer, 164 pp.
        An attempt at a comprehensive reconstruction of staging
    practices based on stage directions and textual allusions
    in published plays and surviving manuscripts. The Swan
    drawing is taken as the basis for the public theatres, the
    Globe in particular. Wegener also examines the second
    Blackfriars. Probable uses of stage structures for scenes
    set in homes, battlefields, and other locations are
    discussed, with the focus on the flexible use of stage doors,
    the traverse, and the upper stage. One of the most moderate
    of the German studies of its time. See 1909.24.

1908

1 ALBRIGHT, VICTOR EMANUEL. A Typical Shakespearian Stage: The
   Outer-Inner Stage. New York: Knickerbocker Press, 42 pp.
       The third chapter of 1909.1 and 2. Albright seeks to
   dismiss the Swan drawing while accepting the Messalina
   title page as valid visual evidence. He argues backwards
   from the Restoration stage, specifically the Duke's Theatre
   of 1671, and advocates the alternation theory.

2 ARCHER, WILLIAM. "The Fortune Theatre, 1600." JDSG 44:159-66.
       Discusses the Fortune contract and attempts a reconstruc-
   tion of the playhouse based on it. Abstracted in 1907.1.

*3 _____. "The Swan Drawing." Tribune (London), 11 January.
       Cited in NCBEL 1, col. 1385.

4 CHAMBERS, E[DMUND] K., and GREG, WALTER W[ILSON], eds.
   "Dramatic Records from the Lansdowne Manuscripts." MSC
   1, pt. 2:143-215.
       Documents drawn from the Burghley Papers, accumulated
   by Sir William Cecil. A total of twenty-two entries are
   included, from 1562 to after 1595. Excluded are all but
   one of the documents published by Feuillerat in 1908.6.

5 DURAND, WALTER YALE. "Some Errors Concerning Richard Edwards."
   MLN 23 (May):129-31.
       Points out minor errors regarding the life and works of
   Edwards in John Farmer's edition of Damon and Pithias.

6 FEUILLERAT, ALBERT, ed. Documents Relating to the Office of
   the Revels in the Time of Queen Elizabeth. Materialien
   zur Kunde des älteren englischen Dramas, no. 21, edited by

Willy Bang[-Kaup.] Louvain: A. Uystpruyst, 513 pp.
    Part I contains the documents related to the Office and
Officers of the Revels, while Part II contains extracts
from the account books from 1558 to 1601. Feuillerat
appends a chronological list of plays and masques mentioned
in the documents, fifty pages of explanatory notes, and
three indexes.

7 G., G. M. The Stage Censor, an Historical Sketch: 1544-1907.
    London: S. Low, Marston & Co., pp. 5-64.
        The relevant section is the first two chapters, dealing
    with the stage censor under the Tudors and Stuarts. This
    is a simple survey, with little depth and less objectivity.
    The writer's purpose seems to be to show how the stage
    censor has from the beginning abrogated the rights of every
    Englishman.

8 GILDERSLEEVE, VIRGINIA CROCHERON. "Government Regulation of
    the Elizabethan Drama." Ph.D. dissertation, Columbia
    University, 259 pp.
        Published: 1908.9.

9 _____. Government Regulation of the Elizabethan Drama.
    Columbia University Studies in English, series 11, no. 4.
    New York: Columbia University Press, 259 pp.
        Published version of 1908.8. An account of the laws and
    regulations, local and national, which affected the drama
    and theatre during the period. The work is based on the
    official documents of the time as they appear in govern-
    ment collections. Gildersleeve first examines the national
    regulations and the office of the Master of the Revels, and
    then moves into the local regulations in London from 1543
    to 1592 and from 1592 to 1642. She concludes with an
    analysis of the Puritan victory over the stage in 1642.

10 GODFREY, WALTER H. "An Elizabethan Playhouse." ArchR 23
    (Spring):239-44.
        A conjectural reconstruction of the Fortune, complete
    with perspective rendering, floor plans, and section
    drawings. Godfrey reprints the relevant section of the
    contract and bases his work on that. His Fortune is
    complete with inner stage, obliquely set doors, curtained
    upper stage, and balcony boxes above the doors. The stage
    pillars are set far to the sides, and there is a railing
    around the stage. Godfrey suggests that the Swan drawing
    is inaccurate, since "the rear wall as there represented is
    merely a temporary stage property with its imitation of
    heavy barred doors, required for the one play, concealing

in this exceptional case the more usual inner stage." He presents little evidence for his reconstruction aside from the contract. Reprinted: 1913.5; see also 1911.2-3; 1912.8; 1916.1.

11 HENSLOWE, PHILIP. Henslowe's Diary. Pt. 2, Commentary. Edited by Walter Wilson Greg. London: A. H. Bullen, 400 pp.
    The four main chapters treat Henslowe's family and private affairs, Henslowe and the stage, and plays and persons mentioned in the diary. A final chapter provides twelve tables of reference. Greg examines the Rose, the Fortune, and the Hope in detail; he also discusses several acting companies associated with Henslowe at one time or another. The chapter on plays lists 280, performed by 12 companies at various playhouses, and the chapter on persons mentioned includes detailed references. See also 1904.7; 1907.15; and other editions of the diary, 1845.3; 1961.13.

12 JARVIS, ROYAL PRESTON. "Investigations on Jigging." Ph.D. dissertation, Columbia University, 71 pp.
    Published: 1908.13.

13 _____. Investigations on Jigging. Transactions of the American Institute of Mining Engineers. New York: AIME, 71 pp.
    Published version of 1908.12. This has nothing to do with the theatrical jig of the Elizabethan period. Instead, the jig discussed is a device used in mining for separating minerals of different specific gravities. Included because of mistaken listing in ADDT, p. 49.

14 LAWRENCE, W[ILLIAM] J[OHN]. "Music in the Elizabethan Theatre." JDSG 44:36-50.
    Examines the use of inter-act music, the use of music to set a mood, and the location of the musicians in the private theatres. Reprinted: 1912.15.

15 _____. "The Situation of the Lord's Room." EStudien 39, no. 3 (Summer):402-12.
    Argues that the boxes for the nobility "were originally situate aloft in the tyring house, and that before 1609 the position had been abandoned." Reprinted: 1912.15.

16 SCHELLING, FELIX E. Elizabethan Drama 1558-1642: A History of the Drama in England from the Accession of Queen Elizabeth to the Closing of the Theaters, to Which Is Prefixed a Résumé of the Earlier Drama from Its Beginnings. Vol. 1. Boston and New York: Houghton, Mifflin & Co., pp. 141-93.

The relevant section is Chapter Four, "The London Playhouse." Schelling bases his discussion of the companies on
Fleay (1890.1) and his discussion of the theatres on
Ordish (1894.2). His examination of the structure of the
stage is drawn from Reynolds (1905.8), but here he includes
more documentation. Schelling also examines costuming and
management practices in his broad survey. Reprinted:
1911.24; 1935.14.

17 SMITH, WINIFRED. "Italian and Elizabethan Comedy." MP 5
(April):555-56.
     Examines Italian commedia actors and their drama in the
sixteenth century for their influence on England. Smith
here discusses character types and improvisation. See also
1912.21.

18 WALLACE, CHARLES WILLIAM. The Children of the Chapel at
Blackfriars 1597-1608: Introductory to the Children of the
Revels, Their Origin, Courses, and Influences. A History
Based upon Original Records, Documents, and Plays, Being a
Contribution to Knowledge of the Stage and Drama of
Shakespeare's Time. UNS, no. 8. Lincoln: University of
Nebraska, 207 pp.
     Published version of 1906.11. Particularly valuable in
its day for the new documentary evidence provided, it
remains an important contribution. Wallace deals with the
Blackfriars building, the organization and maintenance of
the Children of the Chapel under Queen Elizabeth, the
custom of sitting on the stage and its origin, the relationship of the Children at Blackfriars with other companies and
playhouses, and a variety of other issues. The notes are,
as Wallace indicates, the most important part of the book,
since he lays out his evidence in some detail. Certain
parts of the volume, however, such as the discussion of the
stage at Blackfriars and its furnishings, are "reserved for
the complete work" (a standard phrase in German dissertations of the time), projected for three volumes. That
work never appeared, but see also 1909.30-34; 1910.21-25;
1911.29; 1912.24; 1913.18; 1914.25-26. Wallace was an
indefatigable searcher of documents, and while perhaps not
overly modest he made many extremely important contributions to the field. See 1911.4.

19 WILSON, J[OHN] DOVER. "The Missing Title of Thomas Lodge's
Reply to Gosson's School of Abuse." MLR 3 (January):166-68.
     Claims that the work in question is the Honest Excuses
mentioned by Gosson in his Apologie for the School of
Abuse.

<u>1909</u>

1 ALBRIGHT, VICTOR E. "The Shakespearian Stage." Ph.D. dissertation, Columbia University, 194 pp.
Published: 1909.2.

2 _____ . The Shakespearian Stage. Columbia University Studies
in English, series 11, no. 6. New York: Columbia University Press, 194 pp.
Published version of 1909.1. The third chapter reprints
1908.1. The additional information is contained in Chapters Four and Five, "The Shakespearian Method of Stage
Presentation." Basically Albright argues backwards from the
Restoration mode of staging. He is a strong exponent of
the inner stage and the alternation theory.

3 ANON. "The Globe Theatre, Southwark, and Its Site." Builder
97 (25 September):333-34.
Briefly describes the monument to be unveiled at the
supposed site of the Globe. The writer includes a brief
history of the playhouse, including its relationship to the
Fortune contract and the Swan drawing. Rendle is the
authority used to set the site.

4 ANON. "Site of the Globe Theatre, Southwark." Builder 97
(13 November):516.
Briefly reviews Hubbard's (1909.13) and Martin's (1909.
19-21) arguments about the site, favoring Martin.

5 ANON. "Where Did the 'Wooden O.,' the Globe Theatre, Stand?"
Illustrated London News 135 (9 October):500-501.
Several pictures illustrating the dispute over the
location of the Globe (north or south of Maid Lane?), of
interest at the time because of Wallace's charges (in
1909.32) that the memorial tablet was set up in the wrong
location.

6 [ARKWRIGHT, GODFREY EDWARD PELLEW.] "Early Elizabethan Stage
Music." MusAnt 1 (October):30-40.
Discusses the music for five songs extracted from plays
of the boy companies and six others that may have been so
extracted. Arkwright prints "Pandolpho," one of the songs.

7 BOAS, F[REDERICK] S., and GREG, W[ALTER] W[ILSON], eds.
"James I at Oxford in 1605: Property Lists from the
University Archives." MSC 1, pt. 3:247-59.
Extracts from documents in the Oxford University Archives
related to plays performed during the visit of King James

from 27 to 31 August 1605, with commentary. The documents
are concerned with the London hire of apparel and furniture
for the occasion.

8 CHAMBERS, E[DMUND] K. "Court Performances under James I."
   MLR 4 (January):153–66.
         Chambers uses previously neglected records to add to our
   list of plays performed at Court, 1603–1616. The play, the
   date, and the members of the royal family in attendance are
   noted where possible. The new information clarifies the
   status of companies and actors in some cases.

9 _____, and GREG, W[ALTER] W[ILSON], eds. "Dramatic Records
   from the Patent Rolls: Company Licenses." MSC 1, pt. 3:
   260–84.
         Fourteen theatrical licenses from the Patent Rolls, plus
   two from the Signet Office, with commentary.

10 CLARK, ANDREW. "Players or Companies on Tour, 1548–1630."
    N&Q 120 (17 July):41–42.
         Examines the records of the borough of Saffron Walden,
    Essex, for information about theatrical activities from
    1547 to 1631, listing all recorded payments to companies
    and actors. See also 1907.6–9.

11 FLECKNOE, RICHARD. "A Short Discourse of the English Stage."
    In Critical Essays of the Seventeenth Century. Vol. 2.
    Edited by Joel Elias Spingarn. Oxford: Clarendon Press,
    pp. 91–96.
         Reprint of 1664.1.

12 HELMHOLTZ-PHELAN, ANNA AUGUSTA. "The Staging of the Court
    Drama to 1595." PMLA 24 (June):185–206.
         Examines staging at court in the sixteenth century and
    earlier. The relevant section (discussing the reign of
    Elizabeth) is based on the Revels Accounts. Helmholtz-
    Phelan discusses Lyly's Woman in the Moon in detail. She
    speculates on the use of a front curtain and perspective
    scenery.

13 HUBBARD, G[EORGE]. "The Site of the Globe Theatre of
    Shakespeare on Bankside as Shown by Maps of the Period."
    JRIBA, 3d series, 17:26–28.
         Argues for a site north of Maid Lane based on the visual
    evidence of early maps and views of London. See also
    1915.6–12. Hubbard is one of the strongest supporters of
    the north site.

1909

14 JACKSON, RICHARD C. "The Site of Shakespeare's Globe Play-
    house." <u>Athenaeum</u>, 30 October, pp. 525-26.
        Responds to Wallace in 1909.32, 33, questioning the
    validity of both his documents and his diagram, and present-
    ing evidence for a site south of New Park Street, earlier
    known as Maid Lane.

15 LAW, ERNEST. "Shakespeare in London." <u>Times</u> (London), 11
    October, p. 10.
        A letter to the editor, seconding Lee's appeal in
    1909.18 for a thorough search of the Public Records, and
    speculating on Shakespeare's post-1611 connection with the
    King's Men.

16 LAWRENCE W[ILLIAM] J[OHN]. "Early French Players in England."
    <u>Anglia</u> 32:60-89.
        Chronicles French actors in England from the time of
    Henry VII through the Restoration. Reprinted: 1912.15.

17 _____. "Title and Locality Boards on the Pre-Restoration
    Stage." <u>JDSG</u> 45:146-70.
        Examines the evidence for the use of title and location
    boards on the Tudor and Stuart stage. Lawrence concludes
    that title boards were frequently used, but that there is
    insufficient evidence concerning the general use of location
    boards, although we know they were used at Paul's, ca. 1600.
    <u>See</u> 1910.6. Reprinted: 1912.15.

18 LEE, SIDNEY. "Shakespeare in London." <u>Times</u> (London), 5
    October, p. 8.
        A letter to the editor commenting on Wallace's pieces in
    the previous two issues (1909.32-33). Lee challenges
    Wallace's assertion of the value of his discoveries,
    awaiting the full argument, and urges more systematic study
    of the lawsuits and other documents held in the Public
    Record Office.

19 MARTIN, WILLIAM. "Shakespeare in London." <u>Times</u> (London),
    7 October, p. 8.
        A letter to the editor clarifying Tree's letter of the
    previous day (1909.28). Martin interprets Wallace's
    evidence for situating the Globe north of Maid Lane (in
    1909.32-33) as actually referring to a position south of
    that street. <u>See also</u> 1909.21.

20 _____. "Shakespeare in London." <u>Times</u> (London), 8 October,
    p. 10.
        A letter to the editor summarizing the contents of six
    documents that trace the property of the Globe from 1626 to

1787, at which time it can be located exactly. Martin
again places the site to the south of Maid Lane. See also
1909.21.

21 _____. "The Site of Shakespeare's Globe Playhouse." Athenaeum,
9 October, p. 425.
Responds to Wallace in 1909.32-33, arguing for the south
side of Maid Lane, based on maps and views of London,
conveyances of property, tradition, and an alternate reading
of Wallace's evidence. Martin presents much the same
arguments as in 1909.19 and 20.

22 McDONNELL, MICHAEL, F.J. A History of St. Paul's School.
London: Chapman & Hall, pp. 143-55.
The earliest complete history of Paul's. The relevant
section of Chapter Nine deals with the headmastership of
Mulcaster (1596-1608), but there is little mention of
theatrical matters. For more information on Mulcaster's
theatrical connection, see 1943.3; 1970.5; 1972.6; 1974.10.

23 REYHER, PAUL. Les masques anglais: Etude sur les ballets et
la vie de court en Angleterre (1512-1640). Paris: Hachette,
563 pp.
Published version of his Ph.D. dissertation, University
of Paris. Reyher differentiates masques from other forms
of court entertainment, and discusses the literary and
theatrical elements, including scenery, costume, music,
and dance.

24 SKEMP, ARTHUR R. "Some Characteristics of the English Stage
before the Restoration." JDSG 45:101-25.
Examines the Messalina print and what is shows of the
shape of the stage, the character of the upper stage, and
the traverse. Skemp also discusses the heavens, the
mistaken tradition of the front curtain, and later modifications of the public stage. In his section on the private
theatre he stresses the size and shape of the Blackfriars
stage. Primarily a refutation of Wegener (1907.20).

25 STOPES, CHARLOTTE CARMICHAEL. "The Burbages and the Transpor-
tation of 'The Theatre.'" Athenaeum, 16 October, pp. 470-
72.
Discusses the problems involved in moving the playhouse
to its new site south of the river, based on information
found in various court cases. See also 1913.19. Reprinted:
1913.15; 1914.24.

1909

26 STOPES, C[HARLOTTE] C[ARMICHAEL]. "Burbage's 'Theatre.'"
    FortR 92 (1 July):49-59.
        A discussion of the life and achievements of James
    Burbage, father of James and Cuthbert and builder of the
    first public playhouse. Stopes draws much of her informa-
    tion from previously unknown lawsuits in various courts,
    held in the Public Record Office. Reprinted: 1913.15;
    1914.24; see also 1914.22.

27 _____. "Giles and Christopher Alleyn of Holywell." N&Q 120
    (30 October):341-43.
        Biographical notes on the men who leased James Burbage
    the land on which he built the Theatre. Much of the
    information is drawn from various court records.

28 TREE, HERBERT BEERBOHM. "Shakespeare in London." Times
    (London), 6 October, p. 10.
        A letter to the editor disagreeing with Wallace's as-
    sertion that the Globe was located north of Maid Lane (see
    1909.32). While himself not a historian, Tree bases his
    objection on Martin's discovery of a reference to the
    Globe in a Sacrament Token book from Southwark Cathedral.
    See also Martin's letter of the next day, 1909.19.

29 UNWIN, GEORGE. The Gilds and Companies of London. London:
    Methuen; New York: Charles Scribner's Sons, pp. 267-92.
        The relevant section is Chapter 16, dealing with the
    Lord Mayor's Shows. While the entire history of the Shows
    is traced, Unwin pays special attention to the Jacobean
    period, described as "the Golden Age of the Lord Mayor's
    Show." He examines the relationship of the Show to the
    court masque and discusses the contributions of Middleton,
    Munday, Webster, Dekker, and other major playwrights.
    Reprinted: 1925.18; 1938.10; 1963.19.

30 WALLACE, CHARLES WILLIAM. Advance Sheets from Shakespeare,
    the Globe, and Blackfriars. Stratford: Shakespeare Head
    Press, 16 pp.
        A portion of a plea at the Common Law in a case set for
    trial in February 1616. The plaintiff's bill reveals "the
    origin and history of shares in the Globe and Blackfriars
    in outline up to the date of the trial, gives the number of
    shares owned in each by Shakespeare and his associates at
    various dates, estimates the value of a share in 1615-16,
    and places an indefinite but clearly excessive estimate
    upon the profits." Wallace here reprints the Latin text
    "for private circulation only."

31 _____. <u>Globe Theatre Apparel</u>. London: privately printed, 11 pp.
   The documents of the Taylor <u>v</u>. Hemynges case, concerning costumes of the King's Men, from 1612. Wallace prints the Bill of Complaint and two Answers.

32 _____. "Shakespeare in London: Fresh Documents on the Poet and His Theatres, the Globe and the Blackfriars." <u>Times</u> (London), 2 October, p. 9.
   Discusses Shakespeare's financial holdings in the Globe and Blackfriars, based on the discovery of the records of a lawsuit (<u>see</u> 1909.30). Wallace also attempts to locate the Globe, contributing to the controversy that raged for the next fifteen years by placing the building to the north of Maid Lane. Continued in 1909.33. <u>See</u> 1909.14, 18, 21.

33 _____. "Shakespeare in London: Fresh Documents on the Poet and His Theatres, the Globe and Blackfriars." <u>Times</u> (London), 4 October, p. 9.
   Continuation of 1909.32, giving the translated text of the documents. <u>See also</u> 1909.14, 18, 21, 30.

34 _____. "Three London Theatres of Shakespeare's Time." <u>University Studies</u> (Nebraska) 9 (October):287-342.
   Information about the Red Bull, the Fortune, and the Bear Garden, drawn from suits in the Court of Requests, preserved in the Public Record Office. Wallace prints the documents, as well as his deductions from them. He includes the Woodford <u>v</u>. Holland case, bearing on the Red Bull; the Smith <u>v</u>. Beeston suit, dealing with Queen Anne's Men; and the Alleyn <u>v</u>. Henslowe proceedings, about the Fortune and the Red Bull.

<u>1910</u>

1 ANON. "Shakespeare Discoveries." <u>Outlook</u> 94 (26 March):655-56.
   Announces Wallace's discovery of documents described in 1910.22.

2 ANON. "The Site of the Globe Theatre, Bankside." <u>Builder</u> 108 (26 March):353.
   Cites the testimony of Mrs. Thrale in 1781 that she saw the foundations of the Globe, "hexagonal in form without . . . round within." Whatever she saw, it was south of Maid Lane.

1910

3 ARONSTEIN, PHILIP. "Die Organisation des englischen Shauspiels im Zeitalter Shakespeares, I." GRM 2:165-75.
   Discusses government regulation and royal patronage of the drama. Continued in 1910.4.

4 _____. "Die Organisation des englischen Schauspiels im Zeitalter Shakespeares, II." GRM 2:216-31.
   Continuation of 1910.3. Aronstein here discusses the system of sharers, housekeepers, hired men, and boys used in the Elizabethan playhouses.

5 CHILD, HAROLD H. "The Elizabethan Theatre." In Cambridge History of English Literature. Vol. 6, The Drama to 1642, Pt. 2. Edited by A. W. Ward and A. R. Waller. Cambridge: University Press, pp. 241-78.
   Surveys the field: includes discussions of the companies, the playhouses, methods of staging, costumes, the audience, and the financial arrangements. Reprinted: 1919.3; 1932.3; 1934.1; 1949.4; 1950.6.

6 CONRAD, HERMANN. "Bemerkungen zu W. J. Lawrence Aufsatz 'Title and Locality Boards.'" JDSG 46:106-13.
   Responds to Lawrence in 1909.17, claiming that "title" is a general term and does not necessarily refer to a board bearing the title of the play posted in the theatre.

7 FEUILLERAT, ALBERT. Le Bureau des Menus-Plaisirs (Office of the Revels) et la mise en scène à la cour d'Elizabeth. Louvain: A. Uystpruyst, 88 pp.
   Published version of his Ph.D. dissertation, University of Paris. Intended as an introduction to and discussion of the documents in 1908.6. The two major chapters give a brief history of the Office of the Revels and discuss the function and administration of the Office.

8 _____. "Quelques documents nouveaux sur le Théâtre de Blackfriars." In Mélanges littéraires publiés par la Faculté des Lettres de Clermont-Ferrand. Clermont-Ferrand: Université Faculté des Lettres et Sciences Humaines, pp. 267-76.
   Announces the discovery of three documents that establish the existence of the first Blackfriars as a separate theatre in 1576. Feuillerat briefly discloses the transactions between Farrant and Hunnis connected with the playhouse and its early history. See also 1911.13; 1912.6, 17, 23; 1913.3.

9 FORESTIER, A[MEDEE]. "Origins of the English Stage, No. VI:
   A Shakespeare Play at the Old Globe in Shakespeare's Day."
   Illustrated London News 136 (19 March):423.
        A conjectural illustration of 1 Henry IV, showing the
   theatre, stage, actors, and audience, with five lines of
   commentary.

10 LAW, ERNEST. "Shakespeare at Whitehall: Othello on All
   Hallow's Day, 1604." Times (London), 31 October, p. 10.
        Discusses in general terms the performance in the
   Whitehall banqueting house. Law also touches on the
   performance of Merry Wives of Windsor in the Great Hall that
   same year. Continued in 1910.11.

11 _____. "Shakespeare's Christmas, St. Stephen's Day, 1604:
   The First Night Performance of Measure for Measure." Times
   (London), 26 December, p. 10.
        Continuation of 1910.10. Law discusses the December
   twenty-six court performance in the Great Hall, arguing
   that the "gross dialogues" were cut for the occasion.

12 MANLY, J[OHN] M[ATTHEWS]. "The Children of the Chapel Royal
   and Their Masters." In Cambridge History of English
   Literature. Vol. 6, The Drama to 1642, pt. 2. Edited by
   A. W. Ward and A. R. Waller. Cambridge: University Press,
   pp. 279-92.
        Discusses the series of seventeenth-century masters of
   the Children of the Chapel and their possible and known
   dramatic contributions as well as the professional troupe
   which presented public performances at Blackfriars.
   Reprinted: 1919.12; 1932.10; 1934.10; 1949.10; 1950.13.

13 MARTIN, WILLIAM. "The Site of the Globe Playhouse of
   Shakespeare." Surrey Archaeological Collections 23:149-202.
        Reviews the evidence that determined the position of the
   plaque commemorating the site of the Globe on the south
   side of Park Street, formerly Maid Lane. Martin considers
   three classes of evidence: legal, semi-legal, and business
   documents; printed and oral accounts of the site; and
   contemporary maps, views, and plans. He follows Rendle
   (1878.3) in the interpretation of most documents. The
   many illustrations help the reader to follow the argument.
   This is Martin's major contribution to the controversy over
   the site of the Globe and is frequently drawn on by others.
   See Index under Globe Playhouse--Site of.

1910

14 MÜLLER, C. "Zur Geschichte der Hirtenspiele in dem
   Entertainments der Königin Elisabeth und König Jakobs I."
   GRM 10:456-83.
      Examines the songs in the entertainments of Elizabeth
   and James during progresses, with a chronicle of such
   entertainments.

15 MURRAY, JOHN TUCKER. English Dramatic Companies, 1558-1642.
   Vol. 1, London Companies; Vol. 2, Provincial Companies.
   London: Constable & Co.; Boston: Houghton-Mifflin, 804 pp.
      An attempt at a comprehensive history of all dramatic
   companies in London and the provinces during the reigns
   of Elizabeth, James, and Charles. While there is little
   new in the first volume, the second presents the results of
   the first systematic search of records of a dozen provincial cities. The appendixes include many newly discovered
   documents. See 1920.30. Superseded by Chambers (1923.2)
   and Bentley (1941.1).

16 NEUENDORFF, BERNHARD. Die englische Volksbühne im Zeitalter
   Shakespeares nach den Bühnenweisungen. Berlin: E. Felber,
   230 pp.
      Examines the typical Elizabethan stage, based on a study
   of the stage directions in printed texts. Neuendorff supports the inner-outer stage hypothesis and advocates the
   alternation theory.

*17 STOPES, CHARLOTTE CARMICHAEL. "The Rose and the Swan, 1597."
   Stage (London), 6 January.
      Cited in 1917.3.

18 STOPES, CHARLOTTE C[ARMICHAEL]. "Shakespeare's Fellows and
   Followers." JDSG 46:92-105.
      Information drawn from the Lord Chamberlain's papers,
   concerning various actors, managers, and playwrights. See
   also 1931.2.

19 _____. "The Theatre." Archiv 124 (January):129-31.
      A brief review of her research since 1889 on Burbage's
   playhouse and Shakespeare's connection to it. See also
   1913.15, 19.

20 STOPES, C[HARLOTTE] C[ARMICHAEL]. William Hunnis and the
   Revels of the Chapel Royal: A Study of His Period and the
   Influences Which Affected Shakespeare. Materialien zur
   Kunde des älteren englischen Dramas, no. 29, edited by
   Willy Bang[-Kaup]. Louvain: A. Uystpruyst, 362 pp.
      An attempt at a biography of the Master of the Children
   of the Chapel Royal, 1566-1597, with documentary notes.

21 WALLACE, C[HARLES] W[ILLIAM]. "Gervase Markham, Dramatist."
    JDSG 46:345-50.
        Records from the Court of Requests of a suit (1623)
    between Markham and various actors.

22 WALLACE, CHARLES WILLIAM. "New Shakespeare Discoveries:
    Shakespeare as a Man among Men." Harper's 120 (March):489-
    510.
        Discusses the discovery of documents in the Court of
    Requests, preserved in the Public Record Office, bearing on
    Shakespeare's life in London. There is little of theatrical
    interest.

23 WALLACE, CHARLES W[ILLIAM]. "Shakespeare and His London
    Associates as Revealed in Recently Discovered Documents."
    University Studies (Nebraska) 10, no. 4 (October):261-360.
        Transcripts of fifty-six documents of the period bearing
    on theatrical affairs, with commentary. Thirty-nine of the
    documents are from the Belott-Mountjoy case, earlier
    reported in 1910.22. Eight are from the Witter-Heminges
    case, earlier reported in 1910.24. The final nine are from
    the Keysar-Burbage case, earlier reported in 1906.10.

24 WALLACE, CHARLES WILLIAM. "Shakspere and the Blackfriars."
    Century 80 (September):742-52.
        Discusses Shakespeare's association with the Blackfriars,
    based upon a variety of records of court cases discovered
    by Wallace. The most important case centers on a charge of
    conspiracy against the Blackfriars shareholders.

25 _____. "Shakespere's Money Interest in the Globe Theater."
    Century 80 (August):500-12.
        Discusses the business affairs of Shakespeare in the
    organizing, building, rebuilding, and management of the
    Globe, drawn from a variety of records of court cases
    discovered by Wallace. He concludes, for example, that
    Shakespeare in fact owned an interest in the Globe after
    he retired to Stratford, and that his income from his share
    was less than previously supposed.

26 WILSON, J[OHN] D[OVER]. "The Puritan Attack on the Stage."
    In Cambridge History of English Literature. Vol. 6, The
    Drama to 1642. Pt. 2. Edited by A. W. Ward and A. R.
    Waller. Cambridge: University Press, pp. 373-409.
        Discusses the Puritan background and the major publica-
    tions (including those of Gosson, Lodge, Stubbes, Rankins,
    Rainolds, and Prynne) of the attack. Reprinted: 1919.20;
    1932.12; 1934.20; 1949.17; 1950.21.

1911

1 ADAMS, JOSEPH QUINCY, Jr. "The Four Pictorial Representations
   of the Elizabethan Stage." JEGP 10 (April):329-33.
       Examines Albright's treatment of the Swan, Red Bull,
   Messalina, and Roxana drawings in 1909.2 and finds it
   wanting. The Messalina and Roxana illustrations "offer
   practically no proof of Mr. Albright's typical stage,"
   while Albright's rejection of the Swan drawing "will not
   do." Adams rejects Albright's theories.

2 ANON. "At the Sign of St. Paul's." Illustrated London News
   140 (9 September):402.
       Four photographs of James P. Maginnis's model of the
   Fortune, from designs by Godfrey in 1908.10.

3 ANON. "The Elizabethan Playhouse." Architect and Builder's
   Journal, 16 August, pp. 167-71.
       Summarizes 1908.10 and reprints the sections and floor-
   plans from that reconstruction.

4 BASKERVILL, C[HARLES] R[EED]. "The Custom of Sitting on the
   Elizabethan Stage." MP 8 (April):581-90.
       Takes issue with Wallace's conclusion in 1908.18 that
   the custom of sitting on the stage began at the Blackfriars
   in 1597, citing a variety of sources showing a broader
   application.

5 CHAMBERS, E[DMUND] K. "Commissions for the Chapel." MSC 1,
   pts. 4 & 5:357-63.
       Commissions issued to Nathaniel Giles in 1604 and 1606,
   bearing on the use of boys for dramatic purposes.

6 _____. "A Jotting by John Aubrey." MSC 1, pts. 4 & 5:341-47.
       A facsimile of a page of Aubrey's notes, concerning
   Fletcher, Jonson, Shakespeare, and John Ogilby the dancing
   master, with commentary. William Beeston apparently served
   as the source of the information.

7 _____. "Plays of the King's Men in 1641." MSC 1, pts. 4 & 5:
   364-69.
       A warrant and schedule from the Lord Chamberlain's
   Warrant Books in the Public Record Office, with commentary.
   The lists contains sixty plays, apparently all of the
   repertory of the King's Men not yet in print and thus
   reserved for that company.

8 _____. "Two Early Player Lists." MSC 1, pts. 4 & 5:348-56.
   A letter listing the Earl of Leicester's Men in 1572 and
   a certificate listing Queen Elizabeth's Men in 1588, with
   commentary.

9 _____, and GREG, W[ALTER] W[ILSON], eds. "Dramatic Records
   from the Privy Council Register, 1603-42." MSC 1, pts.
   4 & 5:370-95.
   Transcripts of all entries bearing on dramatic history
   from the Privy Council Register during the reigns of James
   and Charles. Chambers and Greg list twenty-four entries in
   all. See also 1912.21.

10 COLLINS, CHURTON. "Shakespearian Theatres." ContempR 99
   (January):96-108.
   A popular general survey of playhouses, acting, and
   theatrical conditions of Shakespeare's time. Collins is
   rather anecdotal, taking the reader on an imaginary tour
   and to an imaginary performance. There are many minor
   errors of fact.

11 CORBIN, JOHN. "Shakespere His Own Stage-Manager." Century
   83 (December):260-70.
   A popular treatment, arguing for the presentation of the
   plays as Shakespeare intended them. Corbin includes
   drawings of a reconstruction with inner stages above and
   below, and octagonal shape. He also describes productions
   he participated in at the New Theatre.

12 CUNLIFFE, J[OHN] W[ILLIAM], ed. "The Queenes Majesties
   Entertainment at Woodstocke." PMLA 26 (March):92-141.
   An edition of the entertainment, based on the 1585 quarto,
   with critical commentary including information of theatrical
   interest.

13 FEUILLERAT, A[LBERT]. "Shakespeare's Blackfriars: Discovery
   of Important Documents." Daily Chronicle (London), no.
   15,552, 22 December, p. 4.
   Announces the discovery of nine documents among the
   Losely manuscripts concerning the history of the first
   Blackfriars. A rough history of the theatre is sketched
   in less than two newspaper columns. A more complete
   history with full documentation is left for another time.
   See also 1912.6, 17, 23; 1913.3.

1911

14 FORESTIER, A[MEDEE]. "Where Money Came from for Dulwich
    College; Chief Rival to Shakespeare's Theatre, the Globe:
    The Fortune." <u>Illustrated London News</u> 140 (12 August):
    276-77.
        Two drawings, a section and a perspective rendering, of
    Forestier's reconstruction, with notes. This version of
    the Fortune has obliquely set doors with balconies above
    them, and large inner stages above and below. It is very
    similar to Godfrey's reconstruction (1908.10).

15 LAW, ERNEST. "Cunningham's Extracts from the Revels Books,
    1842, I." <u>Athenaeum</u>, 9 September, pp. 297-99.
        Responds to Stopes in 1911.26, 27, arguing for the
    genuineness of the Revels extracts. Law answers her
    objections point by point, with reference to many contem-
    porary documents. Here he deals with the genuineness of the
    ink, the punctuation, and the spelling of the 1604-5 entry.
    Continued in 1911.16-17; 1912.13-14. For response <u>see</u>
    1911.29. <u>See</u> <u>also</u> 1911.18; 1912.20; 1913.8; 1920.12-13, 26;
    1922.8; 1925.20; 1928.16; 1930.9.

16 _____. "Cunningham's Extracts from the Revels Books, 1842,
    II." <u>Athenaeum</u>, 16 September, p. 324.
        Continuation of 1911.15, in response to 1911.26-27.
    Here Law examines word usage in the 1604-5 document. For
    response <u>see</u> 1911.29. Continued in 1911.17. <u>See</u> <u>also</u>
    1911.18; 1912.20; 1913.8; 1920.12-13, 26; 1922.8; 1925.20;
    1928.16; 1930.9.

17 _____. "Cunningham's Extracts from the Revels Books, 1842,
    III." <u>Athenaeum</u>, 30 September, p. 388.
        Continuation of 1911.15, 16. Here Law answers Stopes's
    objections to the incompleteness of the 1604-5 document.
    Continued in 1912.13-14; for response <u>see</u> 1911.29. <u>See</u>
    <u>also</u> 1911.18; 1912.20; 1913.8; 1920.12-13, 26; 1922.8;
    1925.20; 1928.16; 1930.9.

18 LAW, ERNEST PHILIP ALPHONSE. <u>Some Supposed Shakespeare</u>
    <u>Forgeries</u>. London: G. Bell & Sons, 80 pp.
        Records the history of the controversy over the sup-
    posedly forged Revels Accounts of 1604 and 1611, ultimately
    arguing for their genuineness. Based on 1911.15-17 and
    1912.13-14. <u>See</u> <u>also</u> 1911.27-29; 1912.20; 1913.8; 1920.
    12-13, 26; 1922.8; 1925.20; 1928.16; 1930.9.

19 LAWRENCE, W[ILLIAM] J[OHN]. "The Evolution and Influence of
    the Elizabethan Playhouse." <u>JDSG</u> 47:18-41.
        Chronicles the changes in the playhouses and the manner

of presentation from the Theatre until the closing of the
playhouses in 1642. Reprinted: 1912.15.

20 ____. "The Seventeenth Century Theatre: Systems of Admission." Anglia 35:526-38.
Discusses the gathering of admissions at the various
points in the Elizabethan playhouse and the survival of
the custom in the Restoration and eighteenth century.
Reprinted: 1913.9.

21 PILCH, LEO. "Shakespeare als Regisseur." ZFEU 10, no. 4
(Fall):385-406.
Examines Shakespeare's function as director, citing
lines from Midsummer Night's Dream, Hamlet, 1 Henry IV,
and Henry V that provide stage directions for action.

22 REESE, GEORG HERMANN. Studien und Beiträge zur Geschichte der
englischen Schauspielkunst im Zeitalter Shakespeares. Jena:
G. Neuerhahn, 36 pp.
Published version of his Jena Ph.D. dissertation. Reese
examines costume practices during the period based on
textual allusions and stage directions in the published
plays. The two sections deal with costumes for Jewish
characters and historical costumes.

23 REYNOLDS, G[EORGE] F[ULLMER]. "What We Know of the Elizabethan Stage." MP 9 (July):47-82.
A review of the literature, divided into three parts:
treatment of sources, construction of the stage, and
principles of stage management. The point of departure
is Reynolds's own argument, presented in 1905.8, for an
essentially medieval method of staging. He emphasizes the
need to consider each playhouse individually and to use
evidence from published plays with great care. In an
appendix Reynolds considers several miscellaneous issues.
This is among the most important of the pre-World War I
articles, indispensible for tracing the history of the
field.

24 SCHELLING, FELIX E. Elizabethan Drama 1558-1642: A History
of the Drama in England from the Ascension of Queen Elizabeth to the Closing of the Theaters, to Which Is Prefixed
a Resume of the Earlier Drama from Its Beginnings. Vol. 1.
Boston and New York: Houghton, Mifflin & Co., pp. 141-93.
Reprint of 1908.16.

25 SPENCER, M. LYLE. Corpus Christi Pageants in England. New
York: Baker & Taylor, 276 pp.

1911

> While the final chapter, dealing with the passing of the
> pageants, covers the sixteenth and seventeenth centuries,
> there is little here of importance to the Elizabethan
> stage. Included because of listing in previous bibliog-
> raphies.

26 [STOPES, CHARLOTTE CARMICHAEL.] "Cunningham's Extracts from
    the Revels Books, 1842, I." Athenaeum, 22 July, pp. 101-2.
      Writing as "Audi Alterem Partem" ["Let the Other Side
    be Heard"], Stopes questions the genuineness of the extracts,
    based on the use of the paper, the handwriting, and the
    spelling. Continued in 1911.27; Law responds in 1911.15-17,
    and Stopes responds to the response in 1911.28. See also
    their books on the subject: Law, 1911.18, 1913.8; Stopes,
    1922.8. Other treatments, with arguments pro and con, may
    be found in 1920.12-13, 26; 1925.20; 1928.16; and 1930.9.

27 _____. "Cunningham's Extracts from the Revels Books, 1842,
    II." Athenaeum, 29 July, pp. 130-31.
      Continuation of 1911.26, written as "Audi Alterem Partem."
    Here Stopes questions the 1604-5 documents on the basis of
    the use of words compared to the usage found in other Revels
    Accounts, as well as their incompleteness. She also chal-
    lenges the 1636 account on the basis of the place of
    performance. See Law's response, 1911.15-17; Stopes's
    rebuttal, 1911.28; and the rest of the controversy, 1911.18;
    1912.13-14, 20; 1913.8; 1920.12-13, 26; 1922.8; 1925.20;
    1928.16; 1930.9.

28 _____. "Cunningham's Extracts from the Revels Books."
    Athenaeum, 7 October, pp. 421-22.
      Writing as "Audi Alterem Partem," Stopes responds to Law
    in 1911.15-17, attempting to refute his argument about the
    genuineness of the 1604-5 document. Law responds in
    1912.13-14; Stopes offers her rebuttal in 1912.20. See
    their books: Law, 1911.18, 1913.8; Stopes, 1922.8; as
    well as other contributions to the controversy in 1920.12-
    13, 26; 1925.20; 1928.16; 1930.9.

29 WALLACE, CHARLES WILLIAM. "The Swan Theatre and the Earl of
    Pembroke's Servants." EStudien 43, no. 3 (July):340-95.
      A set of documents from the Court of Requests, held in
    the Public Record Office, bearing on the Swan, with sixteen
    conclusions about the playhouse and its company that
    Wallace draws from the evidence presented.

1912

1   ADAMS, JOSEPH QUINCY, Jr. "Lordinge (alias 'Lodowick') Barry."
    MP 9 (April):567-70.
        Discusses the common error of calling Lordinge Barry,
    playwright and manager of the King's Revels company at
    Whitefriars, by the wrong name, Lodowick. See also
    1917.8.

2   BELL, WALTER GEORGE. "The Whitefriars Playhouses." In Fleet
    Street in Seven Centuries. London: Isaac Pitman & Sons,
    pp. 305-37.
        Discusses the possible playhouse in 1580, the Whitefriars
    of the Queen's Revels of 1610-13, and the Salisbury Court
    of 1629-64. Most of the information is drawn from Collier
    (1879.2), Fleay (1890.1), and Murray (1910.15). Bell also
    discusses the Dorset Garden Playhouse of the Restoration.

3   BRERETON, J[OHN] LE GAY. "Stage Arrangement in Peele's David
    and Bethsabe, I.i." MLR 7 (July):373-74.
        Draws attention to a 1537 German illustration, in
    relation to a stage direction in Peele's text that indicates
    Bethsabe is discovered bathing, with "David above viewing
    her." The implication is that he sits above an obliquely
    set door in order to see into the discovery space. Re-
    printed: 1948.5.

4   CLAPHAM, ALFRED W. "On the Topography of the Dominican Priory
    of London." Archaeologia 63:57-84.
        A paper read 18 January 1912. Clapham reconstructs the
    Blackfriars precinct, including the site of the playhouse.

5   CULLEN, CHARLES. "Puritanism and the Stage." PRPSG 43:153-81.
        Text of a paper read before the Historical and Philo-
    logical section of the Society, 20 March 1912. Cullen
    sketches the intellectual and cultural backgrounds, briefly
    describes the theatrical situation, and broadly traces the
    arguments of the Puritans, especially Stubbes and Prynne.

6   FEUILLERAT, ALBERT. "The Origins of Shakespeare's Theatre:
    Recent Discovery of Documents." JDSG 48:81-103.
        Discusses the documents found among the Losely Manu-
    scripts that verify the existence of the first Blackfriars
    Playhouse, built by Richard Farrant in 1576-77. Feuil-
    lerat also prints six letters and Farrant's lease for the
    first time. Abridged in 1911.13.

1912

7 FLOOD, W. H. GRATTAN. "Master Sebastian of Paul's." MusAnt
   3 (January):149-57.
      A brief biography of Sebastian Westcott, early Master of
   the Children of Paul's, touching on theatrical matters.

8 GODFREY, WALTER H. "A Scale Model of the Fortune Theatre."
   ArchR 31 (January):53-55.
      Photographs of a scale model built to Godfrey's plans in
   1908.10. See also 1911.3.

9 GRAVES, THORNTON SHIRLEY. "The Court and London Theatres
   during the Reign of Elizabeth." Ph.D. dissertation,
   University of Chicago, 93 pp.
      Published as 1913.6.

10 GRAVES, T[HORNTON] S[HIRLEY]. "A Note on the Swan Theatre."
   MP 9 (January):431-34.
      Discusses a letter of 1602 that demonstrates that the
   Swan was fitted with "hangings and curtains" (which Graves
   takes to be different) for at least one performance.

11 GRAVES, T[HORNTON SHIRLEY]. "Some Allusions to Religious and
   Political Plays." MP 9 (April):545-54.
      Discusses references to anti-Catholic plays in 1559 and
   plays about a possible marriage for Elizabeth (and other
   political matters) in 1565.

12 HUBBARD, GEORGE. "On the Exact Site of the Globe Playhouse
   of Shakespeare." TrLMArchS, n.s. 2, pt. 3:334-57.
      Text of a paper read to the Society, 26 February 1912.
   Hubbard argues for a site north of Maid Lane, based on
   the existence of a property known as "the Park" different
   from the Bishop of Winchester's Park to the south. He
   also cites the discovery of the possible foundations of
   the playhouse in 1907. See Index under Globe Playhouse--
   Site of.

13 LAW, ERNEST. "Cunnigham's Extracts from the Revels Books,
   1842, IV." Athenaeum, 6 April, p. 390.
      Responds to 1911.28, continuing 1911.15-17. Here Law
   argues for the genuineness of the 1611-12 play list.
   Continued in 1912.13; Stopes replies in 1912.20. See also
   1911.18; 1913.8; 1920.12-13, 26; 1922.8; 1925.20; 1928.16;
   1930.9.

14 _____. "Cunningham's Extracts from the Revels Books, 1842,
   V." Athenaeum, 27 April, pp. 470-71.

68

Conclusion of 1911.15-17; 1912.13. Here Law examines the record of 1636/37, which he finds genuine. Stopes based her objection on the place of performance listed, which she found to be false on the basis of payments made to the players. Law reads the same evidence differently, finding the listed place of performance to be genuine. <u>See also</u> 1911.18; 1912.20; 1913.8; 1920.12-13, 26; 1922.8; 1925.20; 1928.16, 1930.9.

15 LAWRENCE, W[ILLIAM] J[OHN]. <u>The Elizabethan Playhouse and Other Studies</u>. Stratford: Shakespeare Head Press, 265 pp.
      A collection composed of one new essay (1912.17) and revisions of eight others (1902.9; 1903.4-5; 1908.14-15; 1909.16-17; 1911.19). Lawrence includes a preface, a bibliography, and an index. <u>See also</u> 1913.9.

16 _____. "Light and Darkness in the Elizabethan Theatre." <u>EStudien</u> 45 (September):181-200.
      Discusses the bringing in of lights as "emblematic of the lateness of the hour," rather than for purposes of illumination. Lawrence argues that stages were never darkened for realistic effect. Reprinted: 1913.9. <u>See also</u> 1913.7; 1915.15.

17 _____. "New Facts about the Blackfriars: Monsieur Feuil-lerat's Discoveries." In <u>The Elizabethan Playhouse and Other Studies</u>. Stratford: Shakespeare Head Press, pp. 225-44.
      Briefly traces the history of the first Blackfriars, as set out by Feuillerat (only 1911.13 had yet been published; 1912.6 was still to come) and then attempts to place that theatre into the general mold of "Elizabethan private theatre."

18 _____. "Windows on the Pre-Restoration Stage." <u>Anglia</u> 36 (November):450-78.
      Examines the issue of the upper stage generally, and the windows belonging to the area particularly. Lawrence discusses casements, bay windows, windows with curtains, gated windows, conjunctive windows, upper back windows, and lower-stage windows, citing a variety of plays from many theatres. Reprinted: 1913.9.

19 SMITH, WINIFRED. <u>The Commedia dell'Arte: A Study in Italian Popular Comedy</u>. Columbia University Studies in English and Comparative Literature, no. 2. New York: Columbia University Press, pp. 170-99.
      The relevant section is Chapter Six, "The Commedia dell'

1912

Arte in Elizabethan and Jacobean England." Smith traces
Italian entertainers in England and commedia influences on
the drama. Based on 1908.17.

20 [STOPES, CHARLOTTE CARMICHAEL.] "Cunningham's Extracts from
the Revels Books." Athenaeum, 27 April, pp. 469-70.
Writing as "Audi Alterem Partem," Stopes responds to
Law (1912.13). She reiterates her reasons for considering
the 1611-12 list a forgery, primarily that only thirteen
of the thirty-two performances are listed and that the list
contains errors. See Law's final response, 1912.14. See
also 1911.18; 1913.8; 1920.12-13, 26; 1922.8; 1925.20;
1928.16; 1930.9.

21 STOPES, C[HARLOTTE] C[ARMICHAEL]. "Dramatic Records from the
Privy Council Register, James I and Charles I." JDSG
48:103-15.
Extracts from the Registers, 1613-1639, bearing on
theatrical affairs, with commentary. See also 1911.9.

22 SULLIVAN, MARY. "Court Masques of James I: Their Influence on
Shakespeare and Public Theatres." Ph.D. dissertation,
University of Nebraska, 259 pp.
Published as 1913.16.

23 WALLACE, CHARLES WILLIAM. The Evolution of the English Drama
up to Shakespeare, with a History of the First Blackfriars
Theatre: A Survey Based upon Original Records Now for the
First Time Collected and Published. Schriften der
deutschen Shakespeare-Gesselschaft, no. 4. Berlin: Georg
Reimer, 246 pp.
Attempts to trace the early history of theatre and drama
in Renaissance England, based on documents rediscovered by
Wallace and his wife over many years. The most important
section from a theatrical perspective is Chapters 14
through 19, dealing with the first Blackfriars. Wallace
prints excerpts from many documents to support his case.
The final chapters contain a table of plays and masques
performed before Elizabeth 1558-1585 and a list of payments
for plays at Court during the same period. This is among
the most important of Wallace's many contributions to
scholarship in the field.

1913

1 ALBRIGHT, VICTOR E. "Two of Percy's Plays as Proof of the
Elizabethan Stage." MP 11 (October):237-46.

Challenges the use of <u>Cuckqueens and Cuckolds Errant</u> and
<u>Faery Pastoral</u>, both manuscript plays by Percy, as evidence
of Elizabethan staging practices, since it is unlikely that
the manuscripts reflect actual productions. <u>See also</u>
1914.21.

2 COWLING, GEORGE HERBERT. <u>Music on the Shakespearian Stage</u>.
   Cambridge: University Press, 116 pp.
      Examines the role of music, both instrumental and vocal,
   on the stage of Shakespeare and his contemporaries. The
   seven chapters treat pre-Shakespearan music; a general view
   of the Elizabethan stage and its music; the instruments of
   the period and their uses; the use of incidental music;
   the musicians, the singers, and the songs in the plays; the
   share in the drama that the music had; and literary allusions
   to music in Elizabethan plays. Cowling concludes that
   music was an important part of Elizabethan performances and
   could be used simply as entertainment, to reveal character,
   or to increase dramatic intensity. <u>See</u> Index under Music.

3 FEUILLERAT, ALBERT. "Blackfriars Records." <u>MSC</u> 2, pt. 1:1–
   136.
      A selection of documents which locate Shakespeare's
   Blackfriars and show its relationship to Farrant's.
   Feuillerat divides the text into four sections, dealing with
   a general survey of the conventual buildings, Farrant's
   playhouse, Burbage's playhouse, and the sale of the property
   adjoining the latter.

4 FOWELL, FRANK, and PALMER, FRANK. <u>Censorship in England</u>.
   London: Frank Palmer, pp. 1–93.
      The relevant section is the first four chapters, dealing
   with the origin of censorship, Sir Henry Herbert and his
   fees, the work of the early censors, and the work of the
   censors during the Interregnum. Chapter Three, "The Early
   Censors at Work," gives numerous examples of the Master of
   the Revel's comments and modifications.

5 GODFREY, WALTER H. "The Fortune Theatre, London (1600)." In
   <u>Some Famous Buildings and Their Story</u>. By Alfred W.
   Clapham and Walter H. Godfrey. Westminster: Technical
   Journals, pp. 13–28.
      Reprint of 1908.10.

6 GRAVES, THORNTON SHIRLEY. <u>The Court and London Theatres
   during the Reign of Queen Elizabeth</u>. Menasha, Wisc.:
   Collegiate Press, 93 pp.
      Published version of 1912.9. Graves approaches the
   London playhouses before 1603 from the perspective of the

1913

court stage, and points out the probability of influence.
He divides his discussion into four parts: the structural
elements of the Elizabethan theatre; the inn-yard and its
relationship to the earliest London theatres; the influence
of the court on the general stage structure; and the
influence of the court on methods of production. The major
development here is the theory of the "canopy" stage, a
permanent curtained booth used for discoveries instead of
an "inner stage."

7 GRAVES, T[HORNTON] S[HIRLEY]. "Night Scenes in the Elizabethan
   Theatres." EStudien 47 (August):63-71.
      Responds to Lawrence (1912.16), suggesting that black
   hangings could also be used to suggest night. Graves also
   argues that there were night performances in the public
   theatres. See also Lawrence's reply, 1915.15.

8 LAW, ERNEST PHILIP ALPHONSE. More about Shakespeare "Forgeries." London: G. Bell & Sons, 70 pp.
      Reprint of 1911.15-17; 1912.13-14.

9 LAWRENCE, W[ILLIAM] J[OHN]. The Elizabethan Playhouse and
   Other Studies. Second Series. Stratford: Shakespeare
   Head Press, 261 pp.
      Contains revisions of three previously published essays
   (1911.20; 1912.16, 18) and three new essays (1913.10-12)
   dealing with the theatre of the period, as well as a
   preface, bibliography, and index.

10 _____. "The Origin of the English Picture-Stage." In The
    Elizabethan Playhouse and Other Studies. Second Series.
    Stratford: Shakespeare Head Press, pp. 119-48.
       Examines possible uses of scenery in the private
    theatres before 1642 and D'Avenant's productions during
    the Interregnum as preparation for a discussion of the
    use of scenery after 1660.

11 _____. "The Origin of the Theatre Programme." In The Eliza-
    bethan Playhouse and Other Studies. Second Series.
    Stratford: Shakespeare Head Press, pp. 55-92.
       Examines the advertising playbills and posters used to
    attract audiences during this period as preparation for
    tracing the later history of the program.

12 _____. "The Persistence of Elizabethan Conventions." In The
    Elizabethan Playhouse and Other Studies. Second Series.
    Stratford: Shakespeare Head Press, pp. 149-88.
       Examines possible influences on later periods of Eliza-

bethan uses of music, masques, the visualization of dreams,
spectators sitting on the stage, passing over the stage,
the bearing of bodies from the stage, the terminal dance,
and the custom of announcing the next performance.

13 MARTIN, WILLIAM. "An Elizabethan Theatre Program." SMNN 24,
no. 277 (January):16-20.
Discusses and prints the Swan "Plot" of England's Joy,
which Martin assumes was printed for the audience like a
modern program.

14 POEL, WILLIAM. Shakespeare in the Theatre. London and
Toronto: Sidgwick & Jackson, pp. 3-28.
The relevant section contains part of "The Elizabethan
Playhouse," a paper read before the Elizabethan Literary
Society on 1 November 1893. Instead of stage structures,
Poel discusses general principles of performance that can
be adapted in the modern theatre.

15 STOPES, C[HARLOTTE] C[ARMICHAEL]. Burbage and Shakespeare's
Stage. London: Alexander Moring, The De la More Press,
272 pp.
Contains reprints of 1909.25-26. The three chapters
examine the lives of James Burbage, builder of the Theatre;
his sons, Richard and Cuthbert; and their descendents. The
last half of the volume consists of twenty-eight documentary
notes, from which Stopes draws her material. The Preface
sheds some light on her competition with the Wallaces.
Stopes includes considerable information about the building
of the Theatre, but she concentrates on biography. See
also Wallace, 1913.19.

16 SULLIVAN, MARY. Court Masques of James I: Their Influence on
Shakespeare and the Public Theatres. New York and London:
G. P. Putnam's Sons, Knickerbocker Press, 259 pp.
Published version of 1912.22. The first four chapters
treat the periods 1603-1608, 1608-1614, 1614-1616, and
1616-1625. The final two chapters examine the cost of
dramatic productions at Court and the influence of diplomatic conditions upon literature. A valuable appendix
prints eighty-seven excerpts from letters, dispatches, and
other documents related to court masques of James I.
Sullivan's central thesis is that the occasion of the masque
is the most important determinant of content.

17 THORNDIKE, ASHLEY HORACE. "From Outdoors to Indoors on the
Elizabethan Stage." In Anniversary Papers by Colleagues
and Pupils of George Lyman Kittredge. Boston: Ginn, pp.
273-79.

1913

Discusses the use of curtains and the inner stage for
the representation of location whenever desired by use of
the principle of alternation, specifically when characters
move from an outdoor location to an indoor location.
Thorndike uses A Yorkshire Tragedy as his main example.
For more details on Thorndike's approach to the Elizabethan
stage, see 1916.16.

18 WALLACE, CHARLES WILLIAM. "A London Pageant of Shakespeare's
Time: New Information from Old Records." Times (London),
28 March, p. 6.
Discusses the pageant on the Thames in 1610 in honor of
the creation of Prince Henry as Prince of Wales. Anthony
Munday was employed as poet, and Richard Burbage and John
Rice were the two orators on behalf of the city.

19 _____. The First London Theatre: Materials for a History.
UNS 13, nos. 1-3, 297 pp.
Presents the documents Wallace found concerning the
Burbage-Brayne controversy and the Burbage-Allen litigation
as well as an essay (pp. 1-35) interpreting the evidence
they present. The 99 documents are printed chronologically.
See 1913.15; 1979.2.

20 WITHINGTON, ROBERT. "English Pageantry, an Historical Outline."
Ph.D. dissertation, Harvard University.
Published as 1918.4 and 1920.32.

1914

1 ANON. "More Light on Shakespeare." Outlook 107 (11 July):
587-89.
Announces additional Wallace discoveries, described in
a variety of scholarly and popular publications.

2 ARKWRIGHT, G[ODFREY] E[DWARD] P[ELLEW]. "Elizabethan Choirboy
Plays and Their Music." PMusA 40:117-38.
A paper read before the association 21 April 1914.
Arkwright traces the history of the Children of the Chapel
and the Children of Paul's, including their dramatic
performances. He then examines the lyrics contained in
the plays.

3 A[RKWRIGHT], G[ODFREY] E[DWARD] P[ELLEW]. "Proposals for
Building an Amphitheatre in London, 1620." N&Q 130
(19 December):481-82.

Three documents related to the proposed Amphitheatre, held in the Bodleian Library, with brief commentary. Arkwright prints the proposal, the King's approval, and the King's ultimate disapproval. Continued in 1914.4.

4 _____. "Proposals for Building an Amphitheatre in London, 1620." N&Q 130 (26 December):502-3. Completes 1914.3.

5 BOAS, FREDERICK S. University Drama in the Tudor Age. Oxford: Clarendon Press, 414 pp.
Primarily a literary study, but Boas does consider "the general relations between the academic and the professional stage." He also includes scattered information concerning stage arrangements, actors, and properties, as well as a discussion of the controversy over the propriety of acting in a University.

6 GRAVES, T[HORNTON] S[HIRLEY]. "The Origin of the Custom of Sitting on the Stage." JEGP 13 (January):104-9.
Examines the possibility that the custom of sitting on the stage originated at the first Blackfriars and demonstrates that it predates even that theatre. Graves cites Bereblock's description of the performance of Palemon and Arcyte (see 1905.1) to show that Elizabeth sat upon the stage in 1566 and concludes that "the gentlemen who occupied the stage were paying for the privilege of sitting where they had seen their superiors sit at private performances."

7 _____. "The Political Use of the Stage during the Reign of James I." Anglia 38:137-56.
Argues that plays were more often used for political purposes than has been supposed, with numerous examples drawn from plays and records of the period.

8 _____. "The Shape of the First London Theatre." SAQ 13 (July):280-82.
Argues briefly that the Theatre was round, based on documents printed by Wallace in 1913.19.

9 HILLEBRAND, HAROLD NEWCOMB. "The Child Actors of the Sixteenth and Seventeenth Centuries." Ph.D. dissertation, Harvard University, 355 pp.
Published as 1926.6.

10 JENKINSON, WILBERFORCE. "The Early Play-Houses and the Drama as Referred to in Tudor and Stuart Literature." ContempR 105 (June):847-56.

1914

           Traces allusions to plays and playhouses from 1547 to 1643.

11   JONAS, MAURICE. "The Red Bull Theatre." N&Q 129 (21 February):150.
        Requests information for the beginning of playing at this theatre, since Lawrence estimates 1600 while everyone else estimates 1609. See 1914.12, 20.

12   JONES, TOM. "The Red Bull Theatre." N&Q 129 (11 April):298.
        Responds to 1914.11, referring Jonas and the reader to 1885.2-4.

13   K., L. L. "Site of the Globe Theatre." N&Q 130 (12 September): 209-10.
        Initiates a series of queries, replies, and counters on this subject in N&Q by requesting more information on the dispute between Stopes and Wallace on the location of the Globe. This is probably the major controversy of the century in the field. See Index under Globe Playhouse-- Site of. The definitive work is Braines (1923.11). Continued in 1914.15. See 1914.18.

14   _____. "Site of the Globe Theatre." N&Q 130 (10 October): 290-91.
        Responds to Martin (1909.21) and Jackson (1909.14), suggesting the north side of Maid Lane, as did Wallace. See Index under Globe Playhouse--Site of. Continued in 1914.15.

15   _____. "Site of the Globe Theatre." N&Q 130 (24 October):335.
        Concludes 1914.13-14. See Index under Globe Playhouse-- Site of.

16   KEITH, WILLIAM GRANT. "The Designs for the First Movable Scenery on the English Public Stage." BMg 25 (April):29-33.
        Primarily concerned with the 1656 production of The Siege of Rhodes, but includes a brief discussion of the pre-Commonwealth designs of Inigo Jones. Continued in 1914.17.

17   _____. "The Designs for the First Movable Scenery on the English Public Stage." BMg 25 (May):85-98.
        Continues 1914.16.

18   MARTIN, WILLIAM. "Site of the Globe Theatre." N&Q 130 (24 October):335.
        Responds to L. L. K. (1914.13-14), referring to his

earlier paper on the subject (1910.13), in which he set out
his reasons for supposing the Globe to have been situated
on the south side of Maid Lane. He also refers L. L. K. to
the new documents discovered by Wallace (1914.25-26). See
Index under Globe Playhouse--Site of.

19 NAIRN, J. ARBUTHNOTT. "Boy Actors under the Tudors and
    Stewarts." TrRSL, 2d series 32:61-78.
        A paper read before the Society, 26 February 1913. Nairn
    divides the boy companies into two types, the choir boys
    and the school boys, and discusses each in turn. He also
    provides a few biographical facts about Nathaniel Field and
    Salathiel Pavy, from the Children of the Chapel, as examples.

20 NORMAN, WILLIAM. "The Red Bull Theatre." N&Q 129 (14 March):
    212.
        Responds to 1914.11, citing three plays produced at the
    Red Bull in 1612, 1620, and 1622.

21 REYNOLDS, GEORGE F[ULLMER]. "William Percy and his Plays, with
    a Summary of the Customs of Elizabethan Staging." MP 12
    (October):241-60.
        Answers Albright's objections (in 1913.1) to the use of
    Percy's manuscript plays as evidence of Elizabethan staging
    practices, pointing out that they contradict Albright's
    alternation theory. The second section of the paper sum-
    marizes Reynolds's findings from a study of the plays
    presented at the Rose, the first Globe, and the first
    Fortune. He again emphasizes the medieval as opposed to
    modern nature of the staging. Reynolds concludes with
    a brief resume of Percy's life. See also his study of the
    Red Bull plays, 1940.10.

22 STOPES, CHARLOTTE CARMICHAEL. "The Burbages, Founders of the
    Modern Stage." TrRSL, 2d series 32:107-45.
        A paper delivered 23 October 1912. Stopes includes a
    discussion of the theatrical world of early Elizabethan
    England, as well as a history of the family's involvement
    with the Theatre, the second Blackfriars, and the Globe.
    She concludes with an evaluation of Richard as a performer.

23 _____. "'The Queen's Players' in 1636 [sic]." Athenaeum, 24
    January, p. 143.
        Despite the title (which was probably an editorial
    error), this transcribes a reference to Queen Jane's players
    in a suit in Chancery in 1536. Reprinted: 1914.24.

1914

24 _____. Shakespeare's Environment. London: G. Bell, 369 pp.
   A collection of thirty previously published essays,
   including 1909.25-26 and 1914.23.

25 WALLACE, CHARLES WILLIAM. "Further New Documents." Times
   (London), 1 May, p. 4.
   Continuation of 1914.26. Wallace here examines the
   history of the Globe property through the eighteenth
   century, as contained in seven documents he discovered in
   1909. They deal with the family of Thomas Brend, and are
   used to argue once again for a site of the Globe north of
   Maid Lane. See Index under Globe Playhouse--Site of.

26 _____. "Shakespeare and the Globe: New Documents Examined."
   Times (London), 30 April, pp. 9-10.
   Reiterates his arguments, set out in 1909.32, that the
   Globe was located north of Maid Lane, in response to the
   heated debate about its location then going on. He here
   brings to bear the Sewer Commission documents, not seen by
   him until 1911. Continued in 1914.25; see also Index
   under Globe Playhouse--Site of.

1915

1 BAYLEY, A[RTHUR] R[UTTER]. "Shakespeare and the Blackfriars
   Theatre." N&Q 132 (7 August):108.
   Responds to 1915.13, stating that while it is possible
   that Shakespeare acted at Blackfriars there is no evidence
   either way.

2 [BRAINES, WILLIAM WESTMORELAND.] Holywell Priory and the Site
   of the Theatre, Shoreditch. Indications of Houses of
   Historical Interest in London, no. 43. London: London
   County Council, 32 pp.
   Through the device of tracing the property through
   transfers, bequests, conveyances, and wills down to a time
   when it is described in terms of boundaries identifiable
   through modern maps, Braines is able to fix the site of
   the Theatre to within a few feet. He cites freely and
   fully from various documents. See also 1917.5 and his
   definitive siting of the Globe, 1921.1 and 1923.11.

3 GRAVES, THORNTON SHIRLEY. "The 'Act-Time' in Elizabethan
   Theatres." SP 12 (July):103-34.
   An attempt to show the weakness of the arguments for
   continuous performance on the Elizabethan stage, by
   establishing "beyond all reasonable doubt that the 'five

act form' with regular act intermissions was the rule in London." See also Lawrence, 1912.15.

4   GRAVES, T[HORNTON] S[HIRLEY]. "Tricks of Elizabethan Showmen." SAQ 14 (April):138-48.
     Discusses questionable advertising methods of Elizabethan players. Graves argues that they often claimed patronage that was not theirs, that they knew the value of catchy and suggestive titles, and that they were not above a quick exit with the cash box. He concludes, as Lawrence did in 1913.11, that "showmanship did not begin with Barnum."

5   HILLEBRAND, HAROLD NEWCOMB. "Sebastian Westcott, Dramatist and Master of the Children of Paul's." JEGP 14 (October):568-84.
     An attempt at a brief biography of the dramatist, including linkage of his name for the first time with The Contention between Liberality and Prodigality, published in 1602 but probably written many years earlier for the Children of Paul's. Hillebrand suggests in passing that the theatre at Paul's might have preceded both the first Blackfriars and Burbage's Theatre.

6   HUBBARD, GEORGE. "The Site of the Globe." N&Q 132 (3 July):11-13.
     Responds to Stopes (1915.23), suggesting that the Globe Alley that presents evidence for the south site was a later, second alley bearing that name, the original being to the north of Maid Lane. He also asserts that the Globe was built on the site of the old Bear Ring, and that two warehouses were built upon the site. Their construction revealed the foundations of the Globe. Continued in 1915.7-12. See also Index under Globe Playhouse--Site of, and 1915.14, 16-19.

7   _____. "The Site of the Globe." N&Q 132 (17 July):50-51.
     Continues 1915.6. Here Hubbard interprets the "Sewar Presentments" evidence for a north site. Continued in 1915.8-12. See also Index under Globe Playhouse--Site of, and 1915.14, 16-19.

8   _____. "The Site of the Globe." N&Q 132 (24 July):70-71.
     Continues 1915.6-7. Hubbard argues for the north site on the basis of visual evidence of maps and views of London. Continued in 1915.9-12; see also Index under Globe Playhouse--Site of, and 1915.14, 16-19.

1915

9 _____. "The Site of the Globe." N&Q 132 (11 September):201-2.
 Replies to Martin (1915.16-19), again arguing for the
 site north of Maid Lane, on the earlier evidence. See
 1915.6-8; see also Index, under Globe Playhouse--Site of,
 and 1915.14, 16-19.

10 _____. "The Site of the Globe." N&Q 132 (18 September):224-
 25.
 Continues 1915.9. See Index, under Globe Playhouse--Site
 of, and 1915.14, 16-19.

11 _____. "The Site of the Globe." N&Q 132 (2 October):264-66.
 Continues 1915.9-10. See Index, under Globe Playhouse--
 Site of, and 1915.14, 16-19.

12 _____. "The Site of the Globe." N&Q 132 (30 October):347-48.
 Responds to L. L. K. (1915.14), reasserting his previous
 arguments in favor of a site north of Maid Lane. See
 1915.6-11, 16-19. See also Index, under Globe Playhouse--
 Site of.

13 JONAS, MAURICE. "Shakespeare and the Blackfriars Theatre."
 N&Q 132 (17 July):47.
 Asks for information on Shakespeare acting at this
 playhouse. See 1915.1.

14 K., L. L. "The Site of the Globe." N&Q 132 (9 October):289.
 Responds to Hubbard (1915.6-8) briefly, pointing out
 that Wallace differs with Hubbard on the position of a
 crucial parcel of land. See Hubbard's response, 1915.12;
 see also Index under Globe Playhouse--Site of.

15 LAWRENCE, W[ILLIAM] J[OHN]. "Night Performances in the Elizabethan Theatres: A Reply to Dr. T. S. Graves." EStudien
 48 (January):213-30.
 Replies to 1913.7, arguing that night performances in
 the public theatres were exceptional and that black
 hangings were not used to signify night.

16 MARTIN, WILLIAM. "The Site of the Globe." N&Q 132 (3 July):
 10-11.
 Responds to Stopes (1915.23), reviewing the argument
 and suggesting again that the evidence for placing the
 Globe north of Maid Lane derives from a clerical accident
 with an upside down map. See Index under Globe Playhouse--
 Site of.

17 ____. "The Site of the Globe." N&Q 132 (14 August):121-23.
Responds to Hubbard (1915.6-8), arguing for a site to
the south of Maid Lane. Here Martin takes issue with the
assumption of an earlier Globe Alley. Continued in 1915.
18-19.

18 ____. "The Site of the Globe." N&Q 132 (21 August):143-44.
Continuation of 1915.17, in response to Hubbard
(1915.6-8). Here Martin questions the assumption of a
second "Park," separate from the Bishop's Park, as well as
Hubbard's interpretation of the Sewer Commission records.
Continued in 1915.19.

19 ____. "The Site of the Globe." N&Q 132 (28 August):161-63.
Continuation of 1915.17-18, in response to Hubbard
(1915.6-8). Here Martin questions Hubbard's treatment of
contemporary maps and views and his assertion that the
foundations of the Globe were discovered, without citing
corroborative evidence. See Hubbard's reply (1915.9), and
definitive work of Braines (1923.11). See also Index under
Globe Playhouse--Site of.

20 POLLOCK, ARTHUR. "The Evolution of the Actor, II: The Rise
of the Modern Actor." Drama 20 (November):651-63.
Includes a brief sketch of Elizabethan actors and acting
conditions. Continued in 1916.12.

21 PORTER, CHARLOTTE. "Playing Hamlet as Shakespeare Staged It
in 1601." Drama 19 (August):511-26.
An anecdotal reconstruction of a performance of Hamlet
at the Globe. Continued in 1915.22.

22 ____. "Playing Hamlet as Shakespeare Staged It, II."
Drama 20 (November):675-89.
Continuation of 1915.21, including a plan of the Globe.

23 STOPES, C[HARLOTTE] C[ARMICHAEL]. "The Site of the Globe."
N&Q 131 (12 June):447-49.
Argues for the site south of Maid Lane, as did Martin
(1909.19-21; 1910.13), based on a court suit, the Sewer
Commission order, various leases, and the archaeological
discoveries of her husband, Henry Stopes, between 1880 and
1890. See particularly Martin's response, 1915.16; see
also Index under Globe Playhouse--Site of.

<u>1916</u>

1 ARCHER, WILLIAM, and LAWRENCE, W[ILLIAM] J[OHN]. "The Playhouse." In <u>Shakespeare's England: An Account of the Life</u>
<u>and Manners of his Age</u>. Vol. 2. Edited by Sidney Lee,
Charles Talbut Onions, and Walter A. Raleigh. Oxford:
Clarendon Press, pp. 283-310.
    Surveys the London playhouses chronologically, from the
Theatre to the Salisbury Court. Archer and Lawrence also
discuss the structure of the playhouse in generalized terms,
including a recessed inner stage. On this point the Swan
drawing is held to be inaccurate. The stage doors and
upper stage, as well as the audience and its management,
are topics for discussion. While intended for the general
reader, this study is fully documented. Archer and Lawrence
also reprint Godfrey's illustration of the Fortune as an
example (<u>see</u> 1908.10). Reprinted: 1950.1.

2 BRERETON, J[OHN] LE GAY. "DeWitt at the Swan." In <u>A Book of</u>
<u>Homage to Shakespeare</u>. Edited by Israel Gollancz. London:
Oxford University Press, pp. 204-6.
    Attempts to reconstruct what DeWitt actually saw on his
visit to the Swan by determining the copying errors of Van
Buchell. Brereton places DeWitt in the second gallery to
the right of center, and makes allowances for this position. In effect, he is trying to provide reasons for the
drawing not conforming to his idea of what it should be.

3 CARGILL, ALEXANDER. "The 'Globe' Theatre on the Bankside."
In <u>Shakespeare the Player and Other Papers Illustrative of</u>
<u>Shakespeare's Individuality</u>. London: Constable & Co., pp.
136-39.
    Appendix B to the volume, with a general discussion and
illustration from the Hollar engraving.

4 _____. "Shakespeare the Player." In <u>Shakespeare the Player</u>
<u>and Other Papers Illustrative of Shakespeare's Individual-</u>
<u>ity</u>. London: Constable & Co., pp. 1-34.
    Reprint of 1891.1.

5 CREIZENACH, WILHELM [MICHAEL ANTON]. <u>The English Drama in</u>
<u>the Age of Shakespeare</u>. Translated by Cecile Hugon.
London: Sidgwick & Jackson, pp. 1-57, 353-430.
    Translation of <u>Geschichte des neueren Dramas</u>, vol. 4
(1903.1). Book I, "The English Theatre from 1570 to 1587,"
and Book VIII, "Staging and Histrionic Art," are the
relevant sections. The former is a general survey of
little interest. The latter is more specifically theatrical,

discussing stage doors, discoveries, the upper stage, and
so on, but the discussion is of generalized "Elizabethan
stage," using evidence from a wide variety of times and
places. Creizenach also discusses acting and actors, particularly Burbage and Alleyn. See also second edition,
1923.4.

6 DICKINSON, THOMAS H. "Some Principles of Shakespeare Staging."
   In Shakespeare Studies by Members of the Department of
   English of the University of Wisconsin. Madison: University of Wisconsin, pp. 125-47.
       Discusses in general terms the flexibility of Elizabethan
   staging and the difference between foreground and background. Much of the essay is then devoted to suggestions
   for modern staging.

7 GRAVES, T[HORNTON] S[HIRLEY]. "The Ass as Actor." SAQ 15
   (April):175-82.
       Briefly traces the ass as character from the medieval
   period through the eighteenth century, including the
   Elizabethan period. While the scholarship is genuine, the
   tone is tongue-in-cheek.

*8 LAWRENCE, W[ILLIAM] J[OHN]. "Acting in Shakespeare's Day:
    Early Histrionic Conditions." Stage (London), 27 April.
    Cited in TN 11 (April 1957):71.

9 _____. "A Forgotten Playhouse Custom of Shakespeare's Day."
   In A Book of Homage to Shakespeare. Edited by Israel
   Gollancz. London: Oxford University Press, pp. 207-11.
       Examines the practice of free admission after the fourth
   act. Lawrence draws his evidence from the extant plots and
   from a legal document of 1612. The custom apparently
   survived until well into the Restoration, when it was
   suppressed.

10 _____. "New Light on the Elizabethan Theatre." FortR 105
    (May):820-29.
        Discusses the difference between the public and private
    playhouses, and argues that changes in the public theatres
    came about because of competition with the private houses.
    The most important change was the roofing of the public
    playhouses, beginning with the Fortune in 1623 and followed
    shortly by the Red Bull.

11 POEL, WILLIAM. Some Notes on Shakespeare's Stage and Plays.
    Manchester: University Press, 17 pp.

A general discussion by the founder and director of the Elizabethan Stage Society. Poel briefly discusses the Globe, the Fortune contract, the costumes, and the acting companies. His main point is that modern productions of Shakespeare should be based on Elizabethan theatrical conditions.

12 POLLOCK, ARTHUR. "The Actor in England." Drama 24 (November): 550-59.
    Continues 1915.20, beginning with Elizabethan actors and acting conditions.

13 PORTER, CHARLOTTE. "How Shakespeare Set and Struck the Scene for Julius Caesar in 1599." MLN 31 (May):281-87.
    Discusses the staging of Julius Caesar based on original stage directions and dialogue references. Porter assumes upper and lower inner stages, and the visual appearance of all properties mentioned in the dialogue.

14 SIMPSON, PERCY. "Actors and Acting." In Shakespeare's England: An Account of the Life and Manners of his Age. Vol. 2. Edited by Sidney Lee, Charles Talbut Onions, and Walter A. Raleigh. Oxford: Clarendon Press, pp. 240-82.
    Examines Puritan attacks on actors and their defense, boy companies, Shakespeare's descriptions of acting, the clowns, and rehearsal and performance procedures. Aimed at the general reader, but well documented. Reprinted: 1950.16.

15 _____. "The Masque." In Shakespeare's England: An Account of the Life and Manners of his Age. Vol. 2. Edited by Sidney Lee, Charles Talbut Onions, and Walter A. Raleigh. Oxford: Clarendon Press, pp. 311-33.
    Discusses mumming and disguises in the sixteenth century as predecessors of the masque, as well as the form and performance of the masque itself. Other sections examine the Office of the Revels and the art of Inigo Jones. Intended for the general reader but well documented. Reprinted: 1950.17.

16 THORNDIKE, ASHLEY H. Shakespeare's Theater. New York: Macmillan, 472 pp.
    An attempt at a comprehensive survey of all that was known of the Elizabethan stage. Thorndike includes chapters on playhouses, the physical stage, stage presentation, court theatres, companies, government regulation, actors and acting, and the audience. He subscribes to most commonplace ideas of his day, such as the inner stage and the alternation theory.

17 YOUNG, KARL. "An Elizabethan Defence of the Stage." In
    Shakespeare Studies by Members of the Department of English
    of the University of Wisconsin. Madison: University of
    Wisconsin, pp. 103-24.
        Two letters, from Rainolds to Thornton and from Gager to
    Rainolds, from 1592 and 1593, concerning Rainolds's attack
    on the stage. See also 1916.18; 1974.3.

18 _____. "William Gager's Defence of the Academic Stage."
    TrWASAL 18, pt. 2:593-638.
        Traces the controversy between Gager and John Rainolds,
    including the text of one substantial letter from Gager in
    defense of the stage. See also 1916.17; 1974.3.

                                1917

1   ADAMS, JOSEPH QUINCY. "The Conventual Buildings of Black-
    friars, London, and the Playhouses Constructed Therein."
    SP 14 (April):64-87.
        An attempt to reconstruct the ancient Dominican Priory
    of Blackfriars, and to point out the location, size, shape,
    and other details of the two playhouses constructed there.
    Because of the discovery of important documents among the
    Losely Manuscripts (see 1913.3), Adams is able to correct
    Clapham's earlier attempt (see 1912.4) in many details.
    Adams places the first Blackfriars Playhouse in the But-
    tery section, a room 46 feet long and 25 feet wide, with
    a platform stage at one end equipped with multiple settings
    after the court fashion. There were no galleries, just
    benches for spectators. The second playhouse was built in
    the Halland Parlor, the combined length of which was 66
    feet, with a width of 46 feet. Adams thinks there were
    two galleries, possible because of the width and height of
    the rooms.

2   ADAMS, JOSEPH QUINCY, ed. The Dramatic Records of Sir Henry
    Herbert, Master of the Revels, 1623-1673. New Haven: Yale
    University Press, 155 pp.
        Composed of the important Office Book, containing
    entries from 1622 to 1642, and two sets of miscellaneous
    documents dated 1622-1642 and 1660-1670. While the Office
    Book itself had, unfortunately, vanished by 1917, Adams
    attempted to reconstruct it as best he could by piecing
    together the quotations from it scattered through the works
    of Malone and Chalmers (see, for example, 1821.1). In a
    brief Introduction Adams traces the history of the office up
    to Herbert and what is known about the Office Book and its

disposal. He divides the Office Book itself into sections
dealing with a variety of areas, the most important being
"Censorship of Plays," "Licenses of Plays," "Licenses of
Playhouses and Companies," and "Plays and Masques at
Court." The Index appears complete and analytical. This
work is certainly among the most important to a study of
the Elizabethan theatre. See also Lawrence (1923.15) for
additions.

3 ADAMS, JOSEPH QUINCY. Shakespearean Playhouses: A History of
English Theatres from the Beginnings to the Restoration.
Boston: Houghton Mifflin, 473 pp.
Includes histories of seventeen permanent playhouses and
five temporary or projected buildings, as well as a general
chapter on the early inn-yard theatres. Adams cites documentary sources at length and is generally quite careful in
his interpretations. He does not attempt to reconstruct
staging practices or make conjectural drawings of the
theatre interiors, but rather contents himself with the
histories of the buildings themselves. He quietly corrects
the errors of Malone, Halliwell-Phillipps, Collier, Fleay,
Ordish, and so on, and modestly hopes to be so corrected
himself when further evidence is discovered or his interpretations are proven wrong. This book stood among the most
important published in the field for years, and still ranks
as indispensable more than sixty years later. The 316-item
bibliography, with the more important items specially
marked, is among the best guides to early scholarship in
the field.

4 BAYLEY, A[RTHUR] R[UTTER]. "Second Fortune Theatre." N&Q
134 (30 December):537.
Responds to 1917.7, suggesting that this playhouse was
dismantled rather than burned in 1649, citing Lawrence
(1912.15). See also 1917.10.

5 BRAINES, WILLIAM WESTMORELAND. "The Site of the Theatre,
Shoreditch." London Topographical Record 11:1-27.
Contains the same information as in 1915.2.

6 GRAVES, THORNTON SHIRLEY. "'Playeng in the Dark' during the
Elizabethan Period." SP 14 (April):88-116.
Discusses performances in the late afternoon during
winter, and evening performances, and speculates about the
artificial lighting that would have been necessary. A
continuation of the running feud between Graves and
Lawrence on the subject; see also 1912.16; 1913.7; 1915.15.

7 JONAS, MAURICE. "Second Fortune Theatre." N&Q 134 (18
   November):408.
       Requests corroboration of the burning of this playhouse.
   See 1917.4, 10 for replies.

8 LAWRENCE, W[ILLIAM] J[OHN]. "The Mystery of Lodowick Barry."
   SP 14 (April):52-63.
       Lawrence shows that the Lording Barry who bought a
   controlling interest in the Whitefriars Playhouse in 1608
   was also the author of Ram Alley. Further, "Lording" is
   not a Christian name (see 1912.1) but a polite title for
   the son of a Lord. Lawrence concludes that the Lo. Barry
   listed as the author was actually David Oge Barry, son of
   Lord Barry, who died in 1610 at the age of 24.

9 LÜDEKE, HENRY. "Ludwig Tiecks Shakespeare-Studien: Zwei
   Kapitel zum Thema: Ludwig Tieck und das englische Theater."
   Ph.D. dissertation, University of Frankfurt, 62 pp.
       The two chapters alluded to in the title deal with
   Tieck's study of the old English theatres throughout his
   life, and the romantic period in Tieck's Shakespeare
   criticism. According to the foreword, these are Chapters
   Two and Four of a longer work. Tieck created a conjectural
   reconstruction of an Elizabethan playhouse in an 1836 short
   story.

10 STEWART, ALAN. "Second Fortune Theatre." N&Q 134 (30 Decem-
    ber):537.
        Responds to 1917.7, suggesting that, according to Prynne,
    this playhouse burned in 1649. See also 1917.4.

11 STRUNK, W[ILLIAM], Jr. "The Elizabethan Showman's Ape." MLN
    32 (April):215-21.
        Discusses the exhibition of trained apes in the period
    and several references to the practice in Shakespeare and
    elsewhere. See 1920.3.

1918

1 LAWRENCE, W[ILLIAM] J[OHN]. "The Elizabethan Stage Throne."
   TR 3 (January):93-108.
       Argues that the stage throne, when required, was placed
   on the rear stage and discovered or thrust out, and was not
   permanently in place. Lawrence uses stage directions and
   allusions from a variety of plays to support his case.

1918

*2   THALER, ALWIN. "Finance and Business Management of the Eliza-
     bethan Theatre." Ph.D. dissertation, Harvard University.
     Cited in ADDT, p. 92.

3   THALER, ALWIN. "Shakespeare's Income." SP 15 (April):82-96.
     Reexamines Shakespeare's income from all sources--as
     actor/sharer, housekeeper, playwright, and investor--placing
     his annual income at about £350. This figure would place
     him among the well off but not the fabulously wealthy.
     Based on research from 1918.2.

4   WITHINGTON, ROBERT. English Pageantry: An Historical Outline.
     Vol. 1. Cambridge: Harvard University Press, pp. 198-238.
     Published version of 1913.20. The relevant section deals
     with Elizabethan pageantry, 1558-1602, and the royal entry
     in the seventeenth century. Nichols (1823.1) is the main
     source for the Elizabethan section. Both chapters present
     chronological listings of pageants and royal entries for
     the years indicated. See also vol. 2 (1920.32).

<u>1919</u>

1   ADAMS, JOSEPH QUINCY. "An 'Hitherto Unknown' Actor of
     Shakespeare's Troupe?" MLN 34 (January):46-48.
     A brief analysis of the letter from William Wilson to
     Edward Alleyn, concluding that Wilson was not, in fact, an
     actor but rather a gatherer or perhaps a stagekeeper.

2   _____. "The Housekeepers of the Globe." MP 17 (May):1-8.
     Discusses the disposition of the housekeeper's shares in
     the Globe from 1598 to 1644.

3   CHILD, HAROLD H. "The Elizabethan Theatre." In Cambridge
     History of English Literature. Vol. 6, The Drama to 1642.
     Pt. 2. Edited by A. W. Ward and A. R. Waller. Cambridge:
     University Press, pp. 241-78.
     Reprint of 1910.5.

4   GRAY, HENRY DAVID. "The Dumb Show in Hamlet." MP 17 (May):
     51-54.
     Rejects the supposition that the dumb show was presented
     above while Claudius was on the throne in the inner stage
     as an explanation of his non-reaction to the recreation of
     his crime.

5   GREG, W[ALTER] W[ILSON]. "'The Seven Deadly Sins.'" TLS (2
     October):532.

A letter to the editor in response to Spens (1919.18), disagreeing with the assertion that this plot was rejected by one company and sold to another.

6 _____. "The 'Stolne and Surreptitious' Shakespearian Texts." TLS (28 August):461.
A letter to the editor, in response to Lawrence (1919. 10), pointing out two fallacies in Lawrence's case.

7 LAWRENCE, W[ILLIAM] J[OHN]. "'He's for a Jig or --.'" TLS (3 July):363-64.
Examines the history and practice of the jig, which was "in essence a primitive ballad-opera." It was a rhymed farce, completely sung, generally arranged for four or five characters, and served strictly as an afterpiece. After 1612, in order to get around an order forbidding the jig after the play, it was presented in the middle. See also Baskervill (1929.1).

8 _____. "Horses on the Elizabethan Stage." TLS (5 June):312.
A refutation of the idea (adopted by many, based on Simon Forman's diary) that horses were used on the Elizabethan stage. Lawrence compares Forman's commentary with the play, concluding that Forman presents "a coloured narrative of the story unfolded."

9 _____. "The King's Revels Players of 1619-1623." MLR 14 (October):416-18.
Argues that with the death of Queen Anne in 1619, the company in her service became the Company of the King's Revels. Lawrence cites title pages of several plays and the records of the Master of the Revels to substantiate his case.

10 _____. "The 'Stolne and Surreptitious' Shakespearian Texts." TLS (21 August):449.
A letter to the editor, in response to Wilson and Pollard's theories of the "bad" quartos as cut copies for touring (see 1919.14-16, 21, 22). Lawrence argues that there was no need for touring cut versions of plays, given adequate doubling. See the responses of Greg (1919.6), Pollard (1919.13), and Wilson (1920.31).

11 _____. "Wilkinson's View of the Supposed Fortune Theatre, and What it Really Represents." ArchR 46 (September):70-71.
Asserts that the picture of the Fortune printed by Wilkinson in 1825.1 was actually a picture of the post-Restoration "Nursery" in Barbican. Lawrence presents no evidence to support his assertion, but claims he has it.

1919

12 MANLY, J[OHN] M[ATTHEWS]. "The Children of the Chapel Royal
    and Their Masters." In Cambridge History of English
    Literature. Vol. 6, The Drama to 1642. Pt. 2. Edited by
    A. W. Ward and A. R. Waller. Cambridge: University Press,
    279–92.
        Reprint of 1910.12.

13 POLLARD, ALFRED W. "The 'Stolne and Surreptitious' Shakespear-
    ian Texts." TLS (28 August):461.
        A letter to the editor, in response to Lawrence (1919.
    10). Pollard defends his view that the "bad" quartos
    represent cut touring versions of the plays.

14 POLLARD, A[LFRED] W., and WILSON, J[OHN] DOVER. "The 'Stolne
    and Surreptitious' Shakespearian Texts, I: Why Some of
    Shakespeare's Plays Were Pirated." TLS (9 January):18.
        Proposes that the "bad" quartos were cut versions of the
    plays, used for the 1593 provincial tour of the Chamberlain's
    Men. They were thus less valuable in London, and more
    easily printed. Continued in 1919.15–16, 21–22.

15 _____. "The 'Stolne and Surreptitious' Shakespearian Texts:
    Henry V (1600)." TLS (13 March):134.
        Continuation of 1919.14, 21. Uses the theories earlier
    advanced to show that the "bad" quarto of Henry V was
    derived from a cut touring version augmented by an actor's
    memory. Continued in 1919.16, 22.

16 _____. "The 'Stolne and Surreptitious' Shakespearian Texts:
    Merry Wives of Windsor." TLS (7 August):420.
        Continuation of 1919.14–15, 21, applying the theories to
    the Merry Wives of Windsor "bad" quarto. For responses
    see 1919.6, 10, 18. Continued in 1919.22.

17 REYNOLDS, GEORGE FULLMER. "Two Conventions of the Elizabethan
    Stage." MP 17 (May):35–43.
        Discusses the use of the stage doors to change locations
    and the conventional suppression of other doors when only
    one was needed for the action on stage. See 1920.1.

18 SPENS, J. "The 'Stolne and Surreptitious' Shakespearian
    Texts." TLS (18 September):500.
        A letter to the editor, in response to Pollard (1919.13).
    Spens suggests that the companies might furnish early out-
    lines, plots, rejected drafts, and cut versions to other
    dramatists for a fee.

19 THALER, ALWIN. "Playwrights' Benefits and 'Interior Gather-
    ing' in the Elizabethan Theatre." SP 16 (April):187-96.
        Examines the beginning of the tradition of playwrights'
    benefits, concluding that they did not begin before 1603,
    and the collection of entrance fees. Thaler differs with
    Lawrence on both issues (see 1913.9). Based on Thaler's
    dissertation (1918.2).

20 WILSON, J[OHN] D[OVER]. "The Puritan Attack upon the Stage."
    In Cambridge History of English Literature. Vol. 6, The
    Drama to 1642. Pt. 2. Edited by A. W. Ward and A. R.
    Waller. Cambridge: University Press, pp. 373-409.
        Reprint of 1910.26.

21 WILSON, J[OHN] DOVER, and POLLARD, A[LFRED] W. "The 'Stolne
    and Surreptitious' Shakespearian Texts, II: How Some of
    Shakespeare's Plays Were Pirated." TLS (16 January):30.
        Continuation of 1919.14. Suggests that the pirate was
    a minor actor of the company, adding to abridged touring
    copies from memory. Continued in 1919.15-16, 22.

22 _____. "The 'Stolne and Surreptitious' Shakespearian Texts:
    Romeo and Juliet, 1597." TLS (14 August):434.
        Continuation of 1919.14, 21, 15-16, applying the theory
    to Romeo and Juliet. There is some evidence that the
    pirate played the role of Capulet.

1920

1 BRERETON, JOHN LE ROY [sic, i.e., GAY.] "One-Door Interiors on
   the Elizabethan Stage." MLN 35 (February):119-20.
       A brief note in response to Reynolds (1919.17), arguing
   that the Swan drawing is incorrect, since it shows only two
   doors instead of the three that Brereton thinks were actually there.

2 GRAVES, THORNTON S[HIRLEY]. "The Devil in the Playhouse."
   SAQ 19 (April):131-40.
       A humorous chronicle of claims of the devil's actual
   appearance in various playhouses throughout history.
   Graves repeats the story about the Fortune's destruction
   (see 1870.4).

3 _____. "The Elizabethan Trained Ape." MLN 35 (April):248-49.
       A brief note adding a few references to those cited by
   Strunk (1917.11).

1920

4   _____. "Notes on the Elizabethan Theatres." SP 17 (April):
     170-82.
        Minor additions to studies of the audience and the play-
     bill.

5   _____. "Organized Applause." SAQ 19 (July):236-48.
        Discusses the use of the claque before the nineteenth
     century, including during the Elizabethan period.

6   _____. "Richard Rawlidge on London Playhouses." MP 18 (May):
     41-48.
        Cites Rawlidge himself, rather than Prynne's misquota-
     tion, to show that he was far from vehemently opposed to the
     London playhouses of his time. Rawlidge's references to
     the putting down of "playhouses" in 1580 probably means
     "gaming-houses."

7   GRAY, HENRY DAVID. "The Sources of The Tempest." MLN 35
     (June):321-30.
        Argues that Shakespeare based his play on the scenarios
     of several commedia dell'arte performances he had seen.
     The scenarios survive in a 1622 manuscript and contain
     most of the dramatic elements Shakespeare employed. See
     also 1920.22.

8   GREG, W[ALTER] WILSON. "Doubled Parts on the Elizabethan
     Stage." TLS (12 February):105.
        A letter to the editor, in response to Lawrence (1919.
     10), pointing out the frequency of sharers doubling parts.
     See also Lawrence's reply (1920.15).

9   GREG, W[ALTER] W[ILSON]. "Doubled Parts on the Elizabethan
     Stage." TLS (4 March):155.
        A letter to the editor, in response to Lawrence's
     response to 1920.8. Greg argues for doubling by sharers on
     the basis of the playhouse documents.

10 _____. "Was Sir Thomas More Ever Acted?" TLS (8 July):440.
        Questions Lawrence's disputation of Greg's opinion,
     expressed in his edition of the play, that Sir Thomas More
     was never acted. See 1920.23.

11 HILLEBRAND, HAROLD N. "The Early History of the Chapel Royal."
     MP 18 (September):233-68.
        Attempts to trace the history of the Chapel Royal from
     the time of Henry I, adding the most information to our
     knowledge of the Chapel in the sixteenth century. Hille-
     brand prints a Bodleian manuscript that adds information to

Rimbault's Cheque Book (1872.1). There is little of specifically theatrical interest.

12 LAW, ERNEST. "Shakespeare's Plays in the Revels Accounts."
TLS (23 December):876.
    A letter to the editor in response to Stopes (1920.26),
again arguing for the genuineness of the Revels Accounts,
on the same evidence. See Index under Revels Accounts for
the entire controversy. Continued in 1920.13.

13 _____. "Shakespeare's Plays in the Revels Accounts." TLS
(30 December):891.
    Continuation of 1920.12. See also Index under Revels
Accounts for the complete controversy.

14 LAWRENCE, W[ILLIAM] J[OHN]. "Dekker on 'Steering the Passage
of Scaenes.'" MLR 15 (April):166-68.
    Points out that the passage from The Guls Horn-booke is
not a literal indication of scenery on the stage, as some
have assumed, but rather a poetic allusion, as is made
clear by the prologue Dekker wrote for All's Lost by Lust
and A Wonder of a Kingdome.

15 _____. "Doubled Parts on the Elizabethan Stage." TLS (26
February):140.
    A letter to the editor, in response to Greg (1920.8).
Lawrence points out that the eleven cast lists from the
period indicate no doubling by sharers. See also Greg's
reply (1920.9).

16 _____. "Early Touring Companies." TLS (5 February):86-87.
    A letter to the editor, in response to Wilson (1920.31).
Lawrence differs with him over the splitting of Shakespeare's company for touring the provinces.

17 _____. "The King's Players at Court in 1610." MLR 15 (January):89-90.
    A brief note discussing the court performance of
Mucedorus and the prologue's mention of an earlier "unwil-
ling errour" of the company.

18 _____. "The Masque in The Tempest." FortR 113 (June):940-46.
    Argues that the betrothal masque in The Tempest was not
originally part of the play, but rather was written "in
anticipation of the coming nuptials of the Elector Palatine
and the Princess Elizabeth." Lawrence bases his theory on
stage directions from the First Folio and several textual
allusions.

1920

19 _____. "Music in the Elizabethan Theatre." MusAnt 6 (April):
192-205.
Discusses the use of music in public and private playhouses. Lawrence examines preliminary, entre-act, and
incidental music, as well as the instruments used.

20 _____. "The Mystery of Macbeth: A Solution." FortR 114
(November):777-83.
Argues that the witch scenes in the play as we have it
were added by another hand after Shakespeare's retirement,
and that Middleton's The Witch was the source. See also
Flatter and Cutts: 1957.6; 1958.6; 1959.5; 1960.5-7.
Reprinted: 1928.9.

*21 _____. "On the Underrated Genius of Dick Tarleton." London
Mercury 2 (May).
Cited in TN 11 (April 1957):72.

22 _____. "Shakespeare and the Italian Comedians." TLS (11
November):736.
Responds to Gray's suggestion (in 1920.7) that The
Tempest was based on five commedia dell'arte scenarios
that survive. Lawrence shows that a company that might
have presented the performances was in London in 1610, the
year before The Tempest was presented at Court. But see
1921.3 for a correction by Chambers.

23 _____. "Was Sir Thomas More Ever Acted?" TLS (1 July):421.
Disputes the validity of Greg's contention in his Malone
Society edition of the play that it was never acted. See
Greg's reply, 1920.10.

*24 _____, and GODFREY, WALTER H. "The Bear Garden Contract of
1606 and What It Implies." ArchR 47 (June).
Cited in TN 11 (April 1957):72.

25 LIEBSCHER, FRIEDA MARGOT. "Wie ersetzt Shakespeare seinem
Publikum Theaterzettel, Bühnendekorationen und künstliche
Beleuchtung? Nachgewiesen am Hamlet, zugleich ein Beitrag
zum Kenntnis des altenglischen Theaters." Ph.D. dissertation, Leipzig, 89 pp.
Examines, among other matters, Shakespeare's setting of
scene with language and implicit stage directions in
dialogue. Handwritten.

26 STOPES, CHARLOTTE CARMICHAEL. "The Seventeenth Century Revels
Books." TLS (2 December):798.
A lengthy letter to the editor, arguing that the three
seventeenth-century accounts published by Cunningham in 1842

were forgeries. See also Law's reply (1920.12–13) and
Index under Revels Accounts for the entire controversy.

27 THALER, ALWIN. "The Elizabethan Dramatic Companies." PMLA
35 (March):123–59.
Discusses the role of the actor/sharer and the business
manager of the company, as well as the value and distribu-
tion of shares. Based in large part on his Ph.D. dissertation (1918.2).

28 _____. "The 'Free-list' and Theatre Tickets in Shakespeare's
Time and After." MLR 15 (April):124–36.
Discusses the development of these two elements of
theatrical management from Shakespeare to Sheridan. Based
in large part on his Ph.D. dissertation (1918.2).

29 _____. "The Players at Court, 1564–1642." JEGP 19 (January):
19–48.
Examines "the financial relations between the court and
the professional players and playwrights from the beginning
of the Shakespearian era to the closing of the theatres in
1642." Thaler includes tables of payments made to companies
for court performances during the reigns of Elizabeth, James,
and Charles. Based on his Ph.D. dissertation (1918.2).

30 _____. "The Travelling Players in Shakespere's England."
MP 17 (January):489–514.
Additions to Murray's information (see 1905.4; 1910.15)
based on research in connection with 1918.2. Thaler
focuses on the financial end of the touring companies, both
London-based and provincial. Reprinted: 1941.13.

31 WILSON, J[OHN] DOVER. "Early Touring Companies." TLS (29
January):68.
A letter to the editor, in response to Lawrence (1919.
10). Wilson reiterates his argument that the four
Shakespeare "bad" quartos were cut-down versions for
touring.

31 WITHINGTON, ROBERT. English Pageantry: An Historical Outline.
Vol. 2. Cambridge: Harvard University Press, pp. 3–42.
Second volume of the published version of 1913.20. The
relevant section deals with the Lord Mayor's Show, 1209–
1635. No records exist 1636–1642. See also 1970.3; 1918.4
(vol. 1); and Index under Lord Mayor's Show.

<u>1921</u>

1 BRAINES, WILLIAM WESTMORELAND. <u>The Site of the Globe Playhouse, Southwark</u>. London: London County Council, 43 pp.
      An attempt to settle the issue of the Globe's location
   north or south of Maid Lane, based on documentary evidence
   only. The case for the north side is made and refuted,
   and the case for the south side prevails. Further, the
   actual site of the property leased for the purpose of
   building the Globe is pinpointed, through bequests, bills
   of sale, and other court documents. G. Topham Forrest adds
   an appendix on the architecture of the playhouse. <u>See also</u>
   second edition (1924.3); and Index under Globe Playhouse--
   Site of.

2 CAMPBELL, LILY BESS. "Scenes and Machines on the English
   Stage during the Renaissance: A Classical Revival." Ph.D.
   dissertation, University of Chicago, 302 pp.
      Published as 1923.1.

3 CHAMBERS, E[DMUND] K. "Italian Players in England." <u>TLS</u> (12
   May):307.
      Corrects Lawrence's assertion (in 1920.22) that an
   Italian company performed in London in 1607-8 by demonstrat-
   ing that "Princes" in a municipal accounts book was misread
   as "Venice."

4 FLOOD, W[ILLIAM] H[ENRY] GRATTAN. "The King's Players at
   Dunwich in 1607." <u>TLS</u> (28 April):276.
      Based on the Corporate Records of Dunwich, Flood lists
   several visits of players to that city, including one by
   the King's Men in 1607.

5 FORREST, G. TOPHAM. "Blackfriars Theatre: Conjectural
   Reconstruction." <u>Times</u> (London), 21 November, p. 5.
      While published by Forrest, the actual reconstruction
   was prepared by J. H. Farrar and R. L. Martin, architects
   of the London County Council. The drawing shows the
   interior of the playhouse, complete with a curtained inner
   stage, two obliquely set doors, and no boxes on the platform level; a curtained space above in the center of the
   gallery; benches in the pit; two audience galleries; and
   candles serving as footlights. For other reconstructions
   of the second Blackfriars, <u>see</u> 1954.17; 1964.14; 1970.13;
   1975.15.

6 GRAVES, THORNTON S[HIRLEY]. "Notes on Puritanism and the
   Stage." <u>SP</u> 18 (April):141-69.
       A few apparently overlooked instances of attack or
   defense of the stage, and a consideration of the defense
   from 1642 to 1660.

7 _____. "The Stage Sword and Dagger." <u>SAQ</u> 20 (July):201-12.
       Anecdotal discussion of fencing in the theatre, includ-
   ing the Elizabethan period.

8 GREG, WALTER W[ILSON]. "'Bengemenes Johnsones Share.'" <u>MLR</u>
   16 (October):323.
       Responds to Thayer's explanation of the entry in
   Henslowe's diary (<u>see</u> 1921.16) by pointing out that it was
   not possible for Jonson to have held a share in the Admiral's Men at the time. Greg suggests that Henslowe had
   arranged to receive certain money out of what was due Jonson
   as a sharer in Pembroke's Men.

9 LAWRENCE, W[ILLIAM] J[OHN]. "The Earliest Private-Theatre
   Play." <u>TLS</u> (11 August):514.
       Argues that <u>The Warres of Cyprus</u> was written by Farrant
   and first presented ca. 1578, making it the earliest
   extant play performed in a private playhouse.

10 _____. "Early Substantive Theatre Masques." <u>TLS</u> (8 December):
    814.
        Discusses details of the initial productions of <u>The World</u>
    <u>Tost at Tennis</u>, <u>The Sun's Darling</u>, and <u>Microcosmus</u>, the
    earliest masques produced in the playhouses.

11 _____. "The Phallus on the Early English Stage." <u>Psyche and</u>
    <u>Eros</u> 2, no. 3 (May-June):161-65.
        Discusses the use of the phallus on the English stage,
    based on the illustration published with <u>The World Tost at</u>
    <u>Tennis</u> showing a devil with erect phallus. The editor of
    the journal (S. A. T.) appends a note indicating that
    Lawrence also detects the use of the phallus in <u>Two Noble</u>
    <u>Kinsmen</u>, III.v.

12 RHODES, R. CROMPTON. "Shakespeare's Prompt Books, I: Stage
    Directions." <u>TLS</u> (21 July):467.
        Examines the stage directions of Shakespeare and sorts
    the plays into three groups, depending upon the adequacy of
    their directions for Elizabethan production. <u>Titus Andro-</u>
    <u>nicus</u>, <u>Henry VI</u>, <u>Tempest</u>, <u>Henry VIII</u>, <u>Coriolanus</u>, and
    <u>Timon of Athens</u> are particularly rich in stage directions,
    while <u>Two Gentlemen of Verona</u>, <u>Merry Wives of Windsor</u>,

1921

Measure for Measure, and Winter's Tale are particularly
scanty. Continued in 1921.13.

13 _____. "Shakespeare's Prompt Books, II: The Curtains." TLS
(28 July):482.
Continuation of 1921.11. Rhodes examines possible uses
of curtains for revealing the "inner stage" at the Globe,
despite the fact that there are no stage directions in the
plays requiring them.

14 ROLLINS, HYDER E. "A Contribution to the History of the
English Commonwealth Drama." SP 18 (July):267-333.
While technically concerned only with events after 1642,
Rollins includes several references to happenings before
that date and to the playhouses involved during the Interregnum, most notably the Phoenix and the Red Bull. Most
comments towards this history of Commonwealth drama are based
upon the Thomason collection in the British Museum.

15 SISSON, CHARLES J[ASPER]. Le goût public et le théâtre élisabéthain jusqu'à la mort de Shakespeare. Dijon: University
of Dijon, 197 pp.
Examines the public taste in relation to English theatre
to 1616. The two major sections deal with public taste in
general and the public's response to theatrical entertainment. The second section contains chapters on the scenic
embellishment, comedy, tragedy, historical drama, and
romance. Sisson concludes that changing public tastes were
reflected in the changing repertories of the public and
private playhouses.

16 THALER, ALWIN. "'Bengemenes Johnsones Share.'" MLR 16
(January):61-65.
Explains an entry in Henslowe's diary by suggesting that
Jonson was an actor-sharer in 1597 and was repaying a loan
he had taken from Henslowe. See also 1921.8. Reprinted:
1941.10.

17 _____. "Was Richard Brome an Actor?" MLN 36 (February):88-91.
A brief note arguing for Brome's having acted, after
serving an apprenticeship with Ben Jonson. Reprinted:
1941.10.

1 GRAVES, THORNTON S[HIRLEY]. "Some Aspects of Extemporal
   Acting." <u>SP</u> 19 (October):429-56.
       Examines the approval of extemporal wit, commedia dell'
   arte, and censorship influences on Elizabethan and later
   acting.

2 ____. "Some References to Elizabethan Theatres." <u>SP</u> 19
   (July):317-27.
       A compilation of more than twenty contemporary refer-
   ences to a variety of Elizabethan playhouses. All are of
   minor importance, and none reveals anything new.

3 HILLEBRAND, HAROLD NEWCOMBE. "The Children of the King's
   Revels at Whitefriars." <u>JEGP</u> 21 (April):318-34.
       Discusses the conduct of business and the plays produced
   by this ill-founded and short-lived group. Hillebrand
   shows that the founder of the company was Thomas Woodford,
   not Michael Drayton as had been supposed, and that the
   company was in operation in August of 1607. He dates the
   beginning of the enterprise as late 1606, with Lording
   Barry, the playwright, taking over from Woodford in 1607.
   Hillebrand cites liberally from various court cases to
   support his assertions. In the final five pages he discusses seven extant plays performed at Whitefriars, although
   he does not attempt to reconstruct staging practices.

4 HIND, ARTHUR MAYGAR. <u>Wenceslaus Hollar and His Views of
   London and Windsor in the Seventeenth Century</u>. London:
   John Lane, 92 pp.
       The first twenty-five pages consists of a sketch of
   Hollar's life and works, valuable background for the theatre
   historian concerned with the period. The heart of the
   volume, however, is the set of sixty-four plates and the
   descriptions of the 132 etchings.

5 LAWRENCE, W[ILLIAM] J[OHN]. "Notes on a Collection of Masque
   Music." <u>M&L</u> 3 (January):49-58.
       Discusses the contents of a manuscript held in the
   British Library, containing music for several masque dances.
   Lawrence lists the contents and comments on each item,
   attempting to assign each to its source entertainment. <u>See
   also</u> 1954.5.

6 ____. "A Plummet for Bottom's Dream." <u>FortR</u> 117 (May):833-
   44.
       Argues that <u>Midsummer Night's Dream</u> was a public play

adapted for private performance, not vice-versa, and that
the quarto text reflects both versions. Reprinted: 1928.9.

7 RHODES, R. CROMPTON. *The Stagery of Shakespeare*. Birmingham:
   Cornish Brothers, 102 pp.
       "An attempt to ascertain the nature of Shakespeare's
   Stagery from an intensive sutdy of the Stage-directions in
   the original texts in Quarto, authorised and unauthorised,
   and in Folio." Rhodes develops the old alternation theory
   into a theory of "the triple stage"--placing far more importance on the upper stage. Rhodes rejects the Swan
   drawing "because in so many particulars it is obviously
   inexact." Includes reprints of 1921.12-13.

8 STOPES, CHARLOTTE CARMICHAEL. *The Seventeenth-Century Accounts
   of the Master of the Revels*. London: Shakespeare Association, 36 pp.
       Examines the three supposed seventeenth-century account
   books that survive, finding them all to be nineteenth-
   century forgeries, probably by Cunningham. For her
   exchanges with Law over the genuineness of the documents,
   and others' opinions, <u>see</u> Index under Revels Accounts.

9 THALER, ALWIN. "Minor Actors and Employees in the Elizabethan
   Theater." <u>MP</u> 20 (August):49-60.
       Brief notes on the hired men, the boy actors, the
   gatherers, tiremen, prompters, stagehands, and musicians.
   Reprinted: 1941.10.

10 _____. *Shakespere to Sheridan: A Book about the Theatre of
    Yesterday and Today*. Cambridge: Harvard University Press,
    339 pp.
       An attempt to show the continuity of theatrical tradition
    from Shakespeare through the eighteenth century. The chap-
    ters on playwrights, players, managers, and playhouses all
    touch on the Elizabethan period. Thaler includes three
    appendixes on rates of admission and capacity that deal
    only with the earlier period.

11 _____. "Strolling Players and Provincial Drama After
    Shakespere." <u>PMLA</u> 37 (June):243-80.
       Primarily concerned with the Restoration and eighteenth
    century, although the general remarks about the types of
    companies and their management are relevant to the earlier
    period.

1923

1 CAMPBELL, LILY B[ESS]. <u>Scenes and Machines on the English Stage during the Renaissance: A Classical Revival</u>. Cambridge: University Press, 302 pp.

Published version of 1921.2. The four parts deal with the classical revival of stage decoration in Italy and stage decoration in England in three successive periods: sixteenth century, pre-Restoration seventeenth century, and post-Restoration seventeenth century. Campbell includes fifteen figures and eight plates. She concludes that "the history of stage spectacle during the sixteenth and seventeenth centuries appears as fundamentally a history of the Renaissance conceptions of the ancient classical stage as these conceptions were modified by the conditions of the age into which they were projected." This work is especially important for its treatment of the masques and the machinery used in the public theatres.

2 CHAMBERS, EDMUND K. <u>The Elizabethan Stage</u>. 4 vols. Oxford: Clarendon Press, 1930 pp.

Synthesis of literally all material on English theatre from 1558 to 1616 available at the time. Composed of twenty-four chapters and thirteen appendixes contained in four volumes. The volumes are further subdivided into five major books. Book I and Book II, in volume 1, deal with the court and the control of the stage respectively. Book III examines the companies, with separate chapters on the boy companies, adult companies, and international companies; it includes a biographical sketch of all known actors of the period. Book IV looks at the playhouses and staging, with chapters on the public theatres, the private theatres, the structure and conduct of the theatres, staging at court, staging in the playhouses in the sixteeenth century, and staging in the playhouses in the seventeenth century. Book III and most of Book IV compose volume 2. Book V, composing the remainder of volume 3 and part of volume 4, deals with plays and playwrights. The three chapters of this Book examine the printing of plays, the individual playwrights and their work, and anonymous works. The appendixes, dealing with miscellaneous information, form the remainder of volume 4. The method of the work is partly documentary and partly interpretive. That is, Chambers presents all available documentary evidence on each subject to enable the reader to make his or her own judgments, but he also presents his own interpretation of the evidence from time to time. While in need of revision in the light of later scholarship, this work remains one of the two or three most important contributions to the field. <u>See</u> 1925.4-5.

1923

3 CHAMBERS, E[DMUND] K., ed. "Four Letters on Theatrical
   Affairs." MSC 2, pt. 2:145-49.
        Letters from 1569, 1576-7 (in Italian), 1599-1601, and
   1608.

4 CREIZENACH, WILHELM MICHAEL ANTON. Geschichte des neuren
   Dramas. 2d ed. Vols. 2 and 3. Halle: S. M. Niemaeyer.
        Second edition of 1903.1; see translation of that edition,
   1916.5.

5 EVANS, M. BLAKEMORE. "Traditions of the Elizabethan Stage in
   Germany." PQ 2 (October):310-14.
        Uses German drama based on English sources to show the
   comic aspect of madness in Elizabethan tragedy and the
   tradition of Pyramus falling on his scabbard rather than
   his sword in Midsummer Night's Dream.

6 GREG, WALTER W[ILSON]. Two Elizabethan Stage Abridgements:
   The Battle of Alcazar & Orlando Furioso: An Essay in
   Critical Bibliography. Oxford: Clarendon Press, 366 pp.
        Contains facsimiles and detailed discussion of the plot
   of The Battle of Alcazar and the actor's part of Orlando,
   especially in relation to the "bad" quartos of both plays.
   Greg includes historical information about the Lord
   Admiral's company 1589-1594 and 1597-1602.

7 HARRISON, G[EORGE] B[AGSHAWE]. Shakespeare's Fellows: Being
   a Brief Chronicle of the Shakespearean Age. London:
   Bodley Head, 207 pp.
        Intended as "a brief introduction to the study of the
   personal side of Elizabethan drama." The relevant chapters
   are the first, discussing "Stage and University," the third,
   examining "The Chamberlain's and the Admiral's," and the
   fourth, "Poetomachia," dealing with the war of the theatres.
   Partially incorporated into 1956.14.

8 HERFORD, C[HARLES] H[AROLD]. Sketch of Recent Shakespearian
   Investigation, 1853-1923. London: Blackie & Son, pp. 8-15.
        Not meant to be a comprehensive bibliography but rather
   "a conspectus of prevailing tendencies." The relevant
   section deals with publications on the Elizabethan stage,
   all of which have been incorporated into the present
   bibliography.

9 HOLZKNECHT, KARL J. "Theatrical Billposting in the Age of
   Elizabeth." PQ 2 (October):267-81.
        Investigates "the origin of the custom of theatrical
   billposting and . . . the character and extent of the

practice in the theatre of the Elizabethan time." Holzknecht
concludes that billposting was common, that posts were
frequently used for the purpose, that the type of play would
be on the bill but not the dramatis personae, that the
bills were posted the morning of the performance by minor
members of the company, and that the printing of bills
became the subject of a monopoly.

10 HOTSON, JOHN LESLIE. "Sir William Davenant and the Common-
    wealth Stage." Ph.D. dissertation, Harvard University.
        Published, in expanded version: 1928.7.

11 HUBBARD, GEORGE. On the Site of the Globe Playhouse of
    Shakespeare. Cambridge: University Press, 47 pp.
        Perhaps the most important of the arguments for placing
    the site of the Globe to the north of Maid Lane, in direct
    response to Braines (1921.1). Braines responded once more,
    in 1924.3, to settle the issue. This exchange is the
    culmination of the controversy over the site of Shakespeare's
    playhouse that dominated the early years of the century.
    See Index under Globe Playhouse--Site of.

12 KINGSLAND, GERTRUDE SOUTHWICK. "The First Quarto of Hamlet in
    the Light of the Stage." Ph.D. dissertation, Columbia
    University.
        Excerpts published as 1923.13.

13 _____. The First Quarto of "Hamlet" in the Light of the Stage.
    Oshkosh: Castle-Pierce Press, 63 pp.
        Published version of 1923.12. Attempts to support the
    theory that the first quarto of Hamlet is an actor's version
    excised from the complete text by comparing it to acting
    versions of the play from the time of Betterton to 1920.
    The five parts of the Introduction are abstracts of the
    five chapters of the complete dissertation. The concluding
    chapter is printed in full.

14 LAMBORN, EDMUND ARNOLD GREENING, and HARRISON, G[EORGE]
    B[AGSWAWE]. Shakespeare: The Man and His Stage. London:
    Oxford University Press, pp. 76-104.
        The relevant section discusses the theatres and actors
    in general terms.

15 LAWRENCE, W[ILLIAM] J[OHN]. "New Facts from Sir Henry Herbert's
    Office Book." TLS (29 November):820.
        Seven additions to 1917.2, discovered by Lawrence in the
    Malone collection at the Bodleian Library. Reprinted:
    1937.5.

1923

16 _____. "A New Shakespeare Test." <u>Criterion</u> 2, no. 5
(October):77-94.
   Discusses the instruments called for in stage directions
for incidental music, focusing on the cornet and trumpet.
Since trumpets were used on the public stage and cornets
on the private stage before 1609, any stage directions that
call for both must be from after that date. Reprinted:
1928.9.

17 _____. "Shakespeare's Workshop." <u>FortR</u> 119 (April):589-99.
   Discusses the influence of the audience, the playhouse,
and the classical leanings of the University Wits on Shakespeare and the drama. Reprinted: 1928.9.

18 LOUNSBURY, THOMAS R. "A Puritan Censor of the Stage." <u>YR</u> 12
(July):790-810.
   Examines Prynne's life and works, particularly
<u>Histriomastix</u>. The tone throughout is derogatory.

19 ROLLINS, HYDER E. "The Commonwealth Drama: Miscellaneous
Notes." <u>SP</u> 20 (January):52-69.
   A variety of notes, some of which pertain to actors of
the earlier period. Rollins also includes notices of
provincial entertainments after the closing of the theatres.

20 SMITH, G. C. MOORE, ed. "The Academic Drama at Cambridge:
Extracts from College Records." <u>MSC</u> 2, pt. 2:150-230.
   Records of plays produced by members of the various
colleges.

<u>1924</u>

1 ADAIR, E[DWARD] R[OBERT]. <u>The Sources for the History of the
Council in the Sixteenth & Early Seventeenth Centuries</u>.
Helps for Students of History, no. 51. London: Society
for Promoting Christian Knowledge, 96 pp.
   An annotated bibliography with an extended introductory
essay. The effect of the Privy Council on English theatrical affairs during this period was far from negligible, but
this volume is of only peripheral interest. Included in
<u>NCBEL</u> 1, col. 1384.

2 ARCHER, WILLIAM. "Elizabethan Stage and Restoration Drama."
<u>QR</u> 24 (April):399-418.
   Essentially a lengthy review article, focusing on
Chambers (1923.2). Archer attacks the Swan drawing, since
it contains no rear stage, which "was from a very early

date, in constant demand," and since the two doors entering
onto the stage are not obliquely set. He also, however,
argues for the primacy of the platform, with inner and
upper stages serving as auxiliary acting spaces.

3   BRAINES, WILLIAM WESTMORELAND. The Site of the Globe Play-
    house, Southwark. 2d ed. London: London County Council,
    47 pp.
         Revised and enlarged edition of 1921.1. The new informa-
    tion includes a discussion of the pictorial evidence of
    the early maps and views of London; a consideration (and
    refutation) of Hubbard (1923.11); and an appendix discus-
    sing the sites of the Southwark Bear Gardens. This work
    stands today as the definitive study of the site of
    Shakespeare's public playhouse. For the entire controversy,
    see Index under Globe Playhouse--Site of.

4   GREG, W[ALTER] W[ILSON]. "The Masque of the Twelve Months."
    TLS (30 October):686.
         A letter to the editor, in response to Lawrence (1924.6).
    Greg admits the reasonableness (but not the inevitability)
    of Lawrence's identification of one of Jones's designs.

5   LAWRENCE, W[ILLIAM] J[OHN]. "Bells on the Elizabethan Stage."
    FortR 122 (July):59-70.
         Discusses the various uses of bells in the theatre for
    dramatic effect. Reprinted: 1935.7.

6   _____. "Inigo Jones: An Identification." TLS (23 October):
    667.
         A letter to the editor, assigning one of Jones's designs
    to The Masque of the Twelve Months. See Greg's response,
    1924.4.

7   _____. "John Kirke, the Caroline Actor-Dramatist." SP 21
    (October):586-93.
         Discusses the acting and playwriting career of the
    author of The Seven Champions of Christendome. Kirke was
    originally a strolling provincial player who became a
    Groom of the Chamber in 1635.

8   _____. "The Rose Theatre of Shakespeare's Day." TLS (21
    February):112.
         A letter to the editor concerning the supposed end of
    the Rose. Lawrence suggests that Collier did not in fact
    forge the poem about the burning of the Rose; the reference
    was actually to the fire at the King's Theatre in 1671-72.

1924

9 ____. "Was Peter Cunningham a Forger?" <u>MLR</u> 29 (January):25-34.
    Argues for the genuineness of the Revels Accounts, in direct answer to Stopes's final attack in 1922.8. Lawrence deals with the three Revels Accounts published by Cunningham in 1842 and finds no reason to doubt their authenticity. <u>See also</u> Index under Revels Accounts for the entire controversy.

10 SIMPSON, PERCY, and BELL, C[HARLES] F[RANCIS]. <u>Designs by Inigo Jones for Masques and Plays at Court.</u> Oxford: Malone and Walpole Societies, 158 pp.
    "A descriptive catalogue of drawings for scenery and costumes mainly in the collection of his Grace the Duke of Devonshire." Simpson and Bell divide their work into two sections, drawings for known masques and plays, and doubtful and unidentified drawings. The detailed introduction traces Jones's artistic achievement. <u>See also</u> 1924.6; 1973.10, 21; and Index under Jones, Inigo.

11 STEELE, MARY SUSAN. "Plays and Masques at Court, 1558-1642." Ph.D. dissertation, Cornell University, 367 pp.
    Published as 1926.10-11.

12 WHANSLAW, HARRY WILLIAM. <u>The Bankside Stage-Book</u>. Redhill, Surrey: Wells Gardner, Darton & Co., 256 pp.
    A guide for children to building a practical model of a Tudor playhouse, based on the Fortune contract and a large dose of speculation. Whanslaw includes a general history of theatre from the Greeks through the early twentieth century. His model includes an inner below and inner above.

<u>1925</u>

1 ARONSTEIN, P[HILIP]. "Das englische Renaissancetheater." <u>NS</u> 33 (July-August):265-80.
    Essentially a lengthy review of Chambers (1923.2), with an outline of previous scholarship in the field, from Malone to Stopes, Greg, Feuillerat, and Wallace.

2 BOAS, F[REDERICK] S. "Crosfield's Diary and the Caroline Stage." <u>FortR</u> 123 (April):514-24.
    Excerpts from the diary of Thomas Crosfield from 1626 to 1640. Crosfield was elected a Fellow of Queen's College, Oxford, in 1627, and he noted many dramatic performances in his diary. Boas includes Crosfield's notes from an interview with Richard Kendall, an actor at Salisbury Court, concerning the London companies in 1634.

3 BRADNER, LEICESTER. "Stages and Stage Scenery in Court Drama
   before 1558." RES 1 (October):447-48.
       Demonstrates that a raised stage and Serlian "houses"
   were used in the Universities before 1550, and speculates
   that the same would have been used at Court.

4 CHAMBERS, E[DMUND] K. "Elizabethan Stage Gleanings." RES 1
   (January):75-78.
       Four notes adding to the information presented in 1923.2.
   Continued in 1925.5.

5 _____. "Some Elizabethan Stage Gleanings." RES 1, (April):
   182-86.
       Continuation of 1925.4, with six additional bits of
   information.

6 GAW, ALLISON. "Actors' Names in Basic Shakespearean Texts,
   with Special Reference to Romeo and Juliet and Much Ado."
   PMLA 40 (September):530-50.
       Argues that the use of actors' names for minor parts
   not taken from Shakespeare's sources reflects the work of
   the playwright, not the prompter.

7 _____. "John Sincklo as One of Shakespeare's Actors." Anglia
   49:289-303.
       Discusses Romeo's description of the Apothecary in the
   second quarto of Romeo and Juliet, and applies the description to John Sincklo, previously one of Strange's Men and
   Pembroke's Men.

8 GRANVILLE-BARKER, HARLEY. "A Note Upon Chapters XX. and XXI.
   of The Elizabethan Stage." RES 1 (January):60-71.
       Dissents from Chambers's view that the inn-yard theatres
   were less important than the court theatres during the
   sixteenth century, asserting that it was in the inn-yards
   that "emotional" acting developed. Granville-Barker brings
   no concrete evidence to bear on the issue; instead, he
   draws upon his extensive production experience.

9 GRAVES, THORNTON SHIRLEY. "Women on the Pre-Restoration
   Stage." SP 22 (April):184-97.
       Reexamines the evidence for female actors before 1642,
   finding that while women were never regularly employed,
   "the sporadic appearance of women on special occasions may
   have been more frequent than has been generally recognized."

1925

10 GREG, W[ALTER] W[ILSON]. "The Elizabethan Stage." RES 1
       (January):97-111.
          An extended review of Chambers (1923.2).

11 ____. "The Evidence of Theatrical Plots for the History of
       the Elizabethan Stage." RES 1 (July):257-74.
          Considers the casts revealed by the seven complete and
       three fragmentary plots in light of the companies and
       vice-versa. Greg is able to clarify the relationship
       between the Admiral's and Strange's company as well as
       tentatively set the date of The Battle of Alcazar as winter,
       1598-99.

12 ____. "Prompt Copies, Private Transcripts, and the Playhouse
       Scrivener." Library, 4th ser. 6 (September):148-56.
          Discusses bibliographical problems of several manuscript
       plays of the period. It seems possible that the playhouses
       kept the author's foul papers as well as a fair copy of the
       play.

13 HAINES, C. M. "The 'Law of Re-Entry' in Shakespeare." RES 1
       (October):449-51.
          Examines a variety of exits at the end of one scene with
       immediate reentrance to start another in Shakespeare,
       concluding that normally this is not the case.

14 KEITH, WILLIAM GRANT. "John Webb and the Court Theatre of
       Charles II." ArchR 57 (February):49-55.
          Traces Webb's career and analyzes several of his scene
       designs. While dealing primarily with the Restoration,
       Keith also touches on Webb's earlier work under Jones. He
       makes the mistake, however, of assigning the construction
       of the Cockpit-in-Court to the later period.

15 MARCHAM, FRANK, and GILSON, J[ULIUS] P[ARNELL], eds. The
       King's Office of the Revels, 1610-22: Fragments of
       Documents in the Department of Manuscripts, British Museum.
       London: Frank Marcham, 48 pp.
          Photographs and transcriptions of eighteen fragments
       from the Cotton Manuscript Tiberius E. X.

16 NICOLL, ALLARDYCE. "The Rights of Beeston and D'avenant in
       Elizabethan Plays." RES 1 (June):84-91.
          While primarily concerned with the Restoration stage
       here, Nicoll does summarize some of the activities of
       William Beeston, Davenant, and Killigrew before 1642.

17 T.-D., G. "Whitehall in 1642." RES 1 (October):462.
    Brief excerpts from a 1642 quarto describing masque
    production.

18 UNWIN, GEORGE. The Gilds and Companies of London. 2d ed.
    London: Methuen, pp. 267-92.
    Reprint of 1909.29.

19 WOOD, D. T. B. "The Revels Books: The Writer of the Malone
    Scrap." RES 1 (January):72-74.
    Identifies Sir William Musgrave as the probable copier
    of this important document. See also 1925.20.

20 _____. "The Suspected Revels Books." RES 1 (April):166-72.
    Examines the external appearance of the Revels Books
    for 1604-5, 1611-12, and 1636, suspected of being forgeries.
    Wood concludes that the documents are probably genuine, but
    if they are not then Sir William Musgrave must have had a
    hand in the forgery. See also 1925.19 and Index under
    Revels Accounts.

21 YATES, FRANCES A. "English Actors in Paris during the Life-
    time of Shakespeare." RES 1 (October):392-403.
    Primarily a summary of what is known of the two English
    companies that performed in Paris before 1616, including a
    suggestion that Richard III might have been one of the
    plays performed. Yates does print two letters, discovered
    in the Public Record Office, that bear on the matter, one
    of which confirms a previously unknown performance in 1603.

1926

1 BALDWIN, T[HOMAS] W[HITFIELD]. "Nathaniel Field and Robert
   Wilson." MLN 41 (January):32-34.
   Brief notes concerning Nathaniel Field, arguing that the
   actor and the printer were in fact the same man, and
   Robert Wilson, arguing that the Queen's Company member in
   1583 had died by 1588, and that later records belong to
   others of that name.

2 BORCHERDT, HANS HEINRICH. Der Renaissancetil des Theaters;
   ein prinzipieller Versuch. Halle: Max Niemeyer, 44 pp.
   Examines the development of the Renaissance playhouse on
   the continent, with comparisons to English practice.

1926

3 DENKINGER, EMMA MARSHALL. "Actors' Names in the Register of
   St. Botolph Aldgate." PMLA 41 (March):91-109.
       A collection of entries in the parish register concern-
   ing fifteen actors from 1592 to 1622. The list is alphabetical, with previously known biographical information
   summarized.

*4 ENGELEN, J[OHANNES]. Die Schauspieler-Ökonomie in Shakespeares
    Dramen. Münster.
        Unlocatable. Cited in NCBEL 1, col. 1395.

5 GRANVILLE-BAKER, HARLEY. "The Stagecraft of Shakespeare."
   FortR 126 (July):1-17.
       A lecture delivered at the Sorbonne, 26 January 1926.
   Granville-Baker here concentrates on the differences between Shakespearean stage conditions and our own, mention-
   ing four: language change; a different sense of the past;
   women's parts played by boys; and primary appeal to the ear
   rather than to the eye. He concludes that to appreciate
   Shakespeare, "we must go back and meet him on his own
   ground."

6 HILLEBRAND, HAROLD NEWCOMB. The Child Actors: A Chapter in
   Elizabethan Stage History. ISLL, vol. 11, nos. 1 and 2.
   Urbana: University of Illinois, 355 pp.
       Published version of 1914.9. Based primarily on previous-
   ly discovered documents, but a fuller treatment than available earlier. Hillebrand begins with a general survey of
   children on the stage since the twelfth century, and gives
   detailed histories of the major boys' troupes during the
   reigns of Henry VIII and Elizabeth. He discusses the
   Children of the Chapel Royal, the Children of Paul's, the
   King's Revels, and the Queen's Revels in turn. In an
   important final chapter Hillebrand deals with the influence
   of the child actors on the plays. Three appendixes contain
   some of the more obscure documents used. See Index under
   Children's Companies for other references.

7 HUNTER, MARK. "Act- and Scene-Division in the Plays of Shakespeare." RES 2 (July):295-310.
       Argues that Elizabethan plays (including Shakespeare's)
   were written in the five-act structure. See 1927.19;
   1928.7, 17-18 for replies.

8 MARCHAM, FRANK. "The King's Office of the Revels." RES 2
   (January):95-96.
       A brief note in response to a review of 1925.15 by
   Chambers.

9 RANNIE, DAVID WATSON. "Scenery in Shakespeare's Plays." In
   Scenery in Shakespeare's Plays and Other Studies. Oxford:
   Basil Blackwell, pp. 125-76.
       Refers not to stage scenery, but to poetic scenery:
   "references, in the speeches of his characters, to exterior
   and interior backgrounds and surroundings, and secondly,
   similes, metaphors or other figures of speech, taken from
   phenomena of landscape or atmosphere."

10 STEELE, MARY SUSAN. Plays and Masques at Court during the
   Reigns of Elizabeth, James, and Charles. Cornell Studies
   in English. Ithaca: Cornell University Press, 300 pp.
       Published version of 1924.11. A chronicle listing of
   all plays and masques presented at Court 1558-1642. Steele
   includes presentations before the sovereign on progress.
   The main sources are the official records from the Revels
   Office books and contemporary allusions from diaries,
   letters, and so on. The three chapters give the details
   of the reigns of Elizabeth, James, and Charles by season.
   The two indexes treat authors and titles. Same as 1926.11.

11 _____. Plays and Masques at Court, 1558-1642. New Haven:
   Yale University Press, 300 pp.
       Same as 1926.10.

12 WILSON, F[RANK] P[ERCY]. "Ralph Crane, Scrivener to the King's
   Players." Library, 4th ser. 7 (September):194-215.
       Examines two manuscripts from the King's Men, shown by
   Greg to be by the same hand (see 1925.12), and claims that
   Ralph Crane was the transcriber. Wilson also ties Crane
   to three other extant manuscripts and shows that he was
   transcribing for the company before 1621. Reprinted:
   1968.3.

13 WRIGHT, LOUIS B. "Will Kempe and the Commedia dell'Arte."
   MLN 41 (December):516-20.
       A brief note arguing for the commedia influence on
   Kempe, and assigning him the parts of Costard and Launce
   as well as Peter and Dogberry.

1927

1 BALDWIN, THOMAS WHITFIELD. The Organization and Personnel of
   the Shakespearean Company. Princeton: Princeton University Press, 464 pp.
       Comprehensive examination of the Chamberlain's/King's
   Men from 1558 to 1642. The major chapters treat government

regulation and theatrical custom, membership, housekeepers, hired men and the bookkeeper, finance, the division of labor, the Beaumont and Fletcher actor lists, and the actors of Shakespeare's plays. The appendixes include discussions of the Admiral's Men before 1595, the apprentices and their roles, and Jonson's plays for the company. Baldwin establishes lines of parts and assigns actors to them. His many charts yield valuable comparisons. While somewhat devalued by more recent research, this work remains an important contribution to the field.

2 BALDWIN, T[HOMAS] W[HITFIELD]. "Posting Henslowe's Accounts." JEGP 26 (January):42-90.
   Uses one of the principles developed in 1927.1 to examine the accounts of the Admiral's Men as revealed in Henslowe's diary. Baldwin clarifies the amounts of loans Henslowe furnished the company, their schedule of repayment, and the actors' income from the galleries. He finally traces the membership of the company.

3 BRETTLE, R[OBERT] E[DWARD]. "Samuel Daniel and the Children of the Queen's Revels, 1604-5." RES 3 (April):162-68.
   Two documents discovered in the declared accounts of the Treasurer of the Chamber that clarify Daniel's standing with the company. Both were previously published by Hillebrand in 1926.2.

4 BYRNE, M[URIEL] St. CLARE. "Shakespeare's Audience." In A Series of Papers on Shakespeare and the Theatre, Together with Papers on Edward Alleyn and Early Records Illustrating the Personal Life of Shakespeare. London: Oxford University Press for the Shakespeare Association, pp. 186-216.
   A reevaluation of the evidence from contemporary accounts and from the plays. Byrne sets out the different classes that attended the theatre and attempts to analyze audience taste as reflected in the plays presented. Rather than a superior imaginative capacity, Byrne would credit the Elizabethan audience with "an immense capacity for . . . the childish faculty of over-looking without effort discrepancies which shatter the illusion of reality." She concludes that the first demand of the audience was for a good story, and that Shakespeare and the other dramatists did their best to oblige.

5 COWLING, G[EORGE] H[ERBERT]. "Shakespeare and the Elizabethan Stage." In A Series of Papers on Shakespeare and the Theatre, Together with Papers on Edward Alleyn and Early Records Illustrating the Personal Life of Shakespeare.

London: Oxford University Press for the Shakespeare Association, pp. 157-85.

Summarizes what was known or thought about the Elizabethan stage in 1927. Cowling describes the public theatres as having two or three doors, a gallery above, and an arras covering the center door and possible a "recess"-- the inner stage. The private theatres, according to Cowling, had "a great curtain which concealed the whole of the rear wall beneath the gallery or balcony." The effect of a proscenium arch was thought to be made by the heavens and the pillars in the public theatres. In the second section Cowling surveys Shakespeare's use of these elements, and in the third he shows how the stage influenced Shakespeare's dramaturgy.

6 GRAY, AUSTIN K. "Robert Armine, the Foole." <u>PMLA</u> 42 (September):673-85.

Discusses the change in Shakespeare's fools when Armin replaced Kempe in the company in about 1600. Armin played Touchstone, Feste, Lear's fool, and the drunken porter, as well as a variety of other roles. Gray also examines Armin's contributions to literature.

7 GREG, W[ALTER] W[ILSON]. "Edward Alleyn." In <u>A Series of Papers on Shakespeare and the Theatre, Together with Papers on Edward Alleyn and Early Records Illustrating the Personal Life of Shakespeare</u>. London: Oxford University Press for the Shakespeare Association, pp. 1-34.

A brief but comprehensive examination of the Alleyn life records. Especially important are the inferences Greg draws from various contemporary records. He traces the travelling of the Lord Admiral's Men from London during times of plague and briefly summarizes Alleyn's relationship with Henslowe and the founding of Dulwich College. <u>See also</u> Index under Alleyn for other references.

8 HAINES, C. M. "The Development of Shakespeare's Stagecraft." In <u>A Series of Papers on Shakespeare and the Theatre, Together with Papers on Edward Alleyn and Early Records Illustrating the Personal Life of Shakespeare</u>. London: Oxford University Press for the Shakespeare Association, pp. 35-61.

Attempts to trace the development of Shakespeare's use of the elements of Elizabethan staging through his plays. Haines assumes, as did most writers on the subject at the time, an inner stage and a balcony flanked by windows and containing an upper inner stage. He goes through the plays by chronological and thematic groups and discusses

1927

Shakespeare's use of the physical features of the stage and
his growing adeptness at localizing action. <u>Macbeth</u>,
<u>Antony and Cleopatra</u>, and <u>Coriolanus</u> are called "his
greatest achievements in this field."

9 HARRISON, G[EORGE] B[AGSHAW]. "Shakespeare's Actors." In <u>A</u>
<u>Series of Papers on Shakespeare and the Theatre, Together</u>
<u>with Papers on Edward Alleyn and Early Records Illustrating</u>
<u>the Personal Life of Shakespeare</u>. Oxford University Press
for the Shakespeare Association, pp. 62-87.
Proposes not to add to our information, but to reexamine
it to see if there are any additional inferences possible.
Harrison concentrates on the years 1597-1605, and he
examines the plays for the impact of the actors on them,
coming to the standard conclusion that Shakespeare wrote
the plays with the actors who would play the parts in mind.
Known biographical facts, then, have an impact on our
understanding of characters and plays, and Harrison discusses what we know of Burbage and Kempe.

10 ISAACS, J[ACOB]. "Shakespeare as Man of the Theatre." In <u>A</u>
<u>Series of Papers on Shakespeare and the Theatre, Together</u>
<u>with Papers on Edward Alleyn and Early Records Illustrating</u>
<u>the Personal Life of Shakespeare</u>. London: Oxford Univer-
sity Press for the Shakespeare Association, pp. 88-119.
Examines Shakespeare's sense of the stage and applies
the modern notion of the director to Shakespeare's art.
Isaacs first establishes a theatrical tradition throughout
Europe before Shakespeare, then fits Shakespeare into that
tradition.

11 _____. "Shakespeare's 'Abridgement' in the Light of Theatrical History." <u>RES</u> 3 (July):339-40.
Relates the French use of outlines (similar to Elizabethan "Plots") to Shakespeare's use of the term in
<u>Hamlet</u> and <u>Midsummer Night's Dream</u>.

12 LAWRENCE, W[ILLIAM] J[OHN]. "John Honeyman, the Caroline
Actor-Dramatist." <u>RES</u> 3 (April):220-22.
A brief note tracing the career of this member of the
King's Men.

13 _____. <u>The Physical Conditions of the Elizabethan Public</u>
<u>Playhouse</u>. Cambridge: Harvard University Press, 129 pp.
Based on a series of lectures given at Harvard and
Radcliffe in 1925-26. While modifying some of his earlier
judgments, Lawrence is still four-square for the inner
stage. His treatment of textual evidence is doubtful, as

he cites stage directions from nineteenth-century editions
in support of several of his contentions, and those directions are not found in the original texts. This is the
only one of Lawrence's many publications where he attempts
a lengthy discussion of his views on the subject; all his
other books are collections of articles, most of which were
previously published.

14 _____. Pre-Restoration Stage Studies. Cambridge: Harvard
University Press, 435 pp.
  Essays selected from the Harvard-Radcliffe lectures of
1925-26, tied together only by their applicability to the
stagecraft of the period. Topics examined include the
innyard plays and playing spaces, the practice of doubling,
the stage jig, Shakespeare's staging of Hamlet, stage
traps, illusions of sound, stage realism, stage spectacle,
the use of properties, and the evaluation of early prompt
books.

15 NOBLE, RICHARD. "Shakespeare's Songs and Stage." In A Series
of Papers on Shakespeare and the Theatre, Together with
Papers on Edward Alleyn and Early Records Illustrating the
Personal Life of Shakespeare. London: Oxford University
Press for the Shakespeare Association, pp. 120-33.
  Examines the development of Shakespeare's use of song
to delineate character, move the plot forward, and help set
the scene. Noble believes the songs were sung to existing
popular tunes, known to the audience.

16 NUNGEZER, EDWIN. "A Dictionary of Actors and of Other Persons
Associated with the Public Representation of Plays in
England before 1642." Ph.D. dissertation, Cornell Univer-
sity, 665 pp.
  Published as 1929.12.

17 SHAKESPEARE ASSOCIATION. A Series of Papers on Shakespeare
and the Theatre, Together with Papers on Edward Alleyn
and Early Records Illustrating the Personal Life of
Shakespeare. London: Oxford University Press for the
Shakespeare Association, 239 pp.
  Contains 1927.4-5, 7-10, 15.

18 SISSON, C[HARLES] J[ASPER]. Introduction to Believe as You
List, by Philip Massinger. Malone Society Reprints.
London: Oxford University Press, v-xxxiv.
  A detailed introduction to an edition of the manuscript
play, including valuable information about the prompter's
notations and the cast. Reprinted: 1968.3.

1927

19 WILSON, J[OHN] DOVER. "Act- and Scene-Divisions in the Plays
    of Shakespeare: A Reply to Sir Mark Hunter." <u>RES</u> 3
    (October):385-97.
        In response to 1926.7, Wilson points out the lack of
    act-division in many manuscript plays of the period 1590-
    1610, when Shakespeare was actively writing. The pause
    between acts was not usual until the King's Men began
    playing at Blackfriars.

20 WRIGHT, LOUIS B. "Animal Actors on the English Stage before
    1642." <u>PMLA</u> 42 (September):656-69.
        Discusses the use of animal actors, especially when it
    approached an "animal act" or extraneous show, as in <u>Two
    Gentlemen of Verona</u>. Wright concludes that "in the variety
    entertainment that helped to attract Elizabethan theatrical
    audiences animal acts held a recognized place."

21 _____. "Elizabethan Sea Drama and Its Staging." <u>Anglia</u> 51:
    104-18.
        Examines the staging of sea drama. Wright concludes
    that "sea atmosphere was induced in Elizabethan theatres
    not only by vivid descriptions, sea songs, etc., but also
    through simulation of actual ship scenes by the arrangement
    and skillful use of the stages, by the use of simple
    properties, and by appropriate costuming." He cites many
    plays of the period.

22 _____. "Juggling Tricks and Conjuring on the English Stage
    before 1642." <u>MP</u> 24 (February):269-84.
        Points out instances of the use of legerdemain, tricks
    of sleight, and elaborate spectacles of conjuring in
    English Renaissance drama. Most such instances were
    gratuitous, included purely for entertainment values.
    Wright cites contemporary sources for methods of feigning
    executions and other stage tricks.

23 _____. "Stage Duelling in the Elizabethan Theatre." <u>MLR</u> 22
    (July):265-75.
        Points out the use of stage combats to furnish duelling
    spectacles in the course of play performances on the
    Elizabethan stage. Players were skilled fencers, and the
    audience enjoyed the spectacle of a good match, as in
    <u>Hamlet</u>. Reprinted: 1968.3.

24 _____. "Variety Entertainment by the Elizabethan Strolling
    Players." <u>JEGP</u> 26 (April):294-303.
        Examines the evidence for variety entertainment (acro-
    batics, music, juggling, magic, dance, and so on) by the
    touring actors, in the provinces and on the continent.

1928

1 BENTLEY, G[ERALD] E[DADES]. "The Dumb Band of Venice." TLS
   (6 December):966.
        Reveals the discovery of a warrant for payment to the
   King's Men for presentation of this previously unknown
   play at Court in 1628. But see 1929.4.

2 _____. "Shakespeare's Fellows." TLS (15 November):856.
        Examines the records of the Church of St. Saviour,
   Southwark, and prints those relating to actors and other
   theatrical personalities who lived in the parish.

3 FREDÉN, GUSTAF. "A propos du théâtre anglais en Allemagne:
   L'auteur inconnu des Comedies et tragedies anglaises de
   1620." RLC 8, no. 3 (July-September):420-32.
        Discusses the possible authorship of a seventeenth-
   century German collection of English plays. See also
   1939.3.

4 GREG, W[ALTER] W[ILSON]. "Act Divisions in Shakespeare." RES
   4 (April):152-58.
        Examines all plays printed 1591-1610 for evidence of act
   division. Only about 45 percent of the plays are divided.
   After excluding plays not intended for the regular stage,
   only about 40 percent are divided. And if plays meant for
   the children's companies are excluded, only about 20
   percent of the plays are divided.

5 HAINES, C. M. "Shakespeare's 'Curtains.'" TLS (10 May):358.
        Responds to Noble (1928.11) suggesting that even if the
   final scene in Othello began with a discovery (which Haines
   considers unlikely), it certainly did not end with the
   drawing of a curtain. The trunk scene in Cymbeline is the
   only Shakespearean scene to both begin and end with the
   curtain. Haines tentatively suggests some sort of
   mechanical device might have allowed the pulling of the
   curtain from backstage.

6 HOTSON, [JOHN] LESLIE. The Commonwealth and Restoration Stage.
   Cambridge: Harvard Universtiy Press, 424 pp.
        Expanded, published version of 1923.10. While on the
   surface dealing with the period after 1642, this book is
   of great importance to the study of the pre-Commonwealth
   stage. Because of Hotson's careful search of public
   records, and his publication of excerpts from many of the
   more than one hundred documents he discovered, we learn
   a great deal about the playhouses and personalities of the

1928

Caroline period. The section dealing with the private
playhouses that survived until the Restoration (the
Phoenix and the Salisbury Court) is especially important.

7 LAWRENCE, W[ILLIAM] J[OHN]. "Act-Intervals in Early Shakespearian Performances." RES 4 (January):78-79.
A brief note, in response to Hunter (1926.17) and
Wilson (1927.19), pointing out that a parody of the lovers
sleeping through the act in Midsummer Night's Dream occurs
in Histriomastix, which must have been written before 1608.
Thus, if it is based on Midsummer Night's Dream, there must
have been an act-time for the lovers to sleep through at
the Globe, since the King's Men did not start playing at
Blackfriars until that date. See Wilson (1928.18) for a
response.

8 ____. Shakespeare's Workshop. Oxford: B. Blackwell; Boston
and New York: Houghton-Mifflin, 161 pp.
Reprints essays from a variety of publications, including four of theatrical interest: 1920.20, 1922.6; 1923.16,
17.

9 ____. "Turrets in Early Elizabethan Theatres." RES 4
(April):208-9.
A brief note suggesting that the Theatre and the Curtain
possessed towers or turrets, based on a passage in Stubbe's
Anatomy of Abuses.

10 MARSCHALL, WILHELM. "Das 'Sir Thomas Moore'-Manuskript und
die englische 'Commedia dell'arte.'" Anglia 52:193-241.
Examines the influence of commedia dell'arte practices on
the Sir Thomas More manuscript and speculates on Shakespeare's part in its writing.

11 NOBLE, RICHARD. "Shakespeare's 'Curtains.'" TLS (3 May):334.
Argues that the final scene of Othello was "discovered
by means of drawing aside the curtain of the inner stage."
See Haines's response, 1928.5.

12 SACK, MARIA. Darstellerzahl und Rollenverteilung bei Shakespeare. Beiträge zur englische Philologie, no. 8. Leipzig:
Bernard Tauchnitz, 76 pp.
Examines the doubling of roles and the actors required
for Shakespeare's plays. Sack includes detailed discussions of King Lear, Macbeth, Midsummer Night's Dream,
Merchant of Venice, Taming of the Shrew, Richard III, and
Romeo and Juliet. Eleven adults and three boys, most of
whom were versatile enough to play several roles, as well as
a few walk-ons, were apparently always available.

13 SHARPE, ROBERT BOIES. "The Real War of the Theatres: The
    Rivalry of the Admiral's Men and the Chamberlain's Men
    during the Last Decade of Queen Elizabeth's Reign, 1594-
    1603." Ph.D. dissertation, Yale University, 259 pp.
    Published as 1935.16.

14 SYMONDS, E. M. "The Diary of John Greene (1635-57)." EHR 43
    (July):385-94.
        Contains notices of Greene's attendance at the Black-
    friars and the Phoenix.

15 TANNENBAUM, SAMUEL A. Shakespeare Forgeries in the Revels
    Accounts. New York: Columbia University Press, 109 pp.
        Examines the supposed Revels Accounts of 1604-5 and
    1611-12, published by Cunningham in 1842, concluding that
    they are in fact forgeries by Collier. Tannenbaum prints
    many transcripts and facsimiles of the documents to support
    his case. For the rest of the controvery, see Index under
    Revels Accounts.

16 TURNER, CELESTE. Anthony Mundy, an Elizabethan Man of Letters.
    University of California Publications in English, vol. 2,
    no. 1. Berkeley: University of California Press, 234 pp.
        Essentially a biographical study of the playwright, with
    some account of the composition of his plays and pageants.
    Of little theatrical interest. Included because of listing
    in NCBEL 1, col. 1402.

17 WILLOUGHBY, EDWIN ELLIOT. "The Heading, Actus Primus, Scaena
    Prima, in the First Folio." RES 4 (July):323-26.
        In response to Hunter (1926.17), Willoughby points out
    that the act divisions of the First Folio are of typo-
    graphical rather than theatrical origin.

18 WILSON, J[OHN] DOVER. "'They Sleepe All the Act.'" RES 4
    (April):191-93.
        A brief response to Lawrence (1928.7) regarding sleeping
    through the act time in Midsummer Night's Dream, suggesting
    that there was probably no act time in Histriomastix and
    that Lawrence's conjecture does not hold up.

19 WINNINGHOF, ELISABETH. Das Theaterkostüm bei Shakespeare.
    Munich: H. Buschmann, 85 pp.
        Published version of a University of Munich Ph.D. dis-
    sertation. Examines general costuming practices of the
    Elizabethan period. Brilliant color and fine detail were
    expected by the audience and presented by the players.
    Costuming was used to delineate characters and identify

1928

social standing, occupation, and history. Royal costumes
for men and women were the most elaborate, followed by
noblemen, clergy, academicians, craftsmen, and servants.
The fool wore an individual costume, and foreigners were
immediately recognizable. Special costumes were used for
fairies, gods, witches, animals, and so on. Winninghof
concludes that costumes were an important part of the
theatre of the time. This was the first comprehensive
treatment of the subject. For other costume references,
see Index under Costumes.

20 WRIGHT, LOUIS B. "Variety-Show Clownery on the Pre-Restoration
Stage." Anglia 52:51-68.
Examines extraneous clownery inserted into Elizabethan
plays to add to audience enjoyment. Wright finds little
change from the beginning of the period until the closing
of the theatres.

21 _____. "Vaudeville Dancing and Acrobatics in Elizabethan
Plays." EStudien 63 (September):59-76.
Discusses the place of incidental dancing and acrobatics
in the regular drama. Wright provides numerous examples
of the use of both, and concludes that they were often used
to enhance entertainment values in a play.

1929

1 BALDWIN, T[HOMAS] W[HITFIELD]. "The Revels Books of 1604-5
and 1611-12." Library, 4th ser. 10 (December):327-38.
Examines the Revels Accounts for the two years that have
been suspected of being forged, arguing for their genuineness. For the complete controversy, see Index under Revels
Accounts.

2 BASKERVILL, CHARLES READ. The Elizabethan Jig and Related
Song Drama. Chicago: University of Chicago Press, 642 pp.
A comprehensive examination of the Elizabethan jig, in
two parts: history and texts. Part I deals with the rise
of the jig, major types and practitioners, and the decline
of the form, while Part II contains the texts of thirty-
six extant English and continental jigs. The many notes
serve as a guide to previous scholarship in the area.

3 BECKWITH, ADA. "A Typical Elizabethan Playhouse." ShAB 4
(January): [inside back cover].
A drawing, after a design by Tannenbaum. Both inner and
upper stages extend the full width of the back wall, fully

curtained, with door and windows inside each. The stage
doors, flanked by smaller windows, are obliquely set.

4 BENTLEY, G[ERALD] E[ADES]. "The Dumbe Band of Venice." TLS
   (21 February):142.
        Responds to 1928.1, following Greg's suggestion that
   this play is probably Henry Shirley's Dumb Baud.

5 _____. "New Actors of the Elizabethan Period." MLN 44 (June):
   368-72.
        Lists information about fourteen previously unknown
   actors found primarily in the registers of London churches.
   Part of the research for his Ph.D. dissertation (1929.7),
   which eventually became 1941.1.

6 _____. "Records of Players in the Parish of St. Giles,
   Cripplegate." PMLA 44 (September):789-826.
        A collection of 288 entries concerning 80 actors and
   dramatists, mostly connected with the Fortune Playhouse.
   Bentley's list is alphabetical, with a brief recital of
   what is known of each individual along with the information
   drawn from the parish register. Part of the research for
   his Ph.D. dissertation (1929.7), which became 1941.1.

7 BENTLEY, GERALD EADES. "Studies in the Theatrical Companies
   and Actors of 'Elizabethan' Times with Special Reference
   to the Period 1616-1642." 2 vols. Ph.D. dissertation,
   University of London, 695 pp.
        Perhaps the most important dissertation ever produced
   in the field, these two volumes served as the basis for
   much of Bentley's later Jacobean and Caroline Stage
   (1941.1). The first volume corrects and supplements the
   then out-of-date histories of the companies by Collier
   (1879.2), Fleay (1890.1), and Murray (1910.15); the second
   volume, dealing with the actors of the later part of the
   period, is wholly original. Almost all information on
   actors and companies comes from primary sources; Bentley
   breaks a good deal of new ground, particularly in the
   parish registers of the London churches (see 1929.5-6).
   Bentley deals with the London companies only in London;
   there is no discussion here of the companies in the
   provinces.

8 BOSWELL, ELEANORE. "'Young Mr. Cartwright.'" MLR 24 (April):
   125-42.
        A biographical sketch of William Cartwright, one of the
   few Restoration actors who began a career before 1642. His
   father was an actor with Henslowe, and the younger man was

1929

at the Salisbury Court Playhouse in the 1630s. After 1642
he became a bookseller, and then joined Killigrew's King's
company in 1660.

9   LAWRENCE, W[ILLIAM] J[OHN]. "The English Jig." TLS (23 May):
    419-20.
       A letter to the editor commenting on a review of Bas-
    kervill (1929.2). Lawrence suggests that "no jig was ever
    acted by living human beings at the Bear Garden until it
    was reconstructed as the Hope Theatre in 1613."

10 MOORE, JOHN ROBERT. "The Songs of the Public Theatres in the
    Time of Shakespeare." JEGP 28 (April):166-202.
       Discusses "the growing sense of dramatic fitness in the
    dramatic songs of Elizabeth's last decade." Moore contends
    that the singer of what he calls the Romantic plays "had
    ceased to be the mere clown of the Moralities and Inter-
    ludes," and had not yet become the "mere singer" of the
    later drama.

11 MOTTER, THOMAS HUBBARD VAIL. The School Drama in England.
    London: Longmans, Green & Co., 325 pp.
       After an initial chapter tracing the development of the
    boy actor, Motter outlines theatrical activities at a
    variety of schools, including Eton, St. Peter's College in
    Westminster, the Merchant Taylors', St. Paul's, Harrow's,
    and Shrewsbury during the Elizabethan period.

12 NUNZEGER, EDWIN. A Dictionary of Actors and Other Persons
    Associated with the Public Representation of Plays in
    England before 1642. Cornell Studies in English, no. 13.
    New Haven: Yale University Press, 438 pp.
       Published version of 1927.16. An attempt to "assemble
    all the available information regarding actors, theatrical
    proprietors, stage attendants, and other persons known to
    have been associated with the representation of plays in
    England before the year 1642," primarily from secondary
    sources. Alleyn is allotted eight pages; Richard Burbage,
    eleven and a half; most receive a scant paragraph. The
    thirty-three page bibliography is perhaps the most useful
    feature.

13 PLATTER, THOMAS. Thomas Platters des Jüngeren Englandfahrt im
    Jahre 1599. Edited by H. Hecht. Halle: M. Niemayer,
    180 pp.
       The standard scholarly edition of Platter's diary, con-
    taining a brief description of a performance at an Eliza-
    bethan playhouse. See 1937.9 for a translation.

14   SISSON, CHARLES [JASPER]. "Henslowe's Will Again." <u>RES</u> 5
     (July):308-11.
        A brief note based on discoveries among the Star Chamber
     proceedings in the Public Record Office.

15   SMITH, WINIFRED. "Italian Actors in Elizabethan England."
     <u>MLN</u> 44 (June):375-77.
        Notes on Drusiano Martinelli and "Scoto of Mantua"
     (Dionisio), two commedia actors found in London in the
     early seventeenth century, drawn from manuscript sources
     held in Italy.

16   WARD, B[ERNARD] M[ORDAUNT]. "John Lyly and the Office of the
     Revels." <u>RES</u> 5 (January):57-59.
        A transcript of a document from the Exchequer Account
     Books, revealing that Blagrave was promoted from Clerk of
     the Revels to Surveyor of the Works in 1586, and that he
     drew salary from both positions until he died in 1590.
     Further, it is possible that John Lyly, on loan from Lord
     Oxford, was involved as Clerk of the Revels from 1590 to
     1603.

<u>1930</u>

1   BENTLEY, GERALD EADES. "Players in the Parish of St. Giles in
    the Fields." <u>RES</u> 6 (April):149-66.
       Information gleaned from the parish registers and from
    a nineteenth-century history of the parish whose author
    apparently had access to other records. Bentley briefly
    summarizes the known facts about each actor listed and
    prints the new information. Based on his dissertation
    (1929.7) and included in 1941.1.

2   DICKSON, M. J. "William Trevell and the Whitefriars Theatre."
    <u>RES</u> 6 (July):309-12.
       A brief history of Trevell's associations with White-
    friars, based on a Court of Requests bill Dickson discov-
    ered. <u>See also</u> 1930.3.

3   DOWLING, MARGARET. "Further Notes on William Trevell." <u>RES</u>
    6 (October):443-46.
       More information on Trevell, based on the same Court of
    Requests bill. <u>See</u> 1930.2.

4   GRAY, HENRY DAVID. "The Roles of William Kemp." <u>MLR</u> 25
    (July):261-73.
       Speculates on the casting of Shakespeare's early clown.

Gray sees Kempe as a comic character actor, and casts him as Polonius/First Gravedigger, Dogberry, Christopher Sly, and Falstaff. See also 1927.1; 1931.1, 8.

5 LAWRENCE, W[ILLIAM] J[OHN]. "The Elizabethan Private Playhouse." Criterion 9, no. 36 (April):420-29.
   Discusses the difference between the terms "private house" and "private playhouse." Lawrence argues that the former was used as a device to get around the law prohibiting London performances: the plays were to be "rehearsed" in the "private house" of the company manager. The revival of the boy companies at the second Blackfriars signaled the change in nomenclature. Reprinted: 1935.7.

6 _____. "The Nut-Cracking Elizabethans." Nation & Athenauem (13 September):729-30.
   Discusses the audience habits of eating and talking through a performance, alluded to in a variety of contemporary documents. Lawrence concludes with a slap at those who hold that scenery was in use before 1642, based on lines from a 1671 play. Reprinted: 1935.7.

7 _____. "The Stage Directions in King Henry VIII." TLS (18 December):1085.
   Argues that the stage directions for the coronation procession were derived from an outside, and authoritative, source.

8 REYNOLDS, GEORGE F[ULLMER]. "'Lines' of Parts in Shakespeare's Plays." ShAB 5 (July):102-103.
   Compares Baldwin's casting in 1927.1 of the Chamberlain's Men in Shakespeare's plays with the 1930 casting of the Stratford-upon-Avon company, concluding that "it is practically impossible on the evidence we have to make even a tentative casting of Shakespeare's or an arrangement of the parts into many significant 'lines.'"

9 STAMPS, ALFRED EDWARD. The Disputed Revels Accounts. London: Oxford University Press for the Shakespeare Association, 42 pp.
   A revised version of a paper read before the Association in 1929, with copies of the complete Accounts for 1604-5 and 1611-12. Stamps argues for the authenticity of the documents, based on analysis of the paper and ink, the handwriting habits of Buc, and other evidence. For the complete controversy, see Index under Revels Accounts.

10 TAYLOR, GEORGE C. "Another Renaissance Attack on the Stage."
    PQ 9 (January):78-81.
        An excerpt from a 1586 treatise that includes an attack
    on the stage couched in usual terms. Taylor speculates
    that there might have been some common source, some yet to
    be discovered "reference books on commonplace themes,"
    since so many of the attacks sound so much alike.

1931

1 BALDWIN, T[HOMAS] W[HITFIELD]. "Will Kemp Not Falstaff." MLR
   26 (April):170-72.
       Differs with Gray (1930.4) over the assignment of the
   role of Falstaff to William Kempe, since the same actor who
   played Falstaff apparently also played Sir Toby Belch in
   1601, by which time Kempe had left the company. See also
   1927.1 and Gray's response, 1931.8.

2 BOSWELL, ELEANOR, and CHAMBERS, E[DMUND] K., eds. "Dramatic
   Records: The Lord Chamberlain's Office." MSC 2, pt. 3:
   321-416.
       Sixteen selections from the records of the Lord Chamber-
   lain of the Household, preserved in the Public Record
   Office. Entries range from 1603 to 1637.

3 CHAMBERS, E[DMUND] K. "Players at Ipswich." MSC 2, pt. 3:
   258-84.
       Extracts from the municipal archives at Ipswich from
   1554 to 1624-25, primarily recording payments to players.

4 COLLINS, FLETCHER, Jr. "The Relation of Tudor Halls to Elizabethan Public Theatres." PQ 10 (July):313-16.
       Argues that the Tudor Hall combined with the innyard to
   influence the Elizabethan public theatre. The Swan
   drawing is an accurate reflection of this influence.
   Collins anticipates Hosley's work by more than thirty
   years; see 1963.15, 1964.17, 1970.13, 1973.12.

5 COOPER, CHARLES WILLIAM. "John Lacy, the Comedian: A Study
   in the Early Restoration Theatrical Tradition." Ph.D.
   dissertation, University of California at Berkeley, 244 pp.
       Examines the career of comic actor and playwright John
   Lacy. Part Three, "John Lacy in the Theatrical Tradition,"
   is especially important, since Cooper traces Lacy's role
   in the transmission of theatrical customs and traditions
   from the pre-Commonwealth stage to the Restoration theatre,
   a largely neglected area. As the principal dancing-master

of the Theatre Royal in the early Restoration, as one of
the foremost men of business at the same playhouse, and as
a leading low comedian, as well as a playwright, Lacy
exerted a strong influence on Restoration theatre practice,
an influence that Cooper claims was strongly rooted in his
earlier experience.

6 EBISCH, WALTHER, and SCHÜCKING, LEVIN L. A Shakespeare Bibliography. Oxford: Clarendon Press, pp. 119-34, 138.
       The relevant section lists works dealing with Shake-
   speare's stage and the production of his plays. Ebisch
   and Schücking provide minimal annotations but they list
   major reviews. The terminal date is 1930. Supplemented:
   1937.3. All relevant items have been incorporated into
   the present bibliography.

7 FITZGIBBON, H. MACAULAY. "Instruments and Their Music in the
   Elizabethan Drama." MusQ 17 (July):319-29.
       Surveys the use of music and catalogues mentions of
   specific instruments in stage directions and texts.

8 GRAY, HENRY DAVID. "Shakespeare and Will Kemp: A Rejoinder."
   MLR 26 (April):172-74.
       Answers Baldwin's objections to his casting of Kempe
   as Falstaff. See 1927.1; 1930.4; 1931.1.

9 GREG, W[ALTER] W[ILSON]. Dramatic Documents from the Elizabethan Playhouse: Stage Plots; Actor's Parts; Prompt
   Books. 2 vols. Oxford: Clarendon Press, 432 pp.
       Facsimiles and transcripts for eight plots, the part of
   Orlando, and selected pages from nine prompt books from
   the Elizabethan period, along with commentary on each.
   This is without question one of the more important works in
   the field, since it presents the actual material used in
   the playhouses. Greg includes a section on the extant
   actor lists, including as much relevant information as
   possible on each actor mentioned. He concludes with a
   complete descriptive list of manuscript plays. Reprinted:
   1969.5.

10 LAWRENCE, W[ILLIAM] J[OHN]. "Old-Time Rehearsal." Stage
   (London), 5 November, p. 20.
       Argues that the playwrights rehearsed their own plays,
   based on Flecknoe's comment to that effect (in 1664.1) and
   Johannes Rhenanus's preface to an adaptation of an old
   English play asserting the same thing. Lawrence also
   discusses rehearsal practices in the Restoration and
   eighteenth century. Reprinted: 1935.4.

11 LEA, KATHLEEN M. "English Players at the Swedish Court."
    MLR 26 (January):78-80.
        Four previously unknown English actors and musicians
    can be placed at the Swedish court between 1592 and 1608
    because of the discovery of their names in correspondence
    among uncalendared Swedish State Papers.

12 McKERROW, RONALD B. "The Elizabethan Printer and Dramatic
    Manuscripts." Library, 4th ser. 12 (December):253-75.
        A paper read before the Bibliographical Society on 19
    October 1931. McKerrow establishes four classes of evi-
    dence in a printed text that mark it as having been set in
    print from prompt copy. Reprinted: 1974.21.

13 MILL, ANNA JEAN, and CHAMBERS, E[DMUND] K., eds. "Dramatic
    Records from the City of London: The Repertories, Journals
    and Letter Books." MSC 2, pt. 3:285-320.
        Sixty extracts from various records of the City of
    London, supplementing those published earlier. Entries
    range from 1522 to 1615.

14 PARADISE, N. BURTON. Thomas Lodge: The History of an Eliza-
    bethan. New Haven: Yale University Press, 254 pp.
        A study of the life and works of one of the earliest
    defenders of the stage against the Puritans. Chapter Five
    specifically examines his work as a playwright, but from a
    literary rather than a theatrical perspective. Included
    because of listing in NCBEL 1, col. 1402.

15 SMITH, MILTON. "Shakespeare in the Schools." ShAB 6 (April):
    39-47.
        Discusses teaching Shakespearean scholarship, including
    the theatrical. Of little scholarly value.

16 THALER, ALWIN. "Faire Em (and Shakspere's Company?) in
    Lancashire." PMLA 46 (September):647-58.
        Discusses Faire Em (presented by Lord Strange's Men,
    1593) as a country play complimenting Sir Edmond Trafford.
    Reprinted: 1941.11.

17 WRIGHT, LOUIS B. "Madmen as Vaudeville Performers on the
    Elizabethan Stage." JEGP 30 (January):48-54.
        Points out "certain examples of the employment of in-
    sanity as extraneous vaudeville entertainment in regular
    play performances." Wright includes The Duchess of Malfi
    and The Changeling among his examples. The introduction of
    madmen and madwomen served to enhance the comic spectacle
    demanded of even serious plays.

1932

1 ADAMS, JOSEPH QUINCY. "Elizabethan Playhouse Manuscripts and
   Their Significance for the Text of Shakespeare." Johns
   Hopkins Alumni Magazine 21 (October):21-52.
      Text of a lecture before the Tudor and Stuart Club,
   Johns Hopkins University, 23 February 1932. Adams clarifies the preparation of dramatic manuscripts for sale to
   the actors and traces them to the printers. The playwright
   first prepares an outline of the plot, gains the approval
   of the company, then composes the speeches of the characters
   in "foul sheets." A "fair copy" is prepared, with stage
   directions in the right margin and speaker designations in
   the left. The finished play is read to the company, sub-
   mitted for license, and used as a prompt book. Abbreviated
   prompt books were frequently prepared for touring. Printed
   plays were set in type from both kinds of prompt books,
   often with editing of stage directions. This is probably
   the clearest discussion of manuscripts and printed plays
   available. See also Bentley (1971.2).

2 BRADBROOK, MURIEL CLARA. Elizabethan Stage Conditions: A
   Study of Their Place in the Interpretation of Shakespeare's
   Plays. Cambridge: University Press; New York: Macmillan,
   149 pp.
      The Harness Prize Essay, 1931. After reviewing Shake-
   spearean criticism in the eighteenth, nineteenth, and
   twentieth centuries, Bradbrook discusses the effect of
   Shakespeare's stage on his dramatic structure and poetry,
   among other matters. Reprinted: 1968.9.

3 CHILD, HAROLD H. "The Elizabethan Theatre." In Cambridge
   History of English Literature. Vol. 6, The Drama to 1642.
   Pt. 2. Edited by A. W. Ward and A. R. Waller. Cambridge:
   University Press, pp. 241-78.
      Reprint of 1910.5.

4 GREG, W[ALTER] W[ILSON]. "Elizabethan Dramatic Documents."
   RES 8 (October):457-58.
      Greg responds in a letter to Lawrence's review of 1931.9,
   clarifying his position on two minor points.

5 HART, ALFRED. "The Length of Elizabethan and Jacobean Plays."
   RES 8 (April):139-54.
      Based on line-counts of 233 plays (all but two of the
   extant plays written for the public stage, 1590-1616),
   Hart comes up with an average length of 2500 lines. He
   examines the repertories of the main companies separately,

and finds that they each conform to this length as well, indicating no substantial difference between lengths of plays at different companies. Continued in 1932.6 and 1934.2. Reprinted: 1934.3; 1970.11.

6 _____. "The Time Alloted for Representation of Elizabethan and Jacobean Plays." RES 8 (October):395-413.
Based on his line-count in 1932.6 and contemporary references, Hart concludes that slightly cut versions of the plays were performed in two hours, plus the time needed for music and the concluding dance. Continued in 1934.2. Reprinted: 1934.3; 1970.11.

7 LAWRENCE, W[ILLIAM] J[OHN]. "A 'Piece of Perspective.'" TLS (21 July):532.
A letter to the editor regarding Jonson's Cynthia's Revels. Lawrence argues that the quotation cannot refer to stage scenery since perspective scenery was unknown in England before 1600.

*8 _____. "Shakespeare's Use of Animals." Dublin Magazine (January-March).
Cited in TN 12 (April 1958):79. Reprinted: 1935.7.

*9 _____. "Stage Dummies." New Statesman (14 May).
Cited in TN 12 (April 1958):80. Reprinted: 1937.5.

10 MANLY, J[OHN] M[ATTHEWS]. "The Children of the Chapel Royal and Their Masters." In Cambridge History of English Literature. Vol. 6, The Drama to 1642. Pt. 2. Edited by A. W. Ward and A. R. Waller. Cambridge: University Press, pp. 279-92.
Reprint of 1910.12.

11 THALER, ALWIN. "The Original Malvolio?" ShAB 7 (April):57-71.
Suggests that William Ffarington, steward to Lord Strange, patron of Shakespeare's company, served as the model for the character. Reprinted: 1941.12.

12 WILSON, J[OHN] D[OVER]. "The Puritan Attack upon the Stage." In Cambridge History of English Literature. Vol. 6, The Drama to 1642. Pt. 2. Edited by A. W. Ward and A. W. Waller. Cambridge: University Press, pp. 373-409.
Reprint of 1910.26.

1933

1 BATY, GASTON. "La scène élizabéthaine." In <u>Le théâtre éliza-
   béthaine: Études et traductions</u>. Edited by Georgette
   Camille. Les Cahiers du Sud, 10. Paris: Les Cahiers du
   Sud, pp. 98-102.
      A general discussion of stages and staging, based on
   Adams (1917.3), Albright (1909.2), Chambers (1923.2),
   Campbell (1923.1), and Mönkmeyer (1905.3).

2 BOAS, F[REDERICK] S. "Tewkesbury Abbey's Theatrical Gear."
   <u>TLS</u> (16 March):184.
      Lists a variety of entries in the Tewkesbury Church-
   wardens Accounts from 1563 to 1703 dealing with theatrical
   costumes and other "gear."

3 ECCLES, MARK. "Sir George Buc, Master of the Revels." In
   <u>Thomas Lodge and Other Elizabethans</u>. Edited by C[harles]
   J[asper] Sisson. Cambridge: Harvard University Press,
   pp. 409-506.
      A biographical study, encompassing Buc's work as Master
   of the Revels, but containing little of specifically
   theatrical interest.

4 ISAACS, JACOB. <u>Production and Stage Management at the Black-
   friars</u>. London: Oxford University Press for the Shakespeare Association, 28 pp.
      Originally a lecture delivered to the Shakespeare Asso-
   ciation on 25 November 1932, with added references and
   corroborative material. Isaacs draws his evidence from
   prologues and stage directions in prompt copies and published plays. He examines 100 texts, "of which some
   seventy were unquestionably performed at the Blackfriars."
   There is no distinction between practices at Blackfriars
   and elsewhere, however. Isaacs examines the production
   staff, lighting, music, prompt books, plots, grouping,
   upper and lower stages (with two sets of curtains), and
   scenery (which was "definitely used" in the 1630s).

5 LAWRENCE, W[ILLIAM] J[OHN]. "A Quaint Old Playhouse Trick."
   <u>Stage</u> (London), 28 September, p. 8.
      Discusses the practice of a character in a play referring
   to the actor who played the character, much to the delight
   of the audience. Thomas Green is Lawrence's prime example,
   but he also cites Nathan Field, William Ostler, and Richard
   Robinson. Reprinted: 1937.5.

6 REYNOLDS, GEORGE F[ULLMER]. "Elizabethan Stage Railings."
    TLS (16 February):108.
        Draws attention to a reference to the stage railing in
    The Hector of Germany, a Red Bull play printed in 1615.

7 SISSON, CHARLES J[ASPER]. "Thomas Lodge and His Family." In
    Thomas Lodge and Other Elizabethans. Edited by C[harles]
    J[asper] Sisson. Cambridge: Harvard University Press,
    pp. 1-63.
        A general discussion of the life of the playwright and
    his works, of only peripheral theatrical interest. Included
    because of listing in NCBEL 1, col. 1402.

8 TILLOTSON, GEOFFREY. "Othello and The Alchemist at Oxford in
    1610." TLS (20 July):494.
        Professional production of these plays at Oxford in 1610
    is verified by William Fulman's transcription of a letter
    from Henry Jackson.

9 WALKER, ALICE. "The Life of Thomas Lodge." RES 9 (October):
    410-32.
        Supplements biographical information provided by
    Paradise (1931.14) and Sisson (1933.7). Continued in
    1934.18.

10 WARD, B[ERNARD] M[ORDAUNT]. "The Chamberlain's Men in 1597."
    RES 9 (January):55-58.
        Extracts from the account books at Faversham, Rye, and
    Dover, bearing on the Lord Chamberlain's company's tour
    in the summer and autumn of 1597.

11 WILLIAMS, IOLO A. "Hollar: A Discovery." Connoisseur 92
    (November):318-21.
        Announces discovery of the Hollar sketch of Southwark
    containing the second Globe, later engraved as the "Long
    Bird's Eye View of London."

1934

1 CHILD, HAROLD H. "The Elizabethan Theatre." In Cambridge
    History of English Literature. Vol. 6, The Drama to 1642.
    Pt. 2. Edited by A. W. Ward and A. R. Waller. Cambridge:
    University Press, pp. 241-78.
        Reprint of 1910.5.

1934

2 HART, ALFRED. "Acting Versions of Elizabethan Plays." <u>RES</u>
   10 (January):1-28.
       Based on his earlier work (1932.5, 6), Hart concludes
   that plays were routinely cut for Elizabethan presentation.
   Evidence to support that conclusion is drawn from extant
   manuscripts containing lines marked for omission and
   comparison of so-called "bad" quartos based on acting
   copies with "good" quartos. Reprinted: 1934.3; 1970.11.

3 _____. "Play Abridgement: The Length of Elizabethan and
   Jacobean Plays, Time Allotted for the Presentation of Eliza-
   bethan and Jacobean Plays, Acting Versions of Elizabethan
   and Jacobean Plays." In <u>Shakespeare and the Homilies, and
   Other Pieces of Research into the Elizabethan Drama</u>.
   Melbourne: Melbourne University Press, pp. 77-153.
       Reprints of 1932.6; 1932.7; 1934.2. <u>See also</u> 1970.11.

4 HARTLEB, HANS. "Landgraf Moritz der Gelehrte von Hessen-
   Kassel als Förderer der englische Komödianten und Erbauer
   des ersten deutschen Theaters." Ph.D. dissertation, Ludwig-
   Maximilians University, Munich, 162 pp.
       Published as 1936.12.

5 LAWRENCE, W[ILLIAM] J[OHN]. "The Italian Comedian of 1610."
   <u>TLS</u> (7 June):408.
       A letter to the editor, referring to a <u>Calendar of State
   Papers</u> entry concerning payments to an "Italian Comedian."
   Lawrence suggests it was an individual, rather than a
   company, referred to also in Jonson's 115th epigram.

6 _____. "The Sharing Table." <u>Stage</u> (London), 6 December, p.
   16.
       Discusses the process of sharing the day's receipts
   after the hired men had been paid. Lawrence finds similarities with the French system of the seventeenth century. Reprinted: 1935.4.

7 _____. "Speeding up Shakespeare." <u>Criterion</u> 14, no. 54
   (October):78-85.
       Argues that "by virtue of Shakespeare's own testimony
   we are compelled to conclude that Shakespeare's plays were
   written in the conventional five acts, and acted in his own
   day with four intervals." Reprinted: 1937.5.

8 LEA, KATHLEEN MARGARITE. <u>Italian Popular Comedy: A Study in
   the Commedia dell'Arte, 1500-1620, with Special Reference
   to the English Stage</u>. Vol. 2. Oxford: Clarendon Press,
   pp. 339-455.

The relevant section forms the bulk of the second volume, wherein Lea discusses the contacts and comparisons with the English drama and theatre. She shows the contact to be "considerable" but the influence, "sporadic and superficial."

9 LEECH, CLIFFORD E. J. "Sir Henry Lee's Entertainment of Elizabeth in 1592." MLR 30 (January):52-55.
      Examines a manuscript of Sir Henry Lee's Devices, held in the British Library, which confirms the history of the 1592 entertainment at Woodstock and clarifies the proceedings of 20 and 21 September.

10 MANLY, J[OHN] M[ATTHEWS]. "The Children of the Chapel Royal and Their Masters." In Cambridge History of English Literature. Vol. 6, The Drama to 1642. Pt. 2. Edited by A. W. Ward and A. R. Waller. Cambridge: University Press, pp. 279-92.
      Reprint of 1910.12.

11 MEPHAM, W[ILLIAM] A. "A XVI Century Village Play at Heybridge, Essex." N&Q 167 (4 August):75-79.
      Enumerates early sixteenth-century performances in Heybridge, based on contemporary accounts preserved in a scrap book. See also 1934.12; 1937.6.

12 _____. "Village Plays at Dunmow, Essex, in the Sixteenth Century." N&Q 166 (19 May):345-48.
      Lists the early sixteenth-century performances, based on the city account book records of payments to actors. See also 1934.11, 1937.6; continued in 1934.13.

13 _____. "Village Plays at Dunmow, Essex, in the Sixteenth Century." N&Q 166 (26 May):362-66.
      Continuation of 1934.12. See also 1934.11; 1937.6.

14 SISSON, C[HARLES] J[ASPER]. "The Theatres and the Companies." In A Companion to Shakespeare Studies. Edited by Harley Granville-Barker and G[eorge] B[agshawe] Harrison. Cambridge: University Press; New York: Macmillan, pp. 9-43.
      A brief general history, divided into sections covering the conditions of Shakespeare's art; the actors, companies, and playhouses; Elizabethan staging; the masques; the repertories; the performances; the actors; the audience; opposition to the stage; and a typical structure of the public theatre, including Godfrey's reconstruction of the Fortune (1908.10). Reprinted: 1960.19.

1934

15 WALKER, ALICE. "The Life of Thomas Lodge, II." <u>RES</u> 10
   (January):46-54.
   Continuation of 1933.9.

16 WHITE, BEATRICE. <u>An Index to "The Elizabethan Stage" and</u>
   <u>"William Shakespeare," by Sir Edmund Chambers</u>. London:
   Oxford University Press, 161 pp.
   Comprehensive index to 1923.2.

17 WILSON, J[OHN] D[OVER]. "The Puritan Attack on the Stage."
   In <u>Cambridge History of English Literature</u>. Vol. 6, <u>The</u>
   <u>Drama to 1642</u>. Pt. 2. Edited by A. W. Ward and A. R.
   Waller. Cambridge: University Press, pp. 373-409.
   Reprint of 1910.26.

<u>1935</u>

1 ADAMS, JOHN CRANFORD. "The Structure of the Globe Playhouse
   Stage." Ph.D. dissertation, Cornell University, 335 pp.
   Expanded version published: 1942.1.

2 BAESECKE, ANNA. <u>Das Schauspiel der englischen Komödianten in</u>
   <u>Deutschland: Seine dramatische Form und seine Entwicklung</u>.
   Studien zur englischen Philologie, no. 8. Halle: Martin
   Sändig, 154 pp.
   Published version of a 1934 Halle Ph.D. dissertation.
   Baesecke examines the form and development of the song-
   drama of the English actors in Germany during the sixteenth
   and seventeenth centuries. She divides the time considered
   into four periods (1560-1600, 1600-1620, 1620-1648, and
   1648-1700) and traces the development of the form during
   each.

3 HUNT, THEODORE B. "The Scenes as Shakespeare Saw Them." In
   <u>The Parrott Presentation Volume</u>. Edited by Harding Craig.
   Princeton: Princeton University Press, pp. 205-12.
   An argument for the reconstruction of Shakespeare's
   imagined settings for scenes based on information included
   in the text. The "lobby" in <u>Hamlet</u>, for example, is shown
   to be "a sunny, elevated portico opening on the ramparts,
   not far from the entrance to the palace," while Polonius's
   "house" is an apartment in the palace.

4 LAWRENCE, W[ILLIAM] J[OHN]. <u>Old Theatre Days and Ways</u>.
   London: George Harrap & Co., 256 pp.
   A collection of previously published essays, some exten-
   sively revised, including 1931.10 and 1935.5. Pertinent

studies examine the use of trumpet and drum to announce the
players, the role of the prompter, the complex systems of
admission used, rehearsal procedures, Elizabethan acrobats,
and the sharing system. Almost all range freely through
time, discussing foreign as well as English production
methods.

5 _____. "The Original Staging of Romeo and Juliet, Act III,
Scene V." TLS (19 September):580.
  Argues for the playing of the second balcony scene
entirely on the upper stage. See also Sampson (1935.13;
1936.21); Adams (1936.3); and Granville-Barker (1936.10).

6 _____. "The Site of the Whitefriars Theatre." RES 11 (April):
186.
  Lawrence sides with Chambers (1923.2) against J. Q.
Adams (1917.3) on the site of the Whitefriars, based upon
the authority of an eighteenth-century history of the
precinct.

7 _____. Those Nut-Cracking Elizabethans: Studies of the Early
Theatre and Drama. London: Argonaut Press, 212 pp.
  A collection of previously published essays, some extensively revised, including 1930.5, 6 and 1932.8. The title
essay examines the eating habits of the audience; others
treat Shakespeare's use of animals, the use of bells, the
stage furniture and its removers, and the development of
the private playhouse.

8 LEECH, CLIFFORD [E. J.] "The Plays of Edward Sharpham:
Alterations Accomplished and Projected." RES 11 (January):
69-74.
  Examines the hasty adaptation of Cupid's Whirligig and
"The Fleire" to the production needs of the moment. The
latter play exists in manuscript in the British Library
and is clearly marked by the adaptor.

9 LEECH, CLIFFORD E. J. "Private Performances and Amateur
Theatricals (Excluding the Academic Stage) from 1580 to
1660, with an Edition of Raguaillo D'Oceano, 1640." Ph.D.
dissertation, London University, 475 pp.
  Examines "those types of dramatic performances in the
period 1580-1660 which were not conditioned by the exigen-
cies of a regular theatre and a paying audience." The
eight major chapters treat the end of the mysteries, May
games, private entertainments, private masques, amateur
and household plays, private professional performances, and
irregular country performances, with the second, sixth, and
eighth chapters containing the most new information.

1935

10 McKERROW, R[ONALD] B. "A Suggestion Regarding Shakespeare's
    Manuscripts." <u>RES</u> 11 (October):459-65.
      Suggests that printed plays where character naming in
    stage directions and speech headings is inconsistent might
    have been printed from the author's foul papers, while
    consistency in naming signals printing from a fair copy,
    perhaps made by a playhouse scribe.

11 NICOLL, ALLARDYCE. "Royal Divertisements." <u>ThArts</u> 19
    (February):139-48.
      Describes the contents of a collection at Turin, bearing
    on the production of masques and ballets at the Savoy
    palace. Of some interest because of the parallels to the
    masques of Jonson and Jones.

12 RENWICK, W[ILLIAM] L[INDSAY]. "Alfonso Ferrabosco." <u>RES</u> 11
    (April):184-85.
      A document in the Vatican Archives explains why the
    Exchequer held up Ferrabosco's annuity after 1583: this
    contributor to Elizabeth's masques left for Italy in that
    year.

13 SAMPSON, GEORGE. "The Staging of <u>Romeo and Juliet</u>." <u>TLS</u> (9
    November):722.
      Responds to Lawrence (1935.5), agreeing with the place-
    ment of the second balcony scene and arguing for continuity
    rather than act division in modern editions.

14 SCHELLING, FELIX E. <u>Elizabethan Drama 1558-1642: A History</u>
    <u>of the Drama in England from the Accession of Queen Eliza-</u>
    <u>beth to the Closing of the Theaters, to Which Is Prefixed</u>
    <u>a Résumé of the Earlier Drama from Its Beginnings</u>. Vol. 1.
    Boston and New York: Houghton, Mifflin & Co., pp. 141-93.
      Reprint of 1908.16.

15 SEH, L. H. "Shakespeares erste Verleger." <u>Weltkunst</u> 9 (8
    December):3.
      A brief note on Heminge and Condell on the "Bibliophile"
    page.

16 SHARPE, ROBERT BOIES. <u>The Real War of the Theatres: Shake-</u>
    <u>speare's Fellows in Rivalry with the Admiral's Men, 1594-</u>
    <u>1603. Repertories, Devices, and Types</u>. Modern Language
    Association Monograph Series, no. 5. Boston: D. C. Heath
    & Co., 260 pp.
      Expanded, published version of 1928.14. A chronological
    survey of the theatrical events of the last decade of
    Elizabeth's rule, focusing on the rivalry between the Lord

Chamberlain's Men and the Lord Admiral's Men. Sharpe sees
political overtones in the rivalry, which culminated in the
history plays that each side presented.

17 SMALL, GEORGE WILLIAM. "Shakespeare's Stage." ShAB 10
    (January):31-35.
        Argues for a rectangular rather than a tapered stage,
    as suggested by the Swan drawing and the Fortune contract.

18 SPRAGUE, ARTHUR COLBY. Shakespeare and the Audience.
    Cambridge: Harvard University Press, 327 pp.
        Not actually a study of the audience, but criticism of
    the plays attempting to establish Shakespeare's intended
    effect on the audience.

1936

1 ADAMS, JOHN C[RANFORD]. "Romeo and Juliet as Played on Shakespeare's Stage." ThArts 20 (November):869-904.
        Discusses Shakespeare's use of what Adams thought were
   the seven stages available to him--the platform, the
   curtained inner stage, the "tarras," the "chamber," the two
   window stages, and the third-level music room. Illustrated
   with diagrams and photographs of a model of Adam's reconstruction of the Globe. Based partially on 1935.1; see
   also 1936.2; 1942.1.

2 _____. "Shakespeare's Stage: New Facts and Figures." ThArts
   20 (October):812-18.
        Describes, without providing evidence, his reconstruction
   of the Globe, complete with seven stages. Based on 1935.1;
   see also 1936.1; 1942.1.

3 _____. "The Staging of Romeo and Juliet." TLS (15 February):
   139.
        In response to Lawrence (1935.5) and Sampson (1935.13),
   Adams explains how the second balcony scene would be staged
   in his reconstruction of the Globe. The entire scene would
   be played on the three upper stages. See also Granville-
   Barker (1936.10) and Lawrence (1936.15) and Adams's
   response, 1936.4.

4 _____. "The Staging of Romeo and Juliet." TLS (23 May):440.
        Responds to Granville-Barker (1936.10) and Lawrence
   (1936.15), reasserting his previous argument (see 1936.3).

1936

5   BRANDL, ALOIS. "Shakespeare-Möglichkeiten." In Forschungen
    und Charakteristiken. Berlin and Leipzig: Walter de
    Gruyter & Co., pp. 177–82.
        Discusses the extant illustrations of the Elizabethan
    stage and how the upper stage would have been used.

6   BROWN, IVOR. "The Boy-Player." ThArts 20 (May):385–91.
        Examines the ways in which Shakespeare's use of boys for
    women's roles shaped the plays. Brown follows Granville-
    Barker in finding that young women in Shakespeare are
    essentially lacking in "sex appeal." See also 1937.1.

7   CRUNDELL, H. W. "Visits of Dramatic Companies to Bristol,
    1584–1600." N&Q 170 (11 July):24.
        Corrects some misreadings in Murray (1910.15), from the
    Audit Books of the Bristol City Chamberlain.

8   ELLIS-FERMOR, UNA M. "The Jacobean Stage." In The Jacobean
    Drama: An Interpretation. London: Methuen, pp. 273–83.
        A general survey of the stage and audience, intended
    to supply background for her literary study in the previous
    chapters. Reprinted: 1947.3; 1953.5; 1958.8; 1961.9;
    1964.10; 1965.8; 1969.4.

9   GAW, ALLISON. "The Impromptu Mask in Shakspere (With Especial
    Reference to the Stagery of Romeo and Juliet, I, iv–v)."
    ShAB 11 (July):149–60.
        Argues that the mask Shakespeare used for getting Romeo
    into the Capulets' house led to an awkward bit of staging
    involving a march around the stage to signify a change of
    locale. With the entry of the Capulet servants, the scene
    becomes the Capulet house, despite the fact that Romeo and
    his group have never left the stage. Further, Gaw claims,
    the scene made heavy demands on the company, and keeping
    the masked characters on stage helped create the illusion
    of a large number of characters.

10 GRANVILLE-BARKER, HARLEY. "The Staging of Romeo and Juliet."
    TLS (22 February):163.
        In answer to Lawrence (1935.5) and Adams (1936.3),
    Granville-Barker argues that the second balcony scene would
    be more effective if staged on the platform rather than on
    the upper stage.

11 HARBAGE, ALFRED. Cavalier Drama: An Historical and Critical
    Supplement to the Study of the Elizabethan and Restoration
    Stage. New York: Modern Language Association, pp. 191–214,
    passim.

Examines the writing and presentation of plays "by fashionable gentry active in the Caroline court and on the Royal side in the Civil Wars--by the 'Cavaliers.'" While not of primary theatrical interest, there are references throughout to playhouses and actors. The most important section for present purposes is Part Two, Chapter V, "Caroline and Commonwealth Private Theatricals."

12 HARTLEB, HANS. <u>Deutschlands erster Theaterbau. Eine Geschichte des Theaterlebens und der englischen Komödianten unter Landgraf Moritz dem Gelehrten von Hessen-Kassel.</u> Berlin and Leipzig: Walter de Gruyter, 162 pp.
     Published version of 1934.4. Hartleb discusses the English actors in Kassel and their repertory in the seventeenth century, and Landgraf Moritz's building of the first German theatre.

13 JOUVET, LOUIS. "The Elizabethan Theatre: Reconstruction after the Manner of Cuvier." <u>ThArts</u> 20 (March):222-23.
     Not a reconstruction but a rather poetic wish for one.

14 LAWRENCE, W[ILLIAM] J[OHN]. "Something New about Shakespeare." <u>London Mercury</u> 34 (July):224-28.
     Argues that the absence of Shakespeare's heroes in the fourth act is purposeful, and has to do with the gradual slowing down of the plot.

15 _____. "The Staging of <u>Romeo and Juliet</u>." <u>TLS</u> (29 February): 184.
     Takes issue with Adams's placement of the second balcony scene in a side window area and his placement of IV.v. on the upper stage. <u>See</u> 1936.3.

16 LEWES, GEORGE HENRY. "Shakespeare: Actor and Critic." <u>ThW</u> 1 (October):41-50.
     Discusses Shakespeare's probable shortcomings as an actor, based primarily on Hamlet's advice to the players. Lewes uses this as a springboard to discuss the general problem of the actor: to play emotions without getting lost in them.

17 LINTHICUM, MARIE CHANNING. "Costume in the Drama of Shakespeare and His Contemporaries." Ph.D. dissertation, University of Iowa, 307 pp.
     Published as 1936.18.

1936

18 LINTHICUM, M[ARIE] CHANNING. <u>Costume in the Drama of Shake-</u>
      <u>speare and His Contemporaries</u>. London: Oxford University
      Press, 307 pp.
         Published version of 1936.17. A comprehensive treatment
      of color, fabric, garment style, and accessories from the
      sixteenth and seventeenth centuries, including selected
      references from the plays of Shakespeare and his contempo-
      raries. Linthicum draws upon many earlier works (including
      manuscripts) for her historical discussion. While not
      dealing precisely with theatre practice, this volume is
      helpful in gaining a full understanding of that practice.
      Linthicum includes two appendixes, but the volume is some-
      what marred by the lack of an introduction or conclusion.

19 NICOLL, ALLARDYCE. "Scenery between Shakespeare and Dryden."
      <u>TLS</u> (15 August):658.
         Discusses two drawings used for staging <u>Candy Restored</u>
      by amateurs in 1640/41.

20 SAMPSON, GEORGE. "The Staging of <u>Romeo and Juliet</u>." <u>TLS</u> (22
      February):163.
         Responds to Adams's response (1936.3) to his previous
      letter (1935.13), reasserting his interest in continuity
      in modern (not Elizabethan) stage directions.

21 SISSON, C[HARLES] J[ASPER]. "Mr. and Mrs. Browne of the
      Boar's Head." <u>L&LT</u> 15, no. 6 (Winter):99-107.
         Discusses the theatre at the Boar's Head, the manager,
      and his wife, based on records of court cases held in the
      Public Record Office. The treatment here is rather
      anecdotal and without notes. <u>See also</u> 1972.29.

<u>1937</u>

1 BOAS, GUY. "The Influence of the Boy-Actor on Shakespeare's
      Plays." <u>ContempR</u> 52 (July):69-77.
         Argues that the range and emotional resources of the boy
      actors were limited, and that the roles they were required
      to play were also limited in order to fit their abilities.

2 CRUNDELL, H. W. "<u>The Taming of the Shrew</u> on the XVII. Century
      Stage." <u>N&Q</u> 173 (18 September):207.
         Argues that the Epilogue (not printed in the First Folio
      but preserved in the text of <u>The Taming of a Shrew</u>) was
      Shakespeare's.

3 EBISCH, WALTHER, and SCHÜCKING, LEVIN L. A Shakespeare Bibliography: Supplement for the Years 1930-1935. Oxford:
   Clarendon Press, pp. 41-44.
       Continuation of 1931.6 until April 1936. All relevant
   items have been incorporated into this bibliography.

4 KERNODLE, GEORGE RILEY. "Perspective in the Renaissance Theatre: The Pictorial Sources and the Development of Scenic
   Forms." Ph.D. dissertation, Yale University, 325 pp.
       Expanded version published: 1944.7.

5 LAWRENCE, W[ILLIAM] J[OHN]. Speeding Up Shakespeare: Studies
   of the Bygone Theatre and Drama. London: Argonaut Press,
   220 pp.
       Collection of previously published essays, some with
   substantial revision, including 1923.15; 1932.9; 1933.5;
   1934.7. Included are discussions of the speed of performance; the habit of actors referring to themselves while in
   character; an evaluation of Richard Tarleton; the use of
   dummies on stage; the origin of the custom of the Grave-
   diggers in Hamlet wearing several waistcoats; and additions
   to Adams's edition of Henry Herbert's office book.

6 MEPHAM, W[ILLIAM] A. "The History of the Drama in Essex from
   the Fifteenth Century to the Present Time." Ph.D. dissertation, London University, pp. 1-284.
       The relevant chapters are two through nine, covering the
   fifteenth through seventeenth centuries. In the sixteenth
   century, London professional companies regularly visited
   Maldon and Saffron Walden, and religious plays were still
   produced by prominent men of the districts. The visits of
   the professional companies ceased by 1639, as Essex was
   predominantly Puritan. Mepham bases most of his conclusions
   on information gathered from a variety of Churchwardens'
   Accounts and municipal archives in Essex. The more modern
   information is largely gleaned from contemporary newspapers.
   See also 1934.11-12.

7 MITCHELL, LEE. "The Advent of Scene Design in England." QJS
   23 (April):189-97.
       Examines Inigo Jones's designs for the court masques,
   with frequent references to Italian practices.

8 NICOLL, ALLARDYCE. The Stuart Masque and the Renaissance
   Stage. London: G. Harrap, 224 pp.
       A study of the staging of the Stuart masques produced at
   Whitehall during the reigns of James I and Charles I.
   After a brief review of the form of the masque,

1937

Nicoll examines in detail the Whitehall banqueting house
and the extant designs for performances there, with frequent
reference to Italian practices. The almost 200 illustrations add significantly to the work.

9 PLATTER, THOMAS. <u>Thomas Platter's Travels in England, 1599.</u>
Translated by Clare Williams. London: Jonathan Cape,
245 pp.
A translation of and commentary on the contemporary
diary containing a brief description of a play that Platter
saw. Based on 1929.13.

<u>1938</u>

1 ADAMS, JOHN C[RANFORD]. "The Staging of <u>The Tempest</u>, III,
iii." <u>RES</u> 14 (October):404-19.
Examines the three important stage directions in the
scene, concluding that the banquet disappeared into a false
table-top; that Ariel descended and ascended with the
flying machinery, in a prone or inclined position; and that
Prospero appeared on a third level rather than on the usual
second level (or upper stage) in order to cue the musicians.

2 ANON. "English Humor 1500 to 1800." <u>TLS</u> (21 May):360.
Includes a brief discussion of Richard Tarlton.

3 BENTLEY, GERALD EADES. "The Diary of a Caroline Theatregoer."
<u>MP</u> 35 (August):61-72.
Extracts from the manuscript diary of Sir Humphrey
Mildmay, held in the British Library, with commentary.
Mildmay attended plays regularly, and his diary records his
attendance from 1633 until the theatres closed in 1642. He
also records his expenses. Mildmay frequented the Blackfriars, but he also visited the Globe and the Phoenix.

4 DAVIES, W. ROBERTSON. <u>Shakespeare's Boy Actors</u>. London: J.
M. Dent & Sons, 207 pp.
Investigates the influence which the convention of the
boy actor for female parts may have exercised over the
Elizabethan dramatist, and the interpretation of the parts
given by the boy actors in general. Davies includes
conjectural accounts of the training given the boys and a
consideration of the devices used by the playwrights to
bring the part within the scope of the young male actor.

5 GREG, W[ALTER] W[ILSON]. "A Fragment from Henslowe's Diary."
   Library, 4th ser. 19 (September):180-84.
      A detailed account and facsimile of an acquitance by
   Dekker for payment, apparently cut from the diary. See also
   1940.1.

6 KELLY, F[RANCIS] M[ICHAEL]. Shakespearian Costume for Stage
   and Screen. London: Adam & Charles Black, pp. 9-58.
      Contains little of historical interest, except the
   section containing an analysis of actual clothing worn
   during the period 1560-1620.

7 MOODY, DOROTHY BELLE. "Shakespeare's Stage Directions: An
   Examination for Bibliographical and Literary Evidence."
   Ph.D. dissertation, Yale University, 434 pp.
      Attempts to show what Shakespeare's stage directions
   "reveal as to the history of his text, and to set forth
   such literary information as they yield . . . . Since the
   matter of staging has been fully discussed elsewhere, for
   the most part I ignore it."

8 R. "Actors in Shakespeare's Plays." N&Q 174 (28 May):387.
      A brief paragraph noting the printing of actors' names
   in the First Folio Much Ado about Nothing.

9 SKOPNIK, GUNTER. "Niederländische Bühnenformen des 16.
   Jahrhunderts." DuV 39 (November):411-26.
      Discusses methods of production in the Netherlands in
   the sixteenth century, including those of touring English
   companies.

10 UNWIM, GEORGE. The Gilds and Companies of London. 3d ed.
   London: G. Allen & Unwin, 397 pp.
      Reprint of 1909.29.

1939

1 EICH, LOUIS M. "Ned Alleyn versus Dick Burbage." SpMon
   6:110-26.
      A comparison of the two great Elizabethan actors, based
   on contemporary references. Alleyn played the stage
   "heavies," such as Barabas, Faustus, Tamburlaine, and
   Hieronimo, and apparently displayed a tendency to "strut
   and bellow." Burbage, on the other hand, was apparently
   more restrained, playing Biron, Romeo, Prince Hal, Brutus,
   and the heroes of the four great tragedies. Eich concludes
   that Burbage was the better actor.

1939

2 ELIOT, SAMUEL A., Jr. "The Lord Chamberlain's Company as
   Portrayed in Every Man Out of His Humour." SCSML 21
   (October):64-80.
       Discusses the casting of Jonson's play, based on a
   published cast list and the types of the characters.

3 FREDÉN, GUSTAF. Friedrich Menius und das Repertorie der
   englischen Komödianten in Deutschland. Stockholm: P. A.
   Palmers, 527 pp.
       Examines the life and work of Menius, an early seven-
   teenth-century German theatrical personality, in relation
   to the touring English players. Fredén pays special
   attention to the plays presented, both straight adapta-
   tions of English originals (such as Titus Andronicus, which
   was very popular) and hybrid German works featuring
   Pickelherring. He concludes that Menius edited the 1620
   collection of plays by the English comedians. See also
   1941.7.

4 GRAY, M[ARGARET] M[URIEL]. "Queen Elizabeth's Players." TLS
   (14 January):25-26.
       A letter to the editor, citing and commenting on a 1589
   letter that demonstrates that the Queen's Men were in
   Scotland in that year.

5 GRIFFIN, WILLIAM JAMES. "Tudor Control of Press and Stage."
   Ph.D. dissertation, University of Iowa, 198 pp.
       A systematic collection of data, arranged historically
   and comparatively, concerning the action and attitude of
   Tudor government toward the press and stage. The most
   useful section is the second chapter, which sets forth a
   calendar of evidence used in the narrative first chapter.
   The study includes data from 1485 to 1603. Griffin has
   used Arber's A Transcript of the Registers of the Company
   of Stationers of London, 1554-1640 extensively.

6 HARBAGE, ALFRED. "Elizabethan Acting." PMLA 54 (September):
   685-708.
       An attempt to define both "formal" and "natural" acting
   styles and to defend the former while attacking the latter.
   Harbage considers Betterton to be the first "natural" actor
   in England, with Burbage, Alleyn, and the rest belonging
   to the "formal" school. He cites the preface to a manuscript play, "The Cyprian Conqueror," and subsequent acting
   manuals, for their formal approach.

7 SOUTHERN, RICHARD. "He, Also, Was a Scene Painter (Wm. Lyzarde 1572)." L&LT 23 (November):294-300.
     An anecdotal look at William Lyzarde, scene painter to Elizabeth, based primarily on his accounts from 1572. Southern concentrates on Lyzarde's pigment order.

8 STUNZ, ARTHUR NESBITT. "The Contemporary Setting of Macbeth." Ph.D. dissertation, University of Iowa, 81 pp.
     Attempts to date Macbeth accurately (he proposes May/June 1606), and to investigate the possible effect of contemporary political attitudes. Of little theatrical interest.

                              1940

1 ADAMS, JOSEPH QUINCY. "Another Fragment from Henslowe's Diary." Library, 4th ser. 20 (September):154-58.
     Discusses a slip of paper containing the signatures of Dekker and two others, held in the Folger Shakespeare Library and apparently removed from the diary. See also Greg (1938.5).

2 BATESON, F[REDERICK] W[ILSE], ed. The Cambridge Bibliography of English Literature. Vol. 1, 600-1660. Cambridge: University Press, pp. 497-513.
     The relevant section is Parts II and III of the Renaissance Drama listings, dealing with "Theatres and Actors" and "The Puritan Attack Upon the Stage." There are also a variety of subsections in each category. Relevant items have been included in this bibliography. See also the Supplement (1957.16) and NCBEL (1974.25).

3 CASTLE, EDUARD. "Zu dem Problem: Shakespeare und seine Truppe." JDSG 76:57-111.
     Examines Shakespeare's plays and company, and attempts to establish lines of business and assign actors to them. Castle includes many pages of tables to help support his contentions. See also Baldwin (1927.1).

4 CHAMBERS, E[DMUND] K. "William Shakespeare: An Epilogue." RES 16 (October):385-401.
     Considers, among many other matters, the acting style of the period, the length of representation of plays, and allusions to the stage and acting in Shakespeare. Reprinted: 1944.6.

1940

5 GORELIK, MODECHAI. <u>New Theatres for Old</u>. New York: S. French,
   pp. 100-105.
   The relevant section is titled "Shakespeare, Liberator."
   Here, as part of a larger argument about the coming of
   naturalism, Gorelik discusses how Shakespeare used his
   resources in a masterful way. Reprinted: 1947.4.

6 GREG, W[ALTER] W[ILSON]. "The Staging of <u>King Lear</u>." <u>RES</u> 16
   (July):300-303.
   Discusses the simplicity of the stage directions for
   <u>King Lear</u>, concluding that no "rear stage," and probably
   no balcony, was available for its initial production.

7 HARBAGE, ALFRED. <u>Annals of English Drama, 975-1700</u>. Philadel-
   phia: University of Pennsylvania Press, 264 pp.
   A comprehensive listing, unannotated and undocumented,
   arranged chronologically, with company and date of performance. The "Index of Dramatic Companies" and "List of
   Theatres" are relevant, although outdated. Revised:
   1964.13.

8 LEWIS, JOHN COLBY. "A Correlation of the Theatre with the
   Graphic Arts, According to the Dominant Artistic Theories
   of Several Times, from the Middle Ages to the Present Day."
   Ph.D. dissertation, Cornell University, pp. 60-105.
   The relevant section deals with the Renaissance, primarily in Italy, although English practice (chiefly in the
   masques) is touched on.

9 PASCAL, R[OY]. "The Stage of the 'Englische Komödianten'--
   Three Problems." <u>MLR</u> 35 (July):367-76.
   Examines the entrances, the balcony, and the curtain
   used by the English actors in Germany during the seventeenth century. Apparently there were usually two or three
   doorways opening on to a booth stage set up in a rectangular
   building open in the center. A balcony was used at times,
   and the open stage was hung with arras. Parallels with
   the Elizabethan stage are clear.

10 REYNOLDS, GEORGE FULLMER. <u>The Staging of Elizabethan Plays at
    the Red Bull Theatre, 1605-25</u>. New York: Modern Language
    Association, 203 pp.
    Widely recognized as a model of scholarship and perhaps
    the most influential staging study ever published. Reynolds
    found, in surveying the state of historical scholarship in
    the thirties, that "many of our present conclusions rest on
    unsound foundations which demand re-examination." In this
    book he proposes to offer "such a re-examination with
    stricter methods of procedure and severer checks on

146

conclusions." Reynolds examines all the evidence presented by a group of plays selected objectively. Each scene of each play is looked at in detail on each point; the plays as a whole are examined; and then all plays are considered in relation to each other. Reynolds is the first to divide the plays of the repertory he establishes for the Red Bull into groups depending upon the reliability of the evidence they provide, and he draws his primary evidence only from those plays that provide the best evidence--the evidence most clearly linked to playhouse practices. Briefly, he concludes that "the Red Bull plays, in spite of their use of spectacle, could be given on a stage structurally like that of the Swan drawing, with the single important addition of a third stage door." Reynolds then speculates that a portable curtained booth might have been used for discoveries.

11 SISSON, C[HARLES] J[ASPER]. "The Mouse-Trap Again." RES 16 (April):129-36.
      Examines the staging of the play-within-a-play scene of Hamlet, focusing on the preliminary dumb show. Sisson places it on the "inner stage" and freezes the action (except for Hamlet and Ophelia) on the "outer stage."

1941

1 BENTLEY, GERALD EADES. The Jacobean and Caroline Stage. Vols. 1-2. Oxford: Clarendon Press, 748 pp.
      The first two volumes of Bentley's seven-volume reference work (see also 1956.4; 1968.2), based on his Ph.D. dissertation (1929.7) but greatly expanded. The major purpose is to carry on the survey begun by Chambers (1923.2) from 1616 to 1642, beginning in these volumes with a survey of the companies (vol. 1) and the actors (vol. 2). Bentley treats the companies in roughly the order of their importance, beginning with the King's Men and continuing through Beeston's Boys. First, he summarizes the history of each company to 1616 (from Chambers), and then he traces it until it disbands or the theatres are closed in 1642. In this latter narrative, all relevant documentary evidence is presented in detail. Each chapter concludes with a series of lists and tables presenting the evidence of the actor lists, provincial notices, plays at court, and so on, and a listing of the company's repertory. Volume two contains the information on the actors, with a minimum of comments by Bentley. Instead he cites "every scrap of biographical evidence" in chronological order. The appendix to volume 2 prints many important documents and discusses plague closings.

1941

2 CAMPBELL, LILY B[ESS]. "Richard Tarlton and the Earthquake of
1580." HLQ 4 (January):293-96.
Establishes the clown Tarlton as the author of a poem on
the earthquake.

3 CRUNDELL, H. W. "Actors' Parts and Elizabethan Texts." N&Q
180 (17 May):350-51.
Argues that Pope first made the suggestion.that some
plays of the First Folio (Merry Wives of Windsor in particular) were assembled from actors' parts.

4 LEECH, CLIFFORD [E. J.] "The Caroline Audience." MLR 36
(July):304-19.
An examination of tone in Caroline plays through a study
of the audience for which they were intended. Leech sees
two reasons for a change in Caroline drama from the Jacobean:
the refinement of the Court and the new group of young
writers. Most evidence for the character of the audience
comes from the prologues and epilogues of the plays. The
most important audience requirement was for variety and a
retreat from the actual. Reprinted: 1950.11.

5 McNEIR, WALDO F. "Gayton on Elizabethan Acting." PMLA 56
(June):579-83.
Responds to Harbage (1939.6) with previously uncited
evidence from a 1654 book by Edmund Gayton, arguing for a
formal acting style.

6 MITCHELL, LEE. "Elizabethan Scenes of Violence and the
Problem of Their Staging." Ph.D. dissertation, Northwestern University, 121 pp.
The three chapters enumerate Elizabethan scenes of
violence by type and discuss the Elizabethan and modern
staging of such scenes. Stabbing is most often used for
sudden and unexpected murders, poisoning for reversal,
shooting for the climax of a struggle, battles and execu-
tions for spectacular terminal catastrophes, and the melee
for surprising terminal action. The use of stage properties, visible blood, and effigies of bodies, heads, and
limbs was common. The expert use of optical illusion or
misdirection of attention was also employed.

7 [PASCAL, ROY.] "Elizabethan Plays in Germany." TLS (26
April):208.
Discusses the career of Fredriech Menius, apparent
editor of an important 1620 collection of English plays
presented in Germany. See also Fredén (1939.3).

8 REYNOLDS, GEORGE F[ULLMER]. "Some Problems of Elizabethan
    Staging." <u>CUS</u>, general series (A), 26, no. 4 (November):
    3-19.
        The sixth annual Research Lecture of the University of
    Colorado, delivered 5 May 1941, based on 1940.10. Reynolds
    includes some interesting personal information as well as
    his concerns with circumspect treatment of the evidence
    for staging practices. Contains nothing new.

9 SCHÜCKING, LEVIN L. "Die Kindertruppenstelle in <u>Hamlet</u>."
    <u>Archiv</u> 179, no. 1:8-14.
        Examines the allusions in <u>Hamlet</u> to the boy companies,
    and places them in historical context.

10 THALER, ALWIN. "Ben Jonson, Richard Brome, and Minor Actors."
    In <u>Shakespeare and Democracy</u>. Knoxville: University of
    Tennessee Press, pp. 266-86.
        Reprint of 1921.16-17; 1922.9.

11 _____. "<u>Faire Em</u> (and Shakespeare's Company?) in Lancashire."
    In <u>Shakespeare and Democracy</u>. Knoxville: University of
    Tennessee Press, pp. 141-56.
        Reprint of 1931.16.

12 _____. "The Original Malvolio?" In <u>Shakespeare and Democracy</u>.
    Knoxville: University of Tennessee Press, pp. 119-37.
        Reprint of 1932.11.

13 _____. "Travelling Players in Shakespeare's England." In
    <u>Shakespeare and Democracy</u>. Knoxville: University of
    Tennessee Press, pp. 157-84.
        Reprint of 1920.30.

1942

1 ADAMS, JOHN CRANFORD. <u>The Globe Playhouse: Its Design and
    Equipment</u>. Cambridge: Harvard University Press, 420 pp.
        Expanded, published version of 1935.1. Perhaps the
    single most influential work in the field, and one of the
    most misleading. In this, the first comprehensive attempt
    to reconstruct the Globe, Adams includes chapters on the
    property and shape of the building; the playhouse frame;
    the auditorium; the platform stage; the exterior of the
    tiring house; the first, second, and third levels and
    stairs of the tiring house; and the superstructure. It was
    Adams who popularized the ideas of the "study," the "tarras,"
    the "chamber," and the "music gallery." The major problem

is Adams's use of evidence from too wide a variety of
sources. While almost completely discredited in scholarly
circles, this reconstruction of the Globe is the most
widely known and accepted, perhaps because of the ubiquitous
models that appeared in high schools throughout the country.
See also the second edition, 1961.1.

2 BENTLEY, GERALD E[ADES]. "A Good Name Lost: Ben Jonson's
Lament for S. P." TLS (30 May):276.
Argues that the first name of the well-known boy actor
was not Salathiel, as had been supposed, but rather Salmon
(Pavy). Bentley cites ten seventeenth-century appearances
of the name, one of which was previously unknown, and
traces the substitution of the Christian name to Gifford's
1816 edition of Jonson.

3 BRAWNER, JAMES PAUL. "The Wars of Cyrus": An Early Classical
Narrative of the Child Actors. ISLL, vol. 28, nos. 3-4.
Urbana: University of Illinois, 163 pp.
A critical edition, with notes and commentary, of the
earliest private theatre play. Section V of the Introduction deals with "Staging of the Play," but Brawner provides
nothing new. He believes that multiple staging would have
been employed.

4 MILES, THEODORE. "Place Realism in a Group of Caroline
Plays." RES 18 (October):428-40.
Examines six private theatre plays from 1631 to 1635
that have London place-names as titles. It has been elsewhere assumed that specific representational scenery might
have been used in staging those plays. See 1972.12.

5 RINGLER, WILLIAM. "The First Phase of the Elizabethan Attack
on the Stage, 1558-79." HLQ 5 (July):391-418.
A different view of the attack on the stage, suggesting
that: 1) it began suddenly in 1577; 2) the causes were
internal, resulting from changes within the theatres
themselves; and 3) the attack was led by laymen, not clergy,
and that it was not initially theological.

6 RINGLER, WILLIAM A. Stephen Gosson: A Biographical and
Critical Study. Princeton Studies in English, no. 35.
Princeton: Princeton University Press, 151 pp.
The most important section from a theatrical perspective
is the fourth chapter, detailing the Puritan attach on the
stage and the role in it of Gosson's Schoole of Abuse.

7 SISSON, C[HARLES] J[ASPER]. "Notes on Early Stuart Stage
     History." <u>MLR</u> 37 (January):25-36.
          The first part consists of a wealth of notes on theat-
     rical personalities of the early seventeenth century,
     derived from the close study of various legal documents.
     The second part (pp. 30-34) discusses the shares in the Red
     Bull company. The final section (pp. 34-36) discusses the
     wages of the hired men. Sisson is particularly noted for
     his skill at dealing with documentary evidence.

8 SISSON, CHARLES J[ASPER]. "Shakespeare's Quartos as Prompt-
     Copies, with Some Account of Cholmeley's Players and a New
     Shakespeare Allusion." <u>RES</u> 18 (April):129-43.
          Argues that the usage of published quartos as prompt
     copies by both provincial and London companies was general.
     Information about Cholmeley's Players (also known as the
     Simpson's Company), a provincial but professional group in
     Yorkshire, is derived from Star Chamber documents.

<u>1943</u>

1 ABEGGLEN, HOMER N. "A Dissertation in Five Parts. 1. The
     Methods of Staging in London Theatres in the Last Half of
     the Nineteenth Century. 2. Theatrical Satire on the
     American Business Man, 1900-1940. 3. The Staging of Medi-
     eval and Elizabethan Plays. 4. A Comparison Between
     Plautine Farce and Romantic Comedy. 5. The Premiere of
     Wycherly's <u>The Plain Dealer</u>." Ph.D. dissertation, Western
     Reserve University, pp. 36-70.
          The relevant part is the third, a highly personalized
     and anecdotal essay examining different types of scenes
     and approaches to their staging. Abegglen simply reports
     on what various scholars have written (he cites fewer than
     ten sources), concluding that "no one method was adhered
     to by all the producers of the seven different theatres."

2 BALD, R[OBERT] C[ECIL]. "Leicester's Men in the Low Countries."
     <u>RES</u> 19 (October):395-97.
          Selections from Halliwell-Phillipps's scrapbooks, con-
     taining excerpts from Leicester's household account book,
     bearing on the company's tour of 1585-86.

3 BRAWNER, JAMES PAUL. "Early Classical Narrative Plays by
     Sebastian Westcott and Richard Mulcaster." <u>MLQ</u> 4
     (December):455-64.
          Claims Westcott and Mulcaster wrote several of the plays
     presented by their children's companies in the sixteenth
     century. <u>See also</u> 1951.4.

1943

4   DAVIS, JOE LEE. "The Case for Comedy in Caroline Theatrical
      Apologetics." PMLA 58 (June):353-71.
          Discusses Prynne's attacks on Caroline comedy in
      Histriomastix and its defence in Randolph's The Muse's
      Looking Glass and Baker's Theatrum Redivivum.

5   GRIFFIN, WILLIAM J. "Notes on Early Tudor Control of the
      Stage." MLN 58 (January):50-54.
          Corrects Gildersleeve (1908.9) on two minor points and
      adds two minor instances of control of the stage in the
      1540s.

6   PARROTT, THOMAS MARC, and BALL, ROBERT HAMILTON. A Short View
      of Elizabethan Drama, Together with Some Account of Its
      Principal Playwrights and the Conditions under Which It
      Was Produced. New York: Charles Scribner's Sons, pp.
      45-62.
          Primarily concerned with major plays and "the person-
      ality of the dramatist," but also considers theatrical
      conditions briefly. The relevant section is Chapter Three,
      "Actors and Theatres," which includes in its general discus-
      sion a drawing and description of J. C. Adams's reconstruc-
      tion of the Globe (see 1942.1). Reprinted: 1958.15.

7   SISSON, C[HARLES] J[ASPER]. "A Note on Sebastian Westcott."
      RES 19 (April):204-5.
          A brief note on the Master of the Children of Paul's,
      derived from a Chancery suit involving his brother.

8   STEVENSON, ALLEN H. "Shirley's Years in Ireland." RES 20
      (January):19-28.
          While Shirley's years as resident dramatist at the
      Werbaugh Theatre, Dublin, are the concern of this essay,
      the dates of his departure and his return to London are
      clarified.

                              1944

1   B[ARRELL], C[HARLES] W[ISNER]. "Documentary Notes on the
      Swan Theatre." ShFQ 5 (January):8-9.
          Discusses the Swan drawing (with a translation of
      DeWitt's description) and the suit against Langley and
      Shakespeare. Barrell thinks that the scene illustrated in
      the drawing is from Twelfth Night and that the Earl of
      Oxford wrote it.

2 BARRELL, CHARLES WISNER. "Lord Oxford as Supervising Patron
of Shakespeare's Theatrical Company." ShFQ 5 (July):33-40.
Argues that Edward de Vere, seventeenth Earl of Oxford,
was the "Lord Chamberlain" who lent his name to Shakespeare's
company.

3 BENNETT, H[ENRY] S[TANLEY]. "Shakespeare's Audience." PBA
30:3-16.
The annual Shakespeare Lecture of the British Academy,
delivered 26 April 1944, examining the audience of the
Theatre, the Curtain, and the Globe, 1595-1609. Bennett
discusses the varied composition of the audience and the
methods the playwright used to appeal to each class. The
end of the essay, however, consists of a plea to avoid
criticism that removes the play from the realm of the
theatre.

4 BETHEL, S[AMUEL] L[ESLIE]. Shakespeare and the Popular
Dramatic Tradition. Westminster: P. S. King and Staples,
pp. 31-41.
The relevant section is chapter two, "Planes of Reality,"
in which Bethel stresses those elements of the playhouse
that Shakespeare used to reinforce his themes. Reprinted:
1948.2.

5 CHAMBERS, E[DMUND] K. "The Stage of the Globe." In Shakespearean Gleanings. London: Oxford University Press,
pp. 98-110.
Reprint of 1907.4.

6 _____. "William Shakespeare: An Epilogue." In Shakespearean
Gleanings. London: Oxford University Press, pp. 35-51.
Reprint of 1940.3.

7 KERNODLE, GEORGE R. From Art to Theatre: Form and Convention
in the Renaissance. Chicago: University of Chicago Press,
pp. 130-53.
Published version of 1937.4. The relevant section
examines the Elizabethan stage in the context of the
architectural symbol, along with the Flemish and Spanish
popular theatres. Kernodle claims the public stage was
similar in many ways to the Flemish Rederyker stage facade,
since they were both derived from the same traditions of
art and pageantry.

1945

1 JENKIN, BERNARD. "Antony and Cleopatra: Some Suggestions on
   the Monument Scenes." RES 21 (January):1-14.
       An imaginative reconstruction of the staging of the
   monument scenes as Shakespeare saw them. Jenkin concludes
   that: 1) the First Folio contains two confused versions
   of the beginning of the scene; 2) the hauling of Antony
   aloft was required by Shakespeare's source and accepted by
   him; and 3) the inner stage and upper stage were used in
   combination in these scenes. See 1964.21.

2 McDOWELL, JOHN H. "Tudor Court Staging: A Study in Perspective." JEGP 44 (April):194-207.
       Considers the causes for the lack of interest in
   perspective in the Tudor period. McDowell begins with a
   survey of the Tudor attitudes toward science, then turns
   to a survey of sixteenth-century court staging practices,
   which he sees as "multiple staging." He concludes with a
   discussion of Serlian methods, ultimately disagreeing with
   Campbell (1923.1) on the use of perspective.

3 SPRAGUE, ARTHUR COLBY. "Off-Stage Sounds." UTQ 15 (October):
   70-75.
       Discusses how sound effects can enhance mood in the
   performance of Shakespeare and other dramatists.

1946

1 ADAMS, JOSEPH QUINCY. "The Author-Plot of an Early Seventeenth-Century Play." Library, 4th ser. 26 (June):17-27.
       Discusses and edits the author plot for a tragi-comedy
   from about 1630, tentatively titled Philander, King of
   Thrace, held in the Folger Shakespeare Library.

2 BARBETTI, EMILIO. "Note storiche sul teatro inglese: 'la
   claque.'" Anglica 1 (April-June):96-99.
       "The existence and organization of the claque in the
   London theatres is traced from Elizabethan times to the
   present century" (from the English abstract).

3 CHAMBRUN, [CLARA] LONGWORTH. "La compagnie de Shakespeare."
   RTh, no. 2 (August-September):176-86.
       Discusses the evolution of Shakespeare's company, from
   Lord Strange's Men through the Lord Chamberlain's Men to
   the King's Men. Chambrun examines the major actors of the
   company, focusing on Burbage and Kempe, but including an

evaluation of Shakespeare as an actor. She includes contemporary portraits of Burbage, Sly, and Lowin.

4 McCALMON, GEORGE. "A Study of the Renaissance and Baroque Factors in the Theatre Style of Inigo Jones." Ph.D. dissertation, Case Western Reserve University, 852 pp.
     Examines the designs for scenery and costumes, tracing Italian and other influences on Jones's work.

5 ORSINI, NAPOLEONE. "La scene italiana in Inghilterra: Il trattato del Serlio." Anglica 1 (April–June):100–102.
     "A mistake in the Jacobean translation of Serlio's treatise on the stage suggests a darker picture of Cinquecento morality than is warranted by the text" (from the English abstract).

6 WATKINS, RONALD. Moonlight at the Globe. London: M. Joseph, 135 pp.
     An imaginative reconstruction of an Elizabethan production of Midsummer Night's Dream, based on J. C. Adams's reconstruction of the Globe (1942.1). Watkins discusses the stage and its settings, the music, and the costumes. Of little historical value. Reprinted: 1947.10.

1947

1 BURRELL, JOHN. "Réflexions sur la mise en scène des tragédies de Shakespeare." RTh 5 (April):169–70.
     A brief note citing Shakespeare's original staging as justification for methods employed at the Old Vic in the 1947 season.

2 DAWSON, GILES E. "Copyright of Plays in the Early Seventeenth Century." EIE. New York: Columbia University Press, 169–92.
     Discusses the practices of the Stationers' Company and, after 1607, the Master of the Revels. Dawson discusses both the establishment and the transfer of copyright, although that particular word is not used until 1734. The copyright history of The Merry Devil of Edmonton is traced as an example.

3 ELLIS-FERMOR, UNA M. "The Jacobean Stage." In The Jacobean Drama: An Interpretation. 2d ed. London: Methuen, pp. 273–83.
     Reprint of 1936.8.

1947

4 GORELIK, MORDECHAI. <u>New Theatres for Old</u>. London: Dennis
   Dobson, pp. 100–105.
      Reprint of 1940.5.

5 HODGES, C[YRIL] WALTER. "The Globe Playhouse: Some Notes on
   a New Reconstruction." <u>TN</u> 1 (July):108–11.
      Hodges sets out his differences from Adams (1942.1) on
   a few small points. His later reconstructions are more
   complete and more original. <u>See also</u> 1953.9; 1968.16.

6 MITCHELL, LEE. "Shakespeare's Sound Effects." <u>SpMon</u> 14:127–
   38.
      Examines the instruments named in Shakespeare's stage
   directions and the function of each, and the nonmusical
   sounds called for and the dramatic purpose of each.
   Mitchell lists information on fifteen sound effects and
   ten instruments, concluding that there was progressively
   greater use of sound effects and an increasing variety
   of instruments available from the early plays to the late.

7 SABOL, ANDREW JOSEPH. "Music for the English Drama from the
   Beginnings to 1642." Ph.D. dissertation, Brown University,
   275 pp.
      Chapters two and three treat secular music in the
   English drama and music for the English masque. Sabol not
   only discusses the music but also provides many examples
   culled from contemporary sources. Especially valuable is
   the music from the boy companies and the music for the
   masques.

8 SOUTHERN, RICHARD. "Observations on Lansdowne MS. No. 1171."
   <u>TN</u> 2 (October):6–19.
      Discusses the evidence of the manuscript for the staging
   of the masques and prints fifteen plates from it. Southern
   deduces a theory of the pre–Restoration groove from one of
   the sketches.

9 STURMAN, BERTA. "Renaissance Prompt Copies: <u>A Looking Glasse
   for London and England</u>." Ph.D. dissertation, University
   of Chicago, 95 pp.
      Examines an undated copy of the play held at the Univer-
   sity of Chicago, which contains manuscript notes in a
   seventeenth–century hand and was apparently used as a prompt
   book during the first half of the century. Sturman examines
   the notes in seven classes: entrances, exits, corrections,
   properties, sound effects, spectacle, and stage business.
   All appear to be the work of a single prompter preparing
   the text for performance and making corrections, perhaps in

rehearsal. Other prompt scripts are also considered, and
Sturman assigns this revival to Queen Anne's Men in 1606.
The third appendix contains a checklist of printed prompt
texts.

10 WATKINS, RONALD. <u>Moonlight at the Globe</u>. London: M. Joseph,
135 pp.
Reprint of 1946.6.

11 WILSON, J[OHN] D[OVER], and HUNT, R[ICHARD] W[ILLIAM]. "The
Authenticity of Simon Forman's Booke of Plaies." <u>RES</u> 23
(July):193-200.
Rejects the notion, put forward by Tannenbaum and others,
that this document is a Collier forgery. The evidence
presented is linguistic and paleographic, Wilson providing
the former and Hunt the latter. See <u>also</u> 1849.6; 1876.1;
1907.8; 1919.8; 1959.1.

<u>1948</u>

1 BENTLEY, GERALD EADES. "Shakespeare and the Blackfriars
Theatre." <u>ShS</u> 1:38-50.
Originally a lecture for the Shakespeare Conference,
Stratford-upon-Avon, August 1947. Bentley places Shakespeare in the context of the London commercial theatre and
the organized professional acting troupe, and discusses
his relationship with the King's Men's private playhouse.
Jonson, Beaumont and Fletcher, and Shakespeare were the
playwrights for the new theatre, and Bentley contends
that all of Shakespeare's post-1608 plays (<u>Cymbeline</u>,
<u>Winter's Tale</u>, <u>Tempest</u>, <u>Two Noble Kinsmen</u>) were written
with the Blackfriars in mind.

2 BETHEL, S[AMUEL] L[ESLIE]. <u>Shakespeare and the Popular
Dramatic Tradition</u>. Westminster: P. S. King & Staples,
pp. 31-41.
Reprint of 1944.4.

3 BOWERS, ROBERT H. "Gesticulation in Elizabethan Acting."
<u>SFQ</u> 12 (Spring):267-77.
Generally supports Harbage's theory of "formal" acting
in the Elizabethan period (<u>see</u> 1939.4), presenting information from the plays on posture and gesture. See <u>also</u> Index
under Acting--Style.

1948

4 BRERETON, J[OHN] LE GAY. "The Elizabethan Playhouse." In
   Writings on Elizabethan Drama. Edited by Robert Guy
   Howarth. Carlton, Victoria: Melbourne University Press,
   pp. 81-88.
       A general discussion of the public theatres based on
   the Swan drawing and of the private theatres based on the
   Roxana and Messalina vignettes. See also 1916.2.

5 _____. "Stage-Arrangement in Peele's David and Bethsabe, I.
   i." In Writings on Elizabethan Drama. Edited by Robert
   Guy Howarth. Carlton, Victoria: Melbourne University
   Press, pp. 93-96.
       Reprint of 1912.3.

6 HODGES, C[YRIL] WALTER. Shakespeare and the Players. London:
   E. Benn, 100 pp.
       A popular treatment for a juvenile audience of Shake-
   speare's career, including an early Hodges attempt at a
   conjectural reconstruction of the Globe, complete with
   inner stages above and below. A detailed discussion of
   the staging of Richard III forms one of the key chapters.
   Reprinted: 1949.6; second edition: 1970.12. See also
   Index, under Hodges, for his more serious work on the
   Globe.

7 McDOWELL, JOHN H. "Conventions of Medieval Art in Shakespearian Staging." JEGP 47 (July):215-29.
       Discusses the influence of medieval art on theatres and
   staging practices of the Elizabethan period. McDowell
   assumes an inner stage used to localize interiors and
   relates it to the convention of the "house" structure in
   art. He similarly relates the curtains used for discoveries, and the iconographic value of stage properties.

8 MITCHELL, LEE. "Shakespeare's Lighting Effects." SpMon 15,
   no. 1:72-84.
       A reexamination of Shakespearean lighting in terms of
   the playwright's intentions. Those lights required by the
   stage action or mentioned in the dialogue are subjected to
   three questions: 1) what are they; 2) why are they there;
   and 3) how are they used? Only three different kinds of
   lights are required: torches, lanterns, and tapers.
   Mitchell describes four purposes for the use of those
   lights: chronographic, symbolic, ceremonial, and meta-
   phoric. In answer to the final question, Mitchell finds
   lights used for important stage business, for spectacle,
   and for providing imagined stage darkness.

9 [NICOLL, ALLARDYCE.] "A Note on the Swan Theatre Drawing."
   ShS 1:23-24.
      A brief note transcribing the text accompanies the
   reproduction.

10 NICOLL, ALLARDYCE. "Studies in the Elizabethan Stage since
    1900." ShS 1:1-16.
       Reviews scholarship in the field from 1900 to 1947 with
    the emphasis on the years following Chambers (1923.2).
    Nicoll concludes with a section considering "The Needs of
    the Future."

11 SHAPIRO, I. A. "The Bankside Theatres: Early Engravings."
    ShS 1:25-38.
       An attempt to survey the pictorial evidence for the
    sixteenth-century Bankside theatres and collate it with
    the documentary data. After rejecting several early views
    as inaccurate, or printed much later, Shapiro uses Norden's
    Civitas Londini to settle the question of the site of the
    Globe while at the same time rejecting its evidence for
    polygonal structure. Hollar's "Long View," as Braines
    suggested (see 1924.3), provides reliable evidence of the
    Bear Garden and the Globe, with the names interchanged.

12 SMITH, WARREN D. "Shakespeare's Stagecraft as Denoted by the
    Dialogue in the Original Printing of His Plays." Ph.D.
    dissertation, University of Pennsylvania, 256 pp.
       Revised version published: 1975.29.

13 STRATMAN, CARL J. "Dramatic Performances at Oxford and
    Cambridge, 1603-1642." Ph.D. dissertation, University of
    Illinois, 416 pp.
       A chronological discussion of professional and amateur
    theatricals at the two major Universities, based on records
    of payment and chronologies of events held in Oxford and
    Cambridge archives.

14 WILSON, J[OHN] DOVER. "Titus Andronicus on the Stage in 1595."
    ShS 1:17-22.
       Discusses the Peachum illustration and its accompanying
    text.

                              1949

1 BACHRACH, A[LFRED] G[USTAV] H[ERBERT]. "The Great Chain of
   Acting." Neophil 33 (Spring):160-72.
      A review of research on Elizabethan acting, focusing on

1949

          Bertram Joseph's 1948 lecture series at Oxford on the
subject (see 1950.10; 1951.18). Bachrach ties acting to
the methods of Renaissance education and the ideas of
Elizabethan psychology. On the whole he describes a formal
style. See also Index under Acting--Style.

2 BAKER, RENNIE. "The Structure of the First Globe Theatre."
     ShAB 24 (April):106-11.
         Argues for an octagonal structure for the Globe, on
the authority of the Fortune contract and pictorial evidence.

3 BENNET, H[ENRY] S[TANLEY]. "Shakespeare's Stage and Audience."
     Neophil 33 (Winter):40-51.
         General discussion of the arrangement and structure of
the Elizabethan stage and of the nature of the audience.
While he cites no sources he is apparently indebted to
Adams (1942.1) in his description of the inner stage and
"tarras." In the second section Bennet considers the use
made of the stage to change time and place at will, and in
the third the composition, nature, and expectations of the
audience.

4 CHILD, HAROLD H. "The Elizabethan Theatre." In Cambridge
     History of English Literature. Vol. 6, The Drama to 1642.
     Pt. 2. Edited by A. W. Ward and A. R. Waller. Cambridge:
     University Press, pp. 241-78.
         Reprint of 1910.5.

5 DARLINGTON, WILLIAM AUBREY. The Actor and His Audience.
     London: Phoenix House, pp. 31-35.
         The relevant section is the first half of Chapter Three,
"Burbage and Betterton." Darlington bases his evaluation
of Burbage's acting on the description in Flecknoe (1664.1)
and Hamlet's advice to the players, delivered by Burbage
and presumably describing him.

6 HODGES, C[YRIL] WALTER. Shakespeare and the Players. New
     York: Coward-McCann, 101 pp.
         Reprint of 1948.6.

7 HOPPE, HARRY R. "English Actors at Ghent in the Seventeenth
     Century." RES 25 (October):305-21.
         Based on research in the Municipal Archives of Ghent and
the Grand Archives at Brussels. Records of payments from
the city treasury for preview performances exist from 1598
on. Several previously unknown English actors on the
continent performed in Ghent, and several new names are
added to the rolls of continental performers.

8 HOTSON, [JOHN] LESLIE. "The Projected Amphitheatre." ShS
   2:24-35.
       Discusses the three letters on the subject revealed by
   Collier and the documents printed in 1914.3-4, as well as
   a new document from the Privy Seal office granting a
   license to build the Amphitheatre. In addition to combats
   and animal acts, the buiding was also to house plays
   presented by a regular acting troupe, perhaps the King's
   Men. The building was to seat 12,000, at a cost of
   £12,000. The license, however, was stayed in 1626; another
   attempt to build the Amphitheatre was made in 1634, and
   another at a later time. Hotson presents new documentary
   evidence for these last three. The building was, of course,
   never constructed.

9 KIRSCHBAUM, LEO. "Shakespeare's Stage Blood and Its Critical
   Significance." PMLA 64 (June):517-29.
       Considers the implications of the particularly bloody
   scenes in Julius Caesar and Coriolanus, concluding that
   Shakespeare intended the blood to be displayed on the stage
   for the purpose of amplifying the theatricality of the
   moment.

10 MANLY, J[OHN] M[ATTHEWS]. "The Children of the Chapel Royal
    and Their Masters." In Cambridge History of English
    Literature. Vol. 6, The Drama to 1642. Pt. 2. Edited by
    A. W. Ward and A. R. Waller. Cambridge: University Press,
    pp. 279-92.
        Reprint of 1910.12.

11 McDOWELL, JOHN H. "Medieval Influences in Shakespearian
    Staging." Players 26 (December):52-53.
        Identifies the "inner stage" with the medieval mansion,
    advocating the alternation theory.

12 MITCHELL, LEE. "Shakespeare's Legerdemain." SpMon 16
    (August):144-61.
        An examination of Shakespeare's use of magic. Mitchell
    finds that ventriloquism, levitation, and the illusion of
    vanishing, among other techniques, were used to mystify--
    and hence to entertain--the audience. The cauldron scene
    in Macbeth and the banquet scene in Tempest are examples
    of important uses of illusion. Magic was always well
    integrated into the scene and never in Shakespeare was
    used for its own sake.

1949

13 REYNOLDS, GEORGE F[ULLMER]. "Staging Elizabethan Plays."
    Listener 42 (11 August):223-24.
        A radio broadcast on the BBC Third Programme. Reynolds
    discusses the division of plays into a large number of
    short scenes and the unchanging background for the action
    that could accommodate any and all locations. Reprinted:
    1949.14.

14 ____. "Staging Elizabethan Plays." ShAB 24 (October):258-63.
    Reprint of 1949.13.

15 SHAPIRO, I. A. "An Original Drawing of the Globe Theatre."
    ShS 2:21-23.
        Reprints and discusses Hollar's drawing of the Globe
    that served as the basis for his "Long View." See also
    1933.11.

16 WILSON, EDWARD M., and TURNER, OLGA. "The Spanish Protest
    against A Game at Chesse." MLR 44 (October):476-82.
        Prints "two reports sent to Madrid by the Spanish
    Ambassador in London" pertaining to the scandal caused
    by this play, with translations.

17 WILSON, J[OHN] D[OVER]. "The Puritan Attack on the Stage."
    In Cambridge History of English Literature. Vol. 6, The
    Drama to 1642. Pt. 2. Edited by A. W. Ward and A. R.
    Waller. Cambridge: University Press, pp. 373-409.
        Reprint of 1910.26.

1950

1 ARCHER, WILLIAM, and LAWRENCE, W[ILLIAM] J[OHN]. "The Playhouse." In Shakespeare's England: An Account of the Life
   and Manners of His Age. Vol. 2. Edited by Sidney Lee,
   Charles Talbut Onions, and Walter A. Raleigh. Oxford:
   Clarendon Press, pp. 283-310.
       Reprint of 1916.1.

2 BETHEL, S[AMUEL] L[ESLIE]. "Shakespeare's Actors." RES,
   n.s. 1 (July):193-205.
       Based on a paper read at the Shakespeare Association
   Conference at Stratford-upon-Avon in the summer of 1948.
   Bethel reexamines the known facts and theories about the
   casting of Shakespeare's plays and the style of Elizabethan
   acting. He doubts the existence of "lines" for actors (see
   Baldwin, 1927.1) and sides with the proponents of the
   "formal" school of acting.

3 BROCK, JAMES WILSON. "A Study of the Use of Sound Effects in
   Elizabethan Drama." Ph.D. dissertation, Northwestern
   University, 156 pp.
   Analyzes musical and nonmusical sound effects in Elizabethan drama "in terms of their dramatic purpose, function,
   and use." Brock eliminates orchestral interludes, songs,
   and dance as stage music instead of sound effects. The
   five major parts examine the dramatic purpose of sound
   effects; the functions as specified in stage directions;
   conjectural effects, based on references in the texts; the
   production of sound effects; and their employment in the
   plays. Brock concludes that the Elizabethan audience
   readily accepted a wider range of conventional sound effects
   than does the contemporary audience, that effects were less
   important in comedy, and that the function of sound
   effects in the Elizabethan theatre is paralleled by their
   function in radio drama and film.

4 BROMBERG, MURRAY. "The Reputation of Philip Henslowe." SQ 1
   (Autumn):135-39.
   Examines Henslowe's contemporary reputation, attempting
   to show that he was not being satirized in Day's Parliament
   of Bees, as Fleay and Chambers thought.

5 BROOK, DONALD. A Pageant of English Actors. London: Rock-
   liffe, pp. 9-35.
   The relevant section is the first four chapters,
   biographies of Richard Burbage, Richard Tarlton, William
   Kempe, and Edward Alleyn. Brook uses only secondary sources
   in this work for a popular audience.

6 CHILD, HAROLD H. "The Elizabethan Theatre." In Cambridge
   History of English Literature. Vol. 6, The Drama to 1642.
   Pt. 2. Edited by A. W. Ward and A. R. Waller. Cambridge:
   University Press, pp. 241-78.
   Reprint of 1910.5.

7 FELDMAN, ABRAHAM. "Hans Ewouts, Artist of the Tudor Court
   Theatre." N&Q 195 (10 June):257-58.
   A biographical sketch of the Dutch painter who influenced the Elizabethan theatre. Ewouts was in the service
   of the court theatre in 1572-74. Feldman conjectures that
   the anonymous Wisdom of Doctor Dodypoll has a Dutch character based on the painter.

1950

*8   FRONIUS, HANS. Zeichungen um Shakespeare. Vienna-Linz:
       Gurlit Verlag.
          Cited in 1963.14. Eight lithographs of Shakespeare and
       the Globe playhouse.

 9   HODGES, C[YRIL] WALTER. "Unworthy Scaffolds: A Theory for
       the Reconstruction of Elizabethan Playhouses." ShS 3:83-94.
          Examines the evidence for the platform itself, rather
       than the tiring house facade. Hodges suggests the booth
       stage as the prototype for the platform. The Swan drawing
       and the Fortune contract support this view. He suggests
       that large props and horses may have been brought into the
       yard.

10   JOSEPH, BERTRAM R. "How the Elizabethans Acted Shakespeare."
       Listener 43 (5 January):17-18.
          A radio broadcast on the BBC Third Programme. Joseph
       argues for a formal acting style based on John Bulwer's
       Chirologia and Chironomia. See also 1951.18 and Index
       under Acting--Style.

11   LEECH, CLIFFORD [E. J.] "The Caroline Audience." In Shake-
       speare's Tragedies and Other Studies in Seventeenth-Century
       Drama. London: Chatto & Windus, pp. 159-81.
          Reprint of 1941.5.

12   LÜDEKE, H[ENRY]. "Shakespeares Globus-Theater: Nach den
       neuesten Ergebuissen der Forschung." JDSG 84-86:131-39.
          Discusses the needs of a reconstruction of the Globe,
       along with photographs of a model built to Adams's speci-
       fications (see 1942.1).

13   MANLY, J[OHN] M[ATTHEWS]. "The Children of the Chapel and
       Their Masters." In Cambridge History of English Literature.
       Vol. 6, The Drama to 1642. Pt. 2. Edited by A. W. Ward
       and A. R. Waller. Cambridge: University Press, pp. 279-92.
          Reprint of 1910.12.

14   PURDOM, C. B. Producing Shakespeare. London: Sir Isaac
       Pitman & Sons, 220 pp.
          Intended primarily as a guide to the modern director,
       containing historical backgroud culled from secondary
       sources only.

15 ROBERTS, J. R. H., and GODFREY, W[ILLIAM] H., eds. Bankside.
   London County Council Survey of London, no. 22. London:
   London County Council, pp. 66-77.
   Chapter Eight, "The Bankside Playhouses and Bear Gardens,"
   contains a brief review of Braines and Chambers on the Rose,
   the Swan, and the Globe, with one or two new pieces of
   information added. The building of the Rose Playhouse is
   set at 1588 rather than 1592, on the basis of a Sewer
   Commission order, and Shakespeare's supposed residence in
   Southwark (proposed by Malone and Collier), while not here
   disproved, cannot be verified, because of documents either
   forged or no longer extant.

16 SIMPSON, PERCY. "Actors and Acting." In Shakespeare's
   England: An Account of the Life and Manners of his Age.
   Vol. 2. Edited by Sidney Lee, Charles Talbut Onions, and
   Walter A. Raleigh. Oxford: Clarendon Press, pp. 240-82.
   Reprint of 1916.14.

17 _____. "The Masque." In Shakespeare's England: An Account
   of the Life and Manners of his Time. Vol. 2. Edited by
   Sidney Lee, Charles Talbut Onions, and Walter A. Raleigh.
   Oxford: Clarendon Press, pp. 311-33.
   Reprint of 1916.15.

18 TRIEBEL, L. A. "Sixteenth-Century Stagecraft in European
   Drama: A Survey." MLQ 11 (March):7-16.
   A general treatment, primarily of continental medieval
   staging, but venturing into Elizabethan staging via the
   Swan drawing. Triebel, however, subscribes to the "inner
   below" and alternation theories, without citing evidence.

19 WATKINS, RONALD. On Producing Shakespeare. London: Michael
   Joseph; New York: Norton, 335 pp.
   Discusses elements of Shakespearean stagecraft, concentrating on methods of staging and acting. Watkins summarizes Adams (1942.1) as his discussion of the playhouse,
   but is more original (if anecdotal) in other areas. As he
   did earlier with Midsummer Night's Dream (1946.6), Watkins
   gives a complete description of the staging of Macbeth.

20 WENTERSDORF, KARL. "Shakespeares erste Truppe: Ein Beitrag
   zur Aufklärung des Problems der sog. 'verlorenen Jahre.'"
   JDSG 84-86:114-30.
   In an attempt to fill in the "lost years" in Shakespeare's biography, Wentersdorf examines the possibility
   that he was a member of Pembroke's Men.

1950

21 WILSON, J[OHN] D[OVER]. "The Puritan Attack on the Stage."
    In Cambridge History of English Literature. Vol. 6, The
    Drama to 1642. Pt. 2. Edited by A. W. Ward and A. R.
    Waller. Cambridge: University Press, 373-409.
        Reprint of 1910.26.

1951

1 ADAMS, JOHN CRANFORD. "'That Virtuous Fabric.'" SQ 2
   (Winter):3-11.
       Adapted from a lecture at the Folger Shakespeare Library
   on 23 April 1950, presenting Adams's reconstruction. See
   1942.1.

2 ALDUS, PAUL JOHN. "The Use of Physical Comic Means in English
   Drama from 1420 to 1603." Ph.D. dissertation, University
   of Chicago, 207 pp.
       Discusses three types of physical comedy: simple
   episodic routines, complex episodic routines, and connate
   routines (by which he means "relevant to the mainstream of
   the play"), as well as the use of properties for comic
   effect, physical scenes of improbability and reversal, and
   the evolution of physical to verbal means. Part of his
   conclusions concern the vast increase in the use of
   physical comedy in plays after 1590.

3 BROMBERG, MURRAY. "Theatrical Wagers: A Sidelight on the
   Elizabethan Drama." N&Q 196 (8 December):533-35.
       Examines various types of theatrical wagers, including
   those between actors and playwrights, from a variety of
   contemporary sources.

4 BROWN, ARTHUR. "A Note on Sebastian Westcott and the Plays
   Presented by the Children of Paul's." MLQ 12 (March):134-
   36.
       A refutation of Brawner's contention (in 1943.3) that
   Sebastian Westcott was the author of several plays performed
   by Paul's Boys while they were under his direction.

5 BUDDE, FRITZ. "Shakespeare und die Frage der Raumbühne." In
   Shakespeare-Studien: Festschrift für Heinrich Mutschmann.
   Edited by Walther Fischer and Karl Wentersdorf. Marburg:
   N. G. Elwert, pp. 21-47.
       The question of stage space referred to in the title is
   the question of scenery. Budde compares the modern
   illusionistic theatre with Shakespeare's staging, finding
   the latter much more flexible.

6 CAPOCCI, VALENTINA. "Poeti e attori nel drama elisabettiano."
   Il Ponte 7 (December):1593-1600.
   Examines the roles of the playwright and the improvisa-
   tions of the actor in Elizabethan drama, with examples
   drawn from Shakespeare, Marlowe, Jonson, and Brome.

7 CHAPMAN, RAYMOND. "Twelfth Night and the Swan Theatre." N&Q
   196 (27 October):468-70.
   Examines the possibility of an early version of Twelfth
   Night at the Swan, seen by DeWitt in 1596 and serving as
   the basis for the Swan drawing. Chapman suggests that this
   early version was the lost Love's Labour's Won, with the
   plot as described by Jonson in Every Man Out of His Humour.

8 DOWNER, ALAN S. "The Tudor Actor: A Taste of His Quality."
   TN 5 (April):76-81.
   Originally a paper read at the MLA convention in 1950,
   concerning acting in the interludes.

9 EDINBOROUGH, ARNOLD.   "The Early Tudor Revels Office." SQ
   2 (Winter):19-25.
   Examines the history of the Revels Office from approxi-
   mately 1540 to 1552. Inventories of the office, the
   accounts of specific court functions, and the accounts of
   the building of a banqueting house in 1552 are presented.

10 EMPSON, WILLIAM. "The Staging of Hamlet." TLS (23 November):
   749.
   Suggests that Shakespeare wanted to stage the closet
   scene in the balcony but the players wouldn't allow such
   an important scene to be played in an auxiliary playing
   space.

11 FLATTER, RICHARD. "The Dumb-Show in Macbeth." TLS (23
   March):181.
   Suggests that the eighth king (who would have been
   James) held a mirror up for the King to see himself.

12 _____. "Outer, Inner, or Upper Stage?" SQ 2 (Spring):171.
   Questions some of J. C. Adams's pronouncements in 1951.1
   on where particular scenes took place, with a request for
   some substantiation for such assertions.

13 FREEMAN, SIDNEY LEE. "The Forms of the Non-Proscenium
   Theatre: Their History and Theories." Ph.D. dissertation,
   Cornell University, pp. 29-32, passim.
   The relevant section discusses the actor-audience rela-
   tionship in general terms; throughout the rest of the

1951

study there are occasional references to the Elizabethan
theatre.

14 GRAY, CECIL G. "Shakespeare's Co-Plaintiffs in the Blackfriars Lawsuit of 1615." N&Q 196 (10 November):490-91.
Identifies the first three complainants as Sir Thomas
Bendishe, Edward Newport, and William Thoresbie, who
owned land in the neighborhood of Dunmow.

15 _____. "The Sixteenth-Century Burbages of Stratford on Avon."
N&Q 196 (10 November):490.
Using a Court of Requests suit of 1610, shows that the
John Burbage, bailiff of Stratford-on-Avon in 1555, was not
related to the William Burbage who was a tenant of Shake-
speare's father.

*16 HAYWARD, WAYNE CLINTON. "The Globe Theatre, 1599-1608." Ph.
D. dissertation, University of Birmingham, 215 pp.
Cited in DEAL, p. 476.

17 HODGES, C[YRIL] WALTER. "DeWitt Again." TN 5 (January):32-34.
A brief note evaluating the Swan drawing. Hodges finds
that the drawing presents us with "a large area of reliable
information," despite some undecipherable or uncertain
elements.

18 JOSEPH, B[ERTRAM] R. Elizabethan Acting. Oxford English
Monographs. London: Oxford University Press, 157 pp.
Examines Elizabethan acting from the point of view of
rhetorical training. Joseph finds that there were
specified manners of speech and gesture for each role, and
that Elizabethan acting was far more formal than what we
would accept as natural. See 1950.10; second edition,
1964.25. For the entire controversy over this subject, see
Index under Acting--Style.

19 LELYVELD, TOBY BOOKHOLZ. "Shylock on the Stage: Significant
Changes in the Interpretation of Shakespeare's Jew." Ph.D.
dissertation, Columbia University, 196 pp.
Traces the significant changes in the manner in which
Shylock has been interepreted in Merchant of Venice in
England and America. While there is a discussion of the
place of the Jew in Elizabethan society, there is no actual
evidence presented for this period.

20 LINN, JOHN GAYWOOD. "The Court Masque and Elizabethan Dramatic Structure." Ph.D. dissertation, Cornell University, 184 pp.

The four major chapters treat the masque before 1595; the masque 1595-1604; and the relationship between the masque and the drama in both periods. Linn concludes that the sharing of elements is not synonymous with "influence," and that prior to the period of the great Jacobean masques there was far less influence in terms of form than has previously been assumed.

*21 LONG, JOHN H. "Shakespeare's Use of Music: A Study of the Music and Its Performance in the Original Performances of Seven Comedies." Ph.D. dissertation, University of Florida, 184 pp.

Cited in ADDT, p. 58.

22 McMANAWAY, JAMES G. "A New Shakespeare Document." SQ 2 (Spring):119-22.

A warrant from the Lord Chamberlain for payment to the King's Men, and the schedule of twenty-one plays presented at the Cockpit-in-Court annexed to it.

23 PRIOR, MOODY E. "The Elizabethan Audience and the Plays of Shakespeare." MP 49 (November):101-23.

Attacks most studies of the audience for having preconceived ideas and engaging in circular reasoning, and surveys attempts to deal with the audience's effect on the plays. A general failing in this type of criticism, Prior says, is a lack of understanding of the limits of the method. See also Index under Audience.

24 PURDOM, C. B. "The Dumb-Show in Macbeth." TLS (20 April):245.

Responds to Ure (1951.31) and Flatter (1951.11).

25 REYNOLDS, GEORGE F[ULLMER]. "Was There a 'Tarras' in Shakespeare's Globe?" ShS 4:97-100.

The "tarras"--the front part of the balcony in most reconstructions of the Globe, stretching more than twenty feet from window to window, three or four feet deep (as in Adams, 1942.1)--is examined. Reynolds finds little evidence for such a structure, suggesting that the context of references to the "tarras" is always theatrical, and that one upper acting area would suffice for all uses. He blames the arguments for the tarras on insistence on modern realistic conventions in the Elizabethan period, which is inappropriate.

1951

26 RICHEY, DOROTHY. "The Dance in the Drama of the Elizabethan
    Public Theatre: A Production Problem." Ph.D. disserta-
    tion, Northwestern University, 212 pp.
      Examines those dances that form an integral part of the
    plots of Elizabethan plays presented at the public play-
    houses and reconstructs, complete with choreographic
    charts, the specific dances suggested by stage directions
    and lines of dialogue. The five chapters deal with the
    pavane, measures, alman, tordion, galliard, volt, basse-
    danse, morris, sword, country dances, coranto, brawl,
    canary, jig, hornpipe, and round. While historical infor-
    mation is included, this study is of more use to the
    director than the theatre historian.

27 SHIELD, H. A. "Links With Shakespeare, VII." N&Q 196 (9
    June):250-52.
      An attempt to identify Agnes Bennet, named in Augustine
    Phillips's will.

28 SMITH, IRWIN. "Notes of the Construction of the Globe Model."
    SQ 2 (Winter):13-18.
      Adapted from a speech delivered at the Hofstra College
    Shakespeare Festival, 24 March 1950, explaining some of
    the decisions behind details of the Adams model of the
    Globe. See 1942.1.

29 SMITH, WARREN D. "Evidence of Scaffolding on Shakespeare's
    Stage." RES, n.s. 2 (January):22-29.
      Presents textual evidence for a raised platform on the
    Globe stage from Hamlet, Richard III, Troilus and Cressida,
    Julius Caesar, and Antony and Cleopatra. Smith envisions
    a small portable platform, perhaps with three steps up.
    The same platform would bear the throne of state when it
    was required.

30 STAMM, RUDOLF. Geschichte des englischen Theaters. Bern: A
    Francke, pp. 55-115.
      The relevant section discusses the theatre of Shake-
    speare's time. Stamm is more concerned with the drama
    than the theatre, despite the title, but he does attempt
    to place the drama in its theatrical context. He includes
    general discussions of playhouses and acting, depending
    heavily on Chambers (1923.2), Bentley (1941.1), and Hotson
    (1928.7), among others.

1952

31 URE, PETER. "The Dumb-Show in Macbeth." TLS (6 April):213.
    Responds to Flatter (1951.11). See also 1951.24.

32 VENEZKY, ALICE S. "Pageantry on the Shakespearean Stage."
    Ph.D. dissertation, Columbia University, 242 pp.
    Published: 1951.33.

33 _____. Pageantry on the Shakespearean Stage. New York:
    Twayne, 242 pp.
    Published version of 1951.32. Analyzes the influence
    of the most popular forms of public display--the procession,
    pageant, and progress--on the Elizabethan drama, 1581-1603.
    The four major chapters cover entries and triumphs; royal
    receptions; pageants, progresses, and plays; and Shake-
    speare's use of pageant imagery. Venezky hopes her
    "comparative examination" will "reveal a fuller signifi-
    cance in many scenes" and "contribute to the appreciation
    and enjoyment of Shakespeare in the study and upon the
    stage."

1952

1   BALD, R[OBERT] C[ECIL]. "The Entrance to the Elizabethan
    Theatre." SQ 3 (Winter):17-20.
    Speculates on the location of the entrances to the
    Elizabethan public theatres, concluding that there were
    two, one on each side, located with the external stair-
    cases. The speculation is based on the Swan drawing and
    the Hollar "Long View" engraving.

2   BORDINAT, PHILIP. "A Study of the Salisbury Court Theatre."
    Ph.D. dissertation, University of Birmingham, 280 pp.
    Examines the last of the pre-Commonwealth playhouses.
    The six major chapters deal with the history of the
    building, its structure and use, the structure of the
    stage, production techniques at this playhouse, and the
    use of the playhouse after the Restoration. Bordinat finds
    that the staging methods used--two doors, an inner stage,
    an upper stage, and a trap, properties and costumes utilized
    for purposes of dramatic illusion, one use of partial
    scenery--were standard for the period.

3   BROWN, ARTHUR. "Sebastian Westcott at York." MLR 47
    (January):49-50.
    A brief note announcing discovery of a document in York
    allowing Westcott, Master of the Children of St. Paul's in
    the 1550s, to take children into his group from anywhere in
    the realm.

1952

4 CROUCH, JACK HERBERT. "Some Shakespearean Stage Conventions
   Developed from a Study of the Architectural Antecedents of
   the Elizabethan Public-Outdoor Playhouse and a Staging
   Study of Romeo and Juliet and Antony and Cleopatra." Ph.D.
   dissertation, Cornell University, pp. 1-73, 253-83.
       The relevant sections discuss the general features of
   the public playhouses and relate them to "manorial-domestic
   architecture," especially the great hall and its screen.
   Playing conventions discussed include direct audience
   address and the neutral playing space localized by dialogue
   and property at each entrance.

5 FELDMAN, ABRAHAM BRONSON. "Dutch Theatrical Architecture in
   Elizabethan London." N&Q 197 (11 October):444-46.
       Discusses Dutch influence on the Elizabethan public
   stage, including the Rhetoric Theatres and the Dutch
   heritage of Peter Street, Burbage's carpenter.

6 FURNISS, W[ARREN] TODD. "Ben Jonson's Masques and Entertainments." Ph.D. dissertation, Yale University, 290 pp.
       Essentially a literary analysis of Jonson's masques,
   concluding that the masques fit into the tradition of the
   literature of monarchy, with its own conventional imagery
   and typical methods. While the study is interesting in
   itself, it is of little theatrical value.

7 GREENSLADE, S. L. "The Elizabethan Theatre." TLS (25 April):
   281.
       Two payments to players from the Chapter Vouchers,
   Durham Cathedral, 1590-91.

8 HARBAGE, ALFRED. Shakespeare and the Rival Traditions. New
   York: Macmillan, 393 pp.
       Presents "a new synthesis of the facts about Elizabethan
   theatres and the content of Elizabethan plays, as a means
   of defining Shakespeare's materials and intentions." The
   main point is the duality of Elizabethan drama and theatre;
   the popular plays of the public stage are contrasted to
   the "coterie" plays of the private stage, and the companies,
   repertories, and styles of the rivals are also contrasted.

9 HOSKING, GEORGE LLEWELLYN. The Life and Times of Edward
   Alleyn. London: Jonathan Cape, 285 pp.
       The first thirteen chapters (pp. 17-133) contain the
   relevant information about Alleyn's theatrical career,
   based primarily on the records held at Dulwich College.
   The most complete information concerns Alleyn's partnership
   with Henslowe. Essentially a popular biography coupled
   with a history of the College.

10 HOSLEY, RICHARD. "A Stage Direction in Romeo and Juliet."
    TLS (13 June):391.
        Sets the entrance of the musicians at IV.v.95
    rather than IV.v.32, on the authority of the "bad"
    first quarto.

11 HOTSON, [JOHN] LESLIE. "False Faces on Shakespeare's Stage."
    TLS (16 May):336.
        Asserts that the curtains for discoveries were drawn by
    two disguised stage-keepers who were visible to the
    audience throughout the performance. Further, the visors
    they wore were often used on stage for purposes of disguise.

12 _____. Shakespeare's Motley. London: Hart-Davis; New York:
    Oxford University Press, 133 pp.
        Examines the fool and his clothing, finding that the
    "motley coat" was a long coat of mixed color, like tweed.
    The most important chapter is the last, "Robert Armin,
    Shakespeare's Fool," which examines the life and works of
    the actor.

13 MEAD, ROBERT SMITH. "A Study of Factors Influencing the
    Development of Acting Techniques in England, 1576-1642,
    with Applications to the Problems of Educational Theatre."
    Ph.D. dissertation, Northwestern University, 306 pp.
        An attempt at a comprehensive view of all factors
    affecting the actor's work during the period. The first
    six chapters introduce the study and examine the changing
    political and social conditions and the development of
    acting style and technique. Mead concludes that "Eliza-
    bethan acting changed greatly during the period and
    developed into an art during the last two decades of the
    sixteenth century."

14 SAUNDERS, F. R. "Capacity of the Second Globe Theatre." TLS
    (14 November):743.
        Presents contemporary evidence from the Spanish State
    Archives (first published in 1949.16) that the Globe held
    3000 people for each of four performances of A Game at
    Chess, 1624.

15 SCHLESS, HOWARD H. "False Faces on Shakespeare's Stage."
    TLS (6 June):377.
        Responds to Hotson (1952.11).

1952

16   SEMPER, I. J.   "Jacobean Playhouses and Catholic Clerics."
     Month, n.s. 8 (July):28-39.
        Examines the controversy over playhouse attendance by
     secular priests in 1617 and 1618, based on manuscripts
     held in the Folger Shakespeare Library. William Harrison,
     on 9 March 1617/18, prohibited their attendance; Thomas
     Lake, on 25 April 1618, wrote a letter of protest; and
     John Colleton, Harrison's assistant, replied. While the
     grounds of the prohibition are similar to the protests of
     the Puritans, Semper maintains that as a general rule
     Catholics did not disapprove of the drama; the prohibition
     of attendance had more to do with maintaining a low profile
     in London. See also 1952.17.

17   _____. "The Jacobean Theatre through the Eyes of Catholic
     Clerics." SQ 3 (Winter):45-51.
        Discusses the controversy among Catholic clerics about
     attending the theatre in the early seventeenth century,
     based on a manuscript held at the Folger Shakespeare
     Library. The prohibition sparked a lively and learned
     debate, and was finally lifted in 1618. See also 1952.16.

18   SMITH, IRWIN. "Theatre into Globe." SQ 3 (Spring):113-20.
        Examines the transformation of the Theatre into the
     Globe, based on a study of Tudor joinery and carpenter's
     marks. Smith concludes that Peter Street supervised the
     tearing down and transportation of the timbers, and that
     the basic frame of the building was reproduced exactly on
     the new site.

19   SOUTHERN, RICHARD. Changeable Scenery: Its Origin and
     Development in the British Theatre. London: Faber &
     Faber, 411 pp.
        Partly based on twelve unpublished volumes by W. J.
     Lawrence, written from 1887 to 1912, and presented to
     Southern by Lawrence in 1939. The relevant section in
     this comprehensive history is Part One, "The Rise of
     Changeable Scenery at Court." The six chapters in this
     section treat an overview of the field; the static scene,
     the house, and the moving cloud; the rise of the shutter
     and its frame; the grooves; the so-called "scenes of
     relieve;" and the great scenic controversy between Jonson
     and Jones. Part One includes detailed discussions of the
     designs of Inigo Jones.

20   _____, and HODGES, C[YRIL] WALTER. "Colour in the Eliza-
     bethan Theatre." TN 6 (January):57-59.

Southern contributes a note on imitation marbled classical columns in the Swan, while Hodges briefly discusses
a seventeenth-century ceiling possibly related to the
decorated "heavens" of the public theatre.

21 WALKER, JOHN ANTHONY. "The Functions of Stage Lighting in
the Changing Concepts of Stage Design." Ph.D. dissertation, Cornell University, pp. 112-36.
The relevant section is Chapter Three, section B, which
examines lighting in Renaissance England. The most
important discussion is of Inigo Jones and lighting in the
court masques. See also 1976.10.

22 WHITE, ERIC WALTER. "A Note on the Reconstruction of Farce
Jigs." TN 6 (January):39-42.
Briefly reviews the current state of knowledge of both
text and music of the Elizabethan jig, suggesting that
"there is enough material extant for some of these jigs
to be edited for stage performance today."

1953

1 BECKERMAN, BERNARD. "The Globe Playhouse at Hofstra College,
II: Notes on Direction." ETJ 5 (March):6-11.
Discusses mounting productions on the full-sized reproduction of J. C. Adams's reconstruction of the Globe. See
also 1942.1; 1953.27.

2 BROWN, JOHN RUSSELL. "On the Acting of Shakespeare's Plays."
QJS 39 (December):477-84.
Argues for an essentially "natural" style, "although
some vestiges of an old formalism remained." Brown
believes that there was a development of methods. Here he
attempts to answer objections to his position, citing a
variety of contemporary texts in support. See also Index
under Acting--Style. Reprinted: 1968.3.

3 CLINTON-BADDELEY, V. C. "Elizabethan Players in Sherborne."
TN 7 (July):83.
Draws attention to several entries in the account books
from the former Church House, showing payments to actors
from 1571 to 1603. The Long Room, in which they played,
still exists.

1953

4 DeBANKE, CECILE. <u>Shakespearean Stage Production: Then and</u>
   <u>Now</u>. New York: McGraw-Hill, 342 pp.
   The four parts examine staging, actors and acting,
   costume, and music and dance, both in Shakespeare's time
   and in the 1950s. DeBanke depends largely on the work of
   others, especially J. C. Adams (1942.1). The work is
   intended as an aid to modern staging rather than a piece
   of historical scholarship.

5 ELLIS-FERMOR, UNA M. "The Jacobean Stage." In <u>The Jacobean</u>
   <u>Drama: An Interpretation</u>. 3d ed. London: Methuen,
   pp. 273-83.
   Reprint of 1936.8.

6 FELDMAN, ABRAHAM B. "Playwrights and Pike-Trailers in the
   Low Countries." <u>N&Q</u> 198 (May):184-87.
   Examines possible Low Country war experiences of George
   Gascoigne, Christopher Marlowe, and Ben Jonson.

7 FLATTER, RICHARD. "Shakespeare, der Schauspieler." <u>JDSG</u>
   89:35-50.
   Examines the documentary and textual evidence for
   Shakespeare as an actor. Flatter argues that the texts of
   the plays show clear signs of Shakespeare's sensitivity to
   the sound of his words and pause patterns, a sensitivity
   that would have been enhanced by his acting experience.

8 HARBAGE, ALFRED. "Shakespeare's Inner Stage." <u>RenN</u> 6
   (Summer):18-19.
   Abstract of Harbage's response to two papers (including
   1953.13) presented at the New England Conference on
   Renaissance Studies, 24 April 1953. He concludes by
   stating that the idea of the "inner stage" may be overempha-
   sized.

9 HODGES, C[YRIL] WALTER. <u>The Globe Restored: A Study of the</u>
   <u>Elizabethan Theatre</u>. London: Ernest Benn, 199 pp.
   A conjectural reconstruction of the first Globe, especially interesting because of the author's awareness of the
   problems of reconstruction and his gathering of relevant
   pictorial evidence. Hodges devotes his central chapters
   to the platform and the tiring house, breaking with Adams
   (1942.1) over the "inner stage" and agreeing with Reynolds
   (1940.10) that a portable curtained booth might have been
   used for discoveries and scenes above. <u>See also</u> revised
   edition, 1968.16.

10 ____. "Some Comments upon Dr. Leslie Hotson's 'Shakespeare
Arena.'" ShStage, no. 3 (December):26-29.
A detailed review of Hotson's 1953.11.

11 HOTSON, [JOHN] LESLIE. "Shakespeare's Arena." SR 61
(Summer):347-61.
Presents Hotson's theory on the use of mansions in the
medieval manner set forth on the platform stage for interior
and above scenes, with the audience on all four sides.
This idea is further developed in 1959.9.

12 ____, ed. Queen Elizabeth's Entertainment at Mitcham: Poet,
Painter and Musician. New Haven: Yale University Press,
57 pp.
An edition of the manuscript entertainment of 12-13
September 1598, from the British Library. Hotson includes
historical and descriptive notes.

13 HOTSON, [JOHN] LESLIE. "Shakespeare's Arena-Stage at Court."
RenN 6 (Summer):17-18.
A summary of 1953.11, delivered at the New England
Conference on Renaissance Studies, 24 April 1953. See
1953.8 for Harbage's response.

14 KREMPEL, DANIEL SPARTAKUS. "The Theatre in Relation to Art
and to the Social Order from the Middle Ages to the
Present." Ph.D. dissertation, University of Illinois,
373 pp.
The chapter dealing with the Elizabethan theatre treats
it primarily as an extension of medieval practice.

15 MARKWARD, WILLIAM BRADLEY. "A Study of the Phoenix Theatre
in Drury Lane, 1617-1638." Ph.D. dissertation, University
of Birmingham, 683 pp.
Examines the Phoenix (or Cockpit) Playhouse in Drury
Lane 1617-1638, with particular stress on the staging of
the plays. The six main chapters treat the history of the
playhouse, the evidence presented by the plays acted there,
the structure of the stage, the use of auditory and visual
effects, and the audience. Markward concludes that the
Phonix stage was divided in the Adams manner into an
outer stage, an inner stage, and an upper stage.
Properties, sound effects, costumes, and even make-up
were frequently used to create realistic effects. The
dates of the study reflect the initial adaptation of the
cockpit into a theatre and the death of the building's
leaseholder and manager, Christopher Beeston.

1953

16 McCULLEN, JOSEPH T., Jr. "The Use of Parlor and Tavern Games
     in Elizabethan and Early Tudor Drama." MLQ 14 (March):7-14.
         A survey of the use of card games, dice, chess, back-
     gammon, and so on, in the Elizabethan and Jacobean theatre.
     The use of games on stage became a convention used to
     promote dramatic action and provide variety. See also
     1953.23.

17 MEADLEY, T. D. "Attack on the Theatre (circa 1580-1680)."
     LQHR 178 (January):36-41.
         A general discussion of government regulation and
     Puritan opposition.

*18 MÖHRING, HANS. "Als Shakespeare zu uns kam. Shakespeare-
     Aufführungen englischer Komödianten in Deutschland."
     Theater der Zeit 8, no. 12 (December):6-12.
         Cited in 1963.14.

19 PROUTY, CHARLES TYLER. "An Early Elizabethan Play-House."
     ShS 6, 64-74.
         Discusses the Accounts of the Churchwardens of St.
     Bodolph without Aldersgate, which demonstrate that a play-
     house was set up in Trinity Hall from 1557 to 1568, and
     apparently used by the provincial companies when performing
     in London. Prouty prints a plan and elevation of the
     building and suggests that a curtain hung from the gallery
     on the west end would provide a playing space.

20 ROTHWELL, WILLIAM FRANCIS, Jr. "Methods of Production in
     the English Theatre from 1550-1598." Ph.D. dissertation,
     Yale University, 496 pp.
         Examines the staging methods, stage picture, and
     physical conditions of the Elizabethan stage before 1598 in
     light of English medieval practices. First Rothwell
     discusses the "courtly" theatre, defined as the court, the
     schools, and the private playhouses, finding precedents
     among the traditional mysteries, the civic pageants, and
     the masques for staging methods after 1550. The Italian
     influence was minimal. Next Rothwell examines the public
     theatres, tracing the traditional staging methods employed
     to the stage of the processional mysteries, with a stage
     house (mansion) and forestage. He concludes that Eliza-
     bethan production methods are rooted in the medieval
     methods, not the Italian.

21   SMITH, WARREN D.   "The Elizabethan Stage and Shakespeare's
     Entrance Announcements."   SQ 4 (Autumn):405-10.
          Examines entrance announcements such as "Look where he
     comes," concluding that they served as a cue for actors
     already on the platform to move forward.

22   _____. "Stage Business in Shakespeare's Dialogue." SQ 4
     (Summer):311-16.
          Examines the nearly 3000 directions for stage business
     in the dialogue (as opposed to the less than 300 marginal
     notations), concluding that such implied directions are
     actually descriptions for members of the audience who could
     not see the action on stage at the moment.

23   SOLEM, DELMAR E.   "Indoor Game Scenes in the Elizabethan
     Drama and the Problem of Their Staging." Ph.D. dissertation,
     Northwestern University, 362 pp.
          Examines, from the point of view of the modern director,
     the production problems inherent in game scenes as part of
     the value of visual elements in Elizabethan plays. The
     four main chapters treat chess, tables, dice, and cards.
     Solem concludes that these games were staged in a conjec-
     tural "inner stage" and that similar games may have been
     staged in widely divergent manners. A valuable glossary is
     included in an appendix. See also 1953.16.

24   SOUTHERN, RICHARD.   "Inigo Jones and Florimène." TN 7
     (April):37-39.
          A brief note, including eight plates of Jones's designs
     for the masque performed by the French in the Great Hall
     at Whitehall, 1635. Southern discusses the shutters and
     relieves used in the performance.

25   SPRAGUE, ARTHUR COLBY.   Shakespearian Players and Performances.
     Cambridge: Harvard University Press, 222 pp.
          Despite the title this work begins with the Restoration.

26   SUMMERSON, JOHN [NEWENHAM].   Architecture in Britain, 1530-
     1830. Pelican History of Art, no. Z3. London and
     Baltimore: Penguin Books, pp. 61-67.
          The relevant section, Part Two, Chapter Seven, "Inigo
     Jones at the Court of James I," contains a general discus-
     sion of Jones's theatre designs. Reprinted: 1955.25;
     1958.22; 1963.18; 1969.16; 1970.30.

1953

27 SWINNEY, DONALD H. "The Globe Playhouse at Hofstra College,
I: Notes on Reconstruction." ETJ 5 (March):1-5.
    Discusses the building of a full-sized replica of the
Globe to the specifications of J. C. Adams (1942.1). Three
sides of the octagon he envisaged were constructed, containing essentially seven separate stages. See also 1953.1.

28 WALTON, CHARLES E. "The Impact of the Court Masque and the
Blackfriars Theatre upon the Staging of the Elizabethan-
Jacobean Drama." Ph.D. dissertation, University of
Missouri, 198 pp.
    Examines the masque and masque-like dramas in relation
to the indoor playhouses. Walton concludes that masques
were inserted into plays to add interest, and that well-
equipped playhouses were required. "If these plays were
produced even with a slight attention to the required
staging, the drama of the period could not have been
without its spectacular moments."

29 WOODFILL, WALTER L. Musicians in English Society from
Elizabeth to Charles I. Princeton: Princeton University
Press, pp. 29-30, 41, 56-58, 65-66, 188, 236-37.
    Brief mentions of the relationship between musicians
and actors and playhouses.

1954

1 ANON. "A Model Elizabethan Playhouse." Listener 51 (29
April):727.
    Describes Southern's model, with quotations from
Southern. He used the Swan drawing as a basis, and
decorated with paint. See also 1954.26.

2 ARMSTRONG, WILLIAM A. "Shakespeare and the Acting of Edward
Alleyn." ShS 7:82-89.
    Attempts to assess the validity of the interpretations
of passages in Hamlet and 2 Henry IV that might be critical
of Alleyn's acting by relating them to contemporary references. Armstrong concludes that recent disparagement of
Alleyn's acting is not justified and that he should be
considered on a par with Burbage, as he was in his own day.

3 ASHE, DORA JEAN. "The Non-Shakespearean Bad Quartos as
Provincial Acting Versions." RenP 1:57-62.
    Examines the twelve non-Shakespearean bad quartos not
previously studied by Greg. Ashe discusses the indications
of prompt-book intent and the signs of provincial adaptation.

4 BRYANT, JOSEPH ALLEN, Jr. "Shakespeare's Falstaff and the
       Mantle of Dick Tarlton." SP 51 (April):149-62.
           Discusses the character of Falstaff in the context of
       the Elizabethan clown, exemplified by Richard Tarlton.
       Bryant suggests that the role was shaped by Shakespeare's
       desire to make use of the clown's antics in support of the
       play rather than in opposition to it, as was often the
       case.

5 CUTTS, JOHN P. "Jacobean Masque and Stage Music." M&L 35
       (July):185-200.
           Discusses a manuscript held in the British Library,
       previously examined by Lawrence (1922.5), containing music
       used for various Jacobean masques. The bulk of the piece
       consists of a listing of the contents of the manuscript
       and commentary (including Cutts's differences with
       Lawrence) on each item.

6 DeBANKE, CECILE. Shakespearean Stage Production: Then and
       Now. London: Hutchinson & Co., pp. 312.
           Reprint of 1953.4.

7 EMPSON, WILLIAM. "The Elizabethan Stage." TLS (10 December):
       801.
           A letter to the editor, challenging Hotson's conclusions
       in 1954.14. Empson suggests that the foreign spectator
       might have been mistaken in his description, and that the
       "eight partitions" cited by Hotson might well have provided
       the usual tiring house facade.

8 FLETCHER, IFAN KYRLE. "Italian Comedians in England in the
       Seventeenth Century." TN 8 (July):86-91.
           Covers the period 1620-1700. The only visit recorded
       prior to 1642 was that of Francis Nicolini, 18 February
       1630.

9 FOAKES, R. A. "The Player's Passion: Some Notes on Eliza-
       bethan Psychology and Acting." E&S, n.s. 7:62-77.
           Steers a middle course through the seas of "natural"
       and "formal" acting styles, advocating "a range of acting
       capable of greater extremes of passion, of much action
       which would now seem forced or grotesque, but realistic
       within a framework of 'reality' that coincides to a large
       extent with ours." Foakes bases his discussion on Eliza-
       bethan psychology. See also Index under Acting--Style.

1954

10 GREG, W[ALTER] W[ILSON]. "Twelfth Night." TLS (31 December):
    853.
        Points out in a letter to the editor that 1599/1600 was
    a leap year, not 1600/01 as Hotson says in 1954.14.

11 HODGES, C[YRIL] WALTER. "New Light on Old Playhouses: Notes
    on Some Research by Richard Southern and Leslie Hotson."
    ShStage, no. 5 (June):41-44.
        Discusses Southern's model of an Elizabethan playhouse
    (1954.26) and Hotson's discovery of an engraving showing
    the Curtain Playhouse and its external staircases (1954.15).

12 HOPPE, HARRY R. "George Jolly at Bruges, 1648." RES n.s. 5
    (July):265-68.
        A brief note revealing further evidence of Jolly's
    pre-Restoration continental touring.

13 HOSLEY, RICHARD. "The Use of the Upper Stage in Romeo and
    Juliet." SQ 5 (Autumn):371-79.
        A paper read at the Southeastern Renaissance Conference
    at Duke University, April 1954. Hosley argues that the two
    balcony scenes (II.ii. and III.v. 1-68) were played on
    the upper level. He suggests that three other scenes
    (III.v. 69-242; IV.iii; IV.v.) sometimes thought to be
    played in this area were played on the platform.

14 HOTSON, [JOHN] LESLIE. The First Night of Twelfth Night.
    London: Rupert Hart-Davis, 256 pp.
        An attempt at a reconstruction of the first performance
    of Shakespeare's comedy at Whitehall, 6 January 1600/01.
    Central to this discussion is the third chapter, "Shake-
    speare's Arena Stage," which parallels Hotson's other
    arguments about the four-sided nature of Elizabethan
    staging, with mansions scattered about the stage serving
    for doors, areas above, and discovery spaces (see 1953.11;
    1959.9). Hotson also prints three documents, in Italian
    and German, that help lead him to his conclusions.

15 ____. "'This Wooden O': Shakespeare's Curtain Theatre
    Identified." Times (London), 26 March, pp. 7, 14.
        Announces the discovery of an engraving of a view of
    London that shows the Curtain playhouse. As was the Swan
    drawing, the engraving was found in the Library of the
    University of Utrecht. Hotson prints the engraving, with
    an enlargement of the area containing the playhouse, along
    with two photographs of Southern's model of an Elizabethan
    public theatre. See 1954.26.

16 MATTINGLY, ALTHEA SMITH. "The Playing Time and Manner of
    Delivery of Shakespeare's Plays in the Elizabethan Theatre."
    SpMon 21 (March):29-38.
        Examines the texts of plays for evidence to support the
    "two hours traffic of our stage" and other similar state-
    ments about playing time. Line count is one indication;
    another is audience expectation. Mattingly examines both
    in detail, as well as what she calls "efficient elocution"
    and the possibility of cutting for performance. She con-
    cludes that the plays were normally cut to 2300 lines, and
    that a rate more rapid than that used in the modern theatre
    was employed. See also 1932.5-6; 1933.3.

17 McCABE, JOHN CHARLES. "A Study of the Blackfriars Theatre,
    1608-1642." Ph.D. dissertation, University of Birmingham,
    330 pp.
        Attempts to bring together the facts fundamental to a
    thorough knowledge of the Blackfriars Playhouse from 1608
    to 1642. The eight chapters examine the history of the
    theatre under the child companies and the King's Men; the
    plays presented there; the dimensions of the playhouse;
    the main platform and the tiring house facade; the use of
    large and small properties and scenic units; the use of
    costume, music, song, dance, and lighting; the audience of
    the theatre; and the staging of a typical Blackfriars play
    by the King's Men. McCabe concludes that the Farrar-Martin
    conjecture of the interior of the Blackfriars (see 1921.5)
    is substantially correct--with a platform stage the full
    width of a rectangular hall; a curtained recess or "inner
    stage," the curtain of which is split in the middle; two
    obliquely set side doors; an upper curtained stage level,
    complete with two angled window stages; and two rows of
    galleries. McCabe places the theatre in a conjectural
    "middle" story of the building rather than in the Parlia-
    ment Chamber on the top floor. See also Index under
    Blackfriars Playhouse--Reconstructions.

18 MILES, BERNARD. "Elizabethan Acting." TLS (2 April):217.
        Cites a bill addressed to Cardinal Wolsey now held in
    the Public Record Office to confirm Joseph's assertion (in
    1951.18) that Elizabethan acting was founded on the art of
    rhetoric and thus was formal in style.

19 MONTGOMERY, ROY F. "A Fair House Built on Another Man's
    Ground." SQ 5 (Spring):207-8.
        Identifies an allusion in Merry Wives of Windsor to the
    situation of the Theatre in 1598, "a fair house built on
    another man's ground."

1954

20 ROBERTSON, JEAN, and GORDON, D. J. "A Calendar of Dramatic
    Records in the Books of the Livery Companies of London
    1485-1640." MSC 3:37-204.
        The relevant section covers the Lord Mayor's Shows from
    1535 to 1640 and miscellaneous records from 1485 to 1639.
    The contributions of ten of the twelve "Great" Livery
    Companies are calendared, the records of the other two
    having been destroyed in the Great Fire of 1666.

21 ROSENBERG, MARVIN. "Elizabethan Actors: Men or Marionettes?"
    PMLA 69 (September):915-27.
        An attack on the "formalist" school of Elizabethan acting
    in favor of the "naturalist" school. See also Index under
    Acting--Style. Reprinted: 1968.3.

22 _____. "Public Night Performances in Shakespeare's Time."
    TN 8 (April):44-45.
        A brief note, drawing attention to evidence for night
    performances in Heywood's Apology for Actors. See also
    Lawrence (1912.16; 1915.15) and Graves (1913.7; 1917.6).

23 ROSENFELD, SYBIL. "Dramatic Companies in the Provinces in the
    Sixteenth and Seventeenth Centuries." TN 8 (April):55-58.
        Summaries of some players' visits to seven provincial
    towns not noted in Murray (1910.15), Chambers (1923.2), or
    Bentley (1941.1).

24 SAUNDERS, J. W. "Vaulting the Rails." ShS 7:69-81.
        Examines the evidence for movement of actors from the
    platform into the yard and back (as in medieval plays).
    The monument scene in Antony and Cleopatra would be
    simplified to the hoisting of the body from the yard to
    the stage. Other similar uses would be made of these two
    areas in Pericles (the barge); Romeo and Juliet (the orchard
    wall); 1 Henry IV (Orleans); Coriolanus (the trenches);
    and others.

25 SISSON, CHARLES J[ASPER]. "The Red Bull Company and the
    Importunate Widow." ShS 7:57-68.
        Discusses the depositions in the Chancery suit of Worth
    v. Baskervile, discovered by Sisson in the Public Record
    Office. The witnesses were almost all members of the Red
    Bull company, and their testimony reveals a number of
    important biographical and theatrical details. The
    "Importunate Widow" of the title is Susan Browne Baskervile,
    widow first of Robert Browne of the Boar's Head and later
    of Thomas Greene of the Red Bull. She was responsible,

with James Baskervile, her third husband, for the tangle
of litigation that tied up Queen Anne's Men for many years.

26 SOUTHERN, RICHARD. "An Elizabethan Playhouse: A New Model
    Reconstruction." Britain Today 216 (April):28-31.
        Describes the model of a generalized Elizabethan play-
    house he made in 1954, with photographs. The model is
    sixteen-sided, with a tiring house facade based on the
    Swan drawing, with hangings added between the two doors.

27 TRACE, ARTHUR STORREY, Jr. "The Continuity of Opposition to
    the Theater in England from Gosson to Collier." Ph.D.
    dissertation, Stanford University, 376 pp.
        Examines opponents of the stage such as Gosson, Stubbes,
    Rainolds, and Prynne, and links their arguments both with
    earlier arguments of the Church Fathers and with the later
    arguments of Collier and his Anglican allies. See also
    Index under Puritan Opposition to the Stage.

1955

1 BRILEY, JOHN. "Of Stake and Stage." ShS 8:106-8.
        A brief note presenting Alleyn's Petition to Lord
    Cranfield (1622) and An Account of Expenses at the Bear-
    Garden, 1615-1621, both bearing on the economics of animal
    baiting.

2 BYRNE, M[URIEL] St. CLARE. "Twelfth Night 'In the Round.'"
    TN 9 (January):46-52.
        Discusses 1954.14 and its arena staging concept. Byrne
    disagrees with Hotson's interpretation of key passages,
    but finds "the preliminary research . . . outstanding."

3 CUTTS, JOHN P. "Some Jacobean and Caroline Dramatic Lyrics."
    N&Q, n.s. 2 (March):106-9.
        Points out how the study of musical settings of dramatic
    lyrics can enhance the study of the lyrics alone. As
    examples Cutts cites extant music for songs from The Rival
    Friends, Duchess of Malfi, The Tragedy of Brennorald, and
    Wild Goose Chase.

4 EMPSON, WILLIAM. "The Elizabethan Stage." Literary Guide
    70 (March):12-14.
        "To keep to the essentials, [Shakespeare] had an inner
    stage and a balcony, both with curtains to open and shut,
    but did most of the acting on an apron-stage." Empson
    also argues for the alternation theory, and he dismisses

the Swan as pictured by DeWitt as "a speculation . . . which
soon failed." His main thrust is toward the importance of
the balcony, and he is prepared to prove that "both the
blinding of Gloucester and the scolding by Hamlet of his
mother in her bedroom" were staged there, although he offers
no evidence for either contention here.

5 FUSILLO, ROBERT JAMES. "Tents on Bosworth Field." SQ 6
   (Spring):193-94.
       A brief note suggesting that no physical tents need
   be present on stage in Act V of Richard III, but that doorways were localized by entrance and exit to serve as tents.
   The multiple staging of the mysteries and at court are
   offered as precedent.

*6 GERSTNER-HIRZEL, ARTHUR. "The Economy of Action and Word in
    Shakespeare's Plays." Ph.D. dissertation, University of
    Basel.
        Abstracted in 1955.7.

7 _____. "Stagecraft and Poetry." JDSG 91:196-211.
       Abstract of 1955.6. Gerstner-Hirzel is concerned with
   the gestures implied in Shakespeare's lines, and he draws
   examples from several plays. He finds the histories have
   an average of 23 gestures per 1000 lines; the comedies, 40;
   the tragedies, 55; and the romances, 45.

8 HOPPE, HARRY R. "English Acting Companies at the Court of
   Brussels in the Seventeenth Century." RES, n.s. 6
   (January):26-33.
       Based on three surviving account books of the royal
   court at Brussels, covering entertainment from 1612 to
   1618 and 1647 to 1652. Hoppe reveals some new information
   on English actors on the continent and their itineraries.

9 HOTSON, [JOHN] LESLIE. "The Elizabethan Stage." TLS
   (7 January):9.
       Announces that he is working on a book on the subject
   of "Shakespeare's Arena." See 1953.11; 1959.9.

10 _____. The First Night of Twelfth Night. London: Rupert
    Hart-Davis, 256 pp.
        Reprint of 1954.14.

11 INGRAM, REGINALD WILLIAM. "Dramatic Use of Music in English
    Drama, 1603-1640." Ph.D. dissertation, University of
    London, 373 pp.
        Discusses music in the theatre in terms of instrumenta-
    tion; musicians and composers; theatrical connections;
    special use of music in the private theatres (with par-
    ticular reference to Marston); the tendency to use music
    for emotional effects in Shakespeare and Fletcher; and
    the use of songs and dances outside of masques. Three
    appendixes include discussions of the use of entre-act
    music; music at the Globe and Blackfriars after 1608; and
    a listing of dances used, song tunes performed, and
    instruments used. Ingram concludes by tracing three
    stages in the development of the dramatic use of music.

12 JOSEPH, BERTRAM. "The Elizabethan Stage and Acting." In
    The Age of Shakespeare. Edited by Boris Ford. Pelican
    Guide to English Literature, no. 2. Aylesbury and London:
    Pelican Books, pp. 147-61.
        An exploration of audience expectations and how the actors
    met them, arguing for a formal acting style. Joseph
    includes a very brief summary of theories of the Elizabethan
    stage. Reprinted: 1956.19; 1961.15; 1962.10; 1975.19.

13 _____. "The Elizabethan Stage and the Art of Elizabethan
    Drama." JDSG 91:145-60.
        Argues that the conventions of the original performance
    must be understood if we are to understand the drama.
    Specifically, Joseph discusses the use of conventional
    gesture in modern productions of Shakespeare.

14 LANGER, LAWRENCE. "Letter to the Editor." ShN 5 (April):11.
        Responds to Hotson in 1954.14, suggesting that Shake-
    speare could not have written the play in a few days,
    that with the Queen in the audience true arena staging would
    not have been possible, and that Orsino's name could have
    been a late change to flatter the real Orsino.

*15 MÜLLER-BELLINGHAUSEN, ANTON. "Die Wortkulisse bei Shake-
    speare." Ph.D. dissertation, University of Freiburg,
    327 pp.
        Partially published: 1955.16.

16 _____. "Die Wortkulisse bei Shakespeare." JDSG 91:182-95.
        Partial publication of 1955.15. Müller-Bellinghausen
    examines Shakespeare's use of words to set the scene and
    his representation of the verbal scene on the actual stage.

1955

*17 NORBERG, LARS. "Shakespearetidens Teater." <u>Borås Tidning</u>
29:10-?
Cited in 1963.14; the title of this Danish publication
translates as "Theatre of Shakespeare's Time."

18 POKORNÝ, JAROSLAV. <u>Shakespearova doba a divadlo</u> [Shakespeare's
Time and Theatre]. Prague: Orbis, 199 pp.
A general discussion of the period, with particular
emphasis on the Globe and the Chamberlain's/King's Men.
In Slovak.

19 RACE, SIDNEY. "The First Night of <u>Twelfth Night</u>." N&Q, n.s.
2 (February):52-55.
Responds to Hotson (1954.14), questioning many of his
conclusions.

20 ROSENFELD, SYBIL M. <u>Foreign Theatrical Companies in Great
Britain in the 17th and 18th Centuries</u>. Pamplet no. 4.
London: Society for Theatre Research, p. 1.
A chronological listing of the visits of foreign
companies. Only four are listed prior to the Restoration;
a French group in 1629; an Italian company in 1630; and
French and Spanish organizations in 1635. Reprinted:
1962.17.

21 ROTHWELL, WILLIAM F. "Decentralized Staging." <u>ShN</u> 5
(April):11.
Responds to Hotson's theory of arena staging (1953.11),
suggesting that a variety of different actor-audience
relationships might have been used at different times.

22 SAUNDERS, J. W. "The Elizabethan Theatre." <u>TLS</u> (11
November):680.
Responds to Hotson (1953.11) and his conjectures about
arena staging in the Elizabethan theatre.

23 [SMET, ROBERT de.] <u>Le théâtre élizabéthain</u>. Collections
Lebèque & Nationale, no. 114. Brussels: Office de
Publicité, pp. 7-23.
Written under the pseudonym Romain Sanvic. The relevant
section is the first chapter, which discusses the Elizabethan theatre in general terms. Smet discusses public
and private playhouses and methods of presentations. The
remainder of the volume concentrates on literary matters,
despite the title.

24 STAMM, RUDOLF. "Dramenforschung." <u>JDSG</u> 91:121-35.
Differentiates between literary and theatrical research.

25 SUMMERSON, JOHN [NEWENHAM]. <u>Architecture in Britain, 1530-</u>
    <u>1830</u>. 2d ed. Pelican History of Art, no. Z3. Harmonds-
    worth: Penguin Books, pp. 61-67.
          Reprint of 1953.26.

26 WHITE, ANNE TERRY. <u>Will Shakespeare and the Globe Theatre</u>.
    Illustrated by C[yril] Walter Hodges. Eau Claire,
    Wisconsin: E. M. Hale; New York: Random House, 182 pp.
          A juvenile treatment, strongly romanticized and of
    little historical value. Hodges's illustrations are
    interesting, but do not compare with those in 1964.15, his
    more sophisticated juvenile work.

27 WILSON, F[RANK] P[ERCY]. "Court Payments for Plays: 1610-
    1611, 1612-1613, 1616-1617." <u>BLR</u> 5 (October):217-21.
          Minor corrections to Chambers (1923.2) and Bentley
    (1941.1) from the Rawlinson Manuscripts held in the
    Bodleian Library. Wilson cites six entries from the
    manuscripts.

28 _____. "The Elizabethan Theatre." <u>Neophil</u> 39 (Winter):40-58.
          Originally a lecture at the University of Amsterdam.
    Wilson begins with a discussion of some theatres of the
    period, then considers problems of staging, and concludes
    with notes on audiences and acting. The original form
    dictated a general rather than specific work. Reprinted:
    1955.29.

29 _____. <u>The Elizabethan Theatre</u>. Groningen: J. B. Wolters,
    21 pp.
          Reprint of 1955.28.

1956

1   ADAMS, JOHN CRANFORD. "Shakespeare's Use of the Upper Stage
    in <u>Romeo and Juliet</u>, III.v." <u>SQ</u> 7 (Spring):145-52.
          Responds to Hosley (1954.13), arguing for the use of
    window stages and a curtained upper stage for the second
    balcony scene.

*2 ANON. <u>The Site of the Office of the Times, 1276-1956</u>. London:
    privately printed.
          Cited in 1963.14. The Blackfriars Playhouse was built
    on this site.

3   BECKERMAN, BERNARD. "The Production of Shakespeare's Plays at
    the Globe Playhouse, 1599-1609." Ph.D. dissertation,
    Columbia University, 468 pp.
       Published as 1962.2.

4   BENTLEY, GERALD EADES. The Jacobean and Caroline Stage. Vols.
    3-5. Oxford: Clarendon Press, 1456 pp.
       A continuation of 1941.1, concluded in 1968.2. These
    volumes examine plays and playwrights, and Bentley tries
    to include "all plays, masques, shows, and dramatic enter-
    tainments which were written between 1616 . . . and the
    closing of the theatres in 1642." Playwrights are listed
    in alphabetical order, with anonymous plays considered at
    the end of volume 5. A brief bibliography and a biography
    for each writer precedes the consideration of the plays,
    also in alphabetical order under each playwright. For
    each play Bentley gives the date of first production, the
    dates of all editions, and a chronological listing of all
    relevant seventeenth-century records. Bentley sees his
    primary task as "the setting of these plays in their
    theatrical context."

5   BLAND, D. S. "The Barriers: Guildhall Library MS 4160."
    GuildMisc 1, no. 6 (February):7-14.
       An edition of the manuscript of the text of the
    "barriers" performed at the ceremony creating Arthur Prince
    of Wales, 4 November 1604. "Barriers" is a formal combat,
    on foot, between contestants who fight across a horizontal
    pole (the "barrier") hung with decorated cloths. It "lies
    on the very frontier of literature and the theatre," since
    it combines elements of the joust and the masque.

6   BORDINAT, PHILIP. "A New Site for the Salisbury Court
    Theatre." N&Q, n.s. 3 (February):51-52.
       From 1952.2. Bordinat challenges Bell's location of
    the playhouse (in 1912.7) by reference to the indenture
    relative to the leasing of the property in 1629 and two
    seventeenth-century maps. He locates the theatre in Water
    Lane (now Whitefriars Street), just south of Tudor Street.
    See also Brownstein, 1977.3.

7   CARTER, JOEL JACKSON. "English Dramatic Music to the
    Seventeenth Century and Its Availability for Modern
    Production." Ph.D. dissertation, Stanford University,
    565 pp.
       Discusses the origins and development of the varying
    types of dramatic music in England before Shakespeare.
    The role of music in the development of Elizabethan drama,

in particular, is seen as important. Eighteen illustrative
examples of dramatic music from before 1600 are reproduced.

8 CUTTS, JOHN P. "An Unpublished Contemporary Setting of a
   Shakespeare Song." ShS 9:86-89.
      Music, probably composed by Robert Johnson, for a song
   in Winter's Tale ("Get you hence, for I must go"), preserved
   in a manuscript held in the New York Public Library. From
   another manuscript an incomplete setting (scored for bass
   and two trebles) provides a previously unknown second
   verse.

9 _____. "Le rôle de la musique dans les masques de Ben Jonson
   et notament dans Oberon (1610-1611)." In Les fêtes de la
   Renaissance. Vol. 1. Edited by Jean Jacquot. Paris:
   CNRS, pp. 285-303.
      Examines music in Jonson's Masque of Queenes (1609/10)
   and Oberon (1610/11). Cutts discusses the payment of
   the musicians and the composition of the music, as well as
   the structure of the masques. He also prints music by
   Robert Johnson and Alfonso Ferrabosco. Reprinted: 1973.2.

10 DODDS, MADELAIN HOPE. "The First Night of Twelfth Night."
    N&Q, n.s. 3 (February):57-59.
       Examines the manuscript on which Hotson based his book
    (1954.14), questioning several of his conclusions.

11 FELVER, CHARLES STANLEY. "William Shakespeare and Robert
    Armin His Fool: A Working Partnership." Ph.D. disserta-
    tion, University of Michigan, 352 pp.
       Examines the extent to which Shakespeare's fools were
    influenced by the writings and comic line of Armin.
    Felver suggests that Shakespeare drew heavily on Armin's
    works in creating an essentially new comic character;
    that the motley coat as costume was a joint development;
    and that a good deal of Shakespeare's fool-lore, including
    the name Touchstone, came from Armin's work. Partially
    published: 1961.10.

12 GORDON, D. J. "Le Masque Mémorable de Chapman." In Les fêtes
    de la Renaissance. Vol. 1. Edited by Jean Jacquot.
    Paris: CNRS, pp. 305-17.
       Discusses the masque Chapman composed for the marriage
    of Elisabeth, only daughter of James I, from a literary
    point of view. Reprinted: 1973.8.

1956

13 GREG, W[ALTER] W[ILSON]. "Fragments from Henslowe's Diary."
    MSC 4:27-32.
        Facsimiles of five pieces removed from the diary,
    containing various signatures, with commentary. See also
    1938.5; 1940.1.

14 HARRISON, G[EORGE] B[AGSHAWE]. Elizabethan Plays and Players.
    Ann Arbor: University of Michigan Press, Ann Arbor Books,
    309 pp.
        Includes parts of 1923.14, greatly expanded. Harrison
    follows a roughly chronological path, going from the
    building of the Theatre and the influence of Lyly to
    separate chapters examining the Lord Admiral's Men, the
    Lord Chamberlain's Men, the Globe, the boy players, and
    the war of the theatres.

15 HOLMES, MARTIN. "A New Theory about the Swan Drawing." TN
    10 (April):80-83.
        Suggests that the drawing represents a rehearsal, with
    actors and not audience members shown in the upper stage.

16 HOSLEY, RICHARD. "More about 'Tents' on Bosworth Field." SQ
    7 (Summer):458-59.
        Comments on Fusillo's suggestion (1955.5) that the tents
    in Richard III might have been represented by the stage
    doors, and draws attention to a similar possibility in
    3 Henry VI.

17 JACQUOT, JEAN, ed. Les fêtes de la Renaissance. Vol. 1.
    Paris: CNRS, pp. 259-317.
        The relevant section contains essays dealing with
    English pageants and masques. Includes 1956.9, 12, 28,
    33-34. Reprinted: 1973.13.

18 JEWKES, WILFRED THOMAS. "Act Division in Elizabethan Plays,
    1583-1616." Ph.D. dissertation, University of Wisconsin,
    387 pp.
        Published: 1958.12.

19 JOSEPH, BERTRAM. "The Elizabethan Stage and Acting." In The
    Age of Shakespeare. Edited by Boris Ford. A Guide to
    English Literature, no. 2. Harmondsworth: Penguin Books,
    pp. 147-61.
        Reprint of 1955.12.

20 KLEIN, DAVID. "Elizabethan Acting." PMLA 71 (March):280-82.
        A brief note, with additional examples supporting
    Rosenberg's argument in 1954.21.

21 LAIRD, DAVID CONNOR. "The Inserted Masque in Elizabethan and
    Jacobean Drama." Ph.D. dissertation, University of
    Wisconsin, 196 pp.
        Primarily a literary study. The only theatrical element
    examined (and that briefly) is the spectacular, or scenic.
    Laird claims that inserted entertainment were used in the
    tragedies of the Inns of Court and the public theatres,
    and in early romantic comedy "to bring to drama the scenic
    display of rival court masques and disguisings."

22 LANE, ROBERT P[HILLIPS]. "A Study of the Repertory of Queen
    Elizabeth's Company, 1583-1593." Ph.D. dissertation,
    University of North Carolina, 326 pp.
        Examines, in five chapters, the personnel of the company,
    the plays of Robert Wilson, chronicle plays in the repertory,
    the plays of Robert Greene, and three miscellaneous plays
    of the repertory. Lane concludes that there is no over-
    riding thematic statement the plays as a group make, that
    there was no structural complexity, but that there was a
    major contribution made to the development of comedy by
    this company.

23 MANIFOLD, JOHN STREETER. The Music in English Drama from
    Shakespeare to Purcell. London: Rockliff, pp. 2-105.
        The relevant section is the first nine chapters, deal-
    ing with music in Shakespeare's theatre. Manifold examines
    the plays of the period for uses of music, instruments
    called for, and effects of music.

24 MERCHANT, W[ILLIAM] M[OELWYN]. "Visual Elements in Shake-
    speare Studies." JDSG 92:280-90.
        Argues that the visual history of Shakespearean produc-
    tion influences our reading of the plays.

25 NAGLER, A[LOIS] M. "Shakespeare's Arena Demolished." ShN 6
    (February):7.
        Briefly replied to Hotson's claims in 1954.14 that
    Twelfth Night was played in the round by citing another
    Italian source that uses similar language to mean that
    the audience was on three sides instead of four.

26 PALME, PER. Triumph of Peace: A Study of the Whitehall
    Banqueting House. Stockholm: Almqvist & Wiksell, 328 pp.
        Published version of an Uppsala Ph.D. dissertation.
    Palme examines Inigo Jones's banqueting house in Whitehall.
    He begins with a simple chronicle of events, proceeds to
    the use of the hall for banquets, masques, and otherwise,
    and then embarks on a conjectural reconstruction, beginning

1956

with the present building and moving backwards to Jones's
preliminary plan, held in the Worcester College, Oxford,
library. Reprinted: 1957.12.

27 REYNOLDS, GEORGE F[ULLMER]. "Hamlet at the Globe." ShS
9:49-53.
Discusses changing perceptions of the original staging
of Hamlet, with special concern for the use of the so-
called "inner stage." Reynolds sets up a possible staging
scheme that requires only a small curtained space and the
bringing on and off of stage properties as needed.

28 ROBERTSON, JEAN. "Rapports de poète et de l'artiste dans la
préparation des cortèges du Lord Maire (Londres 1553-1640)."
In Les fêtes de la Renaissance. Vol. 1. Edited by Jean
Jacquot. Paris: CNRS, pp. 265-78.
Examines the Lord Mayor's pageants, based on the archives
and printed booklets of the corporations of the City of
London. Robertson focuses on the relationships between
modeller, carver, composer, artist, dyer, poet, and
architect, especially payments (both single and group).
Middleton, Jonson, Munday, and Jones are singled out.
Robertson, Jacquot, Yates, and others discuss the ambiguity
of Elizabethan technical vocabulary in a brief postscript.
Reprinted: 1973.22.

29 SCHANZER, ERNEST. "Thomas Platter's Observations on the
Elizabethan Stage." N&Q, n.s. 3 (November):465-67.
Literal translations of Platter's comments on the stage,
with commentary. Chambers's translation in 1923.2 is
unreliable, and Williams's standard edition (1937.9) is
"somewhat freer than seems needful in view of the minute
scrutiny these few passages will continue to receive."

30 SCHNEIDERMAN, ROBERT IVAN. "Elizabethan Legerdemain, and Its
Employment in the Drama, 1576-1642." Ph.D. dissertation,
Northwestern University, 274 pp.
Attempts to give a clear picture of the legerdemain of
the period--its potential value to the playwright, its
psychological bases, its relation to physical staging--and
an exposé of its methods. Specific effects Schneiderman
discusses include appearances, disappearances, levitation,
and scenes of violence involving mutilation. Since
principles of legerdemain have not changed considerably
since the Elizabethan period, their methods are often
effective in modern productions.

31 SMITH, IRWIN. "'Gates' on Shakespeare's Stage." SQ 7
    (Spring):159-76.
        Examines gate scenes in several Shakespeare plays,
    arguing for the existence of property gates set up in the
    inner stage.

32 _____. Shakespeare's Globe Playhouse: A Modern Reconstruction
    in Text and Line Drawings. New York: Charles Scribner's
    Sons, 240 pp.
        Based on the J. C. Adams reconstruction of the Globe
    (1942.1), this work contains photographs of the model that
    Smith and Adams built and detailed drawings based on that
    model. The first thirteen chapters discuss Adams's
    reconstruction in detail, examining some of his evidence,
    with a few minor modifications. The final chapter contains
    fifteen scale drawings. Smith's only personal contribution
    (aside from the drawings) is the use of material drawn from
    his study of Tudor construction (see 1952.18).

33 STEVENS, DENIS. "Pièces de théâtre et 'pageants' a l'epoque
    des Tudor." In Les fêtes de la Renaissance. Vol. 1.
    Edited by Jean Jacquot. Paris: CNRS, pp. 259-64.
        Examines the role of music in plays, masques, and
    other pageantry, especially the work of composers William
    Cornish and John Redford. Primarily concerned with the
    reign of Henry VIII. Reprinted: 1973.29.

34 WICKHAM, GLYNNE. "Contribution de Ben Jonson et de Dekker
    aux fêtes du couronment de Jacques Ier." In Les fêtes de
    la Renaissance. Vol. 1. Edited by Jean Jacquot. Paris:
    CNRS, pp. 279-83.
        Examines Jonson's, Dekker's, and Middleton's contribu-
    tions to James's royal entry into London for his corona-
    tion. Seven tableaux or pageants, much more uniform than
    earlier ones, covered the entire length of the city, from
    London Bridge to Temple Bar. Dekker apparently was in
    overall control, and he and Webster composed odes while
    Jonson and Middleton wrote the tableaux scenarii. During
    the postponement because of the plague, costs nearly
    doubled from the estimated £400 to £784. Reprinted:
    1973.32.

35 WILSON, F[RANK] P[ERCY]. "More Records from the Remembrancia
    of the City of London." MSC 4:55-65.
        Additions to 1907.5, from 1613 to 1616, bearing on the
    Whitefriars and Rosseter's Porter's Hall.

1957

1 ARMSTRONG, WILLIAM A. "'Canopy' in Elizabethan Theatre
   Terminology." N&Q, n.s. 4 (October):433-34.
   Differentiates between the uses of "canopy" to mean a
   curtained discovery space and the awning covering a chair
   of state.

2 BRIDGES-ADAMS, W[ILLIAM]. The Irrestible Theatre. Vol. I,
   From the Conquest to the Commonwealth. London: Secker &
   Warburg; Cleveland: World Publishing Co., pp. 79-392.
   The section on the Elizabethan period in a comprehensive
   history of British theatre and drama. Bridges-Adams
   includes chapters on the Master of the Revels, the boy
   companies, the adult companies, the playhouses, the audience,
   acting styles, management, and the masque, as well as chapters on the major playwrights, the Puritan opposition to
   the stage, and types of drama.

3 CHALLEN, W. H. "Sir George Buck, Kt., Master of the Revels."
   N&Q, n.s. 4 (July):290-92.
   Adds a few non-theatrical details to the biography of
   the early seventeenth-century Master of the Revels.
   Continued in 1957.4.

4 _____. "Sir George Buck, Kt., Master of the Revels." N&Q,
   n.s. 4 (August):324-27.
   Continuation of 1957.3.

5 CUTTS, JOHN P. "Music for Shakespeare's Company, the King's
   Men." 2 vols. Ph.D. dissertation, University of Birming-
   ham.
   Published as 1959.4.

6 FLATTER, RICHARD. "Who Wrote the Hecate-Scene?" JDSG 93:196-
   210.
   Argues that Shakespeare, rather than Middleton, wrote
   the scene. This is the beginning of a controversy with
   Cutts. See also 1958.6; 1959.5; 1960.5, 7.

7 FLECKNOE, RICHARD. "A Short Discourse of the English Stage."
   In Critical Essays of the Seventeenth Century. Vol. 2.
   Edited by J. E. Spingarn. Bloomington: Indiana University
   Press, pp. 91-96.
   Reprint of 1664.1.

8 HOSLEY, RICHARD. "The Gallery over the Stage in the Public
   Playhouse of Shakespeare's Time." SQ 8 (Winter):15-31.
        Examines the pictorial evidence of the Swan drawing and
   the stage directions from a variety of plays to find out
   what they tell us about the acting area above. Hosley
   concludes that "the gallery over the stage in the public
   playhouse of Shakespeare's time functioned primarily as a
   Lord's room, and only secondarily . . . as a raised
   production area; and that during such periods it exercised
   both functions simultaneously."

9 _____. "Shakespeare's Use of a Gallery over the Stage." ShS
   10:77-89.
        Assumes that Shakespeare's plays were "designed for pro-
   duction in a theatre having a gallery over the stage
   essentially similar to the Lord's room shown in the Swan
   drawing," and then discusses how such an acting area would
   have been used. Eighteen of Shakespeare's plays make no
   use of such an area; an additional twelve use it only once.
   All together, Sahkespeare uses this space only thirty-five
   times in his plays. Generally, a secondary action aloft
   is introduced in support of an original action on the
   platform below. Hosley also examines and rejects J. C.
   Adams's assertions about the upper acting area's use as
   the location of interior above scenes.

10 KERR, S. PARNELL. "The Constable Kept an Account." N&Q, n.s.
    4 (April):167-70.
        Among the gifts lavished on the Court by the Spanish in
    1604 were "4780 reales" to "boatmen, musicians, and
    players. . . " Halliwell-Phillips claimed that the King's
    Men performed for the Spanish at Somerset House and that
    he had found a Royal Order for such a performance. Unfor-
    tunately, the Order is now lost, and the Constable's
    account book sheds little light on the matter.

11 MAIN, WILLIAM W. "Dramaturgical Norms in Elizabethan
    Repertory." SP 54 (April):128-48.
        Surveys the norms in plot structure in Elizabethan
    plays from 1598 to 1602. There is little here of theatrical
    interest, although this item is included in NCBEL 1, col.
    1395.

12 PALME, PER. Triumph of Peace: A Study of the Whitehall
    Banqueting House. London: Thames & Hudson, 328 pp.
        Reprint of 1957.26.

1957

13 PATTERSON, REMINGTON P[ERRIGO]. "Philip Henslowe and the
    Rose Theatre." Ph.D. dissertation, Yale University, 348 pp.
       Examines the life of Henslowe as theatrical landlord and
    manager and the history of his Rose Playhouse on the
    Bankside. Includes transcriptions of unpublished (at the
    time) manuscripts from the Dulwich collection as documenta-
    tion. No attempt is made to reconstruct the playhouse or
    to discuss methods of staging employed at the Rose. The
    Diary is used extensively, as are all of the Dulwich
    manuscripts.

14 ROSENFELD, SYBIL. "Unpublished Stage Documents." TN 11
    (April):92-96.
       Includes the Salisbury Court petition (c. 1652) of Eliza-
    beth Heton, William Wintersall, and William Jones that
    shows this playhouse was converted from a barn at a cost
    of £800.

15 TEAGARDEN, JACK E. "Reaction to the Professional Actor in
    Elizabethan London." Ph.D. dissertation, University of
    Florida, 189 pp.
       Examines polemics, apologetics, drama, and popular
    writing 1590-1640 in order to determine the social status
    of Elizabethan actors. In general, reaction was predict-
    able in terms of the individual bias of the reactor.
    Consequently, prose writers and playwrights used actors as
    characters to good effect.

16 WATSON, GEORGE, ed. The Cambridge Bibliography of English
    Literature. Vol. 5 Supplement: A. D. 600-1900. Cambridge:
    University Press, pp. 244-46.
       Supplement to 1940.2. All relevant items have been
    included in this bibliography. See also 1974.25.

*17 WILLIAMS, S. H. "The Lord Mayor's Shows from Peele to Settle:
    A Study of Literary Content, Organisation, and Methods of
    Production." Ph.D. dissertation, University of London.
    Cited in 1963.14.

1958

1   ARMSTRONG, W[ILLIAM] A. The Elizabethan Private Theatres:
    Facts and Problems. Pamphlet no. 6. London: Society for
    Theatre Research, 17 pp.
       Revised text of a paper read before the Society in March
    1957. Armstrong applies the principles used by Isaacs on
    the Blackfriars (see 1933.4) to the other private theatres.

He examines some 150 plays written for the private theatres
and published before the Restoration, but does not attempt
to limit the evidence to a particular theatre or to use
only texts dependent on prompt copy. He concludes that
"the general design of . . . [the private theatre] stage,
complete with platform, stage doors, inner stage, upper
stage, and windows, shows that it had obvious structural
affinities with open air theatres like the Globe." At the
same time, however, the "scenic methods [of the private
playhouses] were more various than those of any other
English theatre of the period." Armstrong cites simultaneous, fixed, successive, and movable painted scenery as
being used in the private theatres.

2 BERNHEIMER, RICHARD. "Another Globe Theatre." SQ 9
   (Spring):19-29.
       An examination of the theatre pictured in Fludd, also
   examined by Yates (1966.28, 1967.17) and Shapiro (1966.20).
   Bernheimer describes the building and suggests that it was
   a remodelled tennis court, standing in Germany and providing space for touring English actors.

3 BOLTON, JANET. "A Historical Study of English Theories and
   Precepts of Vocal and Gestural Expressiveness from Stephen
   Hawes to John Bulwer: 1509-1644." Ph.D. dissertation,
   University of Southern California, 401 pp.
       Examines characteristic English Renaissance theories
   and precepts of pronunciation relevant to the acting of
   the period. Bolton discusses descriptions of the speech
   mechanism in Elizabethan scientific literature, the psychology of humours, physiognomy, grammars and prosodies,
   literary and dramatic criticism, pulpit delivery, and
   rhetoric, concluding that "standards of vocal and gestural
   communication are established by contemporary social ideals."
   The same might be said of the relative naturalness of
   acting, although Bolton does not make the connection.

4 BRETT-EVANS, DAVID. "Der Sommernachstraum in Deutschland
   1600-1650." ZDP 77:317-83.
       Discusses German adaptations of Midsummer Night's Dream
   during the first half of the seventeenth century, including
   performances by English players.

5 BRILEY, JOHN. "Edward Alleyn and Henslowe's Will." SQ 9
   (Autumn):321-30.
       Sheds much additional light on the issue of the division
   of Henslowe's property through revealing the contents of
   newly discovered court documents. In all there were seven

1958

cases in three courts concerning Henslowe's widow, his
nephew, and Edward Alleyn (his son-in-law), and all were
not settled until the three principals were dead. Briley
finds the estate to have been larger, and that it was shared
much more widely, than have previously been supposed.

6 CUTTS, JOHN P. "Who Wrote the Hecate-Scene?" JDSG 94:200-202.
Responds to Flatter (1957.6), arguing that Middleton may
have written the scene since two of his songs are included
in the First Folio version of Macbeth. Cutts agrees with
Lawrence (1920.20) that three additional witches were introduced to sing and dance. See also the rest of the controversy: 1959.5; 1960.5, 7.

7 ECCLES, MARK. "Martin Peerson and the Blackfriars." ShS 11:
100-106.
Examines Peerson's role as sharer in the Revels company
during the early Jacobean period, with information drawn
from various suits held in the Public Record Office.
Peerson, who was a musician, might have composed music for
the company or trained the boys' voices.

8 ELLIS-FERMOR, UNA M. "The Jacobean Stage." In The Jacobean
Drama: An Interpretation. 4th ed. London: Methuen,
pp. 273-83.
Reprint of 1936.8.

9 FEIL, J. P. "Dramatic References from the Scudemore Papers."
ShS 11:107-16.
Cites all dramatic references from the family papers of
the Scudemores of Hereford from 1610 to 1638. A total of
fourteen plays and masques are mentioned, all but one of
which were performed. Five performances were attended by
the Queen and one by the King.

10 GOLDSTEIN, LEONARD. "On the Transition from Formal to
Naturalistic Acting in the Elizabethan and Post-Elizabethan
Theatre." BNYPL 62 (July):330-49.
Examines the social and cultural conditions of the
period and their relevance to the drama and acting.
Goldstein argues that "the drama down to the time of
Shakespeare was . . . essentially didactic" and that "the
acting consonant with this type of drama was formal."
There was a gradual change, however, and by the Jacobean
period "the destructive individualism of the Court emerged.
Here the isolated individual was representative and the
acting depicted the disintegration of that individual. The
acting became psychological and that meant naturalistic."
See also Index under Acting--Style.

11 HOSLEY, RICHARD. "An Elizabethan Tiring-House Facade." SQ
    9 (Autumn):588.
       A brief note with a photograph of a setting designed
    by Richard Southern for the 1958 season of the Bankside
    Players. There is a practicable Lord's room above and two
    sets of double doors flanking a nine foot wide "inner
    stage" below.

12 JEWKES, WILFRED THOMAS. Act Division in Elizabethan and
    Jacobean Plays, 1583-1616. Hamden, Conn.: Shoe String
    Press, 374 pp.
       Published version of 1956.12. Examines 237 plays
    written between 1583 and 1616, in first and other relevant
    editions, with an eye toward act divisions and reasons for
    them. The plays written for the private theatres were
    divided almost without exception. The plays of the
    university wits were also apparently divided, although
    division did not always survive the playhouse into print.
    The public theatre plays, 1590-1607, were apparently not
    divided, although this practice changed after 1607.

13 MITHAL, H. S. D. "'Will, My Lord of Leicester's Jesting
    Player.'" N&Q, n.s. 5 (October):427-29.
       Examines a reference in a letter of Sir Philip Sidney
    from Utrecht, 24 March 1586, suggesting that rather than
    Will Kempe, Robert Wilson might have been referred to. See
    Bruce (1844.1) for an earlier discussion; see also Bald
    (1959.3) for a response, and Mithal's rebuttal (1960.13).

14 NAGLER, A[LOIS] M. Shakespeare's Stage. Translated by Ralph
    Manheim. New Haven and London: Yale University Press,
    117 pp.
       Not an attempt to reconstruct the Globe or Blackfriars,
    which Nagler considers impossible, but rather to recon-
    struct an ideal type of Elizabethan theatre. Richly
    anecdotal, the study examines possibilities for all famil-
    iar elements of the stage: the doors, the platform, the
    discovery space, the upper stage, and the traps. Nagler
    imaginatively reconstructs the staging of Romeo and Juliet
    at the Globe and Tempest at Blackfriars, and he discusses
    costumes, management, and actors and acting, concluding with
    a composite portrait of a typical audience member.

15 PARROTT, THOMAS MARC, and BELL, ROBERT HAMILTON. A Short View
    of Elizabethan Drama, Together with Some Account of Its
    Principal Playwrights and the Conditions under Which It
    Was Produced. New York: Charles Scribner's Sons, pp. 45-62.
       Reprint of 1943.6, with an updated and expanded bib-
    liography.

1958

*16 QUINN, SEABURY GRANDIN, Jr. "Ideological Spectacle: Theories
     of Staging Methods." Ph.D. dissertation, Yale University,
     172 pp.
          Cited in 1963.14.

 17 RACE, SYDNEY. "Simon Forman's 'Bocke of Plaies' Examined."
     N&Q, n.s. 5 (January):9-14.
          Argues that the notes on Richard II, Winter's Tale,
     Cymbeline, and Macbeth are Collier forgeries.

 18 REESE, M. M. Shakespeare: His World and His Work. London:
     Edward Arnold & Co., pp. 97-344, 562-63.
          The relevant section is Part III, "The Elizabethan
     Stage." Reese devotes a chapter each to Elizabethan London,
     the theatres, the players, the plays and playwrights, and
     the audience, as well as an appendix to Shakespeare's
     company. He follows J. C. Adams (1942.1) in most details
     of playhouse reconstruction, and in fact uses secondary
     sources exclusively throughout. Abstracted in Hebrew in
     1965.13.

*19 RICKERT, ROBERT TURNHAM. "A Study of Henslowe's Diary."
     Ph.D. dissertation, University of Birmingham.
          Unlocatable. Cited in DEAL, p. 478. The only known
     copies are missing from the University of Birmingham
     Library and the Shakespeare Institute Library. See also
     Rickert and Foakes's edition of the diary (1961.13).

 20 RUSSELL, DOUGLAS A. "Shakespearean Costume: Contemporary
     or Fancy Dress." ETJ 10 (May):105-12.
          Discusses Elizabethan costume conventions in light of
     what is known of stage decoration and masque costuming.
     While of some historical interest, this piece is intended
     more for the modern costumer than the historian.

 21 SMITH, IRWIN. "Ariel as Ceres." SQ 9 (Autumn):430-32.
          Suggests that the masque was a late insertion into
     Tempest, and that the boy actor who played Ariel was forced
     to change costume and also undertake Ceres.

 22 SUMMERSON, JOHN [NEWENHAM]. Architecture in Britain, 1530-
     1830. 3d ed. Pelican History of Art, no. Z3. Harmonds-
     worth: Penguin Books, pp. 61-67.
          Reprint of 1953.26.

 23 TAYLOR, DICK, Jr. "The Masque and the Lance: The Earl of
     Pembroke in Jacobean Court Entertainments." Tulane Studies
     in English 8:21-53.

1959

Discusses the involvement in the court masques and tilting of William Herbert, third Earl of Pembroke, before he
became Lord Chamberlain in 1615. Pembroke was involved in
both the Jonson-Daniel and Jonson-Jones disputes. He
participated in the major masques of the early Jacobean
years but ended his participation upon taking up the
Chamberlain's staff.

24 WRIGHT, LOUIS B. Shakespeare's Theatre and the Dramatic
   Tradition. Washington: Folger Shakespeare Library, 36 pp.
     A brief pamphlet that treats the medieval antecedents
   of the Elizabethan theatre as well as the history of physical theatres in that period. Seventeen pages of plates
   are appended. Reprinted: 1961.28; 1963.22; 1966.26;
   1969.22; 1972.34; 1979.34.

                           1959

1 ALTON, R. E., ed. "The Academic Drama in Oxford: Extracts
   from the Records of Four Colleges." MSC 5:29-95.
     Records of expenses connected with dramatic entertain-
   ments between 1480 and 1650 at New College, Magdalen College, Christ Church, and St. John's College, with commentary.

2 ARMSTRONG, WILLIAM A. "The Audience of the Elizabethan
   Private Theatres." RES, n.s. 10 (July):234-49.
     Examines contemporary plays, poems, and pamphlets for
   information about the audience of the private theatres as
   a group from 1575 to 1642. Armstrong concludes that the
   audiences were mainly drawn form the parts of London
   adjacent to the playhouses, that the social constitution
   of the audience was like the Restoration audience rather
   than the public theatre audience, and that a certain level
   of decorum was maintained. Reprinted: 1968.3.

3 BALD, R[OBERT] C[ECIL]. "'Will, My Lord of Leicester's
   Jesting Player.'" N&Q, n.s. 6 (March):112.
     Responds to 1958.13, with the information (apparently
   unknown to Mithal) that Kempe was indeed with Sidney in
   November 1585, and that Wilson was as well. See Mithal's
   response, 1960.13.

1959

4   CUTTS, JOHN P. La musique de scène de la troupe de Shake-
      speare: The King's Men sous le règne de Jacques Ier.
      Paris: CNRS, 199 pp.
          Published version of 1957.5. Examines the music of
      eighty-eight plays of the King's Men in a critical intro-
      duction to an edition of over fifty stage songs and
      instrumental compositions. Cutts also considers music in
      interludes, postludes, and choruses, as well as the
      status of the actor-musician. He discusses the use of vocal
      and instrumental music on the stage in some detail, as well
      as the instrumentation required for the plays.

5   FLATTER, RICHARD. "Hecate, 'The Other Three Witches,' and
      Their Songs." JDSG 95:225-37.
          Responds to Cutts (1958.6), who had responded to his
      1957.6. Flatter here denies the existence of the second
      set of three witches, arguing that the First Folio stage
      direction which names them was simply an error. See also
      1960.5, 7.

6   GREG, WALTER W[ILSON]. "Copyright in Unauthorized Texts."
      In Elizabethan and Jacobean Studies Presented to Frank
      Percy Wilson in Honor of his Seventieth Birthday. Edited
      by Herbert Davis and Helen Gardner. Oxford: Clarendon
      Press, pp. 62-64.
          A brief note throwing light on one problem of non-
      dramatic publication copyright in 1631. Included because
      of listing in NCBEL 1, col. 1384.

7   HODGES, C[YRIL] WALTER. "The Lantern of Taste." ShS 12:8-14.
          Examines how changing tastes affect reconstructions of
      Elizabethan playhouses, using Tieck's and Godfrey's recon-
      structions of the Fortune as examples. Hodges discusses
      what he calls "antiquarian revival," "Timbered Cottage
      revival," "Cinema, the Experimental Movement and Flow of
      Action," and "an ornamental baroque reaction against former
      primitivism."

8   HOSLEY, RICHARD. "The Discovery Space in Shakespeare's
      Globe." ShS 12:35-46.
          Published version of a paper read at the International
      Shakespeare Conference at Stratford-upon-Avon, 20 September
      1957. Hosley proposes that discoveries at the first Globe
      were effected by opening a door or by drawing a curtain
      hung up in front of one of two or three doorways. He uses
      as evidence only those thirty plays definitely performed
      at this theatre from 1599 to 1608, when the King's Men
      began to use the Blackfriars. Only nine require discoveries,

and seven require only one each. The hangings often
referred to could be used to effect discoveries, Hosley
declares, "but discovery was not their chief raison
d'être." Reprinted: 1968.3.

9 HOTSON, [JOHN] LESLIE. Shakespeare's Wooden O. New York:
   Macmillan, 335 pp.
      A somewhat curious volume, following Hotson's 1954.14
   in ascribing arena (or in-the-round) production as the norm
   in Elizabethan staging. Hotson uses Middleton's A Game at
   Chess to describe his arena-Globe, with entrances made
   through traps into portable curtained booths set about the
   stage in the medieval manner. The basis for this conjecture
   is the uncontested arena staging employed in earlier
   pageants. Hotson closes by identifying the Fortune and the
   Curtain on a ca. 1600 map of London.

10 JOSEPH, BERTRAM. The Tragic Actor. London: Routledge &
    Kegan Paul; New York: Theatre Arts Books, pp. 1-27.
       The relevant section is the first chapter, "The Age of
    Shakespeare." Joseph reviews the natural/formal debate,
    reversing his previous position by coming down on a middle
    ground, concluding that "the style of the acting expressed
    the style of the work, eliciting in performance the essen-
    tial spirit of the play." He cites a variety of contempo-
    rary sources, especially as regards the rhetorical theory
    of the time, and he compares Burbage and Alleyn.

11 KERNODLE, GEORGE R. "The Open Stage: Elizabethan or
    Existential?" ShS 12:1-7.
       Argues that Shakespeare's stage "was not a blank open
    platform, on which a lonely soul was spotlighted in an
    empty, insubstantial universe." Rather, our open stage is
    a reflection of our age, as Shakespeare's was of his. "Let
    us not forget," says Kernodle, "that the open stage was once
    used as part of a vision of man's central place in a cosmos
    of dignity and order."

12 KINDERMANN, HEINZ. Theatergeschichte Europas. Vol. 3.
    Salzburg: Otto Müller, pp. 42-159.
       The relevant section of a comprehensive history.
    Kindermann discusses the playhouses, playwrights, actors,
    clowns, costumes, masques, government regulations, and
    audience of the period. He reviews various reconstructions
    of theatres, as well as the designs of Inigo Jones.

1959

13 KIRSCHBAUM, LEO. "The Copyright of Elizabethan Plays."
    Library, 5th ser. 14 (December):231-50.
        Originally a paper read before The Bibliographical
    Society, 15 October 1957. The copyright of an Elizabethan
    play belonged to the stationer, not the playwright, and a
    second license was required before publication.

14 LACY, ROBIN THURLOW. "An Encyclopedia of Scenographers,
    534 B.C. to 1900 A.D." Ph.D. dissertation, University of
    Denver, 267 pp.
        Entries are included on Robert Peake, William Lyzarde,
    Inigo Jones, Nicholas Lanier, and John Webb.

15 MERCHANT, W[ILLIAM] M[OELWYN]. Shakespeare and the Artist.
    London: Oxford University Press, pp. 1-19.
        The relevant section is the first chapter, "The Eliza-
    bethan Theatre and the Visual Arts." Merchant briefly
    summarizes the state of architectural scholarship, reprint-
    ing three of Hodges's plates (of the Theatre, the second
    Globe, and the Fortune).

16 MILLER, WILLIAM E. "Periaktoi in the old Blackfriars." MLN
    74 (January):1-3.
        Notes the reference to "the motion of late yeares to
    be seene in the blackfriers" in Abraham Fleming's transla-
    tion of Vergil's Eclogues and Georgics of 1589. Miller
    interprets this as revolving motion, as in periaktoi. See
    also 1964.29.

17 MILLS, L. J. "The Acting in University Comedy of Early
    Seventeenth-Century England." In Studies in the English
    Renaissance Drama in Memory of Karl Julius Holzknecht.
    Edited by Josephine W. Bennet, Oscar Cargill, and Vernon
    Hall, Jr. New York: New York University Press, pp. 212-30.
        Draws evidence primarily from the plays performed at
    Oxford and Cambridge concerning the acting style employed.
    Mills simply points the way for a more thorough study, using
    representative examples to show the apparent exuberance of
    University acting of plays with comic scenes.

18 NICOLL, ALLARDYCE. "'Passing Over the Stage.'" ShS 12:47-55,
        Part of a presidential lecture delivered to the Society
    for Theatre Research on 30 April 1958. Nicoll argues that
    "passing over the stage" meant that actors enter in the
    yard and then walk onto and over the platform.

19 PAFFORD, J. H. P. "Simon Forman's 'Bocke of Plaies.'" RES,
    n.s. 10 (July):289-91.
        A brief note arguing for the authenticity of this
    document, based on the testimony of W. H. Black, who
    transcribed it for Collier in 1832.

20 RHODES, ERNEST LLOYD. "The Staging of Elizabethan Plays at
    the Rose Theatre, 1592-1603." Ph.D. dissertation, Univer-
    sity of Kentucky, 316 pp.
        Published as 1976.21.

21 RIEWALD, J. G. "Some Later Elizabethan and Early Stuart Actors
    and Musicians." ES 40 (February):33-41.
        New information and commentary on sixteen actors and
    musicians, discovered by Riewald on the continent. Useful
    additions to Chambers (1923.2), Nungezer (1929.12), and
    Bentley (1941.1).

22 ROBERTSON, JEAN, ed. "A Calendar of Dramatic Records in the
    Books of the London Cloth-Workers' Company." MSC 5:1-16.
        Addenda to 1954.4, with entries from 1544 to 1634.

23 ROTHWELL, W[ILLIAM] F[RANCIS]. "Was There a Typical Elizabethan
    Stage?" ShS 12:15-21.
        Examines the playhouses before 1598, permanent and
    temporary, and the different production methods utilized,
    using the new information obtained to answer the title's
    question in the negative.

24 SELTZER, DANIEL. "Elizabethan Acting in Othello." SQ 10
    (Spring):201-10.
        Discusses the acting style for this play, based both on
    internal and external evidence. Stage directions implicit
    in the dialogue and comments in other sources indicate
    that relatively realistic business was used.

25 SOUTHERN, RICHARD. "On Reconstructing a Practicable Eliza-
    bethan Playhouse." ShS 12:22-34.
        Attempts "to estimate how far our present knowledge
    allows us to reconstruct a 'typical' Elizabethan playhouse
    sufficiently authentic to permit practical study of pro-
    duction." Using primarily the Fortune and Hope contracts
    and the Swan drawing, Southern comes up with a sixteen-
    sided polygonal structure 92 feet wide, with a stage 43
    feet wide. There are the usual three galleries (with
    standing space behind two rows of seats in the uppermost).
    The tiring house facade has two doors with curtains between,
    obscuring "a small discovery space," and a balcony running
    from side to side.

1959

26 STAMM, RUDOLF. "Elizabethan Stage-Practice and the Transmuta-
      tion of Source Material by the Dramatists." ShS 12:64-70.
        Argues that "the comparison between a play and its
      source renders us particularly sensitive to all those
      features in it that characterize it as a text intended for
      a certain type of stage performance." Antony and Cleopatra
      is the primary example cited. Stamm also stresses the
      importance of discovering implied stage directions
      embedded in the dialogue.

27 STONE, LAWRENCE, ed. "Companies of Players Entertained by the
      Earl of Cumberland and Lord Clifford, 1607-39." MSC 5:17-
      28.
        Extracts from the manuscripts of the Clifford family,
      with commentary. Most entries concern payments given to
      players. There are frequent mentions of company names and
      number of plays given as well as dates and amounts.

28 STYAN, J. L. "The Actor at the Foot of Shakespeare's Platform."
      ShS 12:56-63.
        Examines the actor's use of the depth of the Elizabethan
      stage in order to vary the type of contact with the audi-
      ence. Styan finds six usual situations when the playwright
      sends the actor downstage: 1) the actor introduces himself
      and establishes an emotional relationship with the specta-
      tor; 2) the actor points out another character and estab-
      lishes the relationship between them; 3) a character
      comments on a scene without himself leaving it; 4) the audi-
      ence must distinguish some characters from the rest; 5) the
      audience temporarily collaborates in a deceit because of
      the revelation of a secret; and 6) the playwright suggests
      contrasting values of sincerity between characters. Styan
      draws examples from several plays by Shakespeare and others.

29 WICKHAM, GLYNNE. Early English Stages 1300-1660. Vol. 1,
      1300-1576. London: Routledge and Kegan Paul; New York:
      Columbia University Press, 428 pp.
        The first of a projected five-volume work attempting
      "to trace the history of English stagecraft from its
      beginnings to the advent of the proscenium-arched scenic
      theatres that became public property shortly after the
      Restoration of the Monarchy in 1660." This volume estab-
      lishes the background that the Elizabethans later built
      on. The three books that compose it treat open air enter-
      tainments of the middle ages, indoor entertainments of
      the same period, and dramatic theory and practice to 1576.
      Two more volumes have been published (1963.20 and 1972.32).

1960

1 AUERBACH, LAWRENCE. "The Use of Time in Plays of Four Periods of the Drama." Ph.D. dissertation, University of Wisconsin, 362 pp.
    The periods considered are classical, Elizabethan, realistic, and postrealistic. In each section Auerbach considers the physical stage, the audience, the critics and theorists, and the plays. Essentially he examines the relative advantages of observing the unity of time and its implications.

2 BRADBROOK, M[URIEL] C. "Drama as Offering: The Princely Pleasures at Kenelworth." Rice Institute Pamphlets 46:57-70.
    Discusses the best known of Elizabethan country welcomes and the first text of a court show to survive. Elizabeth visited the Earl of Leicester from 9 to 28 July 1575, and the Earl is said to have spent over £1000 per day. Two accounts survive, one by George Gascoigne, who devised some of the outdoor shows, and Laneham's Letter. Bradbrook claims that the great historical drama of the Elizabethan age was born out of these personal offerings to Elizabeth.

3 BURTON, E. J. The British Theatre: Its Repertory and Practice, 1100-1900 A.D. London: Herbert Jenkins, pp. 59-138.
    Emphasizes presenting period plays today, but includes historical information. The relevant section includes chapters on Interludes, Renaissance drama, Elizabethan theatre, dance and decoration, Shakespeare, and the later Elizabethans.

4 CAIRNCROSS, A. S. "Pembroke's Men and Some Shakespearian Piracies." SQ 11 (Summer):335-49.
    Suggests that four of the earlier Shakespeare quartos--2 Henry VI, 3 Henry VI, Richard III, Romeo and Juliet--were memorial reconstructions made by the same group of actors, members of Pembroke's company, when their group disbanded in 1593.

5 CUTTS, JOHN P. "'Speak--Demand--We'll Answer': Hecat(e) and 'the other three witches.'" JDSG 96:173-76.
    Responds to Flatter, 1959.5, reiterating his argument in 1958.6 for the presence of six witches plus Hecate instead of only three in Macbeth, and for the placement of the "Come away" song (III.v.) before Hecate's exit. See also 1957.6; 1960.7.

1960

6 EDWARDS, H. R. L. "'Atorno, Atorno.'" <u>TLS</u> (10 June):369.
    Responds to Hotson (1954.14), pointing out an inconsis-
    tency in Hotson's use of "round."

7 FLATTER, RICHARD. "Professor Platter's Reply." <u>JDSG</u> 96:192-93.
    Replies to Cutts (1960.5), in the form of a letter
    suggesting an end to the controversy over the "other three
    witches" in <u>Macbeth</u>.

8 FOAKES, R. A. "The Significance of Henslowe's <u>Diary</u>." <u>PP</u>
    3, no. 4:214-22.
    A modified version of a lecture given at Bratislava in
    November 1959. Foakes discusses in general terms the
    classes of evidence for Elizabethan stage conditions
    provided by the diary.

9 GURR, A[NDREW] J. "DeWitt's Sketch of the Swan." <u>N&Q</u>, n.s.
    7 (September):328.
    Argues that what appear to be supports for the stage in
    the Swan drawing are actually the hangings around the
    stage that have been partially drawn open.

10 HOLMES, MARTIN R. <u>Shakespeare's Public: The Touchstone of
    His Genius</u>. London: John Murray, 237 pp.
    Essentially a critical commentary on the plays, within
    the cultural context of the period. The audience serves as
    a point of reference for literary criticism rather than
    the central feature of the investigation. Reprinted with
    corrections: 1964.16.

11 HOSLEY, RICHARD. "Was There a Music Room in Shakespeare's
    Globe?" <u>ShS</u> 13:113-23.
    Examines the evidence for the upper curtained music room
    in Elizabethan theatres in general and at the first Globe
    in particular. Hosley limits his "internal" evidence to
    the thirty extant plays performed at that playhouse 1599-
    1608. These are with one exception unanimous in designat-
    ing off-stage music at the first Globe as "within," which
    indicates the first level of the tiring house rather than
    the second or third, as J. C. Adams proposed (<u>see</u> 1942.1).
    Hosley concludes that "there was probably not a music-room
    over the stage at the First Globe before 1609."

12 M[ARDER], L[OUIS]. "Hotson's Jack-in-the-Box Staging." <u>ShN</u>
    10 (December):44-45.
    Responds to Hotson (1959.9), arguing against his loca-
    tion of the tiring house beneath the stage.

13 MITHAL, H. S. D. "'Mr. Kemp, called Don Gulielmo.'" N&Q,
    n.s. 7 (January):6-8.
        Responds to Bald's response (1959.3) to his earlier note
    (1958.13) by examining the context of a letter cited by
    Bald and suggesting that it was not Will Kempe the actor
    who was referred to but perhaps a priest with the same
    name.

14 PUTZEL, ROSAMUND. "Structural Patterns in the Repertory of
    the Child Actors through 1591." Ph.D. dissertation,
    University of North Carolina, 238 pp.
        Essentially a literary study of plays written for the
    boy companies at Paul's, Eton, Westminster, and elsewhere
    before 1591. Putzel concludes "that basic structural
    patterns changed and multiplied enormously . . . that
    continuity was maintained in traditional English songs and
    comic themes, and there was a strong predilection on the
    part of later audiences for subject matter from classical
    narratives and mythology."

15 RIEWALD, J. G. "New Light on the English Actors in the
    Netherlands, c. 1590-c. 1660." ES, 41, no. 2 (April):65-92.
        Examines the English strolling players on the continent.
    Almost all began their tours in the Netherlands, many
    joining with native actors. Riewald's discussion is
    chronological, based upon newly discovered documents in
    city and national archives.

16 SAUNDERS, J. W. "Staging at the Globe, 1599-1613." SQ 11
    (Autum):401-25.
        Attempts to "explore a way out of the present position
    of scholarly stalemate by outlining certain principles . .
    . and then applying them to a reexamination of the basic
    problems." Saunders's principles are: 1) the plays of one
    theatre at a time should be investigated; 2) deductions
    from staging necessities inferred from the action of the
    play rather than textual references should be made; 3)
    different solutions to staging problems are not necessarily
    mutually exclusive, and similar scenes may have been staged
    differently at different times; and 4) the design of the
    playhouse happened less by choice than by accumulated
    tradition. Saunders concludes that in addition to two
    doorways, there were two "wing" entrances to the Globe
    stage; that action above took place in two bay window side
    stages; that the areas underneath these bays (called
    "lower bays") were used for concealment; and that arras
    were hung across the back wall for discoveries. Reprinted:
    1968.3.

1960

17 SHIRLEY, FRANCES ANN. "Shakespeare's Use of Off-Stage Sound."
    Ph.D. dissertation, Bryn Mawr College, 257 pp.
        Published as 1963.13.

18 SISSON, C[HARLES] J[ASPER]. "The Laws of Elizabethan Copy-
    right: The Stationer's View." Library, 5th ser. 15
    (March):8-20.
        Examines the problem of Elizabethan copyright in the
    light of evidence provided by Thomas Dawson, twice master
    of the Stationers' Company. Of theatrical interest because
    of the problems of using published plays to determine
    staging practices.

19 _____. "The Theatres and the Companies." In A Companion to
    Shakespeare Studies. Edited by Harley Granville-Barker and
    G[eorge] B[agshawe] Harrison. New York: Doubleday, Anchor
    Books, pp. 9-43.
        Reprint of 1934.11.

20 SOUTHERN, RICHARD. "The Mystery of the Elizabethan Stage."
    Listener 63 (24 March):533-35.
        Text of a BBC radio program. The "mystery" of the title
    is what the stage looked like, and Southern reviews the
    possibilities in light of the theories of Lawrence, Hotson,
    and Hosley.

1961

1 ADAMS, JOHN CRANFORD. The Globe Playhouse: Its Design and
   Equipment. 2d ed. New York: Barnes & Noble, 435 pp.
        Second edition of 1942.1. Revises the section on early
   maps and views; adds photographs of his model of the Globe
   and an analysis of the staging of King Lear. Reprinted:
   1964.1.

2 ARMSTRONG, WILLIAM A. "The Enigmatic Elizabethan Stage."
   English 13 (Autumn):216-20.
        A brief "state of the art" survey, focusing on the
   staging of indoor scenes and, in particular, the use of
   the term "canopy." Armstrong suggests the use of a
   projecting curtained space for these scenes, and for discoveries in general, although his evidence is drawn from
   a variety of times and theatres. See also 1957.1.

3 BRADBROOK, M[URIEL] C. "'Silk? Satin? Kersey? Rags?'--The
   Choristers' Theater under Elizabeth and James." SEL 1
   (Spring):53-64.
       Argues that the choristers' theatres declined as the
   common players flourished, because the boys "could not
   compete with the power and range of the masterpieces of
   ripeness and judgment that were written for the popular
   stages." They were "a decaying relic of the older nobility
   faced with a new and flourishing estate." See also 1961.4;
   1962.4.

4 BRADBROOK, MURIEL C. "The Status Seekers: Society and the
   Common Player in the Reign of Elizabeth I." HLQ 24
   (February):111-24.
       Originally a paper read 11 July 1959 at a Huntington
   Library Seminar. Bradbrook examines the rise in status of
   the common players in England in the sixteenth century
   through the pretense of serving some great Lord. See also
   1962.4. Reprinted: 1968.3.

5 COOK, DAVID, ed. "Dramatic Records in the Declared Accounts
   of the Treasury of the Chamber, 1558-1642." MSC 6:1-175.
       Includes records of payments to players and for "apparel-
   lings," and biographical notes, with several appendixes
   detailing references to entertainments in various other
   documents.

6 DAVID, RICHARD. "Shakespeare and the Players." PBA 47:139-59.
       The annual Shakespeare Lecture before the British
   Academy, read 19 April 1961. David examines what we know
   of Shakespeare's acting company, based primarily on Baldwin
   (1927.1) and Joseph (1951.18). He discusses casting, the
   boy actors, rehearsals, and playwriting.

7 DAWSON, GILES E. "Strolling Players in Kent." ORRD 5:7-12.
       While Dawson concentrates here on the fifteenth century,
   he also covers sixteenth-century records. This is but a
   brief report on his research. See also 1965.6.

8 EGGAR, KATHARINE E. "The Blackfriars Plays and Their Music:
   1576-1610." PRMA 87:57-68.
       A paper delivered before the Royal Music Association, 16
   March 1961. Eggar examines the origin, maintenance, and
   disappearance of the boy companies playing at Blackfriars
   during the period. She traces the involvement of the Earl
   of Oxford, William Hunnis, Richard Farrant, Henry Evans,
   Nathaniel Giles, George Peele, John Mundy, and Sebastian
   Westcote in the first Blackfriars, and touches on the second.

1961

9 ELLIS-FERMOR, UNA M. "The Jacobean Stage." In The Jacobean
   Drama: An Interpretation. 4th ed. London: Methuen,
   pp. 273-83.
       Reprint of 1936.8.

10 FELVER, CHARLES S[TANLEY]. Robert Armin, Shakespeare's Fool:
   A Biographical Essay. Kent State University Bulletin 49,
   no. 1: Research Series, no. 5. Kent: Kent State University, 82 pp.
       Partial publication of 1956.11.

11 FOAKES, R. A. "The Profession of Playwright." In Early
   Shakespeare. Stratford-Upon-Avon Studies, no. 3. London:
   Edward Arnold, pp. 11-33.
       Examines theatrical conditions in general rather than,
   as the title suggests, the profession of playwright. Foakes
   includes in his discussion the theatres, companies, finance,
   repertories, and acting.

12 _____, and RICKERT, R[OBERT] T[URNAM]. "An Elizabethan Stage
   Drawing?" ShS 13:111-12.
       Reproduces a sketch from Henslowe's papers that might
   be meant to represent a stage.

13 HENSLOWE, PHILIP. Henslowe's Diary. Edited by R. A. Foakes
   and R[obert] T[urnam] Rickert. Cambridge: University
   Press, 426 pp.
       A new edition based on fresh transcripts of all avail-
   able material. A fifty-nine-page introduction is followed
   by the text of the diary, which is in turn followed by
   three indexes and a glossary. This has become the definitive edition. See also 1790.1; 1845.3; 1904.7; 1907.15;
   1908.11; 1977.8.

14 IVES, E. W. "Tom Skelton--A Seventeenth-Century Jester."
   ShS 13:90-105.
       Examines the costume of the fool based on evidence
   presented in two contemporary paintings of Tom Skelton.
   Patterned motley or patchwork seems to have been the
   uniform of the fool, and it was faithfully recreated on
   the stage.

15 JOSEPH, BERTRAM. "The Elizabethan Stage and Acting." In The
   Age of Shakespeare. Edited by Boris Ford. London:
   Cassell, pp. 139-53.
       Reprint of 1955.12.

16 _____. "The Elizabethan Stage and Acting." In The Age of
   Shakespeare. Edited by Boris Ford. Pelican Guide to
   English Literature, no. 2. London: Pelican Books, pp.
   139-53.
      Reprint of 1955.12.

17 MacKICHAN, L. A. L. "The Elizabethan Stage." TLS (6 October):
   672.
      Provides support for Hotson's theory of arena staging
   (see 1959.9) from Milton's Samson Agonistes.

18 PATERSON, MORTON. "The Stagecraft of the Revels Office during
   the Reign of Elizabeth." In Studies in the Elizabethan
   Theatre. Edited by Charles T. Prouty. Hamden, Conn.: Shoe
   String Press, pp. 1-52.
      Organizes and presents the information from the Revels
   documents relevant to stage practice, based primarily on
   Feuillerat (1908.6) and Chambers (1923.2).

19 PEET, ALICE LIDA. "The History and Development of Simultaneous
   Scenery in the West from the Middle Ages to the Modern
   United States." Ph.D. dissertation, University of Wisconsin,
   393 pp.
      Despite the time frame implied in the title, this work
   does not examine the English Renaissance.

20 PROUTY, CHARLES T., ed. Studies in the Elizabethan Theatre.
   Hamden, Conn.: Shoe String Press, 198 pp.
      Contains a brief introduction and a twelve-page bibli-
   ography (all relevant items of which have been incorporated
   into this one) as well as three essays (1961.18, 22, 25).

21 ROSS, LAWRENCE J. "The Use of a 'Fit-Up' Booth in Othello."
   SQ 12 (Autumn):359-70.
      Examines the possible use of a portable curtained booth
   for the staging of Othello, particularly the last scene.
   Evidence for the presence of this structure is found in
   Iago's line in V.i. ("stand behind this bulk") and in the
   beginning of I.iii. with a discovery. Ross sees the booth
   as a structure of variously modifiable neutrality.

22 SARLOS, ROBERT K. "Development and Operation of the First
   Blackfriars Theatre." In Studies in the Elizabethan
   Theatre. Edited by Charles T. Prouty. Hamden, Conn.:
   Shoe String Press, pp. 137-78.
      An attempt to summarize all that is known about the first
   Blackfriars, primarily from Feuillerat (1910.8; 1912.6;
   1913.3), Wallace (1912.23), and Hillebrand (1926.6).

1961

23 SOUTHERN, RICHARD. <u>The Seven Ages of the Theatre</u>. New York:
    Hill & Wang, pp. 155–214.
        The relevant section is the fourth, "The Organized
    Stage." This is more a thumb-nail sketch than a fully
    developed historical investigation, with quite a different
    purpose. Southern wishes to examine the evolution of the
    forms theatre has taken throughout the world, with an eye
    toward "the establishment of a body of information upon
    which the planning of new theatres can proceed with
    understanding." Consequently, there is a good deal of
    cross-cultural comparison, which is the work's greatest
    strength. For example, the Elizabethan stage is compared
    to the classical Chinese, the Noh, the Teatro Olimpico, the
    classical Indian, and the commedia dell'arte stages.

24 STEVENS, JOHN E. <u>Music and Poetry in the Early Tudor Court</u>.
    Lincoln: University of Nebraska Press; London: Methuen,
    pp. 233–64.
        The relevant section is Chapter 11, "Music in Ceremonies,
    Entertainments, and Plays." Stevens touches on early Eliza-
    bethan court drama.

25 STINSON, JAMES. "Reconstruction of Elizabethan Public Play-
    houses." In <u>Studies in the Elizabethan Theatre</u>. Edited
    by Charles T. Prouty. Hamden, Conn.: Shoe String Press,
    pp. 53–136.
        A summary of major reconstructions, including those by
    Hodges, Southern, Tieck, Archer and Godfrey, Chambers,
    Brodmeier, Albright, Corbin, Smith, Nicoll, Kernodle,
    Forrest, J. Q. Adams, J. C. Adams, and Hotson. A brief
    appendix lists thirty-two commonly reproduced maps and
    views of London, and twelve plates give visualizations of
    some of the reconstructions discussed. Stinson evaluates
    as well as describes each reconstruction. He finds
    Hodges's "the most careful and conservative attempt yet
    made."

26 UNGERER, GUSTAV. "An Unrecorded Elizabethan Performance of
    <u>Titus Andronicus</u>." <u>ShS</u> 14:102–9.
        Prints an eyewitness account (written in French) of a
    pre-1596 performance of the play at a private house in
    Rutland. The letter is included in the Anthony Bacon
    Papers preserved in Lambeth Place Library. The private
    performance was presented by an unknown professional
    company, perhaps the Lord Admiral's Men or the Lord
    Chamberlain's Men.

27 WEINER, A[LBERT] B. "Elizabethan Interior and Aloft Scenes:
A Speculative Essay." ThS 2:15-34.
Examines the use of the discovery space and the acting
area above, and speculates that a solid but hinged and
folding pavillion would solve the problems of staging such
scenes. Such a structure would be appropriate for scenes
on the walls and scenes calling for tents as well. The
Swan drawing does not show this pavilion because it is
folded up and invisible against the tiring house facade.

28 WRIGHT, LOUIS B. Shakespeare's Theatre and the Dramatic
Tradition. Washington: Folger Shakespeare Library,
36 pp.
Reprint of 1958.24.

1962

1 BALL, ROMA. "The Choir-Boy Actors of St. Paul's Cathedral."
ESRS 10, no. 4 (June):5-16.
Based on an M.A. thesis at Kansas State Teachers College,
Emporia, and partially presented at the 1961 meeting of
the Central Renaissance Society. Ball traces several of
the boys through their future careers, finding that seven
became distinguished musicians while only two (or possibly
three) became actors.

2 BECKERMAN, BERNARD. Shakespeare at the Globe, 1599-1609. New
York: Macmillan, 254 pp.
Published version of 1956.3. Examines fifteen Shakespearean and fourteen non-Shakespearean plays first produced at the Globe during the years that the Chamberlain's/
King's Men played only at that theatre. The five major
chapters treat the repertory, the dramaturgy, the stage,
the acting, and the staging, and a brief sixth chapter
defines the style. Beckerman concludes that the style of
production at the Globe was "chiefly characterized by its
reconciliation of the contradictory demands of convention
and reality," defining the style as "at once, ceremonial,
romantic, and epic." He examines each part of the Globe
stage (doors, upper area, pillars, third door or enclosed
space) carefully and thoroughly.

3 BRADBROOK, M[URIEL] C. Elizabethan Stage Conditions: A
Study of Their Place in the Interpretation of Shakespeare's
Plays. Hamden, Conn.: Archon, 149 pp.
Reprint of 1932.2.

1962

4 _____. The Rise of the Common Player: A Study of Actor and
Society in Shakespeare's England. Cambridge: Harvard
University Press, 326 pp.
     Explores "the social envelope within which [the Eliza-
bethan plays] were made." Bradbrook contends that actors
were a new and experimental social group, and that the
opposition they met is a classic example of the force of
unexamined assumptions and social prejudice. The only new
discovery revealed is a letter, previously reprinted but
without indication of authorship, that Bradbrook ascribes
to one of the Earl of Leicester's Men. The letter, as the
only remaining literary production from this first great
Elizabethan acting company, thus becomes a document of
importance to the theatre historian. The book is divided
to correspond with the main social divisions of the drama
in Elizabethan times. The four parts, dealing with the
players and society, common players, household players,
and "general dramatic sports," cover the period from different points of view, revealing different aspects of the
complex social structure.

5 CHILDS, HUBERT E. "On the Elizabethan Staging of Hamlet."
SQ 13 (Autumn):463-74.
     Not a historical piece, but an examination of the play
as staged at Ashland, Oregon, in 1961.

6 GOUSSEFF, JAMES WILLIAM. "The Staging of Prologues in Tudor
and Stuart Plays." Ph.D. dissertation, Northwestern University, 609 pp.
     Investigates costume, makeup, properties employed, and
staging of prologues. The prologue speaker's performance
is traced "from the soundings which heralded his entrance
to the bows which were the precursors of his exit," including choice of entrance and exit doors, contact with the
audience, various forms of salutation, probable position on
stage, and the nature of movement and gesture.

7 HOOK, LUCYLE. "The Curtain." SQ 13 (Autumn):499-504.
     Reveals discovery of a document bearing on this play-
house in The Calendar of Treasury Books that may establish
its location and indicate that it still stood in 1698.
Hook includes a complete review of the information available on the Curtain, with the suggestion that Collier's
account of the end of the playhouses might be fictitious.

8   JONES, ELDRED D. "The Physical Representation of African
    Characters on the English Stage during the 16th and 17th
    Centuries." TN 17 (Autumn):17-21.
       Discusses the use of makeup, wigs, and costumes to
    portray black characters.

9   JONES, MARION, and WICKHAM, GLYNNE. "Stage Furnishings of
    George Chapman's The Tragedy of Charles, Duke of Biron."
    TN 16 (Summer):113-17.
       Discusses the possibility that the 1608 performance and
    printed play were based on a 1602 version referred to in
    Henslowe's diary. It this was the case, a scaffold and bar
    would both have been necessary for its staging.

10 JOSEPH, BERTRAM. "The Elizabethan Stage and Acting." In The
    Age of Shakespeare. Edited by Boris Ford. Pelican Guide
    to English Literature, no. 2. Baltimore: Penguin Books,
    pp. 147-61.
       Reprint of 1955.12.

11 KLEIN, DAVID. "Did Shakespeare Produce His Own Plays?" MLR
    57 (October):556-60.
       Differs with Hart, who claimed there was no direct
    evidence to support the theory that Shakespeare produced
    his own plays. Klein cites Johannes Rhenanus, a German
    visitor who claims to have witnessed a rehearsal; a Nashe
    play; Dekker's Satiromastix; Jonson's Cynthia's Revels;
    Bishop Hall's Virgidemiarum; and a variety of other plays
    by Marston, Shirley, Munday, Middleton and Rowley, Massinger,
    and Jonson as evidence that the playwright normally directed
    his own work.

12 LENNEP, WILLIAM Van. "The Death of the Red Bull." TN 16
    (Summer):126-34.
       Concerns the playhouse after the Restoration.

13 McMANAWAY, JAMES G. "Notes on Two Pre-Restoration Stage
    Curtains." PQ 41 (January):270-74.
       Examines the possibility that the front curtains shown in
    two largely ignored illustrations from the middle of the
    seventeenth century might help clarify staging practices
    in the court masques. Reprinted: 1969.8.

14 McNEIR, WALDO F. "The Staging of the Dover Cliff Scene in
    King Lear." In Studies in English Renaissance Literature.
    Edited by Waldo F. McNeir. Louisiana State University
    Studies, Humanities Series, no. 12. Baton Rouge: Louisi-
    ana State University Press, pp. 87-104.

1962

Originally a lecture at the University of Oregon, 1961.
Suggests the use of a portable curtained booth, with a
seven or eight foot jump, for Gloucester's Dover cliff
scene.

15 REYNOLDS, GEORGE F[ULLMER]. "Two Conventions of the Open
    Stage (as Illustrated in King Lear?)." PQ 41 (January):82-
    95.
    Examines the possible use of curtains in front of a
    central doorway and continuous open staging for King Lear,
    with emphasis on the change of location indicated by a
    character's immediate re-entry through a different doorway
    than the one used for the exit.

16 RIFFE, NANCY LEE. "Shakespeare's Stage: A Bibliography."
    ShN 12 (November):40.
    An unannotated list of books and articles on the physical
    stage from 1940 to 1962. All relevant entries have been
    incorporated into this bibliography.

17 ROSENFELD, SYBIL. Foreign Theatrical Companies in Great
    Britain in the Seventeenth and Eighteenth Centuries.
    Pamphlet Series, no. 4. London: Society for Theatre
    Research, p. 1.
    Reprint of 1955.20.

18 SMITH, HAL H. "Some Principles of Elizabethan Stage Costume."
    JWCI 25 (June):240-57.
    A reevaluation of Elizabethan costuming practice,
    concluding that such plays as Troilus and Cressida were
    costumed in the classical manner as the Renaissance
    understood it. Evidence from the plays and emblem books
    is considered in the light of the Peachum illustration for
    Titus Andronicus and Platter's commentary.

19 STAMM, RUDOLPH. "Dichtung und Theater in Shakespeares Werk."
    JDSG 98:7-23.
    A paper presented 22 February 1962 in Basel. Stamm
    argues for consideration of the theatrical--both in terms
    of staging and acting style--in the interpretation of
    Shakespeare.

20 STOLZENBACH, CONRAD. "A Critical Acting Edition of Antonio
    and Mellida by John Marston (1602)." Ph.D. dissertation,
    University of Michigan, 258 pp.
    Includes in the first section a history of the Children
    of Paul's, the company for which the play was written, and

an analysis of the physical aspects of the playhouse in
which their productions were given. The edited text
contains "extensive and detailed critical annotation for
. . . stage business."

21 WAITH, EUGENE M. "The Staging of Bartholomew Fair." SEL 2
(Spring):181-96.
    A reconstruction of the original production at the
Hope, 31 October 1614, based on information in the text and
from the records of the Court performance the following
day. Waith assigns the Hope two doorways (since it was
supposedly similar to the Swan) and assumes the use of
canvas-covered booths, as in the Court performance. Since
three entrances are required, the arras must have covered
the entire tiring house facade, with entrances through the
middle and at either end. The booths were portable,
being set up and taken down as needed.

22 WEINER, ALBERT B. "Two Tents in Richard III?" SQ 13
(Summer):258-60.
    Responds to Fusillo (1955.5) and Hosley (1956.16),
arguing for the presence of one tent on the stage, pitched
by Richard's men at his command, and used by Richmond as
his tent when Richard exits. The argument is based on
stage directions in the First Folio.

23 WICKLAND, ERIC. Elizabethan Players in Sweden, 1591-92: Facts
and Problems. Stockholm: Almqvist & Wiksell, 199 pp.
    Examines the English company at Nyköping in Sweden
1591-92. Previously believed to have been composed
exclusively of musicians, this company may also have included actors. The recruiting, passage, and performance
of the group is carefully scrutinized. Wickland cautiously
concludes that the question is still open. See 1971.18.

1963

1 BANKS, HOWARD MILTON. "A Historical Survey of the Mise-en-
Scene Employed in Shakespearean Productions from the Elizabethan Period to the Present." Ph.D. dissertation, University of Southern California, 821 pp.
    The relevant section is the first chapter, which surveys
the nature of the Elizabethan playhouse and stage, concluding that "the data concerning the Globe public playhouse
structure revealed a composite picture only of the physical
characteristics attributable to any public playhouse of the
day. Basically, there were Elizabethan playhouses with

1963

certain similarities, employing acting areas, balconies, windows, and doors which were common to all."

2   BENTLEY, G[ERALD] E[ADES]. "Lenten Performances in the Jacobean and Caroline Theaters." In Essays on Shakespeare and the Elizabethan Drama in Honor of Gordon Craig. Edited by Richard Hosley. London: Routledge & Kegan Paul, pp. 351-59.
      A preliminary examination of evidence concerning Lenten performances (later published in more complete form as an appendix to 1968.2). Bentley concludes that the London theatres produced "a reduced number of plays, as well as variety turns, four days a week during the first five and a half weeks of Lent."

3   FLECKNOE, RICHARD. "A Short Discourse of the English Stage." In Critical Essays of the Seventeenth Century. Vol. 2. Edited by J. E. Spingarn. Bloomington: Indiana University Press, pp. 91-96.
      Reprint of 1664.1.

4   FOAKES, R. A. "Henslowe and the Theatre of the 1590s." Renaissance Drama: A Report on Research Opportunities 6:4-6.
      Delineates some of the shortcomings of Greg's work on the Henslowe diary and papers (1904.7; 1907.15; 1908.11) as part of the rationale of his own edition (with Rickert, 1961.13). Ultimately, Foakes sees a need for a comprehensive history of the stage in the volatile 1590s. See in this regard 1964.31.

*5 GURR, ANDREW J. "Elizabethan Acting and Shakespeare's Company." Ph.D. dissertation, Cambridge University.
      Cited in DEAL, p. 535.

6   GURR, A[NDREW] J. "Who Strutted and Bellowed?" ShS 16:95-102.
      Examines the two distinct kinds of acting among the adult companies in the early seventeenth century, in response to Armstrong (1954.2). Gurr cites five references to Tamburlaine's violence to support his claim for exaggeration in the Red Bull style put forward by Alleyn.

7   HARRIS, ANTHONY J. "William Poel's Elizabeth Stage: The First Experiment." TN 17 (Summer):111-15.
      Describes the apron-stage model of the Fortune that Poel used in his 1893 production of Measure for Measure.

8 HOSLEY, RICHARD. "An Approach to the Elizabethan Stage."
   Renaissance Drama: A Report on Research Opportunities
   6:72-78.
       Puts forward Hosley's theory of the use of stage doors
   for discovery spaces by drawing open the hangings in
   front of them. He also discusses briefly the four
   pictorial sources for the Elizabethan stage, reconciling
   their differences. No evidence is presented here, but the
   reader is referred to Hosley's "forthcoming book, Elizabethan Playhouse Stages." While this work has not yet
   appeared, it promises to be a major contribution to the
   field when it does. See Index, under Hosley, for his many
   articles.

9 _____. "The Staging of Desdemona's Bed." SQ 14 (Winter):57-
   65.
       Responds to Ross (1961.21), suggesting that the bed used
   in V.ii. was thrust out, not discovered. Hosley examines
   the staging of bed scenes in all plays written for the
   Chamberlain's/King's Men 1595-1642. Twenty-three uses of
   this property are catalogued, and in sixteen it is stated
   or implied that the bed is not brought on stage; in five,
   there is no evidence that the bed was discovered; and in
   the other two there is no evidence for the use of a
   portable booth.

10 JOSEPH. STEPHEN. The Story of the Playhouse in England.
   London: Barrie & Rockliff, pp. 42-74.
       The relevant section is chapters two through four,
   "First Stages," "Shakespeare and Company," and "Jonson v.
   Jones." Joseph summarizes what is known of the playhouses
   and production practices, and the presentation of masques.
   This is a secondary study aimed at a general or perhaps
   a school audience.

11 KING, THOMAS JAMES. "Production of Plays at the Phoenix,
   1617-42." Ph.D. dissertation, Columbia University, 261 pp.
       Examines textual evidence concerning staging methods
   employed at one of the most important private playhouses,
   the Phoenix in Drury Lane. King selects the thirty-two
   plays from the Phoenix repertory whose title-page claim of
   Phoenix production can be verified in an external historical
   source and which carry markings related to prompt copy.
   Each text is examined for evidence of staging practices.
   King then divides the plays into two groups, depending
   upon staging requirements. The plays of the first group
   require nothing more than two doors and a platform for
   their staging, while the plays of the second group require

1963

an area above, hangings, a discovery space, or some combination of these elements. King suggests that the needs of
the plays of the second group could be met if a portable
curtained booth were set on the stage or if the playhouse
possessed a gallery that could be used to suspend the
hangings in front of a doorway. The first chapter traces
the history of the playhouse, and appendixes deal with
music, dancing, and effects. See also 1965.9; 1971.10.

12 REYNOLDS, GEORGE F[ULLMER]. "The Return of the Open Stage."
    In Essays on Shakespeare and Elizabethan Drama in Honor of
    Gordon Craig. Edited by Richard Hosley. London:
    Routledge & Kegan Paul, pp. 361–68.
       Reviews differing views of the Elizabethan stage, from
    the alternation theory to J. C. Adams to Richard Hosley,
    including practical reconstructions for production
    purposes.

13 SHIRLEY, FRANCES ANN. Shakespeare's Use of Off-Stage Sounds.
    Lincoln: University of Nebraska Press, 258 pp.
       Published version of 1960.17. Shirley discusses both
    the use and production of off-stage sounds, concentrating
    on Julius Caesar, Hamlet, and Macbeth. In an appendix she
    lists all such sounds she finds necessary in Shakespeare.

14 SMITH, GORDON ROSS. A Classified Shakespeare Bibliography,
    1936-1958. University Park: Pennsylvania State University
    Press, pp. 294-308.
       A comprehensive but minimally annotated bibliography of
    scholarship for the years listed, continuing 1937.3. All
    relevant items have been incorporated into this bibliography.

15 SOUTHERN, RICHARD. "The Contribution of the Interludes to
    Elizabethan Staging." In Essays in Shakespeare and Eliza-
    bethan Drama in Honor of Gordon Craig. Edited by Richard
    Hosley. London: Routledge & Kegan Paul, pp. 3-14.
       Suggests that the groundwork for the Elizabethan drama
    was laid down in the interludes of the sixteenth century,
    that the interludes could be played on a portable booth-
    stage as well as before a hall screen, and that the hall
    screen and the booth-stage might have served as the
    prototype of the tiring facade.

*16 SUGA, YASUO. The Shakespearean Theatre and Stage. Kyoto:
    Apollonsha.
       Cited in 1974.18.

1964

17 _____. "Theatre Ways, the Elizabethan and the Japanese."
  ShStud (Tokyo) 2:1-9.
    Compares Elizabethan stage conventions with their
  counterparts on the Kabuki and Noh stages. Suga discusses
  the stage-keepers, the open stage, and symbolic properties.

18 SUMMERSON, JOHN [NEWENHAM]. Architecture in Britain, 1530-
  1830. 4th ed. Pelican History of Art, no. Z3. Baltimore:
  Penguin Books, pp. 61-67.
    Reprint of 1953.26.

19 UNWIN, GEORGE. The Guilds and Companies of London. 4th ed.
  London: Frank Cass & Co., 397 pp.
    Reprint of 1909.29.

20 WICKHAM, GLYNNE. Early English Stages, 1300-1660. Vol. 2, Pt.
  1, 1576-1660. London: Routledge & Kegan Paul; New York:
  Columbia University Press, 408 pp.
    The second of a projected five-volume work, intended to
  apply the information gathered in the first volume (1959.29)
  to the rise of the commercial theatre in London. The Tudor
  Interlude is seen as "the crucible in which a predominantly
  amateur and religious drama came to be translated into a
  predominantly professional and secular one." The two books
  that compose the volume deal with the regulation of the
  theatre and the emblematic tradition, which Wickham sees as
  central. The volume closes with a detailed description of
  the Swan, DeWitt's sketch of which Wickham accepts at face
  value. See also 1972.32.

21 WILSON, F[RANK] P[ERCY]. "Lambarde, the Bel Savage and the
  Theatre." N&Q n.s. 10 (March):92-93.
    Points out that the reference to the Bel Savage Inn used
  as a playhouse in the 1576 edition of Perambulation of Kent
  is one of the earliest allusions to the use of the inn for
  that purpose. The second edition (1596) includes a
  reference to the Theatre.

22 WRIGHT, LOUIS B. Shakespeare's Theatre and the Dramatic
  Tradition. Washington: Folger Shakespeare Library, 36 pp.
    Reprint of 1958.24.

                              1964

1 ADAMS, JOHN CRANFORD. The Globe Playhouse: Its Design and
  Equipment. 2d ed. New York: Barnes & Noble, 435 pp.
    Reprint of 1961.1.

1964

2 ANGLO, SYDNEY. "La salle de banquet et le théâtre construits
   a Greenwich pour les fêtes franco-anglaises de 1527." In
   <u>Le lieu théâtral à la Renaissance</u>. Edited by Jean Jacquot.
   Paris: CNRS, pp. 273-88.
        Discusses the tradition of constructing provisional
   banqueting halls and theatres to house festivities held on
   occasions of diplomatic triumphs on the continent and in
   England during the sixteenth century. Specifically, Anglo
   examines the 1515 banqueting house in Greenwich and the
   1520 banqueting house in Calais, both of which lead up to
   the 1527 Greenwich structure. This last is exceedingly
   well documented, and Anglo describes the festivities in
   detail, including construction practices, payments,
   dimensions, decor and ornamentation, and use. <u>See</u> second
   edition (1968.1) and Hosley (1979.15).

3 ARMSTRONG, WILLIAM A. "Actors and Theatres." <u>ShS</u> 17:191-204.
        A general treatment of these two topics for a volume
   dealing with Elizabethan life. Armstrong examines acting
   styles, favoring the "naturalistic"; simultaneous and
   changeable painted scenery; and such staging devices as
   bowers, tents, thrones, and canopies.

4 BERGERON, DAVID MOORE. "Allegory in English Pageantry 1558-
   1625." Ph.D. dissertation, Vanderbilt University, 303 pp.
        Published, much revised and expanded, as 1971.3. <u>See</u>
   <u>also</u> Index, under Bergeron, for his many articles on the
   subject.

5 BEST, MICHAEL R. "The Development of Ideas and Techniques in
   the Drama of John Lyly: A Critical Study." Ph.D. dissertation, University of Adelaide, pp. 31-112.
        The relevant section is Chapters II and III, "The Stage"
   and "The Plays in Production." Best argues for "a method
   of production which . . . gives to the plays a tautness of
   action, and even of symbolism, of which we would otherwise
   be unaware." He describes this method in his more acces-
   sible 1968.8.

6 BRADBROOK, M[URIEL] C. "Shakespeare and the Elizabethan
   Theatre." <u>English Language and Literature</u> (Korea) 15:3-34.
        Text of a lecture presented to the Shakespeare Society
   of Korea, 6 April 1964, Seoul National University. Bradbrook here examines performances in the public and private
   playhouses, focusing on <u>Richard III</u>, which she sees as
   typical of public theatre plays, with spectacle, color, and
   a firmly established leading part; <u>King Lear</u>; and <u>The</u>
   <u>Tempest</u>, which shows strong influence of the form of the
   court masque.

7 BROWNSTEIN, OSCAR LEE. "Stake and Stage: The Baiting Ring
    and the Public Playhouse in Elizabethan England." Ph.D.
    dissertation, University of Iowa, 460 pp.
        Examines the theory that the general form of the Eliza-
    bethan public playhouse derives from amphitheatres for the
    baiting of bulls and bears. Brownstein first discusses the
    history of organized baiting, then examines the evidence for
    the existence of amphitheatres for baiting predating the
    erection of the Theatre in 1576. He finds that the first
    public playhouse in fact predated the first baiting
    amphitheatre by seven years, so "the theory that baiting
    amphitheatres preceded the Elizabethan playhouse is wholly
    untenable." See also Index, under Brownstein, for several
    articles on this and similar subjects.

8 DAWSON, GILES E. "London's Bull-Baiting and Bear-Baiting
    Arena in 1562." SQ 15 (Winter):97-101.
        The account of Venetian merchant Alessandro Maguo of his
    trip to England in 1562 furnishes a detailed description of
    bull and bear baiting. Dawson correlates this information
    with the surviving illustrations of the baiting rings.

9 DOWNER, ALAN S. "Prolegomena to a Study of Elizabethan
    Acting." MuK 10:625-36.
        Argues against arbitrarily defining Elizabethan acting
    in terms of "formal" or "natural." Instead, Downer suggests
    an eclectic approach, based on what we know the actor
    thought he was supposed to be doing. He cites a number of
    contemporary sources, and concludes that the acting style
    was "not unrelated to other aesthetic manifestations of the
    Renaissance, in dance, in painting, in architecture, in
    poetic imagery, and in music." The actor's purpose was
    "the metaphorical or emblematic enriching of the texture
    of the dramatic situation."

10 ELLIS-FERMOR, UNA M. "The Jacobean Stage." In The Jacobean
    Drama: An Introduction. Vintage History and Criticism
    of Literature, Music, and Art, no. 261. New York: Vintage
    Books, pp. 273-83.
        Reprint of 1936.8.

11 FISCHER, SIDNEY. The Theatre, the Curtain, and the Globe.
    Montreal: McGill University Library, 15 pp.
        Cast in the form of a letter to one Richard (presumably,
    Hosley), dated 26 February 1963. Fischer prints three
    "contemporary and hitherto unrecognized views of the
    Theatre, the Curtain, & the (second) Globe playhouses":

1964

the Utrecht view (pre-1597) showing the Theatre and
Curtain; and the Hollar view (1667) after the Great Fire
showing the Globe. Fischer establishes the point of view of
each drawing and coordinates what is known about location
from other sources.

*12 FRENCH, JOSEPH NATHAN. "The Staging of Magical Effects in
      Elizabethan and Jacobean Drama." Ph.D. dissertation,
      University of Birmingham, 342 pp.
        Cited in DEAL, Supplement 1, p. 194.

 13 HARBAGE, ALFRED. Annals of English Drama, 975-1700. Revised
      by Samuel Schoenbaum. London: Methuen, 321 pp.
        Revised edition of 1940.7.

 14 _____. "Shakespearean Staging." ShN 14 (April-May):31.
        Essentially a review of the literature, from the
      discovery of the Swan drawing in 1888 through Wickham,
      1963.20.

 15 HODGES, C[YRIL] WALTER. Shakespeare's Theatre. London:
      Oxford University Press, 103 pp.
        An introduction to the Elizabethan theatre for a juvenile
      audience, tracing the medieval origins as well as present-
      ing typical production elements at the Globe. While of
      course there is no scholarly apparatus, this volume is one
      of the best introductions to the field available, and the
      scope is very wide for so simple and brief a book. The
      illustrations are from an Encyclopedia Britannica filmstrip
      that Hodges made on the subject.

 16 HOLMES, MARTIN R. Shakespeare's Public: The Touchstone of
      His Genius. London: John Murray, 237 pp.
        Reprint, with corrections, of 1960.10.

 17 HOSLEY, RICHARD. "The Origins of the Shakespearian Playhouse."
      SQ 15 (Spring):29-39.
        Examines specifically the hall screen and the animal-
      baiting houses as contributors to the origin of the Eliza-
      bethan theatres. The baiting houses--open to the sky,
      built in a large number of bays, two stories, with an
      unpaved pit, flying flags--apparently furnished a model for
      the building (but see Brownstein, 1964.7), while the hall
      screen--two doors below, gallery above--furnished a model
      for the tiring house facade.

18 _____. "Reconstitution du théâtre du Swan." In Le lieu
théâtral à la Renaissance. Edited by Jean Jacquot. Paris:
CNRS, pp. 295-316.
     A reconstruction of the Swan, based on the DeWitt sketch.
See 1975.15 for a similar reconstruction in English. See
also second edition, 1968.18.

19 _____. "The Shakespearean Theatre." ShN 14 (April-May):32-33.
     A brief assessment of the state of scholarship in the
field, through the pointing out of eight "landmarks" in
the development of our understanding.

20 _____. "Shakespearian Stage Curtains: Then and Now." CE 25
(April):488-92.
     An examination of the Elizabethan stage curtains used
for discoveries. Hosley claims that production techniques
were essentially the same at all times in all Elizabethan
theatres and that very few plays require discoveries.
Regular stage doors were used for them, with a curtain
hung up in front and drawn open. The "inner stage"
curtain combines this function with the modern proscenium
curtain.

21 _____. "The Staging of the Monument Scenes in Antony and
Cleopatra." Library Chronicle (University of Pennsylvania)
30 (Spring):62-71.
     Conjectural reconstruction of two scenes. Hosley
contends that the tiring house gallery represented the
monument and that Antony was carried in in a chair and
hoisted aloft to Cleopatra with a winch. He cites a Rose
play and the Revels Accounts for substantiation of the
possibility. The second monument scene, says Hosley, was
played on the platform. See 1945.1.

22 JACQUOT, JEAN. "Le théâtre élisabéthain," in "Les types de
lieu théâtral et leurs transformations." In Le lieu
théâtral à la Renaissance. Edited by Jean Jacquot. Paris:
CNRS, pp. 491-96.
     Discusses the approaches of Hosley and Southern to the
problems of the Elizabethan stage, as opposed to those of
Adams and Smith, with a clear preference for the former.
See also second edition, 1968.22.

23 JAMIESON, MICHAEL. "Shakespeare's Celibate Stage." In Papers
Mainly Shakespearian. Edited by G. I. Duthie. Aberdeen
University Studies, no. 147. Edinburgh: Oliver & Boyd,
pp. 21-39.
     "A slightly revised version of a term paper written
several years ago for Professor G. E. Bentley's graduate-

course on Shakespeare (English 525) at Princeton University." Jamieson examines Shakespeare's accommodation to the
use of boy actors in three plays, arguing that the boys
were highly trained, assured, and valuable, and that while
female parts are limited in number and, frequently, length,
there was no limitation imposed on the playwright by lack
of ability or verisimilitude. Reprinted: 1968.3.

*24 JOHNSTON, ELIZABETH CARRINGTON. "The English Masque and the
French Court Ballet, 1581-1640." Ph.D. dissertation,
Harvard University.
    Cited in ADDT, p. 49.

25 JOSEPH, B[ERTRAM] L. Elizabethan Acting. 2d ed. London:
Oxford University Press, 115 pp.
    Second edition of 1951.8. The new edition deletes the
account of the part rhetoric played in the scheme of
humanist learning and considers the intervening twelve
years of scholarship. The picture of Elizabethan acting
presented is essentially unchanged, but Joseph takes pains
to point out that he does not sit exclusively in the
"formalist" school.

26 LAVER, JAMES. "Costumes in Shakespeare's Plays." MuK
10:275-81.
    A historical survey, touching on the Elizabethan period
only briefly.

27 LEECH, CLIFFORD, [E. J.] "The Acting of Marlowe and Shakespeare." ColQ 13, no. 1 (Summer):25-46.
    Originally one of the George Fullmer Reynolds Memorial
Lectures for 1964. Leech discusses the formal requirements
of Marlowe's plays and the increasingly realistic demands
of Shakespeare's later work, primarily from the point of
view of the modern actor.

28 LYONS, CLIFFORD P. "The Trysting Scenes in Troilus and
Cressida." In Shakespearean Essays. Edited by Alwin
Thaler and Norman Sanders. Knoxville: University of
Tennessee Press, pp. 105-20.
    Discusses the divided grouping of III.i., with Pandarus
moving between two groups on stage, and the Troilus-
Cressida trysting scene, with Pandarus acting as go-between
and dumb-show director. Somewhat interesting for its
conjectural reconstruction of implied stage directions.

29 MEHL, DIETER. Die Pantomime im Drama der Shakespearzeit.
    Schriftenreihe der deutschen Shakespeare-Gessellschaft-
    West, n.s. 10. Heidelberg: Quelle & Meyer, 160 pp.
        Published version of a 1960 Munich Ph.D. dissertation.
    See 1966.13 for translation.

30 MILLER, WILLIAM E. "Periaktoi: Around Again." SQ 15
    (Winter):61-65.
        Responds to Hotson's questioning (in 1959.9) of his
    consideration of the use of periaktoi at the first Black-
    riars (see 1959.16).

31 RICKERT, R[OBERT] T. "That Wonderful Year--1596." RenP 1963,
    pp. 53-62.
        A paper presented at the Southeastern Renaissance
    Conference, 1963. Rickert examines information available
    to Chambers (1923.2) about the Lord Admiral's Men and the
    Lord Chamberlain's Men in 1596, challenging Chambers's
    assertion that the year was a smooth one for both companies.
    He concludes that, in fact, 1596 was the most difficult
    year for both companies from 1594 to 1603. An interesting
    speculation that Rickert puts forward is that Henslowe
    deliberately split his company in order to hold the Swan
    against the Chamberlain's Men.

32 SMITH, IRWIN. Shakespeare's Blackfriars Playhouse: Its
    History and Its Design. New York: New York University
    Press, 577 pp.
        An attempt at both a comprehensive history of the
    precinct and the playhouse and a complete reconstruction of
    the theatre based on the plays that were presented there.
    The first twelve chapters deal with the history and the
    last four with the reconstruction. In addition Smith
    prints forty-six documents in an appendix and includes
    twenty-five drawings and eight photographic plates. While
    the historical part of the study takes better than half
    the volume, it is the reconstruction that is generally
    known. Smith follows the lead of Cranford Adams (1942.1)
    in this work, as he did in his similar book on the Globe
    (1952.18). His Blackfriars Playhouse is complete with
    inner above, oblique side doors with windows above, a
    third level, an inner below, and three galleries for
    spectators. See also Index, under Blackfriars Playhouse--
    Reconstructions, for other approaches.

1964

33 SOUTHERN, RICHARD. "Current Controversies about the Eliza-
       bethan Stage." World Theatre 13 (Summer):74-80.
          Discusses the state of "some slight and comparatively
       genial controversy over a number of minor points" of the
       architecture of the Elizabethan stage. The Swan drawing
       and its lack of an "inner stage" is the major controversy,
       and Southern here sums up both sides of the case. A facing
       column French translation is a standard feature of this
       journal.

34 _____. "Les interludes au temps des Tudor." In Le lieu
       théâtral à la Renaissance. Edited by Jean Jacquot. Paris:
       CNRS, pp. 289-94.
          Examines the evolution of the complex Tudor Interlude
       from roughly 1500 to 1580. Southern here emphasizes the
       development of the physical aspects of the performance. He
       describes the typical Great Hall in detail, including the
       dais, the screen, and the buttery. See also 1973.26;
       second edition, 1968.37.

35 THORNBERRY, RICHARD THAYER. "Shakespeare and the Blackfriars
       Tradition." Ph.D. dissertation, Ohio State University,
       339 pp.
          Attempts to determine whether Shakespeare's last five
       plays exhibit features attributable to the taste of the
       Blackfriars audience and whether he wrote them for that
       playhouse, for the Globe, or for both. Thornberry concludes
       that Cymbeline and Henry VIII were written exclusively for
       the Globe; that Winter's Tale, Tempest, and Two Noble
       Kinsmen were written for both playhouses; and that the
       interests of the Blackfriars audience exerted a limited
       but definite influence on four of Shakespeare's last five
       plays.

36 TURNER, ROBERT Y. "Significant Doubling of Roles in Henry VI,
       Part Two." Library Chronicle (University of Pennsylvania)
       30 (Spring):77-84.
          Argues that two actors in 2 Henry VI "doubled roles of
       consistent moral significance." The actor who played
       Richard of York doubled as Jack Cade, and the actor who
       played Humphrey doubled as Lord Say and as Alexander Iden.

37 WICKHAM, GLYNNE. "Emblème et image: Quelques remarques sur
       la manière de figurer et de représenter le lieu sur la
       scène anglaise au XVIe siècle." In Le lieu théâtral à la
       Renaissance. Edited by Jean Jacquot. Paris: CNRS,
       pp. 317-22.

Discusses the emblematic nature of Elizabethan spectacle in the sixteenth and early seventeenth centuries; based on 1963.20. See also second edition, 1968.38.

38 _____. "Exeunt to the Cave: Notes on the Staging of Marlowe's Plays." TDR 8, no. 4 (Summer):184-94.
Examines the stage directions of Marlowe's plays for evidence of their original staging. Wickham finds no evidence for a trap, but ample evidence for an upper acting space, although it is not often used. Large properties (which Wickham calls "emblems") were frequently used. Reprinted: 1969.18.

1965

1 ADAMS, BARRY B. "Doubling in Bale's King Johan." SP 62 (April):111-20.
Discusses the eight of fourteen roles marked for doubling by three actors in the only surviving text of the play and speculates that the remaining roles would also have been doubled; therefore, the entire interlude could have been played by six actors.

2 ANGUS, WILLIAM. "Acting Shakespeare." QQ 72 (January):312-33.
Discusses both Shakespearean acting now and in the Renaissance, coming down firmly on the side of the "natural" school. Angus also offers a brief summary of approaches through the years to acting Shakespeare.

3 ANIKST, A[LEKSANDR ABRAMOVICH]. Teatr ėpokhi Shekspira [Theatre of Shakespeare's Time.] Moscow: Uskysstbo, 328 pp.
A comprehensive survey of English theatre in the period, based on secondary sources. The fifteen chapters examine the playhouses, actors, business practices, government regulation, companies, repertories, staging, costume practices, clowns, music, and Puritan opposition.

4 BENTLEY, GERALD EADES. "Theatrical Conditions and Shakespeare's Plays." SRO 1:21-24.
Argues for approaching Shakespeare's plays "as products designed for Elizabethan theatres."

5 CHARNEY, MAURICE. "Hamlet without Words." ELH 32 (December):457-77.
A paper read at the Eleventh Annual Shakespeare Conference, Stratford-upon-Avon, 1964. Charney discusses indications for sound effects, music, costumes, and properties in both the dialogue and stage directions.

1965

6   DAWSON, GILES E., ed. "Records of Plays and Players in Kent
    1450-1642." MSC 7:1-211.
        Entries in the records of thirteen towns in Kent record-
    ing visits by players or companies during the years
    indicated. Dawson also includes records of other enter-
    tainers, such as minstrels and jugglers. Most entries
    record payments made.

7   DOLAN de AVILA, WANDA. "La vida y teatro de William Shake-
    speare." Humanitas 18:209-20.
        Text of a paper presented at a conference celebrating
    the 400th anniversary of Shakespeare's birth, held at the
    National University of Tucumán in Argentina. Approximately
    the last half presents a general summary (from secondary
    sources) of theatrical conditions of the period.

8   ELLIS-FERMOR, UNA M. "The Jacobean Stage." In The Jacobean
    Drama: An Interpretation. 5th ed. London: Methuen,
    pp. 273-83.
        Reprint of 1936.8.

9   KING, T[HOMAS] J[AMES]. "The Staging of Plays at the Phoenix
    in Drury Lane, 1617-42." TN 19 (Summer):146-66.
        Abstracted from King's Ph.D. dissertation (1963.11) and
    comes to the same conclusions. One difference, however, is
    that only thirty of the thirty-two plays first examined are
    included.

10 LANGHANS, EDWARD A. "A Picture of the Salisbury Court Theatre."
    TN 19 (Spring):100-101.
        Speculates that the Lea and Glynne 1706 map of London
    might by some unknown mistake show a picture of the play-
    house destroyed some forty years earlier. The theatre
    shown, however, appears to be a rectangular three-story
    open air building rather than the enclosed building
    converted from a barn that the Salisbury Court is known
    to have been.

11 LOWER, CHARLES BRUCE. "Editorial Principles and Practices for
    Indicating Significant Elizabethan Staging in a Reader's
    Edition of Shakespeare." Ph.D. dissertation, University of
    North Carolina, 542 pp.
        Since "Shakespeare's stagecraft is essential to his
    artistry," Lower first establishes a consensus about the
    characteristics of the stage and then suggests the editorial
    implications of each technique of stagecraft. Specifically,
    he suggests printing Shakespeare's plays without act divi-
    sion or location designation, without speech-prefixes for

some minor characters, and with detailed stage directions
indicating stage groupings and essential movement.

12 McMILLIN, HARVEY SCOTT, Jr. "The Staging of Elizabethan Plays
    at the Rose Theatre." Ph.D. dissertation, Stanford Univer-
    sity, 163 pp.
        Discusses staging techniques at the Rose, based on
    thirty-six printed plays and manuscript plots (eleven of
    which "almost certainly reflect playing conditions at the
    Rose alone"). McMillin finds that the Rose looked much
    like the Swan drawing, with the addition of a larger
    central doorway "capable of accommodating mass entrances,
    introducing large properties onto the platform, and
    revealing occasional discoveries." There was apparently
    a trap, "heavens" and its flying machinery, and a long
    gallery at the second level. Simultaneous settings were
    also utilized. McMillin concludes that "drama performed
    within the stage conditions of the Rose creates a world of
    potential moral order, organized by openly theatrical
    conventions in which both actor and spectator participate."
    See also Rhodes (1959.20; 1976.21).

13 REESE, M. M. "The Elizabethan Playhouse." In ha-'Olam
    ha-shekspiri [The Shakespearean World.] Edited by Murray
    Roston. Tel Aviv: Am Hassefer, pp. 59-76.
        A general survey of public and private theatres and
    audiences. Reese focuses on the Globe. See 1958.18 for a
    discussion in English of the same material.

14 TATARKIEWICZ, W. "Theatrica: The Science of Entertainment
    from the 12th to the 17th Century." JHI 26 (April-June):
    263-72.
        Traces the idea of a science of entertainment from Hugh
    of St. Victor through John Henry Alsted. There is nothing
    here of specifically theatrical interest. Included because
    of listing in NCBEL 1, col. 1393.

15 WREN, ROBERT MERIWETHER. "The Blackfriars Theatre and Its
    Repertory, 1600-1608." Ph.D. dissertation, Princeton
    University, 515 pp.
        Investigates the accommodations made by playwrights to
    the theatre, actors, and theatrical conditions of the
    Blackfriars company 1600-1608. First Wren discusses the
    management of the company, then he establishes the repertory
    of twenty plays written for the Blackfriars during this
    period. The heart of the study is the analysis of the
    plays, revealing a main playing space with five entries

1965

and distinct playing areas, "architectonically defined."
There was apparently a "correspondence of literary tech-
nique to the age and relative maturity of the actors, and
to the peculiar talents of the leading actor, Nathan Field."

<u>1966</u>

1 BARTHOLOMEUSZ, DENNIS STEPHEN. "<u>Macbeth</u> and the Actors: A
    Critical Study of Players' Interpretations of the Roles of
    Macbeth and Lady Macbeth on the English Stage from 1611 to
    the Present." Ph.D. dissertation, University of London,
    pp. 1-40.
        Published as 1969.1.

2 BAUR-HEINHOLD, MARGARETE. <u>Theater des Barock: Festliches
    Bühnenspiel im 17. und 18. Jahrhundert</u>. Munich: G. D. W.
    Callwey, pp. 117-19.
        Barely three pages of the volume are given to
    "Shakespearbühne," linking it to the medieval tradition
    and comparing it with Spanish corrales.

3 BECKERMAN, BERNARD. <u>Shakespeare at the Globe, 1599-1609</u>. New
    York: Collier Books, 254 pp.
        Reprint of 1962.2.

4 BERRY, HERBERT. "The Stage and Boxes at Blackfriars." <u>SP</u>
    63 (April):163-86.
        Discloses discovery of a document at the Public Record
    Office that bears on the most important of the private
    playhouses. A newsletter from John Pory to Viscount
    Scudmore dated 4 February 1632 contains details of a
    brawl at Blackfriars that provides evidence that the boxes
    were contiguous to the stage and stood level with it, and
    that audience members stood on the stage. Berry speculates
    that boxes might have been at the back, rather than at the
    sides, of the stage.

5 CUTTS, JOHN P. "New Findings with Regard to the 1624
    Protection List." <u>ShS</u> 19:101-7.
        Attempts to reassess identifications of musicians in
    the 1624 List, to provide evidence for further identifica-
    tions, and to explore the possibility of a permanent
    theatre orchestra. Seven of the twenty-four people men-
    tioned in the Protection List "can definitely be identified
    as musicians," and a potential band of eleven musicians is
    inferred.

236

6 FUSILLO, ROBERT J. "The Staging of Battle Scenes on the
   Shakespearean Stage." Ph.D. dissertation, University of
   Birmingham, 530 pp.
      Examines the staging of battle scenes in publicly
   performed plays in the Elizabethan theatre, 1576-1642.
   During the first forty years of this period over one-third
   of all extant plays include such scenes, requiring "warlike
   conflict between two opposing forces of some size." This
   thesis brings together all available evidence from the
   plays (in reliable editions) and contemporary reports and
   analyzes the convention as a whole and its component
   parts. Six major chapters focus on the preliminaries to
   battle, the stage directions, the beginnings of battle,
   on-stage fighting, other on-stage activity, and the ends
   of battles. Fusillo concludes that, although usually most
   of a battle takes place off-stage with only highlights and
   climaxes shown on-stage, "constant attempts were made to
   improve and increase the realistic appearance and depiction
   of battles, probably in an attempt to adjust to the
   changing substance of drama." The prominence of battle
   scenes decreased as the plays became less romantic after
   the turn of the seventeenth century.

7 GREG, WALTER WILSON. Collected Papers. Edited by J. C.
   Maxwell. Oxford: Clarendon Press, pp. 1-28, 95-109,
   226-38.
      Reprints 1900.2; 1923.6; 1931.9.

8 GURR, ANDREW J. "Elizabethan Action." SP 63 (April):144-56.
      Examines the evolution of "playing" into "acting" from
   1550 to 1650. Gurr compares the "action" of the orator as
   outlined in the rhetorical treatises of the period with
   the "feigned imitation" of the players, and he traces the
   linguistic changes accompanying the improvement in acting
   (at least in repute) around 1600.

9 H[ODGES], C[YRIL] W[ALTER]. "Playhouse Structure." In The
   Readers Encyclopedia of Shakespeare. Edited by Oscar J.
   Campbell and Edward G. Quinn. New York: Thomas Y. Crowell,
   pp. 636-43.
      Aimed at the general reader. Hodges presents a balanced
   summary of what is known of the public and private playhouses, concentrating on recent theories of reconstruction,
   including Adams (1942.1), Hotson (1959.9), and himself
   (1953.9). The Encyclopedia also includes brief anonymous
   articles on a number of theatrical matters: acting; acting
   companies; the Globe, Theatre, Curtain, Fortune, Swan,
   Blackfriars, Salisbury Court, Phoenix, Cockpit-in-Court,

1966

Boar's Head, and Hope Playhouses; Revels Accounts and
Revels Office; the Burbages, Edward Alleyn, Philip
Henslowe; and so on.

10 HUNT, J. A. "Staging by the Paul's Boys in the Seventeenth
Century." Ph.D. dissertation, University of Birmingham,
584 pp.
Examines the plays associated with the Children of
Paul's during the years 1600-1606 for what they tell us
about the physical aspects of the theatre and the company's
production resources and techniques. The four chapters
deal with the history and operation of the company, the
repertory performed by them and the state of their
published and manuscript plays, the stage and tiring house
facade, and the production resources available to the
company (such as properties, costumes, lighting, music,
and special effects). Hunt concludes that, while the
location of the theatre remains obscure, the plays written
for it presume the availability of what he calls "the
more basic elements of the seventeenth century stage":
three doors; a large enough platform to hold twenty actors
and a standing prop; a trap, probably without a mechanical
lifting device; acting space above, including a window for
interiors and a balcony for exteriors; one discovery space
(a permanent projecting structure); and two other possibly
curtained spaces flanking the center space. Few elaborate
properties were used, but music and elaborate costumes were
important parts of performance at this playhouse.

11 KING, T[HOMAS] J[AMES]. "Review Article: Irwin Smith,
Shakespeare's Blackfriars Playhouse." RenD 9:291-309.
Included because the review contains a close analysis
of the staging requirements of fourteen King's Men plays
whose texts carry markings related to prompt copy and for
which records of performance exist. King, following the
pattern he set in his previous work on the Phoenix (1963.11;
1965.9), sets forth the minimal stage features necessary
for production of the plays he considers, including two
stage doors, a trap, several large properties, an acting
area above, and hangings. Discoveries, he says, could be
effected by opening the hangings in front of an unused
doorway, or by the use of a portable curtained booth.
King's review of Smith (1964.32) concludes: "only by a
detailed analysis of the available historical and bibliographical evidence concerning each play can we gain a
clear understanding of how this important body of dramatic
literature was first staged." See also Hosley (1975.16).

12 KOPECKÝ, JAN. "Shakespeare's Forgotten Theatre: A Contribu-
     tion to the Problems of the Theatre Today." In <u>Charles</u>
     <u>University on Shakespeare</u>. Edited by Zdenek Stríbrný and
     Jamelia Emmerová. Prague: Charles University, pp. 93-113.
          A paper read at the Shakespeare Conference of Charles
     University, 23-24 April 1964. Kopecký argues that "Shake-
     speare's work implies the theory of his practices," and
     that by studying the plays we can see the theory in action.
     In particular, the theatrical scenes from the plays can
     tell us a good deal about Shakespeare's theatrical condi-
     tions.

13 MEHL, DIETER. <u>The Elizabethan Dumb Show: The History of a</u>
     <u>Dramatic Convention</u>. Cambridge: Harvard University Press,
     207 pp.
          Translation of 1964.29. Mehl traces the sources of the
     dumb show and then examines selected plays to show the uses
     to which the convention could be put.

14 MORGAN, EDMUND S. "Puritan Hostility to the Theatre." <u>PAPS</u>
     110, no. 5 (27 October):340-47.
          A paper read before the American Philosophical Society,
     22 April 1966. Morgan traces the hostility toward the
     theatre from 1579 to the end of the seventeenth century,
     and later. He ascribes it at least partly to the competi-
     tion furnished by the theatres to the churches.

15 PRESLEY, HORTON EDWARD. "'O Showes, Mighty Showes': A Study
     of the Relationship of the Jones-Jonson Controversy to the
     Rise of Illusionistic Staging in the Seventeenth-Century
     British Drama." Ph.D. dissertation, University of Kansas,
     308 pp.
          Examines the Jonson-Jones quarrel with regard to the
     increasing audience demand for spectacle. Chapter Five in
     particular discusses the state of both the demand and the
     spectacle when Jones began his work in the early seven-
     teenth century, while Chapters Six and Seven document his
     designs for masques and plays and trace his influence on the
     public stage later in the century.

16 RIBNER, IRVING. <u>Tudor and Stuart Drama</u>. Goldentree Bibli-
     ographies in Language and Literature. Northbrook, Ill.,
     A. H. M. Publishing, pp. 5-10.
          Selective unannotated bibliography, with emphasis on
     major works since 1920. Ribner lists 116 entries in the
     relevant section, "Dramatic Companies, Theatres, Conditions
     of Performance." All relevant entries have been incorpo-
     rated into this bibliography. <u>See</u> second edition, 1978.22.

1966

17 RICHTER, BODO L. O. "Recent Studies on Renaissance Sceno-
      graphy." <u>RenN</u> 19 (Winter):344-58.
          Essentially a lengthy review article, commenting on
      Jacquot's collection of essays (<u>see</u> 1964.2, 18, 22, 34,
      37).

18 SCHAAR, CLAES. "'They hang him in the arbor.'" <u>ES</u> 47
      (February):27-28.
          Proposes the transposing of the two stage directions
      "They hang him in the arbor" and "They stab him" in
      <u>Spanish Tragedy</u> as more likely to reflect Kyd's intentions.
      <u>See</u> 1966.21.

19 SELTZER, DANIEL. "The Staging of the Last Plays." <u>The Later</u>
      <u>Shakespeare</u>. Stratford-on-Avon Studies, no. 8. London:
      Edward Arnold, pp. 127-66.
          Examines the last six of Shakespeare's plays with special
      reference to the techniques of the actors and the use of
      spectacle and music. Seltzer uses stage directions, both
      explicit and implicit, to recreate stage business, voice,
      blocking, and what he calls "address." He concludes that
      "the acting techniques . . . reveal an art conservative
      in its uses of the past, yet thoroughly capable of a wide
      range of flexible stage movements, small details of busi-
      ness, modulation of facial expression and address, and
      stage moves. . . . Always the intention was to represent
      realistically the motion of the mind and the very shape
      of nature."

20 SHAPIRO, I. A. "Robert Fludd's Stage-Illustration." <u>ShSt</u>
      2:192-209.
          Takes issue with Yates's identification of the illustra-
      tion as the Globe (in 1966.28), arguing instead for the
      Blackfriars. <u>See also</u> 1958.2; 1967.1; 1967.17.

21 SMITH, JAMES L. "'They hang him in the arbor': A Defense of
      the Accepted Text." <u>ES</u> 47 (October):372-73.
          Defends the traditional order of the stage directions
      "They hang him in the arbor" and "They stab him" in <u>Spanish</u>
      <u>Tragedy</u> on the basis of an imaginative visualization of the
      scene. Schaar, who proposed the transposition (<u>see</u>
      1966.18), replies briefly.

22 SOMERSET, JOHN ALAN BEAUFORT. "The Comic Turn in English
    Drama, 1470-1616." Ph.D. dissertation, University of
    Birmingham, 839 pp.
        Focuses primarily on the development of the low comic
    scene through the interaction of the actors and the play-
    wright. While primarily literary in orientation,
    Somerset does examine the improvisations of the clowns and
    direct audience address that are of theatrical interest.
    Also helpful is his tracing of the Elizabethan clown from
    the medieval vice.

23 SOMERSET, J[OHN] A[LAN] B[EAUFORT]. "William Poel's First
    Full Platform Stage." TN 21 (Spring):118-21.
        Discusses Poel's use of a full platform stage in 1927
    for his production of Rowley's When You See Me, You Know
    Me.

24 SPRAGUE, ARTHUR COLBY. The Doubling of Parts in Shakespeare's
    Plays. London: Society for Theatre Research, 35 pp.
        Primarily concerned with the later stage history of
    doubling rather than with doubling in Shakespeare's day.
    Only the last three pages examine Elizabethan practice,
    and that generally.

25 WHALLY, JOYCE I. "The Swan Theatre in the Sixteenth Century."
    TN 20 (Winter):73.
        Transcribes the text of the Swan drawing, and prints
    photographs of both the drawing and the text.

26 WRIGHT, LOUIS B. Shakespeare's Theatre and the Dramatic
    Tradition. Washington: Folger Shakespeare Library, 36 pp.
        Reprint of 1958.24.

27 WRIGHT, W. S. "Edward Alleyn, Actor and Benefactor, 1566-
    1626." TN 20 (Summer):155-60.
        A reappraisal of Alleyn's life, based on the holdings of
    the Dulwich College Library. See also Index, under Alleyn,
    for earlier and more complete treatments.

28 YATES, FRANCES. "New Light on the Globe Theatre." NYRB
    6, no. 9 (26 May):16-22.
        Excerpted from a chapter of her The Art of Memory, and
    containing the same information on Fludd's 1619 Ars
    Memoriae. Fludd printed illustrations of several "memory
    theatres," one of which looks rather like our typical idea
    of an Elizabethan playhouse, with two doorways, a gated
    discovery space, and an upper gallery. Yates suggests that
    it may shed light on the structure of the Globe. See also
    1966.20; 1967.1, 17; 1958.2.

1967

1 BERRY, HERBERT. "Dr. Fludd's Engravings and Their Beholders."
 ShSt 3:11–21.
   Argues against the illustrations in Fludd's Ars Memoriae
   as being of English theatres, responding to Yates (1966.28)
   and Shapiro (1966.20). See also Yates's response (1967.17),
   and Bernheimer (1958.2).

2 HAWLEY, JAMES ABGRIFFITH. "Inigo Jones and the New English
   Stagecraft." Ph.D. dissertation, Ohio State University,
   154 pp.
   "An examination of the total staging contributions of the
   masques reached through an analysis of Inigo Jones's precise
   methods of staging." Hawley identifies definite periods of
   design style in Jones, from the early scaffold stage
   displaying large units in a shuttered enclosed area, to
   the later "full shutter nest" with flat wings. While some
   of this change in style can be traced to the development
   of the later masques, much of it occurred because of Jones's
   experimentation with continental devices.

3 HOSLEY, RICHARD. "Elizabethan Theatres and Audiences." RORD
   10:9–16.
   Text of a paper read at the 1966 MLA convention. Hosley
   here examines the size of the audience at both public
   (2500–3000) and private (about 720) playhouses and the
   influences exerted on the plays by these two classes of
   theatre. He also discusses the use of entre-act music
   in the private playhouses.

4 KIRSCH, ARTHUR C. "Cymbeline and Coterie Dramaturgy." ELH
   34 (September):285–306.
   Assumes Cymbeline was written for the particular audience of the Blackfriars and examines the text for evidence
   of how Shakespeare catered to this coterie. Deliberate
   self-consciousness, in the style of Fletcher and Marston, is
   one way. Another is the use of the tragicomic form. Still
   another is the conspicuousness of the workings of Provi-
   dence. Kirsch sees the influence of the private theatre
   audience as important.

5 KLEIN, DAVID. "Time Allotted for an Elizabethan Performance."
   SQ 18 (Autumn):434–38.
   Responds to Hart (1932.6), arguing for a presentation
   time of more than two hours.

6 MATSON, MARSHALL NYVADL. "A Critical Edition of The Wisdom of
   Doctor Dodypoll (1600) with a Study of Dodypoll's Place in
   the Repertory of Paul's Boys." Ph.D. dissertation, Northwestern University, 359 pp.
       A critical old-spelling edition of the play, with a
   study of the Paul's repertory "with particular attention
   to the revival of boys' theatrical activities in late 1599
   and Dodypoll's part in that revival." An appendix examines
   staging and music.

7 MULLIN, DONALD C. "An Observation on the Origin of the Elizabethan Theatre." ETJ 19 (October):322-26.
       Discusses the state of theories of the origin of the
   Elizabethan public theatres and rejects the idea of genera-
   tion from inn-yards and baiting rings. Mullin sees a more
   direct classical influence, particularly from Roman arenas.

8 REYNOLDS, GEORGE F[ULLMER]. On Shakespeare's Stage. Edited
   by Richard K. Knaub. Boulder: University of Colorado
   Press, 109 pp.
       Texts of four lectures at Stratford-upon-Avon, July 1954.
   Reynolds first examines the available evidence (pictorial
   and textual) concerning Shakespeare's stage, and then
   applies the evidence to two critical questions: the nature
   of the rear stage, and the use of the main platform.
   Reynolds also considers the use of scene boards to localize
   entrances and exits. He returns to his stress of the
   primacy of the platform, and reiterates his theory of the
   portable curtained booth. See also Index, under Reynolds,
   for more of his more original and well-known contributions.

9 ROWAN, D. F. "The 'Swan' Revisited." RORD 10:33-48.
       Text of a paper read at the 1966 MLA convention. Rowan
   reviews the state of scholarship on the Swan drawing,
   focusing on the debate over the lack of an "inner stage."
   He also discusses the only play known to have been produced
   at the Swan, The Chaste Maid of Cheapside, and concludes
   that the play could have been staged at the Swan as
   DeWitt drew it.

10 SHAPIRO, MICHAEL. "The Plays Acted by the Children of Paul's,
   1599-1607." Ph.D. dissertation, Columbia University,
   398 pp.
       Expanded version published: 1977.32.

1967

11 SHAW, JOHN. "The Staging of Parody and Parallels in 1 Henry
    IV." ShS 20:61-73.
        Examines Prince Hal's interviews with Falstaff posing
    as the king and with the real king, and contemporary
    attitudes toward parody, to show that the scenes are meant
    to be similarly staged in order to reinforce the parallels.
    Shaw then examines two other scenes, the Hotspur-Kate
    interview and the Francis-Hal scene in the tavern, assert-
    ing that parallel staging will bring out a strong parallel
    in structure and meaning.

12 SMITH, IRWIN. "Their Exits and Reentrances." SQ 18
    (Winter):7-16.
        Examines exits by characters at the end of one scene
    and immediate reentrances at the beginning of the next in
    Shakespeare. Smith discusses the sixteen possible viola-
    tions of the so-called "Law of Reentry," and concludes that
    none of them, in fact, is a violation. This, to Smith,
    is evidence of a lack of act intermissions in the public
    playhouses.

13 STYAN, J. L. Shakespeare's Stagecraft. Cambridge: University
    Press, 244 pp.
        Intended as a guide to exploration of Shakespeare's
    stage practices. The three parts review scholarship on the
    Elizabethan stage and acting conventions and discuss Shake-
    speare's visual and aural craft from the point of view of
    the director and actor. The main point is that "the
    requirement of Shakespearian scholarship . . . is first to
    be able to read the texts through the eyes of an Eliza-
    bethan actor." This is precisely what Styan attempts here.

14 TAYLOR, ALISON. The Story of the English Stage. Oxford:
    Pergamon Press, pp. 20-33.
        A general treatment for an adolescent audience, complete
    with study questions at the end of each chapter. The
    relevant section is Chapter Three, "The Elizabethan
    Theatre." Taylor discusses the playhouse (reprinting the
    Swan drawing), the companies and actors, and production
    practices.

15 WICKHAM, GLYNNE. "The Cockpit Reconstructed." NTM 7
    (Spring):26-36.
        A correlation of the information in the Accounts of the
    Office of Works with the Inigo Jones design for the Cockpit-
    in-Court allows Wickham to reconstruct that playhouse down
    to fine details. The date of the theatre's opening is set

at 1630, rather than 1632, and the familiar design of the playhouse is discussed in terms of the records of its construction.

16 WREN, ROBERT M. "The Five-Entry Stage at Blackfriars." <u>TR</u> 8, no. 3:130-38.
    Based on Wren's Ph.D. dissertation (1965.15). Discusses plays presented by the Children of the Chapel at Black-friars, 1600-1608. Wren concludes that "the Blackfriars theatre had a five-entry, architectonically-segmented facade stage, markedly unlike the Swan drawing or any reconstruction based on the Swan." He proposes the Amster-dam Schouwburg as a model, suggesting that it might be thought related to the Blackfriars. <u>See</u> <u>also</u> Hosley (1975.15) and King (1966.11).

17 YATES, FRANCES A. "The Stage in Robert Fludd's Memory System." <u>ShSt</u> 3:138-66.
    Responds to Shapiro (1966.20), answering his objections to her identification of the illustration in <u>Ars Memoriae</u> as the Globe and refuting his identification of it as the Blackfriars. <u>See</u> <u>also</u> Berry (1967.1) and Bernheim (1958.2).

1968

1 ANGLO, SYDNEY. "La salle de banquet et le théâtre construits a Greenwich pour les fêtes franco-anglais de 1527." In <u>Le lieu théâtral à la Renaissance</u>. 2d ed. Edited by Jean Jacquot. Paris: CNRS, pp. 273-88.
    Reprint of 1964.2.

2 BENTLEY, GERALD EADES. <u>The Jacobean and Caroline Stage</u>. Vols. 6-7. Oxford: Clarendon Press, 699 pp.
    The final volumes of Bentley's reference work, begun in 1941.1 and continued in 1956.4. Volume 6 deals with the theatres of the period 1616-42, and volume 7 contains appendixes to volume 6 and an analytical index to all seven volumes. As in earlier volumes, the treatment of the playhouses in volume 6 is primarily documentary. That is, Bentley has presented all available documentary evidence for each theatre and has briefly weighed the conflicting hypotheses that have been put forward about each, but he has refrained from drawing any conclusions of his own. While there are entries for eight private theatres, sixteen public theatres, four court theatres, and two projected theatres, naturally not all are discussed in

detail. For example, the entries on the first Blackfriars
and the Theatre merely refer the reader to Chambers
(1923.2) and J. Q. Adams (1917.3). The most space is
devoted to the second Blackfriars, the Phoenix, the
Salisbury Court, the second Fortune, and the second Globe.
Each entry begins with a brief bibliography (up to 1962)
and then presents all available evidence. The appendixes
in volume 7 include discussions of Sunday and Lenten
performances and "Annals of Jacobean and Caroline Theatrical
Affairs," perhaps the most valuable section of the entire
series since it lays out all the material in chronological
order. These seven volumes are without question the most
important work in the field to date.

3   _____, ed. The Seventeenth-Century Stage: A Collection of
     Critical Essays. Patterns of Literary Criticism, no. 6.
     Chicago: University of Chicago Press, 287 pp.
          Reprints of 1926.12; 1927.18, 23; 1953.2; 1954.21;
     1958.8; 1960.16; 1961.4; 1964.23. Also contains 1968.31,
     as well as an introduction by the editor and four seven-
     teenth-century commentaries. These include selections from
     The Gull's Horn Book and An Apology for Actors, the Induc-
     tion to Bartholomew Fair, and the Praeludium for The Care-
     less Shepherdess. Bentley's Introduction lucidly describes
     the methods and history of scholarship in the field.

4   BERGERON, DAVID M. "The Christmas Family: Artificers in
     English Civic Pageantry." ELH, 35, no. 3 (September):354-64.
          Discusses the contributions Gerard Christmas and his two
     sons made to civic pageantry, illuminating the relationship
     between poet and architect in the process. The Christmases
     worked with Middleton, Dekker, and Heywood on the mayoral
     shows, and were frequently commended for their work. The
     role of artificer increased significantly during their
     tenure.

5   _____. "The Emblematic Nature of English Civic Pageantry."
     RenD, n.s. 1:167-98.
          Some preliminary suggestions about the connection between
     emblems and civic pageantry, 1558-1640. Bergeron estab-
     lishes that "the method of the emblem and the pageant is
     fundamentally the same," and while no direct link can be
     established, he argues for mutual inspiration.

6   _____. "Harrison, Jonson and Dekker: The Magnificent Enter-
     tainment for King James (1604)." JWCI 31:445-48.
          A note on James's royal entry into London on 15 March
     1603/4. Stephen Harrison designed and built the triumphal
     arches, while Jonson, Dekker, and Middleton collaborated

on the text. There are inconsistencies, however, between Harrison's drawings and the textual descriptions, and Bergeron tentatively suggests that Harrison is more accurate.

7 _____. "Prince Henry and English Civic Pageantry." TSL 13:109-16.
Discusses the relation of the Prince of Wales to the pageantry of the early Stuart era. Bergeron traces the homage paid to Henry in Royal Entries and Lord Mayor's Shows from 1610 until 1624, some fourteen years after the Prince's death.

8 BEST, MICHAEL R. "The Staging and Production of the Plays of John Lyly." TR 9, no. 2:104-17.
Based on Best's Ph.D. dissertation, 1964.5. He assumes that the first Blackfriars, the stages at Court, and the stage at Paul's were "substantially the same in structure," and then uses Lyly's plays to reconstruct them. Best finds that a stage with two entrances from off-stage and with two houses set in opposition across the stage would have been sufficient for the staging of Lyly's plays.

9 BRADBROOK, M[URIEL] C. Elizabethan Stage Conditions: A Study of Their Place in the Interpretation of Shakespeare's Plays. Cambridge: University Press, 149 pp.
Reprint of 1932.2.

10 DEMADRE, ANTOINE. "Un témoin: Thomas Nashe." In Dramaturgie et société: Rapports entre l'oeuvre théâtrale, son interprétation et son public aux XVIe et XVIIe siècles. Vol. 2. Edited by Jean Jacquot. Paris: CNRS, pp. 577-88.
Nashe's writings bear witness to changing theatrical conditions in late sixteenth-century London. His works shed light on dates, places, attributions, aspects and opponents of the theatre, and, representatively on a "University Wit" in a changing theatre and on an "author-victim" who lived in poverty and persecution and who died miserably.

11 DUCKLES, VINCENT. "The Music for the Lyrics in Early Seventeenth-Century English Drama: A Bibliography of Primary Sources." In Music in English Renaissance Drama. Edited by John H. Long. Lexington: University of Kentucky Press, pp. 117-60.
Lists manuscript sources, modern editions, and period editions of music for the songs in plays of the period. The list is broken down by playwright and play.

1968

12 FREEHAFER, JOHN. "Brome, Suckling, and Davenant's Theater
    Project of 1639." TSLL 10 (Fall):367-84.
        Identifies Brome's Court Beggar as the banned play
    presented at the Cockpit in 1640 and relates it to Brome's
    opposition to Davenant's project for bringing the innovations
    of the court into the public theatres. Freehafer explores
    the details of the Brome-Davenant rivalry and the plan for
    the projected playhouse, and concludes that Davenant's
    Duke's Theatre of 1661 was the realization of that plan.

13 _____. "The Italian Night Piece and Suckling's Aglaura."
    JEGP 67 (Spring):249-65.
        Identifies The Italian Night Piece with Suckling's
    Aglaura, and asserts it was acted by the King's Men at
    Blackfriars and later in a new version with changeable
    scenery from a masque at court.

14 GAIR, W. R. "La Compagnie des Enfants de St. Paul, Londres
    (1559 à 1606)." In Dramaturgie et société: Rapports entre
    l'oeuvre théâtrale, son interprétation et son public aux
    XVIe et XVIIe siècles. Vol. 2. Edited by Jean Jacquot.
    Paris: CNRS, 655-74.
        Examines the theatre operated by the Children of Paul's
    and this company's role in the "War of the Theatres."
    Originally, St. Paul's Boys had a refined, aristocratic
    image, catering to those wanting to savor the entertainment
    played at court. External and internal pressures, however,
    caused the clientele and repertory to change from elite to
    sensation-seekers, from amateurs' aristocratic literary
    activities to a collection of scandals. Gair claims that
    St. Paul's failed as an amateur theatre because it became
    too popular.

15 HAAKER, ANN. "The Plague, the Theater, and the Poet." RenD,
    n.s. 1:283-306.
        Discusses two 1640 documents which reveal a good deal
    about the relationship between the Salisbury Court Play-
    house and its resident dramatist, Richard Brome. The first
    is a complaint filed by the actors and owners of Queen
    Henrietta's Men, and the second is Brome's reply. Much of
    the conflict concerns the closing of the theatres for the
    plague outbursts of 1636-37. Haaker also prints C. W.
    Wallace's transcripts of both documents in full.

16 HODGES, C[YRIL] WALTER. The Globe Restored. 2d ed. New York:
    Coward-McCann, 177 pp.
        Revised and enlarged edition of 1953.9. There are
    additional illustrations, already one of the work's great-
    est strengths, and a new chapter offering a conjectural
    reconstruction of the Globe that Hodges thought best to
    leave out of the first version.

17 HOSLEY, RICHARD. "The Origins of the So-Called Elizabethan
    Multiple Stage." TDR 12, no. 2 (Winter):28-50.
        Originally a paper read at the November 1966 meeting
    of the American Society for Theatre Research. Hosley
    examines the derivation of the component parts of the
    multiple stage proposed by J. C. Adams (1942.1) and others.
    He first lists the "external" evidence (the pictures) for
    the Elizabethan stage and then examines the obliquely set
    doors, the traps, the inner stage, the upper stage, and
    the music room, all common elements in reconstructions.
    He concludes that these elements were introduced by
    reasoning backwards from post-Restoration practices.

18 _____. "Reconstitution du théâtre du Swan." In Le lieu
    théâtral à la Renaissance. 2d ed. Edited by Jean Jacquot.
    Paris: CNRS, pp. 295-316.
        Reprint of 1964.17.

19 INGRAM, R[EGINALD] W[ILLIAM]. "Patterns of Music and Action
    in Fletcherian Drama." In Music in English Renaissance
    Drama. Edited by John H. Long. Lexington: University of
    Kentucky Press, pp. 75-94.
        Discusses the use of music for mood heightening in
    several of Fletcher's plays. Ingram argues that in
    Fletcher "music was a homogeneous part of the dramatic
    context."

20 JACQUOT, JEAN, ed. Dramaturgie et société: Rapports entre
    l'oeuvre théâtrale, son interprétation et son public aux
    XVIe et XVIIe siècles. Vol. 2. Paris: CNRS, pp. 525-888.
        The relevant section examines England, including five
    essays of theatrical rather than literary interest:
    1968.10, 14, 21, 24, 32.

21 JACQUOT, JEAN. "Le répertorie des compagnies d'enfants à
    Londres (1660-1610): Essai d'interprétation socio-drama-
    tique." In Dramaturgie et société: Rapports entre l'oeuvre
    théâtrale, son interprétation et son public aux XVIe et
    XVIIe siècles. Vol. 2. Edited by Jean Jacquot. Paris:
    CNRS, pp. 729-82.

1968

Examines the repertories of the Children of Paul's and
the Children of the Chapel and attempts by comparing common characteristics to pinpoint their creative influence.
Histrio-Mastix gives us an idea of the children's companies'
authors' view of society, of themselves, and of their
audience. Jacquot views audience taste as leading to the
development of tragicomedy and, eventually, comedy of
manners.

22 ____. "Les théâtres élisabéthain," in "Les types de lieu
théâtral et leurs transformations." In Le lieu théâtral à
la Renaissance. 2d ed. Edited by Jean Jacquot. Paris:
CNRS, pp. 291-96.
Reprint of 1964.21.

23 JENSEN, EJNER J. "The Style of the Boy Actors." CompD 2
(Summer):100-14.
Argues for a natural style of acting in the children's
companies, similar to the style employed by the adult
actors.

24 LECOCQ, LOUIS. "Le théâtre de Blackfriars de 1596 à 1606."
In Dramaturgie et société: Rapports entre l'oeuvre
théâtrale, son interprétation et son public aux XVIe et
XVIIe siècles. Vol. 2. Edited by Jean Jacquot. Paris:
CNRS, pp. 675-704.
Examines the theatre building, the actors, the repertory,
and the audience of the second Blackfriars under the
Children. Lecocq summarizes the dealings of the Burbages
with Henry Evans and the Children of the Queen's Revels
from a variety of secondary sources.

25 LONG, JOHN H., ed. Music in English Renaissance Drama.
Lexington: University of Kentucky Press, 184 pp.
Includes 1968.11, 19.

26 McMILLIN, [HARVEY] SCOTT. "Jonson's Early Entertainments:
New Information from Hatfield House." RenD, n.s. 1:153-66.
Discusses newly discovered documents bearing on four
of Jonson's early entertainments for the Earl of Salisbury,
1606-1609. McMillin includes information about the actors,
Inigo Jones's collaboration, payments to Jonson and Jones,
and the staging and costumes employed. Both Edward Alleyn
and Nathan Field were involved. The documents do not
contain the texts of the entertainments.

27 NOSWORTHY, J. M. "Dornackes and Colysenes in Henslowe's
    Diary." N&Q n.s. 15 (July):247-48.
        Suggests that "dornackes" in the diary means "dornick,"
    a fabric used for hangings, and that "colysenes" means
    "cullisance," a corruption of "cognizance."

28 ORGEL, STEPHEN. "To Make Boards to Speak: Inigo Jones's
    Stage and the Jonsonian Masque." RenD, n.s. 1:121-52.
        Considers the "interaction between the inventions of the
    poet and of the designer," concentrating on the period
    1610-18. Orgel sees both as moving toward a significant
    redefinition of the form of the masque, which "in great
    measure determined the course of English drama for the
    next three hundred years."

29 PETIT, J. B. "'This Wooden O': Théâtre et signe dans les
    choeurs de Henry V." EA 21 (July-September):268-92.
        Examines the six speeches of the Chorus in Henry V
    for what they tell us about the means of presentation in
    the Elizabethan playhouse. Petit argues that Shakespeare
    dismissed the limitations of the theatre by the act of
    calling attention to them.

30 RICHARDS, KENNETH R. "Changeable Scenery for Plays on the
    Caroline Stage." TN 23 (Autumn):6-20.
        Reexamines the case for the use of changeable scenery
    on the stage of the Caroline private playhouses. Richards
    identifies only twelve plays "for which there is good
    evidence that they were performed with changeable painted
    scenery," and all twelve were presented at court or in a
    private residence. He concludes that there is little
    reason to believe that changeable painted scenery was
    used in the playhouses.

31 RINGLER, W[ILLIAM] A. "The Number of Actors in Shakespeare's
    Early Plays." In The Seventeenth Century Stage. Edited by
    G[erald] E[ades] Bentley. Patterns of Literary Criticism,
    no. 6. Chicago: University of Chicago Press, pp. 110-36.
        Examines the plays Shakespeare wrote for the Lord
    Chamberlain's Men to determine the number of actors avail-
    able in that troupe. Eighteen pre-Globe plays are examined,
    and through the creation of scene-by-scene charts and
    doubling schemes (the charts for Julius Caesar are printed)
    Ringler finds that sixteen actors represents the usual size
    of this company. Finally, the doubling in Love's Labour's
    Lost and Midsummer Night's Dream is examined for what it
    can tell us about Shakespeare's original productions.

1968

32 SALINGAR, L. G.; HARRISON, GERALD; and COCHRANE, BRUCE. "Les
    comédiens et leur public en Angleterre de 1520 à 1640." In
    Dramaturgie et société: Rapports entre l'oeuvre théâtrale,
    son interprétation et son public aux XVIe et XVIIe siècles.
    Vol. 2. Edited by Jean Jacquot. Paris: CNRS, pp. 525-76.
       A comprehensive, statistical treatment of the vitality,
    development, and downfall of the dramatic arts during the
    Elizabethan age. The authors examine audience demand,
    intellectual quality of the public, the social composition
    of the audience, and the economics of the theatre. The
    tables and statistics focus attention on development during
    the period. Most information is secondary, drawn from
    Harbage and Schoenbaum (1964.13), Murray (1910.15), Chambers
    (1923.3), Bentley (1941.1; 1956.4; 1968.2), and Wickham
    (1959.29; 1963.20; 1972.32).

33 SCHANZER, ERNEST. "Hercules and His Load." RES, n.s. 19
    (February):51-53.
       A brief note suggesting that George Steevens, not
    Edmond Malone, was the first to state that the sign of the
    Globe Playhouse was a picture of Hercules carrying the
    globe.

34 SCOUTEN, E. H. "Some Assumptions behind Accounts of the Eliza-
    bethan Stage." In On Stage and Off: Eight Essays on
    English Literature. Edited by John W. Ehrstine and Emmet
    Langdon Avery. Pullman: Washington State University Press,
    pp. 4-11.
       A paper presented at the University of Toronto, 9
    November 1967. Scouten uses Morse Peckham's theory of
    constructs to discover the unstated assumptions underlying
    standard histories of the Elizabethan stage, particularly
    Chambers (1923.2). The most important assumption is evolu-
    tion: there has been a gradual development in complexity,
    and the Elizabethan stage falls between the medieval and
    the Restoration. Scouten also attacks "the myth of the
    innyards" and the division of Shakespeare's texts into
    acts and scenes.

35 SHAPIRO, MICHAEL. "Music and Song in Plays Acted by
    Children's Companies during the English Renaissance." CM
    7:97-110.
       Examines the songs of the boy companies. Shapiro iden-
    tifies four types of songs (complaints, servant songs,
    pastoral and supernatural songs, and religious songs) and
    discusses the use of instrumental music. One of his
    purposes "is to invite musicologists to collaborate with

literary scholars in investigating music and song and
their uses in non-Shakespearean drama of the English
Renaissance."

36 SLOVER, GEORGE W. "The Elizabethan Playhouse and the Tradition of Liturgical Stage Structure." Ph.D. dissertation,
Indiana University, 448 pp.
    Discusses the idea of "stage and theater structure as
symbolic form," with the Elizabethan stage in the tradition
of the Greek, Roman, and medieval stages. "The stage of
the Elizabethan playhouse is . . . an emblem . . . [belong-
ing] to the emblem family representing state." Slover sees
the Elizabethan stage as appearing in the transition from
"Medieval" to "Modern." The supplanting of it by the
picture-frame stage is part of the same transition.

37 SOUTHERN, RICHARD. "Les interludes au temps des Tudor." In
Le lieu théâtral à la Renaissance. 2d ed. Edited by Jean
Jacquot. Paris: CNRS, pp. 284-94.
    Reprint of 1964.34.

38 WICKHAM, GLYNNE. "Emblème et image: Quelques remarques sur
la manière de figurer et de représenter le lieu sur la scène
anglaise au XVIᵉ siècle." In Le lieu théâtral à la
Renaissance. 2d ed. Edited by Jean Jacquot. Paris:
CNRS, pp. 317-22.
    Reprint of 1964.36.

39 ZUCKER, DAVID HARD. "Stage and Image in the Plays of
Christopher Marlowe." Ph.D. dissertation, University of
Syracuse, 231 pp.
    Published as 1972.35.

1969

1 BARTHOLOMEUSZ, DENNIS [STEPHEN]. "Macbeth" and the Players.
Cambridge: University Press, pp. 1-13.
    Published version of 1966.1. The relevant section deals
with Macbeth at the Globe. Simon Forman's description of
a performance in 1611 is the basis for initial speculation
that Macbeth first enters on horseback and that Banquo's
ghost is sitting in Macbeth's chair after Macbeth drinks
his health. The final part of the treatment involves less
specific information, primarily about the acting of Richard
Burbage.

1969

2 BOURGY, VICTOR. <u>Le bouffon sur la scène anglaise au XVI</u>e
   <u>siècle (c. 1495-1594)</u>. Paris: OCDL; Lille: University
   of Lille, pp. 354-445.
   A University of Lille Ph.D. dissertation. Bourgy
   examines all aspects of the clown or buffoon in English
   drama in the sixteenth century, including the contributions
   of the actors, especially Tarlton, in Chapter Five.
   Reprinted: 1975.3.

3 DEWEY, NICHOLAS. "The Academic Drama of the Early Stuart
   Period (1603-1642): A Checklist of Secondary Sources."
   <u>RORD</u> 12:33-42.
   Divided into two sections: general criticism and
   scholarship, and bibliography and chronology. This checklist contains a total of 110 items, some of theatrical
   interest, sporadically annotated. All relevant items
   have been incorporated into this bibliography.

4 ELLIS-FERMOR, UNA M. "The Jacobean Stage." In <u>The Jacobean</u>
   <u>Drama: An Interpretation</u>. London: Methuen, pp. 273-83.
   Reprint of 1936.8.

5 GREG, W[ALTER] W[ILSON]. <u>Dramatic Documents from the Eliza-</u>
   <u>bethan Playhouse: Stage Plots: Actors' Parts: Prompt</u>
   <u>Books</u>. 2 vols. Oxford: Clarendon Press, 432 pp.
   Reprint of 1931.9.

6 KAHRL, STANLEY J., ed. "Records of Plays and Players in
   Lincolnshire 1300-1585." <u>MSC</u> 9:1-108.
   Entries from the records of fourteen towns in Lincolnshire, regarding payment made to players and companies from
   1300 to 1585. Very few entries are from the relevant period.

7 MARKLAND, MURRAY F. "Two Italian Glimpses of the English
   Theatre." <u>TR</u> 10, no. 1:32-36.
   Examines two manuscripts from the Biblioteca Riccardiana
   in Florence for what they tell us about English theatre
   in the seventeenth and eighteenth centuries. The relevant
   document, MS Ricc. 1493, is the diary of the travels of
   Guilio de Medici in England. He arrived in London on 7
   July 1621 and on 23 July he went to a play, apparently
   about Henry VIII. Markland suspects there are many such
   untranslated documents in Italian archives.

8 McMANAWAY, JAMES G. <u>Studies in Shakespeare, Bibliography, and</u>
   <u>Theater</u>. Edited by Richard Hosley, Arthur C. Kirsch, and
   John W. Velz. New York: Shakespeare Association of
   America, pp. 215-22.

Contains a reprint of 1962.13 as well as many other
McManaway essays not directly relevant to English Renaissance theatre.

9 RIBNER, IRVING. "Elizabethan Theatres and Theatre Companies."
   In William Shakespeare: An Introduction to His Life, Times,
   and Theatre. Waltham, Mass.: Blaisdell Publishing Co.,
   pp. 130-61.
        A general discussion summarizing the work of scholars
   in the field. The chapter includes subdivisions discussing
   medieval spectacle and staging, the rise of professional
   companies, the innyards, the public playhouse, the
   children's companies, productions at Blackfriars, Elizabethan acting, and the audience.

10 ROWAN, D. F. "A Neglected Jones/Webb Theatre Project: Barber-
   Surgeons Hall Writ Large." NTM 9, no. 3 (Summer):6-15.
        Tentatively identifies the Inigo Jones drawing held at
   Worcester College, Oxford, as the designs for Barber-
   Surgeons Hall. Rowan also points out the similarity of
   the drawing to Hosley's reconstruction of the second
   Blackfriars (see 1970.13). For Rowan's later thoughts on
   the drawing, see 1970.27; for another view, see 1977.25.

11 SCHUMAN, SAMUEL. "Emblems and the English Renaissance Drama:
   A Checklist." RORD 12:43-56.
        Contains a total of 116 items, some of theatrical
   interest, sporadically annotated. All relevant items have
   been incorporated into this bibliography.

12 SHAPIRO, MICHAEL. "Children's Troupes: Dramatic Illusion
   and Acting Style." CompD 3 (Spring):42-53.
        Examines devices used by playwrights of the boy
   companies to draw attention to the actors as children.
   Shapiro finds four most commonly used: adults alongside
   children, bawdry, self-reference, and inductions. These
   are most often found in comedies. The style used by the
   boys varied, depending on the type of play. It was
   frequently formal, but at times, especially in the city
   comedies, could be natural.

13 SJÖRGREN, GUNNAR. "Thomas Bull and Other 'English Instrumentalists' in Denmark in the 1580s." ShS 22:119-24.
        A new study of the Danish documents previously drawn on
   by Bolte (1888.2) and Ravn (1906.9), establishing that one
   of the "English Instrumentalists," John Bull, was beheaded
   for murder in 1586.

1969

14 SOENS, ADOLPH E. "Tybalt's Spanish Fencing in Romeo and
    Juliet." SQ 20 (Spring):121-27.
        Argues that Tybalt's fencing style is Spanish, not
    French or Italian. Soens then considers implications for
    the staging of the fights with Mercutio and Romeo. See
    also 1927.23.

15 SPRINCHORN, EVERT. "'Wrapt in a Canapie.'" TN 24 (Autumn):
    36-37.
        Suggest that canopy and arras were not in fact inter-
    changeable terms, as they are often thought. See also
    1957.1; 1964.3.

16 SUMMERSON, JOHN [NEWENHAM]. Architecture in Britain, 1530-
    1830. Pelican History of Art, no. Z3. Harmondsworth:
    Penguin Books, pp. 61-67.
        Reprint of 1953.26.

17 WICKHAM, GLYNNE. "Notes on Inigo Jones' Designs for the
    Cockpit-in-Court." In Shakespeare's Dramatic Heritage:
    Collected Studies in Mediaeval, Tudor, and Shakespearean
    Drama. London: Routledge & Kegan Paul; New York: Barnes
    & Noble, pp. 151-62.
        Reprint of 1967.15.

18 _____. "Notes on the Staging of Marlowe's Plays." In
    Shakespeare's Dramatic Heritage: Collected Studies in
    Mediaeval, Tudor, and Shakespearean Drama. London:
    Routledge & Kegan Paul; New York: Barnes & Noble, pp.
    121-31.
        Reprint of 1964.38.

19 _____. "Shakespeare's Stage." In Shakespeare's Dramatic
    Heritage: Collected Studies in Mediaeval, Tudor, and
    Shakespearean Drama. London: Routledge & Kegan Paul;
    New York: Barnes & Noble, pp. 132-50.
        A general discussion of the Elizabethan playhouse, with
    emphasis on the Swan drawing, the actors for whom the
    plays were written, and their use of large properties or
    "scenic emblems" which enabled them to perform virtually
    anywhere.

20 _____. "The Stuart Mask." In Shakespeare's Dramatic Heritage:
    Collected Studies in Mediaeval, Tudor, and Shakespearean
    Drama. London: Routledge & Kegan Paul; New York: Barnes
    & Noble, pp. 103-17.
        An attempt "to distill the essence . . . of Masks of the
    Jacobean and Caroline period, relating the blossom itself

1969

to the roots from which it sprang and to the seed which it
left against the future." Wickham sees the masque as a
turning point, translating the English theatre from "one
of suggestion, visual and poetic, into one of verisimilitude,
realistic and prosaic." The masques grew out of the
resolve of the privileged elite to assert its privilege,
regardless of cost, and should not be judged by strictly
literary standards.

21 WREN, ROBERT M. "Salisbury and the Blackfriars Theatre." <u>TN</u>
    23 (Spring):103-9.
    Discusses the role of the Earl of Salisbury in the
    affairs of the Blackfriars Playhouse, and demonstrates that
    he was clearly satirized on the stage of that theatre.

22 WRIGHT, LOUIS B. <u>Shakespeare's Theatre and the Dramatic Tradi-
    tion</u>. Washington: Folger Shakespeare Library, 36 pp.
    Reprint of 1958.24.

23 YATES, FRANCES A. <u>The Theatre of the World</u>. Chicago: Univer-
    sity of Chicago Press, 186 pp.
    Based on the chapter in her <u>Art of Memory</u> (<u>see</u> 1966.27)
    that argues that the stage illustration in Robert Fludd's
    <u>Ars Memoriae</u> can throw light on Shakespeare's Globe Play-
    house. Primarily centered on John Dee and Fludd as
    representatives of Renaissance philosophy in England,
    particularly with regard to the influence of Vitruvius,
    this work does not attempt to present a full reconstruction
    of the Globe. The most that is offered is a new approach
    to the ground plan of the building and its stage. Yates
    sees the public theatres of London as "adaptations of the
    ancient theatre made within the sphere of the popular
    Vitruvianism generated by the Dee movement." The ground
    plan she offers consists of a circle inscribed within a
    hexagon (based on the largely discredited evidence of
    Mrs. Thrale, friend of Dr. Johnson, who claimed to have
    seen the foundations of the Globe) with a smaller circle
    inside that, determined by the intersections of four
    equilateral triangles inscribed within the larger circle.

*24 YOH, SUK-KEE. "Shakespearean Stage." In <u>An Introduction to
    Shakespeare</u>. Seoul (Korea): n.p., pp. 170-92.
    Cited in 1974.18.

<u>1970</u>

1 ARNOTT, JAMES FULLARTON, and ROBINSON, JOHN WILLIAM. <u>English</u>
   <u>Theatrical Literature, 1559-1900: A Bibliography; Incorpo-</u>
   <u>rating Robert W. Lowe's "A Bibliographical Account of</u>
   <u>English Theatrical Literature," 1888</u>. London: Society for
   Theatre Research, 486 pp.
       Includes 1888.9. The dates in the title refer not to
   events of theatrical history, but to the date of publication of the work included. In all there are 4506 entries,
   encompassing all phases of English, Irish, and Scottish
   theatre. Relevant entries are to be found throughout. The
   author, short-title, and place of publication indexes are
   useful, but a subject index would have been more useful
   still.

2 BERGERON, DAVID M. "Charles I's Royal Entries into London."
   <u>GuildMisc</u> 3, no. 2 (June):91-97.
       Examines the planned and aborted entries of Charles into
   London in 1626, 1633, and 1641. The records demonstrate
   clearly the involvement of the city government, Aldermen
   and Council, and livery companies in the preparations, as
   well as the expenses and methods of financing used.

3 _____. "The Elizabethan Lord Mayor's Show." <u>SEL</u> 10 (Spring):
   269-86.
       Traces the development of the Lord Mayor's Show in the
   sixteenth century from a simple procession to complex and
   sophisticated plays concentrating on history, mythology,
   and moral allegory. Particularly important is the 1585
   pageant written by Peele. One measure of the development
   of the form is the cost, which went from £151 in 1561 to
   £747 in 1602.

4 BERRY, HERBERT. "The Playhouse in the Boar's Head Inn,
   Whitechapel." In <u>The Elizabethan Theatre, [I]</u>. Edited by
   David Galloway. Toronto: Macmillan; Hamden, Conn.:
   Archon, pp. 45-73.
       The first of two articles on the Boar's Head (<u>see also</u>
   1973.1), which Berry calls "one of the more successful
   Elizabethan playhouses," based on documents discovered by
   Sisson (<u>see</u> 1972.29) and supplemented by Hotson (1959.9)
   and Berry himself. Berry untangles the complicated
   litigation surrounding the Boar's Head, and a picture
   emerges of an inn located just outside the London city
   limits converted into a permanent playhouse. The major
   figures in the theatre's history were Oliver Woodliffe,
   who leased the building in 1594; Richard Samwell, who

subleased from Woodliffe; John Mags, a contractor who was to expand the upper galleries; Frances Langley, builder of the Swan who was looking for a new investment; and Robert Browne, head of the acting company involved at the Boar's Head.

5 DeMOLEN, RICHARD LEE. "Richard Mulcaster: An Elizabethan Savant." Ph.D. dissertation, University of Michigan, 319 pp.
   The relevant section is the fourth chapter, where DeMolen discusses Mulcaster's use of literary and theatrical forms. He claims that "Mulcaster employed pageantry, poetry and drama for hortatory and didactic reasons as well as for purposes of flattery and persuasion." DeMolen sees the revival of the acting company at St. Paul's as Mulcaster's responsibility. See also 1972.6; 1974.10.

6 DODD, KENNETH M. "Another Elizabethan Theatre in the Round." SQ 21 (Spring):125-56.
   Discusses the "Game Place" in Suffolk, described in a 1581 manuscript. This open air theatre had a stage made of a circular stone retaining wall filled with earth and was related to the medieval method of staging rather than the Elizabethan.

7 FOAKES, R. A. "Tragedy of the Children's Theatres after 1600: A Challenge to the Adult Stage." In The Elizabethan Theatre, II. Edited by David Galloway. Toronto: Macmillan; Hamden, Conn.: Archon, pp. 37-59.
   Suggests that Harbage's "rival traditions" (see 1952.8) need reexamination. The impact of the revival of the children's companies in 1600 was very great, and the adult companies had to take over the style and techniques of the boys in order to compete. Thus the children's companies and their playwrights had a strong influence on the drama and theatre of the seventeenth century.

8 GALLOWAY, DAVID, ed. The Elizabethan Theatre, [I]. Toronto: Macmillan; Hamden, Conn.: Archon, 130 pp.
   "Papers given at the International Conference on Elizabethan Theatre held at the University of Waterloo, Ontario, in July 1968." Contains 1970.4, 13, 25, 29, 31, as well as an introduction by the editor and two other non-theatrical articles.

1970

9   _____. The Elizabethan Theatre, II. Toronto: Macmillan;
     Hamden, Conn.: Archon, 148 pp.
        "Papers delivered at the Second International Conference
     on Elizabethan Theatre held at the University of Waterloo,
     Ontario, in July 1969." Contains 1970.7, 18-20, 27, as
     well as other nontheatrical papers and an introduction by
     the editor.

10 GURR, ANDREW [J]. The Shakespearean Stage, 1574-1642.
     Cambridge: University Press, 192 pp.
        Primarily a summary of Bentley (1941.1; 1956.4; 1968.2),
     Chambers (1923.2), and other such works. According to
     Gurr this work "should be read as a preliminary, outlining
     study of the background circumstances out of which the plays
     first appeared." He includes chapters on the companies,
     actors, playhouses, staging, and audience.

11 HART, ALFRED. "Play Abridgement: The Length of Elizabethan
     and Jacobean Plays, Time Alloted for the Representation of
     Elizabethan and Jacobean Plays, Acting Versions of Eliza-
     bethan and Jacobean Plays." In Shakespeare and the Homilies,
     and Other Pieces of Research in the Elizabethan Drama.
     New York: Octagon, pp. 77-153.
        Reprint of 1934.3, which in turn reprints 1932.5-6;
     1934.2.

12 HODGES, C[YRIL] WALTER. Shakespeare and the Players. 2d ed.
     New York: Coward-McCann, 110 pp.
        Second edition of 1949.6. Retains the original illus-
     trations but adds a few new ones, and makes a few minor
     additions to the text. The most important addition is an
     appendix of eleven extracts from theatrical documents of
     the period.

13 HOSLEY, RICHARD. "A Reconstruction of the Second Black-
     friars." In The Elizabethan Theatre [I]. Edited by David
     Galloway. Toronto: Macmillan; Hamden, Conn.: Archon,
     pp. 74-88.
        Conjectural reconstruction of Shakespeare's private
     playhouse, based on the size of the hall, the influence of
     the hall screen, and analogues in the Fortune contract.
     Hosley locates the theatre in the upper Parliament Chamber,
     places the stage at one end, and endows it with three
     doorways in the tiring house facade, three upper acting
     spaces (one above each doorway), and three galleries. The
     acting area on the stage is assumed to be 29 feet wide
     (with a gallery at stage level on either side) and 18½ feet
     deep to the tiring house facade. No information from the

plays staged at the Blackfriars is here considered (but see
his 1975.15). Illustrations of Hosley's conjectures are
provided by Richard Southern. See Index, under Blackfriars
Playhouse--Reconstructions, for alternative conjectures.

14 HUBBARD, BARBARA. "The Boar's Head Redefined." M.A. thesis,
    University of Iowa, 185 pp.
       Reexamines the available evidence concerning this inn-
    yard playhouse, including location, structure, history, and
    theatrical activities. Hubbard includes transcriptions
    of published and unpublished documents of the Boar's Head
    and sections of several contemporary maps and views. While
    only a master's thesis, this work is as comprehensive as
    many doctoral dissertations.

15 INGRAM, [REGINALD] WILLIAM. "The Playhouse at Newington Butts:
    A New Proposal." SQ 21 (Autumn):385-98.
       Following up a reference in a 1955 London County Council
    Survey of London, Ingram was led to a series of documents
    that suggest that this playhouse was built by actor Jerome
    Savage: that it may have preceded Burbage's Theatre; that
    Savage's company, Warwick's Men, played at Newington Butts
    without incident from 1576 to 1580; and that the Earl of
    Oxford's Men took over in the latter year. Further,
    Ingram suggests that Henslowe never had a proprietary
    interest in this playhouse, it being managed by Peter
    Hunninghorn until 1595 and Paul Buck until 1597, at which
    time it was dismantled.

16 JENSEN, EJNER J. "A New Allusion to the Sign of the Globe
    Theater." SQ 21 (Winter):95-97.
       Points out a possible allusion to the Globe sign in the
    Introduction to Marston's Antonio and Mellida.

17 JOHNSON, ROBERT CARL. "Audience Involvement in the Tudor
    Interludes." TN 24 (Spring):101-10.
       Discusses the interplay between actors and audience in
    the Interludes, relevant because of the parallel to the
    Elizabethan actor-audience relationship.

18 LAVIN, J. A. "The Elizabethan Theatre and the Inductive
    Method." In The Elizabethan Theatre, II. Edited by David
    Galloway. Toronto: Macmillan; Camden, Conn.: Archon,
    pp. 74-86.
       An attack on the inductive method--"extracting general
    laws from particular instances"--in the study of Eliza-
    bethan theatre history. Lavin takes J. C. Adams, Irwin
    Smith, T. W. Baldwin, and Bertram Joseph in particular to

task, although even such contemporary luminaries as Richard
Hosley are prone to inductive reasoning errors. Lavin
concludes that "attempts to generalize about Elizabethan
theatres, acting, dramatic companies, and theatrical texts
are at the best naive, and at the worst positively mis-
leading."

19 LENNAM, TREVOR. "The Children of Paul's, 1551-1582." In The
    Elizabethan Theatre, II. Edited by David Galloway.
    Toronto: Macmillan; Camden, Conn.: Archon, pp. 20-36.
        Examines the career of Sebastian Westcott and discusses
    the repertory and composition of his company of boys.
    While "the precise location of the Paul's playhouse remains
    obscure," Lennam examines and rejects several sites and
    suggests two new possibilities. See also 1975.22.

20 MARKER, LISA-LONE. "Nature and Decorum in the Theory of Eliza-
    bethan Acting." In The Elizabethan Theatre, II. Edited by
    David Galloway. Toronto: Macmillan; Camden, Conn.:
    Archon, pp. 87-107.
        A broad view of Elizabethan acting techniques. Marker
    sees a more homogeneous style than many other writers on
    the subject, one that changed little over the years and
    was deeply rooted in past practice. Contemporary rhetori-
    cians are examined for their contributions.

21 McKENZIE, D. F. "A Cambridge Playhouse of 1638." RenD, n.s.
    3:263-72.
        Discusses the building constructed for the performance
    of plays at Queen's College in 1638, based on later
    drawings of the building and contemporary records. McKenzie
    finds that the playhouse apparently shares many features
    with the Cockpit-in-Court and that the tiring house facade
    corresponds with the Swan drawing.

22 MULLIN, DONALD C. The Development of the Playhouse: A Survey
    of Theatre Architecture from the Renaissance to the Present.
    Berkeley and Los Angeles: University of California Press,
    pp. 32-42.
        The relevant section is Chapter III, "The Triumph of
    Albion." Mullin presents a general summary of the play-
    houses of the period, illustrated with contemporary and
    modern drawings. He discusses how various reconstructors
    have used stage directions and allusions to postulate
    certain physical features of the stage without endorsing
    those methods. Mullin concludes with a discussion of
    staging in the court masques.

23 PINCISS, G. M. "The Queen's Men, 1583-1592." ThS 11
    (May):50-65.
        Examines the provincial and London records of this
    unusually large group of twelve men drawn from the other
    companies. They were clearly the most important adult
    company during the later 1580s, but were soon eclipsed by
    the Lord Chamberlain's Men.

24 RIDDELL, JAMES A. "Some Actors in Ben Jonson's Plays." ShSt
    5:285-98.
        Discusses the names of actors written in a copy of the
    1616 Jonson folio, apparently with the parts distributed as
    they were between 1610 and 1615. Riddell concludes that
    while the ascription of actors to roles in the seventeenth-
    century hand is possible, it cannot be proven or disproven
    with the available evidence.

25 ROWAN, D. F. "The Cockpit-in-Court." In The Elizabethan
    Theatre [I]. Edited by David Galloway. Toronto: Macmillan;
    Hamden, Conn.: Archon, pp. 89-102.
        Examines the Inigo Jones drawings for this theatre held
    at Worcester College, Oxford, concluding that this was "an
    actual Elizabethan theatre which was not . . . a classical
    'coterie' theatre for elegant amateurs, but was, in fact,
    a traditional 'popular' theatre for experienced profes-
    sionals, which only happened to be located at Court."
    Rowan examines the staging of The Lost Lady in detail. See
    also Wickham (1967.15) and Star (1972.30; 1974.23) on this
    theatre.

26 _____. "A Neglected Jones/Webb Theatre Project: Barber-
    Surgeon's Hall Writ Large." ShS 23:125-29.
        Abridged from 1969.10.

27 _____. "A Neglected Jones/Webb Theatre Project, Part II: A
    Theatrical Missing Link." In The Elizabethan Theatre, II.
    Edited by David Galloway. Toronto: Macmillan; Hamden,
    Conn.: Archon, pp. 60-73.
        Reexamines his earlier identification of the Inigo Jones
    drawings of the unidentified private playhouse with the
    Barber-Surgeon's Hall. Instead, Rowan now sees these
    drawings as a "missing link" between the two best pieces
    of visual evidence we have of the Elizabethan theatre: the
    Swan drawing and the Cockpit-in-Court drawings. There was
    apparently a continuous tradition in theatre architecture
    from the 1590s to the 1630s.

1970

28 SHAPIRO, MICHAEL. "Three Notes on the Theatre at Paul's c.
     1569-c. 1607." <u>TN</u> 24 (Summer):147-53.
          Notes on the location, auditorium, and admission price
     and audience of the theatre at Paul's. Based on Shapiro's
     Ph.D. dissertation, 1967.6.

29 SPENCER, T. J. B. "Shakespeare: The Elizabethan Theatre-
     Poet." In <u>The Elizabethan Theatre [I]</u>. Edited by David
     Galloway. Toronto: Macmillan; Hamden, Conn.: Archon,
     pp. 1-20.
          Examines the divergent courses of Shakespearean produc-
     tion and criticism, revealing "artistic connections between
     stage and dramatic form."

30 SUMMERSON, JOHN [NEWENHAM]. <u>Architecture in Britain, 1530-
     1830</u>. Pelican History of Art, no. Z3. Harmondsworth:
     Penguin Books, pp. 61-67.
          Reprint of 1953.26.

31 WICKHAM, GLYNNE. "The Privy Council Order of 1597 for the
     Destruction of All London's Theatres." In <u>The Elizabethan
     Theatre, [I]</u>. Edited by David Galloway. Toronto:
     Macmillan; Hamden, Conn.: Archon, pp. 21-44.
          Explains why the order was never carried out and sug-
     gests that the Privy Council never intended it to be.
     Wickham points out that since the public and private
     theatres were held to be rehearsal halls for the various
     companies to prepare for Court performances, information on
     those performances might yield valuable information on
     performances in the public and private playhouses.

<u>1971</u>

1 BECKERMAN, BERNARD. "Philip Henslowe." In <u>The Theatrical
    Manager in England and America: Players of a Perilous Game</u>.
    Edited by Joseph W. Donohue, Jr. Princeton: Princeton
    University Press, pp. 19-62.
          Examines the various roles (banker, impresario,
    entrepeneur, etc.) played by Henslowe in the theatrical
    life of the period. Beckerman breaks Henslowe's career
    into four phases (1592-1596/7, 1597/8-1604, 1604-1611, and
    1611-1616) and discusses each, with the emphasis on the
    first (the Rose period) and fourth (the Hope period). He
    concludes by distinguishing the historical meaning of
    Henslowe's position as manager from his personal style.
    While historically he represents "the manager of the future
    at an early stage of development," we must recognize the
    prosaic qualities of his style.

2 BENTLEY, GERALD EADES. The Profession of Dramatist in Shakespeare's Time, 1590-1642. Princeton: Princeton University
Press, 329 pp.
"An explication of the normal working environment
circumscribing the activities of those literary artists who
were making their living by writing for the London theatres"
from the time of Shakespeare to the closing of the playhouses. Bentley examines relations with the company, pay,
working conditions, contractual obligations, status, regulation and censorship, collaboration, revision, and publication. The final chapter, where Bentley traces the
publication patterns of eleven playwrights, is particularly
important. See also J. Q. Adams (1932.1).

3 BERGERON, DAVID M. English Civic Pageantry: 1558-1642.
London: Edward Arnold; Columbia: University of South
Carolina Press, 325 pp.
Expanded published version of 1964.4, incorporating the
findings of several of his published articles, including
1968.4-7; 1970.2, 3. Here he attempts a comprehensive
treatment of pageants, including progresses, royal entries,
and Lord Mayor's shows. This is the most complete work in
the area of pageantry yet produced.

4 BROWNSTEIN, O[SCAR] L. "A Record of London Inn-Playhouses c.
1565-1580." SQ 22 (Winter):17-24.
Examines "The Register of the Masters of Defense" (MS
Sloane 2530 in the British Library) for references to early
playhouses. "It is," says Brownstein, "the only systematic
account of activities of any kind at four of the earliest
Elizabethan playhouses during the period of the origin of
these playhouses." Apparently the only distinction made
between the innyard theatres of the city (the Bull, the
Bell-Savage, the Cross Keys, the Bell, the Boar's Head) and
the suburban playhouses (the Theatre, the Newington Butts,
the Swan) was their location, not their facilities.
Brownstein also suggests that the Bell-Savage Inn contained
a public theatre that pre-dated Burbage's Theatre.

5 _____. "The Saracen's Head, Islington: A Pre-Elizabethan
Inn Playhouse." TN 24 (Winter):68-72.
Discusses what is known about the management, location,
and activities at the inn, where it is known theatrical
performances were given as early as 1557. Brownstein opens
and closes with a plea for additional research into the
innyard playhouses.

1971

6 FREEHAFER, JOHN. "Inigo Jones's Scenery for The Cid." TN
   24 (Spring):84-92.
       Argues that Simpson and Bell's Inigo Jones design no.
   361, frequently thought to represent the first scene of
   The Queen of Aragon, actually was designed for The Cid in
   1639.

7 HOSLEY, RICHARD. "Three Kinds of Outdoor Theatre before
   Shakespeare." ThS 12 (May):1-33.
       Examines the Place-and-scaffolds theatre, the pageant
   wagons, and the booth stages of the middle ages. The last
   is relevant, since most scholars believe that the Elizabethan playhouses were influenced by the booth stage.
   Unfortunately, Hosley sheds little light on the issue here.

8 HUDSON, KATHERINE. The Story of the Elizabethan Boy-Actors.
   Illustrated by Robert Micklewright. London: Oxford
   University Press, 90 pp.
       A popular treatment intended for a juvenile audience.
   Hudson begins with the middle ages and traces the Children
   of Paul's and the Children of the Chapel through the
   seventeenth century.

9 INGRAM, [REGINALD] WILLIAM. "The Closing of the Theatres in
   1597: A Dissenting View." MP 69 (November):105-15.
       Ingram reviews the Isle of Dogs incident and speculates
   that the performance took place after the decision of 28
   July to close the playhouses. Sir Robert Cecil took
   advantage of the incident to break Francis Langley, already
   in trouble with the Crown over a stolen diamond. Documentary evidence from the Public Record Office and the collection of the Marquis of Salisbury substantiate the case.
   See also 1970.31.

10 KING, T[HOMAS] J[AMES]. Shakespearean Staging, 1599-1642.
   Cambridge: Harvard University Press, 163 pp.
       A "systematic survey of theatrical requirements for 276
   plays first performed by professional actors in the period
   between the Autumn of 1599 . . . and 2 September 1642."
   King's primary aim is to find positive correlations between
   the internal evidence of the texts of the plays presented
   during this period and the external evidence as provided
   by surviving illustrations. He makes no attempt to deal
   with the plays by playhouse of presentation. King presents
   the evidence in order of increasing complexity: subsequent
   chapters treat entrances, areas above, hangings and
   discoveries, and traps. He also includes an imaginative
   reconstruction of the staging of Twelfth Night at the
   Middle Temple and a review of the major scholarship in the

266

field since 1940. King concludes that all the plays he examines could with minor adjustments have been staged upon any of the nine stages represented in the surviving illustrations. See also 1971.11; 1972.17.

11 _____. "Shakespearean Staging, 1599-1642." SRO 5-6:30-35.
Summarizes conclusions from 1971.10, with suggestions for further research.

12 KOHLER, RICHARD CHARLES. "The Fortune Contract and Vitruvian Symmetry." ShSt 6:311-26.
As a test of Yates's ideas on the use of Vitruvian principles in the Elizabethan theatre (see 1969.23), Kohler compares her ground plan of the Globe to the Fortune contract and the Swan drawing, and estimates the sizes of the Fortune, Swan, Rose, and Globe. He concludes that there is exact correspondence between two of the measurements found in the Fortune contract and the Vitruvian scheme, and that there is no conflict with any other data. Consequently, Roman influence on the Elizabethan theatre is quite possible.

13 ORDISH, T. FAIRMAN. Early London Theatres--In the Fields. London: White Lion Publishers, 316 pp.
Reprint of 1894.4, with a new Foreword by Hodges.

14 SHAPIRO, MICHAEL. "Le prince d'amour and the Resumption of Playing at Paul's." N&Q, n.s. 18 (January):14-16.
Suggests that the Children of Paul's resumed playing by the fall of 1597 instead of 1599-1600 as previously thought.

15 _____. "What We Know about the Children's Troupes and Their Plays." SRO 5-6:36-45.
A review of the literature on and state of knowledge of the boy companies.

16 SKURA, MERIDETH ANNE. "Shakespeare's Clowns." Ph.D. dissertation, Yale University, 231 pp.
A literary study of little theatrical or historical interest.

17 WHITTY, JOHN CHRISTOPHER. "The Lord Admiral's Men, 1594-1600: What the Actor Did." Ph.D. dissertation, University of Iowa, 356 pp.
Examines a body of eleven plays produced by a single company in a limited period of time to find out what instructions to the actors are contained in the texts. Using this information and other historical records, Whitty

has described as completely as possible what the actors who
first appeared in these plays actually did physically and
vocally. This is an attempt to deal with "the substance
rather than the style of Elizabethan acting." The most
important contribution of this work is the development of
a system for script analysis, codifying the hit-and-miss
intuitive methods of most historians. The major conclusion
is that "physical modes of behavior creating visual effects
formed a considerable part of the actor's craft." The
bulk of the work consists of four appendixes containing
tables of cues and various verifications.

18 WIKLAND, ERIC. Elizabethan Players in Sweden, 1591-92.
    Translated by Patrick Hort. 2d ed., revised and enlarged.
    Stockholm: Almqvist & Wiksell, 281 pp.
        Revised edition of 1962.23. Additional material extends
    the coverage to 1594 and 1617, and Wikland prints addi-
    tional illustrations.

1972

1 BAKER, Sir RICHARD. Theatrum Redivivum, or The Theatre
   Vindicated. New York: Johnson Reprint Corp., 141 pp.
       Reprint of the 1662 edition, with an introduction by
   Peter Davison.

2 BALE, JOHN, and LODGE, THOMAS. "The Epistle Exhortatory of
   an English Christian" and "Reply to Gosson." New York:
   Johnson Reprint Corp., 124 pp.
       Reprints of the 1544 and 1579-80 editions, with intro-
   ductions by Peter Davidson.

3 CHETTLE, HENRY, and RANKINS, WILLIAM. "Kind Heart's Dream"
   and "Mirror of Monsters." New York: Johnson Reprint Corp.,
   246 pp.
       Reprints of the 1587 and 1592 editions, with introduc-
   tions by Peter Davison.

4 CRASHAW, WILLIAM. Sermon Preached at the Cross, February 14,
   1607. New York: Johnson Reprint Corp., 188 pp.
       Reprint of the 1608 edition, with an introduction by
   Peter Davison.

5 DAVISON, PETER, ed. Critics and Apologists of the English
   Theatre: A Selection of Seventeenth-Century Pamphlets in
   Facsimile. New York: Johnson Reprint Corp., 107 pp.

Reprints of six printed texts and one manuscript dealing
with the attack and defense of the English stage. Included
are The Actors' Remonstrance, 1643; the forged Mr. William
Prynne, His Defence of Stage Plays, 1649; The Players
Petition to Parliament, 1643; A Short Treatise Against
Stage-Plays, 1625; The Stage-Players' Complaint, 1641; and
Testimonies of Pagans, of Infidels, of Christian Fathers,
on the Nature and Tendency of Theatrical Amusements, 1819.
The editor includes a brief introduction to each selection.

6 DeMOLEN, RICHARD L. "Richard Mulcaster and the Elizabethan
   Theatre." ThS 13 (May):28-41.
       Examines the role Mulcaster played as Headmaster of the
   Merchant Taylor's School from 1561 to 1585, and of St.
   Paul's, 1596 to 1608. While he may have written some plays,
   he almost certainly adapted some to suit his young actors,
   and he was responsible for the revival of the boy companies
   in 1600. DeMolen also claims that Shakespeare modeled
   Holofernes in Love's Labour's Lost on Mulcaster.

7 FEATHER, JOHN. "Robert Armin and the Chamberlain's Men."
   N&Q, n.s. 19 (December):448-50.
       Examines Armin's movement from Lord Chandos's Men to the
   Lord Chamberlain's company, suggesting that the transfer
   took place in 1598 rather than 1599.

8 FEILDE, JOHN, and W., T. "A Godly Exhortation by Ocassion of
   the Late Judgement of God Showed at Paris-Garden, the
   Thirteenth Day of January" and "A Sermon Preached at Paul's
   Cross, 3 November 1577." New York: Johnson Reprint Corp.,
   160 pp.
       Reprints of the 1583 and 1578 editions, with introduc-
   tions by Peter Davison.

9 FENTON, GEORGE. Form of Christian Policy Gathered Out of
   French. New York: Johnson Reprint Corp., 142 pp.
       Reprint of the 1574 edition, with an introduction by
   Peter Davison.

10 GOSSON, STEPHEN. Plays Confuted in Five Actions. New York:
    Johnson Reprint Corp., 128 pp.
        Reprint of the 1582 edition, with an introduction by
    Peter Davison.

1972

11 HABICHT, WERNER. "Tree Properties and Tree Scenes in Elizabethan Theater." RenD, n.s. 4:69-92.
An attempt "to point out the use to which a constantly
recurring type of property was put in an important phase
of the history of the theater." Habicht discusses the
emblematic and literary uses of trees, not their use as a
property in actual stage practice.

12 HAMMER, GAEL WARREN. "The Staging of Elizabethan Plays in the
Private Theatres, 1632-1642." Ph.D. dissertation, University of Iowa, 194 pp.
Examines the staging of plays at the Blackfriars,
Phoenix, and Salisbury Court Playhouses during the last
ten years of their legitimate existence, with special
reference to the possible use of painted perspective scenery.
He establishes a group of "place-realism" plays that might
have used such scenery during this period, and infers from
internal evidence in Nabbes's Microcosmus what it might have
been like. Hammer also attempts to determine the structural
features of the playhouse stages, using the method of
script analysis proposed by Whitty (1971.17). He concludes
that the three playhouses were similar in structure and
staging methods.

13 HEYWOOD, THOMAS, and G[REENE], J[OHN]. "An Apology for Actors"
and "A Refutation of the Apology for Actors." New York:
Johnson Reprint Corp., 144 pp.
Reprints of the 1612 and 1615 editions, with introduc-
tions by J. W. Binns.

14 HOSLEY, RICHARD. "The Interpretation of Pictorial Evidence
for Theatrical Design." RORD 13-14:123-25.
Summary of a paper presented at the 1969 MLA convention.
Hosley discusses distortion of scale in a painting of a
1615 pageant wagon, distortion of point of view in the Swan
drawing, and distortion of shape in Hollar's "Long Bird's
Eye View of London."

15 INGRAM, [REGINALD] WILLIAM. "'Neere the Playe House': The
Swan Theatre and Community Blight." RenD, n.s. 4:53-68.
A detailed examination of the charge that the Swan was
the cause of the decline of the neighborhood in which it
was located. Ingram shows how Frances Langley's "neglect-
ful and exploitive attitudes" were responsible for the bad
reputation of his playhouse and how that reputation improved
considerably when Hugh Browker, "a respected member of the
community," took over.

16 KINCAID, A. N. "A Revels Office Scrap Deciphered." N&Q, n.s.
    19 (December):461-63.
       Reexamines one of Sir George Buc's Revels Office entries,
    changing the name from Bald's reading. An unknown play,
    Cupid's Festival, was approved 18 December 1614, and held
    at the Revels Office for "Dwarf Bob" the actor, also
    unknown.

17 KING, T[HOMAS] J[AMES]. "The Stage in the Time of Shakespeare:
    A Survey of Major Scholarship." RenD, n. s. 4:199-235.
       Reprinted in part from 1971.10. King reviews major
    scholarship by nineteen writers "to show how the failure of
    some scholars to apply consistent criteria for the evalua-
    tion of evidence has led to widely divergent and sometimes
    mutually contradictory theories." Includes reviews of
    Albright, Thorndike, Chambers, Lawrence, Greg, Reynolds,
    J. C. Adams, Kernodle, Southern, Hodges, Hotson, Harbage
    Irwin Smith, Hosley, Nagler, Beckerman, Wickham, Yates, and
    Gurr in a roughly chronological treatment. See Index,
    under each writer, for specific references.

18 MANNING, THOMAS JOHN. "Staging of Plays at Christ Church,
    Oxford: 1582-1592." Ph.D. dissertation, University of
    Michigan, 223 pp.
       Examines three plays by William Gager performed at
    Christ Church, Oxford, 1582-92, in order to reconstruct the
    staging practices employed. Essentially medieval techniques
    of simultaneous staging were apparently used. One mansion
    was equipped with curtains for a discovery, and there was
    an upper acting space available.

19 McMILLIN, [HARVEY] SCOTT. "Casting for Pembroke's Men: The
    Henry VI Quartos and The Taming of a Shrew." SQ 23
    (Spring):141-59.
       Examines three reported or "bad" quartos to see what
    they tell us about the casting of Pembroke's Men. McMillin
    concludes that a company of eleven actors could double all
    parts in these plays, assisted by four boys in female parts
    and five hired men for walk-ons. He also speculates on
    the origin and membership of the company.

20 MONTANUS, JOANNES FERRARIUS. Work Touching the Good Ordering
    of a Common Weal. Translated by William Bauande. New
    York: Johnson Reprint Corp., 88 pp.
       Reprint of the 1559 edition, with an introduction by
    Peter Davison.

1972

21 NAOGERGUS, THOMAS. <u>Popish Kingdom; or, Reign of Antichrist</u>
    <u>Written in Latin Verse</u>. Translated by B. Googe. New York:
    Johnson Reprint Corp., 124 pp.
       Reprint of the 1570 edition, with an introduction by
    Peter Davison.

22 PRYNNE, WILLIAM. <u>Histrio-Mastix: The Player's Scourge, or,</u>
    <u>Actor's Tragedy</u>. 2 vols. New York: Johnson Reprint
    Corp., 1006 pp.
       Reprint of the 1633 edition, with an introduction by
    Peter Davison.

23 RAINOLDS, JOHN. <u>The Overthrow of Stage-Plays</u>. New York:
    Johnson Reprint Corp., 190 pp.
       Reprint of the 1599 edition, with an introduction by
    J. W. Binns.

24 ROWAN, D. F. "The English Playhouse: 1595-1630." <u>RenD</u>, n.s.
    4:37-51.
       Argues for considering both "public" and "private"
    theatres together, and restricts the time frame in this
    examination to the limitations imposed by the Swan drawing
    and the Inigo Jones design for the Cockpit-in-Court.
    Rowan views the unidentified Jones drawings held at
    Worcester College, Oxford, as "a theatrical missing-link
    between the Swan and the Cockpit-in-Court." It is now, he
    says, possible to discuss the physical features of the
    Elizabethan playhouse stage with some assurance. <u>See also</u>
    1970.27.

25 _____. "The Tiring-House Wall and the Galleries in the Second
    Blackfriars: Two Points in Dispute." <u>TN</u> 26 (Spring):101-4.
       Rowan differs with Hosley (1970.13) in placing the
    tiring house wall at the end of the sixty-six-foot Par-
    liament Chamber and in surrounding the pit with three
    galleries.

26 SALOMON, BROWNELL. "Visual and Aural Signs in the Performed
    English Renaissance Play." <u>RenD</u>, n.s. 5:143-69.
       Defines "sign" as a sensory datum explicitly demanded by
    the playwright's text that assumes interpretative relevance,
    and discusses that concept (from semiotics) in selected
    plays. Specifically, Salomon discusses language, vocal
    tone, gesture, movement, makeup, costume, hand properties,
    the decor, lighting, music, and sound effects. He concludes
    that "thematically relevant details can be organized so
    they will more effectively demonstrate how or to what extent
    theatre poets have realized dramatic meaning in phenomenal
    terms, in a total, histrionic frame."

27 SALVIANUS and EUTHEO [pseuds.]. Second and Third Blast of
    Retreat from Plays and Theatres. New York: Johnson
    Reprint Corp., 142 pp.
        Reprint of the 1580 edition, with an introduction by
    Peter Davison.

28 SIMMONS, J. L. "Elizabethan Stage Practice and Marlowe's
    The Jew of Malta." RenD, n.s. 4:93-104.
        Examines the staging of one scene of the play for what
    it tells us of the playhouse. Simmons contends that the
    supposedly dead body of Barabas was thrown from the stage
    into the yard, reentering from a trap. Similarly, Calymath
    and his Turks enter into the yard and assault the stage
    from the front.

29 SISSON, C[HARLES] J[ASPER]. The Boar's Head Theatre: An Inn-
    Yard Theatre of the Elizabethan Age. Edited by Stanley
    Wells. London and Boston: Routledge & Kegan Paul, 100 pp.
        Posthumous cumulation of Sisson's previous work on the
    Boar's Head (see 1936.21; 1954.25), edited by his student
    and friend. The four chapters examine the inn-yard theatres
    in general, the George Inn in Whitechapel, the history of
    the Boar's Head, and the legal battle for control of the
    theatre. Sisson makes the important point that the inn
    was given over entirely to the presentation of plays, with
    no other business conducted. The work is based on a
    series of documents discovered by Sisson in the Public
    Record Office, rediscovered more recently by Berry (see
    1970.4; 1973.1).

30 STAR, L[EONIE] R[ACHEL]. "A Note on the Use of Scenery at the
    Cockpit-in-Court." TN 26 (Spring):89-91.
        Suggests the use of "backcloths" rather than changeable
    painted scenery behind three of the five doorways at the
    Cockpit-in-Court. Based on research leading to her Ph.D.
    dissertation (1974.21). See also Freehafer (1971.6), against
    whom she argues, and his answer (1973.6).

31 STUBBES, PHILIP. The Anatomy of Abuses. New York: Johnson
    Reprint Corp., 120 pp.
        Reprint of the 1583 edition, with an introduction by
    Peter Davison.

32 WICKHAM, GLYNNE. Early English Stages, 1300-1660. Vol. 2,
    Pt. 2, 1576-1660. London: Routledge & Kegan Paul; New
    York: Columbia University Press, 266 pp.
        The third of a projected five-volume work, following
    1959.29 and 1963.20. Wickham here treats the development
    from multi-purpose gamehouses to single-purpose theatres.

1972

He examines the inns used as playhouses as well as public and private theatres built specifically for the purpose. While the many excellent drawings and photographs lend an air of authority, many statements made here are conjectural. Nonetheless, Wickham explores a great many intriguing possibilities, and when the evidence from the plays is added, as is promised for a subsequent volume, Early English Stages may well end up as one of the most comprehensive contributions to the field.

33 WRIGHT, JAMES, and FLECKNOE, RICHARD. "Historia Histrionica" and "A Short Discourse of the English Stage Appended to Love's Kingdom." New York: Johnson Reprint Corp., 46 pp.
        Reprints of 1664.1 and 1699.1, with introductions by Peter Davison.

34 WRIGHT, LOUIS B. Shakespeare's Theatre and the Dramatic Tradition. Washington: Folger Shakespeare Library, 36 pp.
        Reprint of 1958.24.

35 ZUCKER, DAVID HARD. Stage and Image in the Plays of Christopher Marlowe. Salzburg Studies in English Literature, no. 7. Salzburg: Institut für englische Sprache und Literatur, Universität Salzburg, pp. 10-15, passim.
        Published version of 1968.39. As part of a literary study of Marlowe, Zucker (drawing entirely on secondary sources) discusses the stage he wrote for. The remainder of the study examines visual iconography in the plays.

1973

1 BERRY, HERBERT. "The Boar's Head Again." In The Elizabethan Theatre, III. Edited by David Galloway. Toronto: Macmillan; Hamden, Conn.: Archon, pp. 33-65.
        Continuation of 1970.4. Berry traces the major figures in the Boar's Head from 1562 to 1621 and uses the Ogilby and Morgan 1676 map of London, several subsequent maps and surveys, and various legal documents to discover more about the property and playhouse.

2 CUTTS, JOHN P. "Le rôle de la musique dans le masques de Ben Jonson et notament dans Oberon (1610-1611)." In Les fêtes de la Renaissance. Vol. 1. Edited by Jean Jacquot. Paris: CNRS, pp. 285-303.
        Reprint of 1956.9.

3 DOEBLER, JOHN. "A Lost Paragraph in the Revels Constitution."
   SQ 24 (Summer):333-34.
       Transcribes this important document, held at the Folger
   Shakespeare Library. Kempe (1836.1), and all subsequent
   transcriptions based on Kempe including that by Chambers
   (1923.2), leave out the third paragraph. See also 1974.11.

4 EVANS, G. BLAKEMORE. "An Elizabethan Theatrical Stocklist."
   HLB 21 (July):254-70.
       An attempt to establish the provenance of the folio leaf
   held by the Houghton Library, to determine its connection
   with Edward Alleyn, and to examine its influence on the
   study of Elizabethan theatre history. The leaf contains
   a price stock list of costumes and properties and a nota-
   tion of estate accounts and rents. While not part of
   Henslowe's diary, as had been suspected, the list was in
   Alleyn's possession, as his handwriting attests. Evans
   suggests that the list represents costumes and properties
   assembled by John Alleyn, Edward's brother, and sold to
   some acting group, perhaps for provincial touring.

5 FLECKNOE, RICHARD. "A Short Discourse of the English Stage."
   In Love's Kingdom. New York: Garland, pp. 99-109.
       Reprint of 1664.1, with a preface by Arthur Freeman.

6 FREEHAFER, JOHN. "Perspective Scenery and the Caroline Playhouses." TN 27 (Spring):98-113.
       Examines the influence of Italian perspective scenery
   and theatre building on the Caroline work of Inigo Jones.
   Freehafer argues against Star (1972.30) and King (1965.9,
   1971.10), claiming changeable perspective scenery was used
   at the Cockpit-in-Court for several productions, at the
   Phoenix at least for Hannibal and Scipio, and at the
   Salisbury Court for Microcosmus. He also accepts Wickham's
   conjecture (in 1972.32) that the Inigo Jones drawings held
   at Worcester College were designs for the Salisbury Court
   Playhouse, lending credence to the possible use of scenery
   there. But see 1977.25.

7 GALLOWAY, DAVID, ed. The Elizabethan Theatre, III. Toronto:
   Macmillan; Hamden, Conn.: Archon, 149 pp.
       Contains three essays of theatrical interest (1973.1,
   14, 15) and five others, as well as an introduction by the
   editor. The theme of the volume, as of the conference
   whose papers it publishes (Third International Conference
   on Elizabethan Theatre, University of Waterloo, Ontario,
   July 1970), is "Theatre and Society."

8 GORDON, D. J. "Le Masque Mémorable de Chapman." In Les fêtes
   de la Renaissance. Vol. 2. Edited by Jean Jacquot. Paris:
   CNRS, pp. 305-17.
      Reprint of 1956.12.

9 GOSSETT, SUZANNE. "Drama in the English College, Rome, 1591-
   1660." ELR 3 (Winter):60-93.
      Identifies eleven specific productions, 1612-1648,
   including an English play, The New Moon, 1633. After 1634
   a removable stage with changeable scenery was used; before
   that date the plays were performed "in the tradition of the
   Elizabethan manner," but Gossett is not more specific.

10 HARRIS, JOHN; ORGEL, STEPHEN; and STRONG, ROY, eds. The King's
   Arcadia: Inigo Jones and the Stuart Court. London: Arts
   Council of Great Britain, 232 pp.
      Catalogue of the exhibition in the Whitehall Banqueting
   Hall, 12 July-2 September 1973. Composed of three parts:
   "Jones in the Making," "The British Vitruvius," and "The
   King's Arcadia." Parts II and III deal with the theatre
   architecture and the masque designs. The many illustra-
   tions are the work's greatest strength. See also 1973.21.

11 HODGES, C[YRIL] WALTER. Shakespeare's Second Globe: The
   Missing Monument. London: Oxford University Press, 100 pp.
      A reconstruction of the Second Globe, erected on the
   same site after the first playhouse by that name burned.
   Hodges bases his conjectures on the preliminary sketch and
   subsequent etching of Wenceslaus Hollar of 1647 ("The Long
   View of London"). An important second chapter clearly
   establishes the credibility of the source, and Hodges goes
   on to solve problems of proportion, size, the superstructure, and the interior. He proposes a sixteen-sided
   building, 92 feet in diameter, with three galleries, eleven,
   ten, and nine feet high respectively. He omits pillars
   supporting the "Heavens," which in this reconstruction are
   open to view. The size of the stage here (43' x 27'6")
   is taken from the Fortune contract. The tiring house facade
   contains two doors and a built-in projecting booth in front
   of a larger center door that could be fitted with hangings
   and used for discoveries. The booth also provides an
   acting area above, as does the open gallery behind it, with
   openings above the side doors. Despite the fact that no
   use is made of the plays known to have been staged at the
   Second Globe, and that Hodges had by 1980 modified some of
   his conclusions (regarding the number of sides and the
   diameter of the playhouse, the use of pillars to support
   the heavens, and the type of flying machinery available),
   this is perhaps the most authoritative reconstruction of
   the Globe to date.

12 HOSLEY, RICHARD. "Three Renaissance English Indoor Playhouses."
    ELR 3 (Winter):166-82.
        Distinguishes five classes of hall screen (with one, two,
    or three doors), with detailed descriptions of the screens
    of the Hampton Court Great Hall, the Trinity Hall of St.
    Bodolph-without-Aldersgate, and the unidentified hall pic-
    tured on The Wits frontispiece. The five-class descriptive
    model enables Hosley to depict the playhouses set up in
    these halls.

13 JACQUOT, JEAN, ed. Les fêtes de la Renaissance. Vol. 1.
    Paris: CNRS, pp. 259-317.
        Reprint of 1956.17, including 1956.9, 12, 28, 33-34.

14 KING, T[HOMAS] J[AMES]. "Shakespearean Staging, 1599-1642."
    In The Elizabethan Theatre, III. Edited by David Galloway.
    Toronto: Macmillan; Hamden, Conn.: Archon, pp. 1-13.
        A report on the contents of King's book (1971.10).

15 LAVIN, J. A. "Shakespeare and the Second Blackfriars." In
    The Elizabethan Theatre, III. Edited by David Galloway.
    Toronto: Macmillan; Hamden, Conn.: Archon, pp. 66-81.
        Argues against the theory, put forth most persuasively
    by Bentley (1948.1), that Shakespeare's craft was strongly
    influenced by the acquisition of the Blackfriars Playhouse
    by his company. Further, Lavin "assert[s] categorically
    that there is not a shred of evidence to show that the
    dramaturgy of Elizabethan playwrights was materially
    affected by the physical arrangement of the public
    playhouses."

16 LEACROFT, RICHARD. The Development of the English Playhouse.
    Ithaca: Cornell University Press, pp. 25-77.
        The relevant section surveys the development of the
    Elizabethan stage. Leacroft provides scale-drawing
    reconstructions of the Swan and the second Globe (which he
    gives four doors and a door-sized discovery space, each of
    which has a corresponding curtained balcony above it). A
    separate chapter considers the staging of the masques. He
    also considers (and provides scale-drawing reconstructions
    of) the Cockpit-in-Court and the unidentified playhouse,
    both designed by Inigo Jones.

17 LELL, GORDON. "'Ganymede' on the Elizabethan Stage: Homo-
    sexual Implications of the Use of Boy-Actors." Aegis
    (Moorehead, Minn.) 1 (Spring):5-15.
        Argues that "Elizabethans were not completely naive
    concerning suggestions of homosexuality," and that

1973

Shakespeare and the other dramatists regularly exploited
the irony of a boy impersonating a woman.

18 MacKINTOSH, IAIN. "Inigo Jones--Theatre Architect." TABS 31,
no. 3 (September):99-105.
An attempt to draw attention to Jones as the architect
of theatres other than the masquing houses, one of which--
the Banqueting House--still exists. Mackintosh discusses
the Jones drawings of the Cockpit-in-Court and the
unidentified private playhouse at length. He suggests
that the latter drawings are of the Phoenix in Drury Lane,
and that it was intended as a flexible theatre--to be used
both for Elizabethan staging and for the use of changeable
scenery. See also Orrell (1977.25).

19 MEAGHER, JOHN C. "The Lord Mayor's Show of 1590." ELR 3
(Winter):94-104.
An edition of the British Library copy of the text with
commentary.

20 O'DONNELL, C. PATRICK, Jr. "The Repertory of the Jacobean
King's Company." Ph.D. dissertation, Princeton University,
413 pp.
Investigates Philip Henslowe's valuable records of the
finances of the Lord Admiral's Men and applies the
findings to the King's Men, with attention to the special
circumstances of that group. The heart of the study is
the third chapter, an annotated bibliography of plays from
the King's company's repertory containing the documentation
for the conclusions reached in the previous chapter.

21 ORGEL, STEPHEN, and STRONG, ROY. Inigo Jones: The Theatre
of the Stuart Court. 2 vols. Berkeley: University of
California Press, 843 pp.
The first volume contains four chapters of text (on
the poetics of spectacle, the mechanism of Platonism, the
arts of design, and Platonic politics), and a catalogue of
Jones's masques from 1605 to 1631, text and designs of
which were reproduced primarily from the collection of the
Duke of Devonshire. The second volume continues the
catalogue to 1640. Orgel and Strong see Jones as "the most
important single person in the arts in seventeenth-century
England" and attempt to view his work from a variety of
perspectives. This is a seminal work essential to an
understanding of the Stuart masques.

22 ROBERTSON, JEAN. "Rapports de poète et de l'artiste dans le
    préparation des cortèges du Lord Maire (Londres 1553-1640)."
    In Les fêtes de la Renaissance. Vol. 1. Edited by Jean
    Jacquot. Paris: CNRS, pp. 265-78.
       Reprint of 1956.28.

23 SCHOENHERR, DOUGLAS EDGAR. "The Pageant of the People: A
    Study of Queen Elizabeth I's Royal Entries." Ph.D. dis-
    sertation, Yale University, 209 pp.
       Examines the Elizabethan royal entries from the point of
    view of the roles into which the Queen was cast in the
    various pageants. Schoenherr reconstructs the five
    Coronation pageants and the two most important provincial
    entries from contemporary descriptions. English pageantry
    in the sixteenth century is seen as extremely traditional
    and conservative, adapting types introduced over a century
    earlier to new uses.

24 SCRAGG, LEAH. "Macbeth on Horseback." ShS 26:81-88.
       Discusses the implications of Simon Forman's "Bocke of
    Plaies" for the original staging of Macbeth. Scraggs
    differs with Bartholomeusz (1969.1) on the possible use of
    a horse, contending that Forman's description cannot be
    taken literally.

25 SNYDER, FREDERICK E. "Composition des fêtes et cortèges
    d'apparat élizabéthains." RHT 25:244-56.
       Discusses the city and country royal entries, festivals,
    and processions early in Elizabeth's reign. The reasons
    for these include reinforcement of the idea of reciprocity
    between Queen and subjects, affirmation of the Queen's new
    rites, and filling the royal treasury. All theatrical
    elements were located outdoors, in front of monuments and
    on specially built stages. A major purpose of such
    entertainments was to satisfy public taste for amusement
    and spectacle.

26 SOUTHERN, RICHARD. The Staging of Plays before Shakespeare.
    New York: Theatre Arts Books, pp. 399-595.
       The relevant sections are Parts Three and Four, dealing
    with the rise of the stage from the interludes and the
    building of the Theatre. Southern deals comprehensively
    with the development of staging practices from 1466 to
    1589. He clearly delineates the differences in the
    traditions of the travelling professional Interlude players
    performing in private halls and those of the Inns of Court,
    the Universities, and the Court performances. The general

conclusion, that the building of the Theatre and the other professional playhouses was strongly influenced by the experiences of the Interluders playing before hall screens, cannot be doubted.

27 SPINUCCI, PIETRO. *Teatro elisabettiano, teatro di stato: La polemica dei puritani inglesi contro il teatro nei secc. XVI e XVII.* Pubblicazioni dell'istituto di lingua e letteratura inglese e di letteratura anglo-americana, no. 2. Florence: Leo S. Olschki, pp. 61-91.
     The relevant section is Chapter Three, on the political control of the Elizabethan and Jacobean theatre.

28 STEVENS, DAVID. "A Study of Christopher Beeston and the Phoenix or Cockpit Theatre." Ph.D. dissertation, Bowling Green University, 326 pp.
     An attempt to find out as much as possible about the management, repertory, staging practices, and audience of the Phoenix, from an examination of extant records and the body of ninety-one plays produced at this playhouse. Stevens concludes that the stage had three doorways and an upper gallery; that discoveries could be effected by drawing a curtain that had been hung up in front of the center door; that Christopher Beeston, the playhouse manager until his death in 1637, was particularly sophisticated in his business practices; that appropriate costumes, properties, and music were used for virtually all of the plays staged at this playhouse; and that the audience of the Phoenix was sophisticated and demanding.

29 STEVENS, DENIS. "Pièces de théâtre et 'pageants' a l'epoque des Tudor." In *Les fêtes de la Renaissance*. Vol. 1. Edited by Jean Jacquot. Paris: CNRS, pp. 259-64.
     Reprint of 1956.33.

30 WERTHEIM, ALBERT. "James Shirley and the Caroline Masques of Ben Jonson." TN 27 (Summer):157-61.
     Discusses the picture of the Jonsonian masque in Shirley's *Love's Cruelty*, suggesting that it gives us a good sense of what the Jonson-Jones masques must have been like.

31 WHITMARSH-KNIGHT, DAVID. "The Second Blackfriars: The Globe Indoors." TN 27 (Spring):94-97.
     Clarifies his differences with Hosley (1970.13) and Smith (1964.22), arguing that there was no substantial difference between the Globe and the Second Blackfriars in size or symmetry.

32 WICKHAM, GLYNNE. "Contributions de Ben Jonson et de Dekker
    aux fêtes du couronnement de Jacques Ier." In <u>Les fêtes de</u>
    <u>la Renaissance</u>. Vol. 1. Edited by Jean Jacquot. Paris:
    CNRS, pp. 279-83.
        Reprint of 1956.34.

33 YARROW, DAVID ALEXANDER. "A Stage History of Shakespeare's
    <u>Romeo and Juliet</u> in London, 1597 to 1800." Ph.D. disserta-
    tion, University of New Brunswick, 244 pp.
        Since there is almost no evidence concerning the staging
    of this play before the Restoration, most of the study falls
    beyond the scope of the present listing.

<u>1974</u>

1 ANON. "Theatre and Play Production in Shakespeare's Time."
    In <u>The New Century Shakespeare Handbook</u>. Edited by Sandra
    Clark. Englewood Cliffs, NJ: Prentice-Hall, pp. 18-42.
        A survey (for the general reader) of the playhouse, the
    stage and stagecraft, the audience, and the actors and
    companies.

2 ASTINGTON, JOHN HAROLD. "The Staging of the Beaumont and
    Fletcher Collaborations, 1606-1616." Ph.D. dissertation,
    University of Toronto, 253 pp.
        Examines nine collaborations, in relation to the
    theatres and companies associated with their initial
    performances. It is assumed that Beaumont and Fletcher
    wrote particularly for private playhouses and that this
    was of help to the King's Men when they began playing at
    Blackfriars in 1609. Astington examines the acting style
    associated with boy and adult companies and concentrates
    on the uses made of the various physical features of the
    stage by the dramatists. He concludes that they write with
    a strong sense of the play as a piece of physical action
    and that there were probably no differences in presentation
    between the adult and boy companies.

3 BINNS, J. W. "Women or Transvestites on the Elizabethan
    Stage? An Oxford Controversy." <u>SCJ</u> 5 (October):95-120.
        Discusses the controversy among Rainolds, Gager, and
    Alberico Gentili over "stage transvestitism." Rainolds
    and Gentili corresponded in Latin, and Binns translates
    several sections and comments on them. Essentially, Genti-
    li argues that the law of Deuteronomy prohibiting the
    wearing of women's garments by men should not be taken
    literally in the case of the theatre.

4 BLISSETT, WILLIAM. "Your Majesty Is Welcome to a Fair." In
   The Elizabethan Theatre, IV. Edited by G[eorge] R. Hibbard.
   Toronto: Macmillan; Hamden, Conn.: Archon, pp. 80-105.
      Examines the court performance of Bartholomew Fair in
   1614.

5 CAVANO, JANET M. JEFFREY. "Macbeth: The Book of the Play and
   the King's Men: A Study of the Stage-Copy in Production
   and Performance." Ph.D. dissertation, University of North
   Carolina, 497 pp.
      Since the First Folio text of Macbeth was almost certain-
   ly set in type from the prompt-book, careful study of it can
   help us understand in what ways it could serve as a guide to
   the company in production and performance. Cavano finds
   no support for such common assertions as "A stage-copy
   should be precise" or "the book-keeper adapts the author's
   manuscript for performance." Staging notations are incomplete, and entrance and exit notations inconsistent.

6 COOK, ANN JENNALIE. "The Audience of Shakespeare's Plays: A
   Reconsideration." ShSt 7:283-305.
      Reexamines Harbage's hypothesis (in 1941.4) that the
   working class formed the majority of Shakespeare's audience.
   Cook first arrives at a definition of the working class at
   the time, and concludes that they did not form a majority
   of the population of London. Next she examines the admissions structure, concluding that it was not especially
   designed for the working class. Ultimately, she concludes
   that the working class did not form the majority of
   Shakespeare's audience.

7 COPE, JACKSON I. "Marlowe's Dido and the Titillating
   Children." ELR 4 (Autumn):315-25.
      Discusses the compatibility of declamation and farce.
   Cope sees the success of the play as "dependent upon a cast
   of child actors."

8 CROSSLEY, D. W. "Ralph Hogge's Ironworks Accounts, 1576-
   1581." Sussex Archaeological Collections 112:48-79.
      Discusses the material from Henslowe's diary from
   before Henslowe began to use it. Crossley transcribed the
   accounts and comments on them. See also 1977.8.

9 CUTTS, JOHN P. "An Entertainment for Queen Elizabeth, 1591."
   SMC 4, no. 3:554-60.
      A paper presented at the Fourth Conference on Medieval
   Studies, 13-15 March 1968, Western Michigan University.
   Cutts examines the question of authorship, rejecting

Nicholas Breton and supporting John Lyly. His major
contribution here concerns the "consort of six musicians
provided by the Lord of Hertford to entertain her Majesty."
Cutts argues for John Johnson's authorship of two songs and
his participation in the Elvetham Entertainment.

10 DeMOLEN, RICHARD L. "Richard Mulcaster and Elizabethan
Pageantry." SEL 14 (Spring):209-21.
Examines Mulcaster's use of pageantry. He participated
in all three types: royal entries, Lord Mayor's pageants,
and royal progresses. Mulcaster wrote pageants "for
purposes of flattery and amusement and as a device for
persuasion," according to DeMolen. Based in part on 1970.5.

11 DOEBLER, JOHN. "A Lost Paragraph in the Revels Constitution."
SQ 25 (Spring):286-87.
Reprint of 1973.3, with corrected lineation and line
references.

12 DOLLERUP, CAY. "Danish Costume on the Elizabethan Stage." RES
n.s. 25 (February):53-58.
Suggests that "pludderhoser," a low hat with an ostrich
feather, and gold chains around the neck were the typical
costume indications of Danes on the Elizabethan stage.

13 DOLMAN, ROBERT CHRISTOPHER SIBSON. "Formal Implications of
Staging in the Elizabethan Metatheatre." Ph.D. dissertation, Johns Hopkins University, 287 pp.
Examines Elizabethan assumptions about the mimetic
nature of the stage as a metaphor for life. Of greatest
theatrical interest is the discussion of emblematic staging
conventions before 1590 and the end of that tradition with
the installation of flying thrones in the Rose and Swan
about 1595.

14 EDMOND, MARY. "Pembroke's Men." RES, n.s. 25 (May):129-36.
Based on the discovery of Simon Jewell's will, and
illuminates Pembroke's Men. Especially interesting is the
suggestion that Ben Jonson began his career as a hired man
with this group in 1592, a suggestion here supported by
overlooked entries about Jonson in the records of the
Tilers' and the Bricklayers' Company. See also 1976.16.

15 GEORGE, DAVID. "Early Cast Lists for Two Beaumont and
Fletcher Plays." TN 28 (Winter):9-11.
Discusses apparent cast lists for Philaster and The
Maid's Tragedy, dating from ca. 1640 and ca. 1660, held in
the Folger Shakespeare Library. The lists are written in

1974

quarto editions of the plays included in a scrapbook
possibly assembled by Halliwell-Phillipps.

16 HIBBARD, G[EORGE] R., ed. The Elizabethan Theatre, IV.
Toronto: Macmillan; Hamden, Conn.: Archon, 175 pp.
"Papers given at the Fourth International Conference on
Elizabethan Theatre held at the University of Waterloo,
Ontario in July 1972." This volume focuses on Ben Jonson,
and only one paper--1974.4--is of theatrical interest.

17 KERNAN, A. B. "This Goodly Frame, the Stage: The Interior
Theatre of Imagination in English Renaissance Drama."
SQ 25 (Winter):1-5.
Originally a paper presented at the meeting of the Shakespeare Association of America, March 1973. Kernan is
concerned not with the physical theatre building but with
theatrical metaphors in the plays.

18 KOLIN, PHILIP C., and WYATT, R. O., II. "A Bibliography of
Scholarship on the Elizabethan Stage since Chambers."
RORD 15-16:33-59.
Contains a total of 361 items, unannotated but including
reviews of relevant items. They "included only those
works which deal with the stage as a material object of
empirical investigation." The listing is alphabetical.
All relevant entries have been incorporated into this
bibliography.

19 McKERROW, RONALD B. "The Elizabethan Printer and Dramatic
Manuscripts." In Ronald Brunlees McKerrow: A Selection of
His Essays. Compiled by John Philip Immroth. Great
Bibliographers Series, no. 1. Metuchen, N.J.: Scarecrow
Press, pp. 139-58.
Reprint of 1931.12.

20 MORSEBERGER, ROBERT E. Swordplay and the Elizabethan and
Jacobean Stage. Jacobean Drama Studies, no. 37. Salzburg:
Institut für englische Sprache und Literatur, Universität
Salzburg, 129 pp.
After three chapters of background on styles of fencing,
Morseberger examines fencing methods used in the theatres,
the swordplay of actors and the techniques of Elizabethan
fencing, the performance of stage fights, and the duel in
Hamlet.

21 PINCISS, G. M. "Shakespeare, Her Majesties Players, and
    Pembroke's Men." ShS 27:129-36.
        Examines the evidence for Shakespeare's association with
    the Queen's Men, 1583-92, which comes from the close inter-
    connection he had with at least four plays from the
    repertory of that company. Pinciss then discusses the rise
    of Pembroke's Men as a division of the Queen's company,
    with Shakespeare following the split section in 1593, and
    then moving on to the Chamberlain's Men in 1594.

22 SHAW, JOHN. "'In Every Corner of the Stage': Antony and
    Cleopatra. IV, iii." ShSt 7:227-32.
        Examines the implications of the stage direction of the
    title. Shakespeare appears to have been influenced by the
    book of Revelation, and he used the emblematic tradition
    to clarify his point.

23 STAR, LEONIE RACHEL. "The Staging of Plays at the Cockpit-in-
    Court." Ph.D. dissertation, University of New Brunswick,
    228 pp.
        Attempts to examine and evaluate all available evidence
    concerning the Cockpit-in-Court from 1630, when it was
    remodelled by Inigo Jones, until the closing of the
    theatres in 1642. Twenty-six extant plays were performed
    there, and Star examines them for evidence of staging at
    this theatre. She finds "no essential difference between
    the mounting of plays at court, and in the professional
    'public' and 'private' theatres of the time." She does,
    however, consider some of Jones's designs in relation to
    the Cockpit-in-Court.

24 VISWANATHAN, S. "The Seating of Andrea's Ghost and Revenge
    in The Spanish Tragedy." ThS 15 (November):171-76.
        Suggests that the two Inductor-Presenter-Chorus char-
    acters were seated in the gallery rather than at opposite
    sides of the stage as has sometimes been supposed. The
    suggestion is partly based on the theories of Yates
    (1969.23).

25 WATSON, GEORGE, ed. The New Cambridge Bibliography of English
    Literature. Vol. 1, 600-1660. Cambridge: University
    Press, columns 1379-1400.
        As in the CBEL (1940.2), the relevant section is Parts
    II and III of the Renaissance Drama listings. The earlier
    volume and its Supplement (1957.16) are brought up to date.
    All new relevant items are included in this bibliography.

1974

26 WEIXLMANN, JOSEPH. "How the Romans Were Beat Back to Their
      Trenches: An Historical Note on <u>Coriolanus</u>, I. iv." <u>N&Q</u>,
      n.s. 20 (April):133-34.
         Suggests (following Saunders, 1954.24) that the Roman
      soldiers jumped off the stage but that the officers made
      their retreat through a stage door.

                              1975

1 BARKER, KATHLEEN M. D. "An Early Seventeenth Century Provin-
     cial Playhouse." <u>TN</u> 29 (Spring-Summer):81-84.
        Discusses a privately-owned playhouse in Bristol from
     some time after 1598 until 1619. The lease of the
     property, payment records in the Hospital School Treasurer's
     Book, and the owner's will all attest to its existence, as
     does the patent for the only licensed provincial company.

2 BERGERON, DAVID M. "Civic Pageants and Historical Drama."
     <u>JMRS</u> 5 (Spring):89-105.
        Argues that the "city pageants constitute a genre of
     history play and should be considered a part of the
     development of historical drama." Bergeron links the city
     pageant with the medieval mysteries, both in content and
     iconography.

3 BOURGY, VICTOR. <u>Le bouffon sur la scène anglaise au XVIe</u>
     <u>siècle (c. 1495-1594)</u>. Lille: University of Lille, 544 pp.
        Reprint of 1969.2.

4 BRADBROOK, MURIEL C. "The Triple Bond: Audience, Actors,
     Author in the Elizabethan Playhouse." In <u>The Triple Bond:</u>
     <u>Plays, Mainly Shakespearean, in Performance</u>. Edited by
     Joseph G. Price. London and University Park: Pennsylvania
     State University Press, pp. 50-69.
        Discusses the relationship between actors, audience, and
     playwright in the sixteenth century. She concludes that
     "the relationship of actors to audience moved from the
     customary to the contractual. The actors' role became
     increasingly interpretative, that of the audience differen-
     tiated, while in certain kinds of play the author acquired
     independent status."

5 BÜCHLER, KLAUS. "Explizite und implizite Bühnen- und Spielen-
     weisungen in Shakespeares <u>Tempest</u>." <u>JDSh</u> 1975, pp. 174-78.
        Examines <u>The Tempest</u> for cues for actors implicit in the
     dialogue as well as explicitly stated in stage directions.
     Büchler finds several detailed descriptions of appearance
     and behavior.

                              286

6 CHARNEY, MAURICE. "The Children's Plays in Performance."
     RORD 18:19-24.
         Examines differences in effect on the audience of the
     children's plays, arguing that the boy companies had a
     "witty, musical, and very distanced style." Charney
     concludes that "the hard lines of distinction between the
     repertories of the children and the adult companies need to
     be reexamined."

7 COGHILL, NEVILL. "Macbeth at the Globe, 1606-1616(?): Three
     Questions." In The Triple Bond: Plays, Mainly Shake-
     spearean, in Performance. Edited by Joseph G. Price.
     London and University Park: Pennsylvania State University
     Press, pp. 223-39.
         Discusses the questions of the witches' flying, Malcolm's
     army entering into the yard before passing over the stage,
     and the loss of part of one scene.

8 COLDEWEY, JOHN C. "The Last Rise and Final Demise of Essex
     Town Drama." MLQ 36 (September):239-60.
         An assessment of the influences affecting town drama in
     the county of Essex in the first two decades of Elizabeth's
     reign. While there was Puritan opposition, Coldewey feels
     that, at least in Essex, local drama died out as much from
     the Vestiarian controversy as from church objections, simply
     because of material convenience.

9 CRAIK, T. W. "The Reconstruction of Stage Action from Early
     Dramatic Texts." In The Elizabethan Theatre, V. Edited by
     G[eorge] R. Hibbard. Toronto: Macmillan; Hamden, Conn.:
     Archon, pp. 76-91.
         Looks at the evidence of the original text and stage
     directions for what they can tell us about stage action.
     Peele's David and Bethsabe, Kyd's Spanish Tragedy, and
     Marlowe's Doctor Faustus, The Jew of Malta, and Edward II
     serve as examples. Craik considers various staging
     problems.

10 DESSEN, ALAN C. "Two Falls and a Trap: Shakespeare and the
     Spectacle of Realism." ELR 5 (Autumn):291-307.
         Argues for "a mixed mode of presentation not limited to
     the tenets of realism." Dessen specifically discusses the
     stage falls in Titus Andronicus and King Lear as he feels
     Shakespeare intended they be played.

1975

11 ETHERIDGE, CHARLES LARIMORE. "The Image of Truth: The
     Evidence of a Natural Style of Acting in the Elizabethan
     Theatre c. 1600." Ph.D. dissertation, Cornell University,
     253 pp.
          Attempts to establish the distinguishing characteristics
     of the professional actor in Shakespeare's London. "Formal"
     and "natural" are the alternative styles considered, with
     no new historical information introduced. Etheridge
     examines material specifically related to the professional
     players at the close of the sixteenth century. The
     players' sequence in Hamlet is the central piece of evi-
     dence. He finds that the material he examines can be read
     at face value, without dismissing or reinterpreting any of
     it, and that it clearly points toward the use of a "natural"
     style. See also Index under Acting--Style.

12 EWBANK, INGA-STINA. "'What words, what looks, what wonders?':
     Language and Spectacle in the Theatre of George Peele." In
     The Elizabethan Theatre, V. Edited by G[eorge] R. Hibbard.
     Toronto: Macmillan; Hamden, Conn.: Archon, pp. 124-54.
          Argues that Peele's achievement has been underrated
     because too much attention has been paid to his use of
     language and not enough to his use of theatrical spectacle.
     Peele's main purpose was to create a sense of wonder in the
     audience, as he did in his pageants. David and Bethsabe
     is seen as "a link between the Mysteries and Shakespeare's
     last plays."

13 GREBANIER, BERNARD. Then Came Each Actor: Shakespearean
     Actors, Great and Otherwise, Including Players and Princes,
     Rogues, Vagabonds and Actors Motley, from Will Kempe to
     Olivier and Gielgud and After. New York: David McKay,
     pp. 15-24.
          The relevant section is Chapter Four, "In Shakespeare's
     Day." Grebanier discusses Richard Burbage and a few other
     members of the Chamberlain's/King's Men in general terms.

14 HIBBARD, G[EORGE] R., ed. The Elizabethan Theatre, V.
     Toronto: Macmillan; Hamden, Conn.: Archon, 158 pp.
          "Papers given at the Fifth International Conference on
     Elizabethan Theatre held at the University of Waterloo,
     Ontario, in July 1973." Contains 1975.9, 12, 26, as well
     as other papers concerned with the medieval period and an
     introduction by the editor.

15 HOSLEY, RICHARD. "The Playhouses." In <u>Revels History of Drama in English</u>. Vol. 3, <u>1576-1613</u>. Edited by Clifford [E. J.] Leech and T. W. Craik. London: Methuen, pp. 119-236.

Discusses the playhouses generally and includes detailed reconstructions of the Swan, the first Globe, and the second Blackfriars. The Swan reconstruction is made on the basis of the well-known sketch and the Fortune contract, and is complete down to fine architectural details. It is based on Hosley's earlier 1964.18. The Globe reconstruction is based on the internal evidence of twenty-nine plays produced at this playhouse 1599-1608 and the assumption of similarity between the first Globe and the Swan. The second Blackfriars reconstruction is based on both internal and external evidence, and it differs from the Swan and Globe primarily in size, capacity, and the existence of a third stage door. Twenty plays performed at Blackfriars 1600-1608 are used in the reconstruction. Hosley concludes by defining the "upper station" and the "discovery space" as parasitic uses of the boxes intended for spectators or musicians and the entries to the stage. In his view, the day of the "upper stage" and "inner stage" is over.

16 _____. "The Second Globe." <u>TN</u> 29 (Autumn):140-45.

Essentially an extended review of Hodges (1973.11). Hosley questions the theory of the postless superstructure and rejects Hodges's open ceiling. The diameter of the building and its number of sides are also subject to varying interpretations.

17 JENSEN, EJNER J. "The Boy Actors: Plays and Playing." <u>RORD</u> 18:5-12.

Discusses repertories and performances, with emphasis on the techniques of the playwrights.

18 JOSEPH, BERTRAM. "The Elizabethan Stage and Acting." In <u>The Age of Shakespeare</u>. Edited by Boris Ford. The Pelican Guide to English Literature, no. 2. Harmondsworth and Baltimore: Penguin Books, pp. 147-61.

Reprint of 1955.12.

19 KING, T[HOMAS] J[AMES]. "<u>Hannibal and Scipio</u> (1637): How 'The Places Sometimes Changed.'" <u>TN</u> 29 (Winter):20-22.

Responds to Freehafer (1973.6), showing how Nabbes altered accounts in Livy, thus "changing the places," rather than requiring the use of scenery.

1975

20 LATTER, D. A. "Sight-Lines in a Conjectural Reconstruction
of an Elizabethan Playhouse." ShS 28:125-35.
A generalized reconstruction of a typical public playhouse, with twelve sides and a diameter of 90 feet. Most
dimensions correspond to the Fortune or Hope contract.
Latter attempts to maximize the audience size, especially
in the higher-priced areas, with consideration of sight-
lines as his primary criterion. While Latter argues
against an inner stage, he considers the arrangement of the
tiring house facade only briefly.

21 LEGGATT, ALEXANDER. "Companies and Actors." In Revels History
of Drama in English. Vol. 3, 1576-1613. Edited by Clifford
[E. J.] Leech and T. W. Craik. London: Methuen, pp. 95-
118.
Focuses on the Admiral's Men with Edward Alleyn and the
Chamberlain's Men with Richard Burbage, but Leggatt also
considers clowns Tarlton and Kempe and the boy companies.
He discusses methods of rehearsal and performance and the
style of acting employed, taking a middle-of-the-road
approach to the formal versus natural debate.

22 LENNAM, TREVOR [N. S.]. Sebastian Westcott, the Children of
Paul's, and "The Marriage of Wit and Science." Toronto
and Buffalo: University of Toronto Press, pp. 5-80.
The relevant section is the first half, "Sebastian
Westcott and the Children of Paul's," containing chapters
on Westcott's life and his relationship with the boy
company. Includes slightly expanded reprint of 1970.19.

*23 MERZLAK, ANTHONY GEORGE. "A Theatrical History of Macbeth,
1606-1853." Ph.D. dissertation, Harvard University.
Cited in Comprehensive Dissertation Index, 1975 Supplement 5:301.

24 ORGEL, STEPHEN. The Illusion of Power: Political Theater in
the English Renaissance. Berkeley: University of California Press, 95 pp.
An extension and development of certain ideas in his
Inigo Jones (1973.21). Deals with theatre at court;
specifically, the three chapters treat theatres and audiences, royal spectacle, and the role of the King. Orgel's
thesis is that the marvels of the new stagecraft, imported
from Italy by Inigo Jones, are the supreme examples of
Renaissance kingship.

*25   OZAKI, MAKOTO. "Puritans and the Stage in Elizabethan Period."
     AnRS (Kyoto, Japan) 26, no. 1:64-79.
          Cited in 1976 MLA International Bibliography 1, entry
     3066. In Japanese.

26   ROWAN, D. F. "The Staging of The Spanish Tragedy." In The
     Elizabethan Theatre, V. Edited by G[eorge] R. Hibbard.
     Toronto: Macmillan; Hamden, Conn.: Archon, pp. 112-23.
          Questions about staging are answered by a return to the
     original stage directions. Rowan concludes that the Ghost
     and Revenge sit on the main stage (see 1974.24) and that
     the "arbour" is possibly the most important element used in
     the staging of the play.

27   SALGADO, GAMINI. Eyewitnesses of Shakespeare: First Hand
     Accounts of Performances, 1590-1890. New York: Harper &
     Row--Barnes & Noble Import Division, pp. 15-65.
          Compilation of records of Shakespeare's plays in per-
     formance. The material in Part I (1590-1700) is, of
     course, the least detailed, but it is nonetheless of
     interest since it brings together all extant contemporary
     accounts.

28   SHAPIRO, MICHAEL. "Theatrical Perspectives of Children's
     Companies." RORD 18:13-18.
          Examines "the unique qualities of the children's
     troupes and their plays," concentrating on "the atmosphere
     that surrounded performances." Shapiro discusses the
     audience's sense of the theatrical occasion, its attitudes
     and behavior in the playhouse, and its awareness of the
     actors as actors.

29   SMITH, WARREN D. Shakespeare's Playhouse Practice. Hanover,
     N.H.: University Press of New England, 119 pp.
          Examines cues for actors and technicians in Shakespeare
     for hints on how the plays were staged. One conclusion
     that Smith reaches is that Shakespeare probably described
     in dialogue as much of the action as possible to help those
     who might not have been able to see the stage clearly.
     Other sections examine his methods of bringing characters
     on and off stage. Based on Smith's Ph.D. dissertation
     (1948.12).

30   STAR, LEONIE [RACHEL]. "The Use of Bibliographical Methods
     in Studies of English Renaissance Staging." Parergon
     (Journal of the Australian and New Zealand Association
     for Medieval and Renaissance Studies) 12:32-38.

1975

Reviews the state of bibliographical scholarship in
theatre reconstruction, based on her Ph.D. dissertation
(1974.23). Star follows the method proposed by Reynolds
(1940.10) and refined by King (1965.9) but does not
recognize the inherent contradiction in her work on the
Cockpit-in-Court, all the plays of whose repertory were
staged at other playhouses and thus present printed texts
of doubtful value for the reconstructor.

31 WILSON, F[RANK] P[ERCY], and HILL, R. F., eds. "Dramatic
Records in the Declared Accounts of the Office of Works,
1560-1640." MSC 10:1-59.
Extracts from the Declared Accounts of the Office of
Works, from its inception under Queen Elizabeth until 1640.
All references regarding plays and masques and the preparations for their performances are included. Among these are
the records for the construction of the Cockpit-in-Court
(drawn upon by Wickham in 1967.15) and Inigo Jones's
banqueting houses.

1976

1 ADAMS, VICTOR. "When 'The Players' Came to Blandford."
Dorset Year Book (1975-76), pp. 25-30.
The only relevant item appears in the first paragraph,
noting that £11.7s.1d was earned for six performances at a
race meeting in 1603.

*2 AZZI VISENTINI, MARGHERITA. "Il teatro di Inigo Jones."
Comunità 30:273-93.
Cited in 1976 MLA International Bibliography 1, item
3789.

3 BERRY, HERBERT. "Americans in the Playhouses." ShSt 9:31-44.
Discusses the contributions of Americans (including
Canadians) to the study of the Elizabethan playhouse. Berry
breaks studies of the playhouse down into three periods:
1882-1923, dominated by the Germans and the alternation
theory, closed by Chambers; 1923-1968, dominated by J. C.
Adams and the inner below and upper stages, closed by
Bentley; and 1968-present, dominated by tightly controlled
evidence and single-playhouse studies.

4 BERRY, HERBERT; BROWNSTEIN, OSCAR; HOSLEY, RICHARD; INGRAM,
   [REGINALD] WILLIAM; and WICKHAM, GLYNNE. "Abstracts of
   Papers at the International Shakespeare Association Congress.
   The First Public Playhouse: The Theatre 1576-1976."
   ShN 36, no. 3 (May):27.
      Abstracts of papers printed in 1979.4.

5 BODDY, G. W. "Players of Interludes in North Yorkshire in
   the Early Seventeenth Century." NYCROJ 3:95-130.
      Examines Cholmley's Men, a North Yorkshire provincial
   company, and their leaders, Robert and Christopher Simpson.
   Boddy uses information from various lawsuits to discuss the
   players and their repertory. He is able to plot two of
   the company's tours.

6 BRADBROOK, MURIEL C. The Living Monument: Shakespeare and the
   Theatre of His Time. Cambridge: University Press, 287 pp.
      Deals with the "sociology of theatre" (by which she
   means the relationship between actors and audience and its
   effect on plays and playwrights) rather than its "archaeol-
   ogy." Part One explores this topic, with emphasis on the
   development of Shakespeare's history plays and the early
   masques. Part Two examines the Jacobean Shakespeare, and
   Part Three returns to the masque, but in its new form.
   Perhaps best viewed as a companion piece to Bradbrook's
   Rise of the Common Player (1962.4).

7 CARRÈRE, FÉLIX. "Vitruve et le théâtre élisabéthain." In
   De Shakespeare à T. S. Eliot: Mélanges offerts à Henri
   Fluchère. Edited by Marie-Jeanne Durry, et al. Études
   anglaises, no. 63. Paris: Didier, pp. 11-18.
      Examines the influence of Vitruvius on the Elizabethan
   theatre, emphasizing the microcosmic nature of the drama.

8 CARSON, NEIL. "The Elizabethan Soliloquy: Direct Address or
   Monologue?" TN 30 (Winter):12-18.
      Discusses Heywood's The Silver Age as an example of the
   movement away from direct address to monologue, a more
   realistic form of speech.

9 _____. "The Staircases of the Frame: New Light on the
   Structure of the Globe." ShS 29:127-32.
      Examines the drawing in Henslowe's diary, speculating
   that instead of having to do with the stage, as has been
   supposed, it instead illustrates the relationship of the
   staircase in the frame to the benches. Carson hypothesizes

1976

that this is a drawing of the Globe made to illustrate
the Fortune contract. See also 1960.8.

10 GRAVES, ROBERT BRUCE. "English Stage Lighting: 1576–1642."
Ph.D. dissertation, Northwestern University, 380 pp.
Traces the contrasting traditions of sunlit and candle-
lit plays, and estimates their effect. Graves assesses
the quality and quantity of Elizabethan general lighting,
drawing on extant documents, contracts, maps, and occasional
references in the plays. The number and placement of
windows and candles in private playhouses are inferred from
ecclesiastical and Tudor architecture. The conventions of
outdoor and indoor lighting are found to be similar, with
an adequately lit stage without contrasts of light and dark.
Graves concludes with an examination of a scene from
Duchess of Malfi for its lighting requirements. See
1978.13.

11 HARBAGE, ALFRED. "Copper into Gold." In English Renaissance
Drama: Essays in Honor of Madeleine Doran and Marc Eccles.
Edited by Standish Henning, Robert Kimbrough, and Richard
Knowles. Carbondale: Southern Illinois University Press;
London and Amsterdam: Feffer & Simons, pp. 1–14.
Examines the decade of the 1570s, when the strolling
players became resident companies. This in turn led to the
development of professional playwrights for the first time,
launching the Golden Age of English drama.

12 HONIGMANN, E. A. J. "Re-Enter the Stage Direction: Shakespeare and Some Contemporaries." ShS 29:117–25.
Discusses the placement of stage directions (including
speech prefixes) in modern critical editions.

13 HUNTER, G[EORGE] K. "Were There Act-Pauses on Shakespeare's
Stage?" In English Renaissance Drama: Essays in Honor of
Madeleine Doran and Marc Eccles. Edited by Standish
Henning, Robert Kimbrough, and Richard Knowles. Carbondale:
Southern Illinois University Press; London and Amsterdam:
Feffer & Simons, pp. 15–35.
Reexamines the evidence for pauses between the acts,
ultimately begging the historical question. Hunter then
argues that pauses are often needed in production to
reinforce meaning.

14 KOLIN, PHILIP C. "An Annotated Bibliography of Scholarship
on the Children's Companies and Their Theatres." RORD 19:
57–82.

Divided into three sections: Background Studies (68
items), Critical Studies (67 items), and Music Studies
(32 items). Kolin surveys the scholarship since Hillebrand
(1926.6), although a few earlier works are included.
Relevant entries have been incorporated into this bibliography.

15 LAMB, MARGARET A. "Shakespeare's Antony and Cleopatra on the
English Stage." Ph.D. dissertation, New York University,
363 pp.
Examines major English productions from 1606-7 through
1973. While there is no direct evidence that the King's
Men ever performed the play, an original production by that
group is assumed, since "the play, with its wide-ranging
action, is clearly suited to the neutral facade, swift
speech and economical battles of Shakespeare's theatre."

16 McMILLIN, [HARVEY] SCOTT. "Simon Jewell and the Queen's Men."
RES, n.s. 27 (May):174-77.
A note in response to 1974.3, suggesting that the Queen's
Men, rather than Pembroke's, might have been the company
referred to in Simon Jewell's will. McMillin further
speculates that the "Johnson" referred to was not Ben but
William, an early member of the Queen's Men.

17 ORRELL, JOHN. "Inigo Jones and Amerigo Salvetti: A Note on
the Later Masque Designs." TN 30 (Autumn):109-14.
Discusses the correspondence between Salvetti and the
Duke of Florence from 1616, which includes commentary on
masques and plays at court. Salvetti apparently furnished
Jones with designs from Italy which Jones used in the late
1630s. See 1979.23.

18 _____. "Productions at the Paved Court Theatre, Somerset
House, 1632/3." N&Q, n.s. 24:223-25.
Reviews Reyher's arguments (in 1909.23) that the
pastoral produced on 9 January was not repeated on 5 March,
but that a masque was presented in the altered theatre
instead. Newsletters of the time, the accounts of the
Office of Works, and dispatches from the Florentine
Resident in London are all cited in support.

19 PALUMBO, RONALD J. "From Melodrama to Burlesque: A Theatrical Gesture in Kyd, Shakespeare, and Marston." ThS 17
(November):220-23.
Examines the frequently used theatrical gesture of an
actor throwing himself to the ground in grief or sorrow.
Palumbo traces the evolution of the gesture from melodrama
in Kyd's Spanish Tragedy to burlesque in Marston's

1975

Antonio and Mellida, by way of Richard II and Romeo and
Juliet.

20 PENNINGER, FRIEDA ELAINE. English Drama to 1660 (Excluding
    Shakespeare): A Guide to Information Sources. American
    Literature, English Literature, and World Literature in
    English: An Information Guide Series, no. 5. Detroit:
    Gale Research, pp. 175-86.
        Selected, annotated bibliography, with the relevant
    section Part I, Chapter 11, "Theatre and Stagecraft."
    Only thirty-seven books are included, to cover both
    medieval and Renaissance periods in England. All relevant
    entries have been incorporated into this bibliography.

21 RHODES, ERNEST L. Henslowe's Rose: The Stage and Staging.
    Lexington. University Press of Kentucky, 286 pp.
        Revised, published version of 1959.20. Rhodes assumes,
    following Yates (1969.23), that the public theatres were
    based upon classical Vitruvian models. He also makes use
    of what he calls "the documents of the Rose," to be found
    among Henslowe's personal papers and diary. The study
    concludes that the stage of the Rose had five entrances,
    consisting of a central set of gates flanked by a pair of
    curtained discovery spaces, flanked in turn by a pair of
    doorways. That doorways could serve as either gates or
    discovery spaces appears not to have occurred to him. A
    "penthouse" with a window was located above the gates, and
    a gallery was available over both doors and discovery
    spaces. All elements of the stage were used to represent
    specific places. See also McMillin (1965.12) for different
    interpretations of the same evidence.

22 SMITH, MARY E. "Staging Marlowe's Dido Queene of Carthage."
    SEL 16 (Spring):177-90.
        An imaginative recreation of the play as it might have
    been acted in the Elizabethan theatre, despite the fact
    that it may never have been so acted. Smith divides the
    acting area by a wall, running from the back of the stage
    to the front. This wall is an open, ornamental structure
    with a large functional gate allowing the action to pass
    freely from one side to the other. On one side is a
    pastoral setting, represented by an emblematic bush. On
    the other is Carthage, consisting of a palace and a
    banquet hall. This staging is supposed in an Elizabethan
    Great Hall, in front of a hall screen with two doorways.
    Smith also draws inferences about costume and spectacle
    from the text of the play.

23 STAR, LEONIE [R]. "The Middle of the Yard, Part II: The
      Calculation of Stage Sizes for English Renaissance Play-
      houses." TN 30 (Spring-Summer):65-69.
          Continuation of 1976.24. Star argues that calculations
      of the size of the stage should be based on the six sizes
      we are sure of rather than on other considerations, and
      that permanent theatres always had spectators on three
      sides of the stage. Permanent stages were also always as
      wide or wider than they were deep. Thus, a working
      hypothesis for the stage size at the second Blackfriars
      would be 30 feet wide by 30 feet (at most) deep.

24 STAR, L[EONIE] R. "The Middle of the Yard: A Second Inner
      Stage?" TN 30 (Winter):5-9.
          Discusses the phrase "the middle of the yard," from the
      Fortune contract, suggesting that it was not necessarily
      standard practice for stages to extend to that point.
      Continued as 1976.23.

25 TWEEDIE, ELEANOR M. "'Action is Eloquence': The Staging of
      Thomas Kyd's Spanish Tragedy." SEL 16 (Spring):223-39.
          An imaginative recreation of the play in the theatre,
      concerned with what Tweedie calls "stage imagery": props,
      setting, and action. One of the most important things in
      the play is Kyd's use of repeated images; the audience is
      forced to make comparisons. Tweedie discusses the use of
      large properties in the play and concludes with a possible
      method of staging the play-within-a-play.

1977

1 ADAMS, VICTOR J. "When the Players Came to Bridport." Dorset
      Year Book (1977), pp. 61-66.
          The relevant section is the first page, noting the
      appearance of a troupe of puppet-players, led by William
      Sands, in 1630. Sands and two members of the company got
      into a fight with the local Puritan preacher, and the
      group was ordered to quit the county.

2 BENTLEY, G[ERALD] E[ADES]. "The Salisbury Court Theatre and
      Its Boy Players." HLQ 40 (February):129-49.
          Additional information about the Salisbury Court, its
      company, and one of the actors, from two suits in the Court
      of Requests in 1632, discovered and transcribed by Wallace
      in 1910 but never published. The dates of the lease of the
      building and its terms are verified, and a new estimate of
      the cost of conversions (£300) is made. The origins of the

Revels Children as a boy company meant to supply the King's
Men is clarified. Finally, the position of Stephen Ham-
merton, popular actor in the King's company, at Salisbury
Court is clarified.

3 BROWNSTEIN, OSCAR L. "New Light on the Salisbury Court Playhouse." ETJ 29 (May):231-42.
    Announces discovery of a document in the Guildhall
Library that finally pinpoints the location of the playhouse and casts some light upon "the dimensions, the
internal arrangements, and . . . the role of this last
Caroline playhouse in the preservation of the theatrical
traditions of the private playhouse during the Interregnum."
Important conclusions in addition to the location of the
playhouse include William Beeston's probable presentation
of plays to "persons of honor" from 1652 onwards, and a
correction of Hotson (1928.7) on the matter of raising the
roof thirty feet when the playhouse was repaired in 1652.
Brownstein argues that it was raised three feet instead, a
more reasonable figure. He feels that the "thirty" was
mistakenly copied from the line above.

4 CARSON, NEIL. "Literary Management in the Lord Admiral's
Company, 1596-1603." ThR 2, no. 3 (May):186-97.
    Examines the questions of play selection and alteration,
based on a reconsideration of Henslowe's diary. Carson
suggests that it was always the company, not Henslowe the
financier, who commissioned plays, and that after 1599 the
loose system of payment for scripts was reformed because
of the company's financial difficulties. He identifies
Robert Shaw, Thomas Downton, and Samuel Rowley as the
primary policymakers among the shareholders, and speculates
as to their reasons for failing to combine the functions
of resident playwright and literary manager. Carson
concludes with a statistical analysis of the authorization
and purchase of plays by the company from 1597 to 1603.

5 COLDEWEY, J[OHN] C. "Playing Companies at Aldeburgh, 1566-
1635." MSC 9:16-23.
    Records of provincial plays and players at Aldeburgh,
primarily from the Chamberlain's Accounts preserved in the
East Suffolk Record Office, Ipswich. The accounts covering
1593-1623 have not survived, but except for those years all
references to plays and players, mostly records of payment,
are transcribed.

6 COLDEWEY, JOHN C. "That Enterprising Property Player: Semi-
   Professional Drama in Sixteenth-Century England." TN 31
   (Winter):5-12.
       Originally a paper presented at the Tenth Conference on
   Medieval Studies at Western Michigan University, May 1975.
   Coldewey examines the professional directors of London who
   worked with amateur actors in the provinces before 1576.
   Three of the four centers of local drama in sixteenth-
   century Essex used such "property players," as did other
   cities in Kent and Suffolk. His duties included finance
   as well as staging.

7 CUMMINGS, L. A. "'Parte of a Play': A Possible Dramatic
   Fragment (c. 1550) from the Office of the Master of the
   Revels." REEDN 2:2-15.
       An edition of a fragment from the office, with
   facsimiles and commentary. See also Proudfoot (1977.28).

8 FOAKES, R. A., ed. The Henslowe Papers. 2 vols. London:
   Scolar Press; New York: British Book Centre, unpaged.
       Facsimiles of Henslowe's diary and the other theatrical
   papers held at Dulwich College. The first volume is the
   diary and associated papers and the second is MSS One and
   Two, the theatre papers and the Bear Garden papers of
   Henslowe and Alleyn.

9 GALLOWAY, DAVID. "The 'Game Place' and 'House' at Great
   Yarmouth, 1493-1595." TN 31, no. 2 (Spring-Summer):6-9.
       Discusses references in various records to a "game
   place" at Great Yarmouth, suggesting that it was not used
   mainly for staging plays.

10 GEORGE, DAVID. "Pre-1642 Cast Lists and a New One for The
   Maid's Tragedy." TN 31, no. 3 (Autumn):22-27.
       Reviews all known cast lists and adds one. George also
   draws attention to a prologue for Philaster "which sheds
   light on pre-Restoration actors for that play." The Maid's
   Tragedy list is written in, and has been cropped so that
   only fragments remain, but George attempts identification
   of King's Men in the roles.

11 KING, T[HOMAS] J[AMES]. "The King's Players at Stratford-
   upon-Avon, 1622." TN 31, no. 2 (Spring-Summer):4-6.
       A brief note examining records of performances in Shake-
   speare's home town, suggesting that the company that
   visited in 1622 was a provincial troupe headed by Richard
   Errington rather than the London King's Men.

12 KIPLING, GORDON. "Triumphal Drama: Form in English Civic
    Pageantry." <u>RenD</u>, n.s. 8:37–56.
        Discusses the civic triumph in London in the sixteenth
    century, from a primarily literary point of view.

13 LANCASHIRE, IAN. "Records of Drama and Minstrelsy in
    Nottinghamshire to 1642." <u>REEDN</u> 2:15–28.
        Discusses the evidence for theatrical performances in
    Nottinghamshire to be found in various town records.
    Lancashire corrects Murray (1910.15) in several particu-
    lars, and adds one new provincial company to those known.
    He prints a "semi-dramatic fragment" from a private house-
    hold in 1622 or 1623.

14 LEVIN, MARTHA WASKO. "Patterns in the Comedies Staged at the
    Theater of Paul's Children and at Blackfriars 1599–1606."
    Ph.D. dissertation, University of Colorado, 200 pp.
        Separates the comedies staged at the two theatres and
    examines them to determine the differences between the two
    groups. Levin finds a variety of patterns both between
    the companies and within their repertories, including the
    treatment of dance and song, the use of boy actors, the
    treatment of humanistic themes, and the emphasis given to
    satiric or city comedy.

15 LIMON, JERZY. "Przypuszczalne zwiazki teatru gdanskiej
    'Szkoły Fechtunku' z teatrem 'Fortune' w Londynie."
    <u>Pamiętnik Teatralny</u> 26, no. 1:29–38.
        Discusses the existence of a possible copy of the
    Fortune playhouse in Gdansk in the seventeenth century.
    <u>See</u> 1979.18 for an article on the same subject in English.

16 LINNELL, ROSEMARY. <u>The Curtain Playhouse</u>. London: privately
    printed by the Curtain Theatre, 64 pp.
        Attempts "to bring together as much as possible of the
    known history of the Curtain" along with Elizabethan
    theatre in general to see if any additional conclusions
    may be drawn. Linnell reviews information about acting in
    general and the Curtain in particular, and then develops
    a conjectural reconstruction of the Curtain as an octagonal
    structure, forty feet or so high and only some forty feet
    wide. Differing entertainments could be set up in differ-
    ent arrangements in the twenty-foot interior. The recons-
    truction is based on a "View of the City of London from the
    North Toward the South," so identified by Hotson in 1950.

17 METZ, G. HAROLD. "Stage History of Titus Andronicus." SQ 28
(Spring):154-69.
The relevant section (I) lists recorded and unrecorded
performances in England from 1594 to at least 1620.

18 MILLS, A. D. "A Corpus Christi Play and Other Dramatic
Activities in Sixteenth-Century Sherborne, Dorset." MSC
9:1-15.
Extracts from the Churchwardens' Accounts for Sherborne
relating to the performance of a Corpus Christi play and
interludes, to performances by touring companies, and to
other matters apparently related to plays. Dates range from
early sixteenth century to 1617.

19 MULHOLLAND, P. A. "The Date of The Roaring Girl." RES, n.s.
28 (February):18-31.
Redates the play 1611, based on the correction of a
misdating of the incident on which it was based and several
textual allusions. Mary Firth, alias Moll Cutpurse, the
Roaring Girl, apparently appeared on the Fortune stage in
early 1611. Mulholland also prints the corrected court
record.

20 MURAD, ORLENE. "The 'Theatre Letter' of Archduchess Maria
Magdalena: A Report on the Activities of the English
Comedians in Graz, Austria, in 1608." Mosaic 10 (Summer):
119-31.
The complete text of the letter in English translation,
with commentary. The Archduchess refers by plot summary
to several plays performed by the English actors in Graz.
Reprinted: 1978.19.

21 MURPHY, J. L., ed. "A Seventeenth-Century Play from the
Essex Record Office." MSC 9:30-51.
The incomplete dramatic manuscript, probably written
sometime during 1642, held in the Essex Record Office,
Chelmsford. Murphy suggests, based on unspecified internal
evidence "to be set forth elsewhere," that the author of the
piece was John Tatham. A company of twelve, half of whom
were boys, was required for performance.

22 NOSWORTHY, J. M., ed. "An Elizabethan Jig from the National
Library of Wales." MSC 9:24-29.
A previously overlooked Elizabethan farce jig, presum-
ably from the end of the sixteenth century.

1977

23 ORBISON, TUCKER. "Research Opportunities at the Inns of
    Court." RORD 20:27-33.
       Lists manuscripts held in the libraries of the Inns of
    Court, as well as the catalogues of those libraries, with
    suggestions for research.

24 ORRELL, JOHN. "The Agent of Savoy at The Somerset Masque."
    RES, n.s. 28 (August):301-4.
       A description of Campion's Somerset Masque from the
    dispatch of the Agent of Savoy who attended its performance
    in 1613. Orrell prints the original Italian and provides
    a translation.

25 _____. "Inigo Jones at the Cockpit." ShS 30:157-68.
       Suggests that the Inigo Jones drawings of an unidentified
    indoor playhouse held in the Worcester College, Oxford,
    Library, are probably for the Phoenix, or Cockpit, in Drury
    Lane. Orrell bases his suggestion on a dating of the
    drawings by John Harris (see 1973.10) and careful measure-
    ments of the actual drawings which reveal Vitruvian influ-
    ences. There is also a possible connection between the
    Phoenix manager, Christopher Beeston, and Jones. Finally,
    the designs for The Siege of Rhodes appear to fit the Jones
    drawing exactly, as do the rough sketches Jones made for an
    unknown production for "ye cockpitt" in 1639. See also
    1973.18.

26 PAFFORD, J. H. P. "Blandford Forum. Early Records of the
    Drama." N&QSD 30 (September):283-87.
       Extracts from the Chamberlain's Accounts 1564-1752,
    recording payments to companies and players. The relevant
    extracts cover the years 1588 to 1621 and name several
    provincial companies including Lord Mounteagle's Men and
    Lord Stafford's Men. See also 1976.1.

27 PRINDLE, RODERIC MARVIN. "Apes and Boys, Men and Monsters:
    The Aesthetics of Elizabethan Acting." Ph.D. dissertation,
    University of California at Berkeley, 1010 pp.
       Defines three principal modes of Elizabethan acting:
    the old, required by the plays of Marlowe, Kyd, and so on,
    practiced by men on the public stage and exemplified by
    Alleyn; the new, developed by Shakespeare and Burbage,
    practiced by men on the public stage; and the coterie,
    required by the plays of Marston, Jonson, and Chapman, and
    presented privately by boys aged ten to fifteen. Both
    specific techniques and audience expectations and response
    are examined as each mode of acting is discussed by itself
    and in relation to the other two. Prindle rejects the usual

terms "natural" and "formal." He posits the "formula" of
Heraclitus (God:man=man:ape/boy) as the pattern for the
mutual relationship he finds, and the figure of Hercules is
described as a major element in the aesthetic of Elizabethan
meta-theatre. See also Index under Acting--Style.

28 PROUDFOOT, G. R., ed. "Five Dramatic Fragments from the
    Folger Shakespeare Library and the Henry E. Huntington
    Library." MSC 9:52-75.
        The fifth fragment, described by Harbage as "'Masque',
    ca. 1625," contains stage directions calling for flying
    machinery. It may have been an evening Christmas perfor-
    mance by children, put on by Andrew, seventh Lord Grey.

29 RICHARDS, KENNETH. "A Sunday Play Performance at the Caroline
    Court." N&Q, n.s. 24 (December):535.
        Notes a reference to a Sunday performance in 1633 in the
    autobiography of Richard Baxter, the divine.

30 _____. "Theatre Audiences in Caroline and Early Restoration
    London: Continuity and Change." In Das Theater und sein
    Publikum: Referate der Internationalen theaterwissenschaft-
    lichen Dozentenkonferenzen in Venedig 1975 und Wien 1976.
    Veröffentlichungen des Inst. für Publikumsforschungen 5,
    SÖAW 327. Vienna: Österr. Akad. der Wissenschaften,
    pp. 162-87.
        Compares the evidence regarding audience composition
    immediately before and after the Commonwealth to illuminate
    the audiences of both periods. Richards cites prologues,
    dedicatory epistles, and epilogues for much of his evidence.
    He concludes that "the interregnum was not a great divide,
    and that both continuity and change were as much features
    of the composition of theater audiences as they were of
    organisation, acting, and the dramatic repertory."

31 SHADY, RAYMOND C. "The Stage History of Heywood's Love's
    Mistress." ThS 18, no. 2 (November):86-95.
        Traces the stage history of Heywood's masque from its
    initial production in 1635 at the Phoenix through the end
    of the seventeenth century. Shady examines the possible
    use of three unidentified Inigo Jones designs for the
    second performance at Denmark House.

32 SHAPIRO, MICHAEL. Children of the Revels: The Boy Companies
    of Shakespeare's Time and Their Plays. New York: Columbia
    University Press, 313 pp.
        Greatly expanded published version of 1967.10; it is so
    much changed, however, as to be better described as

1977

inspired by 1967.10. Shapiro concentrates more on the plays
than the companies, rendering his study of more interest
to the student of dramatic literature than the theatre
historian, but he does discuss the companies, the occasion,
and the audience in three preliminary chapters, and he
examines the "natural" vs. "formal" debate in relation to
the boy actors. Three appendixes discuss song and music
in the children's plays and list court performances and
repertories of the companies. The terminal date is 1613.

*33 SHIBATA, TOSHIHIKO. "Elizabeth-cho no Kankyaku: Oboegaki."
In Shakespeare no Engekiteki Fudo. Tokyo: Kenkyusha, pp.
97-112.
      Cited in 1977 MLA International Bibliography 1, entry
2742. Title translates as Dramatic Climate of Shakespeare;
the subject of the relevant article is the Elizabethan
audience.

34 STEVENS, DAVID. "The Stagecraft of James Shirley." ETJ 29
(December):493-516.
      Examines the twenty-two plays of James Shirley staged at
the Phoenix from 1625 to 1637, when Shirley left London for
Ireland. "Shirley is of special interest because his plays
abound with sophisticated use of the physical features of
the Elizabethan playhouse stage and effective theatrical
use of auditory and visual effects indicated by both
dialogue and stage directions in the printed texts . . . .
Shirley can thus serve as an exemplary resource for the
study of Elizabethan staging techniques." Stevens
concentrates more on the style and texture of a production
at the Phoenix than on determining precisely what the
physical structure of the stage was, although he clarifies
his differences with King (1965.9), primarily over the
existence of a third stage door.

35 SUMMERSON, JOHN [NEWENHAM]. Architecture in Britain, 1530-
1830. 6th ed. Pelican History of Art, no. Z3.
Harmondsworth and New York: Penguin Books, pp. 61-67.
      Reprint of 1953.26.

1978

1 BARTHOLOMEUSZ, DENNIS [STEPHEN]. "Macbeth" and the Players.
Cambridge: University Press, pp. 1-13.
      Reprint of 1969.1.

2 BENTLEY, GERALD EADES. "The Troubles of a Caroline Acting
    Troupe: Prince Charles's Company." HLQ 41 (May):217-49.
      New information on the acting company, from a suit
    preserved in the Public Record Office, discovered by
    Wallace in about 1910 but never published. While never
    serious rivals of the King's Men, Prince Charles's company
    at least managed to stay together through the 1630s and
    early 1640s, which is a better record than most of their
    contemporaries had.

3 BERGERON, DAVID M. "Elizabeth's Coronation Entry (1559): New
    Manuscript Evidence." ELR 8 (Winter):3-8.
      Discusses evidence from the Losely collection in the
    Folger Shakespeare Library that demonstrates that Elizabeth
    herself assisted in the preparations for her coronation
    entry by loaning costumes from the Revels Office.

4 BILLINGTON, SANDRA. "Sixteenth-Century Drama in St. John's
    College, Cambridge." RES, n.s. 29 (February):1-10.
      Discusses the inventories of goods and furniture belong-
    ing to the College, including several bearing on theatrical
    performances. Costumes are most frequently mentioned.
    Billington suggests that two of Terence's comedies were
    among the plays performed.

5 BLACKSTONE, MARY ANNA. "The Eighth Fairy: Stage Music and
    A Midsummer Night's Dream to 1880." Ph.D. dissertation,
    University of New Brunswick, 268 pp.
      The relevant section examines the use of music in the
    original text. Shakespeare used the music as a dramatic
    device unifying the plot, characterization, and theme of
    the play.

6 BRADBROOK, M[URIEL] C. "Shakespeare and the Multiple Theatres
    of Jacobean London." In The Elizabethan Theatre, VI.
    Edited by G[eorge] R. Hibbard. Toronto: Macmillan;
    Hamden, Conn.: Archon, pp. 88-104.
      Examines the relationship between the playwright and his
    audience, focusing on the influence of the court masque.
    Bradbrook claims that masques were a subject for irony in
    Jacobean plays rather than a direct influence.

7 _____. Shakespeare: The Poet in His World. New York:
    Columbia University Press; London: Weidenfeld & Nicolson,
    pp. 91-201.
      The most relevant section is the second, "The World He
    Made," where Bradbrook examines Shakespeare's successful

years with the Lord Chamberlain's/King's Men. She inter-
weaves a wealth of historical and cultural material into
her biographical narrative.

8   DESSEN, ALAN C. "The Logic of Elizabethan Stage Violence:
    Some Alarums and Excursions for Modern Critics, Editors,
    and Directors." RenD, n.s. 9:39-70.
       Discusses realistic duels and selectivity in battle
    scenes as well as what might be called "symbolic" violence.
    Dessen argues for an other than straightforwardly realistic
    approach to the staging of scenes of violence in Elizabethan
    plays.

9   FORDYCE, RACHEL. Caroline Drama: A Bibliographic History of
    Criticism. Boston: G. K. Hall, pp. 157-70.
       The relevant section, "Stage History," contains a total
    of fifty-five annotated entries; a few other relevant
    entries are scattered throughout the other sections. This
    is a highly selective listing, and at times the criteria
    for selection are difficult to discern. All relevant items
    have been incorporated into this bibliography.

10 GAIR, [W.] REAVLEY. "Chorister-Actors at Paul's." N&Q n.s.
    25 (October):440-41.
       Notes on the names of previously unknown Paul's
    choristers in the parish records of St. Gregory-by-Paul's.
    Gair also determines a range of ages for them from six to
    twelve.

11 _____. "The Presentation of Plays at Second Paul's: The
    Early Phase (1599-1602)." In The Elizabethan Theatre, VI.
    Edited by G[eorge] R. Hibbard. Toronto: Macmillan;
    Hamden, Conn.: Archon, pp. 21-47.
       Presents an account of the setting up of the second
    playhouse in 1599 and uses the plays presented there as
    evidence of staging methods employed. Gair finds that the
    playhouse had two doors on either side of a small stage
    (at least one of which contained or was near a grate); a
    third, larger door between them, sometimes curtained for
    discoveries; a trap, operated from below; an upper acting
    area the entire width of the stage, with one or two case-
    ments opening onto the stage. Gair also locates the play-
    house and discusses Antonio and Mellida and Antonio's
    Revenge in more detail.

12 GEORGE, DAVID. "Another Elizabethan Stage." <u>TN</u> 32, no. 2
    (Spring-Summer):63-67.
         A sketch from a copy of the 1600 quarto of <u>2 Henry IV</u>,
    previously printed by Halliwell-Phillipps in 1861. George
    suggests that it is a diagram of the stage action at that
    point, made by the prompter, and thus gives us a possible
    diagram of the stage of the Globe. He further suggests
    that the sketch is upside down, which would give the stage
    of that playhouse two small side stages, perhaps for
    audience members.

13 GRAVES, R[OBERT] B[RUCE]. "<u>The Duchess of Malfi</u> at the Globe
    and Blackfriars." <u>RenD</u>, n.s. 9:193-209.
         Examines the "dead man's hand" scene in relation to what
    is known of illumination at the King's Men's two playhouses.
    Graves suggests that the scene was not originally staged
    in a completely darkened auditorium at Blackfriars, since
    the audience reaction would be enhanced by enough light to
    see by. He further suggests that, at least in this one
    respect, staging methods in the public and private play-
    houses may not have been quite so divergent as has sometimes
    been thought. Based on 1976.10.

14 HIBBARD, G[EORGE] R., ed. <u>The Elizabethan Theatre, VI</u>.
    Toronto: Macmillan; Hamden, Conn.: Archon, 161 pp.
         "Papers given at the Sixth International Conference on
    Elizabethan Theatre held at the University of Waterloo,
    Ontario, in July 1975." Contains 1978.6, 11, 15, as well
    as other nontheatrical papers and an introduction by the
    editor.

15 HOSLEY, RICHARD. "A Reconstruction of the Fortune Playhouse:
    Part I." In <u>The Elizabethan Theatre, VI</u>. Edited by
    G[eorge] R. Hibbard. Toronto: Macmillan; Hamden, Conn.:
    Archon, pp. 1-20.
         Examines "some basic questions which have arisen in an
    attempt to reconstruct the first Fortune playhouse: depth
    of stage, height of tiring-house storeys, number and size
    of bays of the playhouse frame, location of yard entrances,
    and location of staircases." The remainder of the
    reconstruction is to be treated in Part II, to be pub-
    lished later. Hosley illustrates his conclusions with
    eleven line drawings. He argues for a ten-inch overhang on
    both second and third storeys, for a platform extending to
    the middle of the yard but only 25'10" deep rather than the
    27'6" usually assumed, for twenty-four-bay construction,
    and for the entrances to the playhouse being located oppo-
    site the stage, thus placing the stage on the north end.

1978

16   INGRAM, [REGINALD] WILLIAM. <u>A London Life in the Brazen Age:</u>
     <u>Frances Langley, 1548-1602</u>. Cambridge, Mass., and London:
     Harvard University Press, 335 pp.
        A biography of the theatrical entrepeneur, based largely
     on various historical records examined by the author.
     Chapters seven through fifteen contain the details of
     Langley's theatrical affairs, which included the building
     and management of the Swan and the management of the Boar's
     Head. This is an apparently complete and well-documented
     study of a sometimes forgotten major theatrical figure.
     Ingram incorporates material from 1971.9 and 1972.15 into
     this work.

17   MARDER, LOUIS. "The Henslowe Papers: 200 Years of Editing."
     <u>ShN</u> 28 (February):2-3.
        On the occasion of the publication of the facsimile
     edition (1977.8), the editor of the <u>Newsletter</u> briefly
     discusses the earlier editions, including those of Malone
     (1790.1; 1821.1), Collier (1841.1), Greg (1904.7; 1907.15;
     1908.11), and Foakes and Rickert (1961.13).

18   MOYNES, JON CRAIG. "The Reception of Elizabeth I at Norwich."
     Ph.D. dissertation, University of Toronto, 192 pp.
        An edition of the two surviving accounts of the Queen's
     1578 reception in Norwich, including the royal entry
     prepared by Bernard Garter and a series of outdoor enter-
     tainments conceived by Thomas Churchyard.

19   MURAD, ORLENE. <u>The English Comedians at the Habsburg</u>
     <u>Court in Graz, 1607-1608</u>. Elizabethan and Renaissance
     Studies, no. 81. Salzburg: Institut für englische Sprache
     und Literatur, Universität Salzburg, 101 pp.
        Reprints 1977.20 and chronicles the eleven plays known
     to have been performed by English actors in Graz, Austria,
     1607-1608, based on letters and other documents.

20   NEILL, MICHAEL. "'Wits most accomplished Senate': The Audi-
     ence of the Caroline Private Theaters." <u>SEL</u> 18 (Spring):
     341-60.
        A reevaluation of the previously labelled "decadent"
     audience of the pre-Commonwealth theatre. Neill asserts
     that, while there are different groups discernable in the
     audience, far more important than any one of them is the
     audience's sense of itself as a so-called "court of taste."
     The audience craved novelty but often preferred old plays
     to new. The rise of published dedications, epistles to
     the reader, prologues, and epilogues shows the concern of
     the theatres for the audiences. Neill concludes with a

discussion of "wit," which he claims was the chief concern
of the Caroline audience.

21 PARRY, GRAHAM. "A New View of Bankside." ShS 31:139-40.
    A sketch of the Bankside, including the Globe in rough
outline, from one of Hollar's notebooks preserved in the
John Rylands Library. It apparently dates from 1642-43,
and is drawn from the point of view of the tower of St.
Mary's Southwark. The roundness of the building and the
double gable of the stage roof are substantiated.

22 RIBNER, IRVING, and HUFFMAN, CLIFFORD CHALMERS. Tudor and
    Stuart Drama. 2d ed. Goldentree Bibliographies in Language
    and Literature. Arlington Heights, Ill.: A. H. M.
    Publishing Corp., pp. 6-12.
    Second edition of 1966.16, revised and enlarged.

23 SMITH, DUNCAN BRUCE. "Shakespeare's Comic Cast: A Study of
    the Relationship between Actor and Character in the Early
    Comedies." Ph.D. dissertation, University of California
    at Berkeley, 317 pp.
    Examines four early comedies in order to determine the
extent to which Shakespeare may have considered the stage
personalities of the actors of his company as he created
the characters. Smith concludes that while he took careful
account of the composition of the company he did not treat
all of the actors equally. The clowns especially were
exploited in this manner.

24 SMITH, M[ARY] E. "Personnel at the Second Blackfriars: Some
    Biographical Notes." N&Q, n.s. 25 (October):441-44.
    Presents information about the lives outside the theatre
of Edward Kirkham, Thomas Kendall, and Henry Evans, all of
whom were involved in the management of the boy company
ousted by the King's Men.

25 STAR, LEONIE [R.] "Inigo Jones and the Use of Scenery at the
    Cockpit-in-Court." ThS 19 (May):35-48.
    Partly based on 1974.23, her Ph.D. dissertation. Star
examines the possible use of painted perspective scenery
at the Cockpit, particularly the possible use of scene
designs by Inigo Jones in the Duke of Devonshire's collection. She concludes that Jones probably maintained the
distinction between masques and plays, and that the Cockpit-
in-Court was designed in the typical Elizabethan manner
for professional acting companies who performed at Court.
Consequently, painted perspective scenery was rarely, if
ever, used.

1978

26 STREITBERGER, W. R. "On Edmond Tyllney's Biography." <u>RES</u>
    n.s. 29 (February):11-35.
        Attempts a more complete biography of the Elizabethan
    Master of the Revels, concentrating on the cross-pressures
    Tyllney faced from the Court, the City, and the Church.

27 _____. "Renaissance Revels Documents, 1485-1642." <u>RORD</u>
    21:11-16.
        A brief history of the Office of the Revels and a list-
    ing of available documents, with commentary and references
    to discussions of the documents elsewhere.

28 TEAGUE, FRANCES. "Ben Jonson's Stagecraft in <u>Epicoene</u>." <u>RenD</u>,
    n.s. 9:175-92.
        Discusses Jonson's use of the various elements of the
    Whitefriars Playhouse (as described in Wickham, 1963.20).
    "Jonson tried to use peripheral stage areas or to exploit
    the theater's small size when he thought it might further
    the dramatic action or ensure that his audience would
    respond as he wanted them to." Teague also discusses the
    use of the child acting company and the use of songs in
    the play.

29 VISSER, COLIN. "The Killigrew Folio: Private Playhouses and
    the Restoration Stage." <u>ThS</u> 19 (November):119-38.
        Examines the Worcester College, Oxford, copy of the
    1664 folio of Killigrew's plays annotated in his own hand.
    Visser shows that the plays originally meant for the
    private playhouses of pre-Commonwealth London could have
    been adapted easily for Restoration production. He uses
    the stage directions to establish two doors, a discovery
    space, an upper acting area, bay windows over the
    doors, and traps in the private playhouse (probably Black-
    friars) that these plays were written for. Killigrew's
    handwritten directions then yield information on how the
    plays were adapted for the scenic stage.

30 WILLIAMS, PATRICK R. "Ben Jonson's Satiric Choreography."
    <u>RenD</u>, n.s. 9:121-45.
        An attempt to find an approach to Jonson's plays that
    accounts for both their theatrical characteristics and
    for their satiric humor, one in terms of the other.
    Williams does so by contrasting the flexibility of the
    stage itself with the playwright's insistence on maintain-
    ing the unity of place. "Open" and "closed" compositions
    use the tiring house facade to create a variety of
    tensions on the stage.

1979

1 ALSOP, J. D. "A Sunday Play Performance at the Jacobean
   Court." N&Q, n.s. 26 (October):427.
   A brief note regarding a previously unnoticed reference
   to a Sunday performance (17 December 1615) before Queen
   Anne in the accounts of her receiver-general, held in the
   Public Record Office.

2 BERRY, HERBERT. "A Handlist of Documents about the Theatre in
   Shoreditch." In The First Public Playhouse: The Theatre
   in Shoreditch, 1576-1598. Edited by Herbert Berry.
   Montreal: McGill-Queen's University Press, pp. 97-133.
   Catalogues the documents concerning the Theatre held in
   the Public Record Office, according to the four categories
   suggested by Chambers (1923.2). All previous transcriptions
   (Wallace, 1913.19; Stopes, 1913.15) are checked for accu-
   racy, with discrepancies noted, although no new transcriptions are offered. Berry interprets the evidence held in
   the documents in 1979.3.

3 _____. "Aspects of the Design and Use of the First Public
   Playhouse." In The First Public Playhouse: The Theatre
   in Shoreditch, 1576-1598. Edited by Herbert Berry.
   Montreal: McGill-Queen's University Press, pp. 30-45.
   Interprets the documentary evidence catalogued in 1979.2.
   Berry includes little new material, but he draws some new
   conclusions, particularly concerning the profitability of
   the playhouse. He suggests £190 per year as a reasonable
   guess at the housekeepers' profits.

4 _____, ed. The First Public Playhouse: The Theatre in Shore-
   ditch, 1576-1598. Montreal: McGill-Queen's University
   Press, 139 pp.
   Contains 1979.2-3, 8, 16-17, 33.

5 BERRY, HERBERT; LIMON, JERZY; KING, T[HOMAS] J[AMES]; ORREL,
   JOHN; HOSLEY, RICHARD; and YOUNG, ALAN R. "The Public
   Playhouse: Architectural Problems." ShN 19 (May):20.
   Abstracts of papers presented at the Shakespeare
   Association of America meeting in San Francisco, 13 April
   1979. Berry reconstructed the Boar's Head (with drawings
   by Hodges); Limon discussed his 1979.18; King compared the
   superstructure of the second Globe with Herbert's House,
   York; Orrel discussed his 1979.25; Hosley discussed the
   ground plan of the Swan from 1975.15; and Young calculated
   sun dial configurations for London, "useful for calculat-
   ing the amount of light and the angle of the sun's rays
   in the theatre."

1979

6   BOOTH, STEPHEN. "Speculations on Doubling in Shakespeare's
    Plays." In Shakespeare: The Theatrical Dimension. Edited
    by Philip C. McGuire and David A. Samuelson. AMS Studies
    in the Renaissance, no. 3. New York: AMS, pp. 103-31.
        Speculates on unverified doubling for theatrical effect
    in Midsummer Night's Dream, King Lear, Winter's Tale,
    Twelfth Night, and Cymbeline. Booth's purpose is not to
    suggest historical practice but to stimulate contemporary
    experimentation in casting.

*7 BOYLE, ROBERT RAYMOND. "The End of the Elizabethan Theatre:
    The Interaction of Cultural Conditions and Theatrical
    Productions in London 1632-1642." Ph.D. dissertation,
    New York University, 486 pp.
        Cited in DAI 40, no. 11A:5649.

8   BROWNSTEIN, OSCAR [L.]. "Why Didn't Burbage Lease the
    Beargarden? A Conjecture in Comparative Architecture." In
    The First Public Playhouse: The Theatre in Shoreditch,
    1576-1598. Edited by Herbert Berry. Montreal: McGill-
    Queen's University Press, pp. 81-96.
        Questions the assumption that the form of the Elizabethan
    public playhouse was adapted from the animal-baiting rings.
    Brownstein shows that baiting rings were available and
    would have been cheaper to adapt. The question is, "if
    baiting arenas were so readily adaptable for stage plays,
    why didn't Burbage merely lease a beargarden?" Brownstein
    hypothesizes that playhouses and baiting rings accommodated
    their customers in fundamentally different ways, and that
    rather than being similar they were in fact quite different
    structures.

9   CARSON, NEIL. "Production Finance at the Rose Theatre,
    1596-98." ThR, n.s. 4, no. 3 (May):172-83.
        Examines daily income records from the Rose, from
    Henslowe's diary. Carson points out that the company
    borrowed from Henslowe only when low attendance or irregu-
    lar playing schedules reduced their weekly income, and that
    their repayment was prompt. The players also regularly
    mounted new productions without resort to borrowing from
    the manager.

10 CARTELLI, THOMAS PAUL. "Marlowe's Theater: The Limits of
    Possibility." Ph.D. dissertation, University of California
    at Santa Cruz, 419 pp.
        Attempts to balance our critical estimate of Marlowe by
    establishing a theatrical perspective from which to view
    his major plays. While Cartelli does consider commercial

questions, the physical layout of the playhouse, the use of
the stage, and the nature of the audience, his study is
essentially literary rather than theatrical in nature.

11 CHARNEY, MAURICE. "Female Roles and the Children's Companies:
     Lyly's Pandora in The Woman in the Moon." RORD 22:37-44.
        Examines the seven separate roles Pandora plays, as well
     as Lyly's complete stage directions.

12 CHILLINGTON, CAROL ANNE. "Philip Henslowe and his 'Diary.'"
     Ph.D. dissertation, University of Michigan, 294 pp.
        A comprehensive examination of Henslowe's life and
     diary, balancing the standard portrait with a picture of
     the courtier, landowner, magistrate, and churchwarden.
     The heart of the study analyzes the playhouse accounts in
     detail, both the daily receipts of 1592-97 and the loan
     and repayment accounts of 1597-1603. Chillington also
     discusses the players' performance schedules, especially
     the problems they faced when two companies amalgamated.
     The remainder of the study discusses the process of play-
     writing and collaboration in the public theatre. Chil-
     lington also transcribes Henslowe's will.

*13 GEORGE, DAVID. "Records of Interest at the Lancashire Records
     Office." REEDN 2:2-6.
        Cited in 1979 MLA International Bibliography 1, entry
     4735.

14 GLENN, SUSAN MacDONALD. "The Designation of General Scene in
     English Dramatic Texts, 1500-1685." Ph.D. dissertation,
     University of Arizona, 133 pp.
        Examines the origins of designating scenes by tracing
     the use of scene-designations in continental and English
     texts, and explores rationales for the practice by
     analyzing the wording of such designations. Glenn argues
     that one reason for scene-designation is as an indication
     that the play in question observes the unity of place.

15 HASLER, JÖRG. "The Serpent's Tongue: Shakespeare and the
     Actor." ES 60 (August):389-401.
        Examines Shakespeare's plays for images of actors and
     acting (finding many) and traces of Shakespeare's acting
     experiences (finding a few). The main focus is literary,
     tracing the theatrical image of the audience hissing a
     poor performance.

1979

16 HOSLEY, RICHARD. "The Theatre and the Tradition of Playhouse
    Design." In The First Public Playhouse: The Theatre in
    Shoreditch, 1576-1598. Edited by Herbert Berry. Montreal:
    McGill-Queen's University Press, pp. 47-79.
        The first part of the essay relates what we know of
    the design of the building to what is known of later
    Elizabethan and Jacobean public playhouses. Hosley reminds
    us that the Theatre and the first and second Globes must
    have all been of the same size and shape, since the second
    Globe was built on the foundation of the first, and the
    first Globe was built with the timbers of the dismantled
    Theatre. The second part of the essay examines Henry VIII's
    Calais banqueting house (1520) as an antecedent of public
    playhouse design. This was a sixteen-sided structure 121
    feet in diameter with three galleries; as Hosley says, it was
    "fairly close to our understanding of the . . . tradition
    of public-playhouse design."

17 INGRAM, [REGINALD] WILLIAM. Henry Lanman's Curtain Playhouse
    as an 'Easer' to the Theatre, 1585-1592." In The First
    Public Playhouse: The Theatre in Shoreditch, 1576-1598.
    Edited by Herbert Berry. Montreal: McGill-Queen's
    University Press, pp. 17-28.
        Examines the profit-sharing arrangement James Burbage
    and Lanman entered into in 1585 and suggests that it was
    actually a sale, with Lanman settling for seven years'
    profits rather that the more usual fifteen. According to
    this theory, Burbage financed his later purchase of the
    Blackfriars by selling the Curtain to the players.

*18 KNIGHT, W. NICHOLAS. "Comic Twins at the Inns of Court."
    PMPA 4:74-82.
        Cited in 1979 MLA International Bibliography 1, entry
    4289.

19 LIMON, JERZY. "Pictorial Evidence for a Possible Replica of
    the London Fortune Theatre in Gdansk." ShS 32:189-99.
        Based on 1977.15. Limon discusses an engraving by a
    Dutch artist of a Gdansk theatre between 1664 and 1687. He
    cites stage directions from plays presented there in order
    to reconstruct staging practices, finding familiar Eliza-
    bethan usages such as doors, machinery, simple emblematic
    properties, and a trap. Limon suggests that some of the
    many English actors who played in the city had also played
    at the Fortune and provided information for a close copy of
    the playhouse in Gdansk. He concludes with a chronology
    of English performances there, 1600-1612. See also 1895.1.

20 LINDLEY, DAVID. "Who Paid for Campion's Lord Hay's Masque?"
    N&Q, n.s. 26 (April):144-45.
        Argues that the Earls of Exeter, Salisbury, and Suffolk
    footed the bills for the wedding masque of James Hay and
    Honora Denny on Twelfth Night, 1607, "as part of their
    political activity to gain the King's favour."

21 MIRABELLA, BELLA MARYANNE. Part I, "Mute Rhetoric: Dance in
    Shakespeare and Marston;" Part II, "The Machine in the
    Garden: The Theme of Work in Tess of the d'Urbervilles;"
    Part III, "Art and Imitation in Edith Wharton's The House
    of Mirth." Ph.D. dissertation, Rutgers University, pp.
    1-141.
        The first part considers dance as a literary conven-
    tion and a dramatic device. Mirabella also examines
    the linkage between dance and disguise in Love's Labour's
    Lost, Much Ado about Nothing, and Malcontent.

22 NIEMEYER, CHRISTIAN BERNARD. "Shakespeare and the Chamberlain's
    Men (1594-1603): A Reexamination of the Evidence." Ph.D.
    dissertation, Vanderbilt University, 469 pp.
        Reexamines the evidence for when and where Shakespeare's
    company acted between 1594 and 1603 and the evidence for
    the dates of eleven of his plays that certainly appeared
    during that time. Part One details the Chamberlain's Men's
    movements from their formation in 1594 from the Newington
    Butts to the Cross Keys to the Theatre to the Swan to the
    Globe. Niemeyer also documents the political and plague-
    related restrictions of acting as wells as the summer
    provincial tours of the company.

23 ORRELL, JOHN. "Amerigo Salvetti and the London Court Theatre,
    1616-1640." ThS 20 (May):1-26.
        Translation of parts of British Library Additional MS
    27962, the diplomatic dispatches sent from London to
    Florence by Tuscan agents in the seventeenth century. The
    selections deal with the Court drama of the period. Orrell
    makes many additions to Bentley and The Calendar of State
    Papers Venetian. See 1976.17.

24 _____. "Court Entertainment in the Summer of 1614: The
    Detailed Works Accounts." REEDN 1:1-9.
        Fifteen extracts from a manuscript ledger giving accounts
    of work performed at Whitehall and Somerset House for
    various Court entertainments from April to August, with
    commentary.

1979

25 _____. "On the Construction of Elizabethan Theatres." ShN
29 (May):20.
A brief note reporting results of his research into the
ad triangulum and ad quadratum methods of laying out
buildings. Orrell suggests that Peter Street used these
methods in building both the Globe and the Fortune, and he
cites figures from the Fortune contract in support. A
fuller treatment is to be published in ShS, presumably in
the 1980 volume.

26 _____. "The London Court Stage in the Savoy Correspondence,
1613-1675." ThR, n.s. 4, no. 2 (May):79-93.
Extracts and translates passages on the English theatre
from the correspondence of the Savoy agent in London during
the dates indicated. All but one entry predates 1642.
Five individuals, most importantly Giovanni Battiste Gabaleone, contributed to the correspondence.

27 PHELPS, WAYNE H. "The Second Night of Davenant's Salmacida
Spolia." N&Q, n.s. 26 (December):512-13.
Pinpoints the date of the second performance of this
masque as 18 February 1639/40, based on references in the
Sidney Papers at Penshurst.

28 SCHOENBAUM, S[AMUEL]. Shakespeare: The Globe and the World.
New York and Oxford: Oxford University Press, 208 pp.
Prepared for the touring Folger Shakespeare Library
exhibition of the same name. Includes general discussions
of the Globe and the acting company.

29 SHAW, CATHERINE M. "Some Vanitie of Mine Art": The Masque
in English Renaissance Drama. 2 vols. Jacobean Drama
Studies, no. 81. Salzburg: Institut für Anglistik und
und Amerikanistik, 580 pp.
Primarily a literary study of the inserted masque, but
Shaw includes discussions of staging possibilities throughout.

30 SHOAP, JEFFREY. "The Children's Plays of Marston, Chapman
and Middleton, 1600-1605." Ph.D. dissertation, University
of Massachusetts, 286 pp.
Essentially a literary study, but Shoap does briefly
examine the effects of theatre design, child actors, and
audience sophistication on the plays.

31 SMEATH, FRANCES ANN. "Great Reckonings in Little Rooms:
    Christopher Marlowe, Thomas Kyd, and Certain Circles of
    Association, 1583-1593." Ph.D. dissertation, Brigham
    Young University, 225 pp.
       Examines a group of documents arising out of the
    arrest of Kyd and the arrest of Marlowe for evidence about
    the acting company patron for whom the two dramatists
    worked.

32 STEVENS, DAVID. "The Staging of Plays at the Salisbury
    Court Theatre, 1630-1642." <u>TJ</u> 31 (December):511-25.
       Examines stage directions and textual allusions in
    twenty-five plays known to have been staged at this play-
    house. Stevens concludes that the physical features neces-
    sary for the staging of these plays are "neither startling
    nor very different from what is known about the other
    private theatres." The tiring house facade probably
    resembled the Inigo Jones designs (held in the Worcester
    College Library and here reproduced) for the unknown
    private playhouse, with three doors below and an open
    gallery above. The center door, fitted with hangings,
    could serve as a discovery space.

33 WICKHAM, GLYNNE. "'Heavens,' Machinery, and Pillars in the
    Theatre and Other Early Playhouses." In <u>The First Public
    Playhouse: The Theatre in Shoreditch, 1576-1642</u>. Edited
    by Herbert Berry. Montreal: McGill-Queen's University
    Press, pp. 1-15.
       Gathers the evidence regarding the existence of these
    elements in the early playhouses. Of the forty-five plays
    written for public performance from 1576 to 1591, only two
    seem to require pillars, and in each case the dialogue
    references could have been satisfied by the use of a
    standing prop. Similarly, no machinery for ascents and
    descents is even vaguely suggested in a play before 1595.
    Wickham suggests that Henslowe's modification of the Rose
    in the 1590s was for purposes of increased spectacle,
    which led to the incorporation of machinery and supporting
    posts in subsequent playhouses.

35 WRIGHT, LOUIS B. <u>Shakespeare's Theatre and the Dramatic
    Tradition</u>. Washington: Folger Shakespeare Library, 36 pp.
       Reprint of 1958.24.

1979

35 YOUNG, ALAN R. "The Orientation of the Elizabethan Stage:
    'That Glory to the Sober West.'" <u>TN</u> 33, no. 2 (Spring-
    Summer):80-85.
        Discusses the apparently conventional placement of the
    stage on the west side of Elizabethan theatre buildings.
    Young links the lighting problem to the orientation and
    offers three speculations: 1) the placement of the stage
    involved a preconceived iconography, derived from church
    architecture; 2) the placement resulted from Elizabethan
    interpretations of Vitruvian theory; and 3) protection from
    rain required artificial lighting.

Index

Abegglen, Homer N., 1943.1
Acting, 1885.10; 1904.9; 1907.11;
    1915.20; 1916.5, 12, 14-15;
    1920.8-9, 15; 1922.1; 1925.9;
    1927.14; 1931.10; 1939.1;
    1940.4; 1949.7; 1950.16;
    1951.6, 8, 30; 1952.17;
    1953.4, 7; 1955.13, 28;
    1957.15; 1958.3; 1961.11;
    1962.2; 1963.5; 1964.27, 36;
    1965.1-2; 1966.1, 8-9, 22, 24;
    1967.13; 1969.1, 9; 1971.17;
    1972.19; 1974.20; 1975.5, 29;
    1976.8, 19; 1979.6
-Companies, 1881.2; 1907.16;
    1908.11; 1910.5, 15; 1916.11,
    15; 1920.27; 1923.2; 1927.1;
    1929.7; 1934.14; 1940.7;
    1941.1; 1946.3; 1957.2;
    1961.4, 11; 1962.4; 1965.3;
    1966.9; 1967.14; 1970.10;
    1972.19; 1974.1-2; 1975.21
    See also the names of indi-
    vidual companies, such as
    Lord Admiral's Men, King's
    Men, etc.
-Style, 1903.2; 1925.8; 1939.6;
    1940.4; 1941.4; 1948.3;
    1949.1; 1950.2, 10; 1951.18;
    1952.17; 1953.2; 1954.2, 9,
    18, 21; 1955.12; 1956.20;
    1957.2; 1958.10; 1959.10, 17,
    24; 1962.2, 19; 1963.6; 1964.3,
    9, 25; 1965.2, 8; 1968.23;
    1969.12; 1970.20; 1971.17;
    1974.2; 1975.11, 21; 1977.27

Actors, 1846.1; 1879.1; 1881.1-2;
    1904.9; 1916.12, 14-15;
    1919.1; 1922.9; 1923.2;
    1926.3-4; 1927.1, 9, 16, 18;
    1928.2, 13; 1929.5-7, 12;
    1930.1, 8; 1931.1, 9; 1934.14;
    1938.8; 1940.3; 1941.1, 10;
    1943.3, 6; 1950.2, 5, 16;
    1953.3-4; 1958.18; 1959.12;
    1961.4; 1962.4; 1964.3;
    1965.3; 1967.14; 1968.24, 26,
    31; 1969.2, 19; 1970.10, 24;
    1974.1; 1975.4, 11, 13, 21;
    1976.6, 11; 1977.10; 1978.23
    See also the names of indi-
    vidual actors, such as Richard
    Burbage, Edward Alleyn, Will
    Kempe, etc.
-Boy, 1929.11; 1936.6; 1937.1;
    1938.4; 1958.21; 1961.6;
    1964.23; 1973.17; 1974.3
-English, on Continent, 1880.1;
    1884.4-5; 1886.1, 9; 1887.2,
    11-12; 1888.2; 1889.1;
    1893.2; 1895.1; 1900.1;
    1902.6; 1903.3; 1904.4;
    1906.9; 1907.13-14; 1909.16;
    1923.2; 1925.21; 1927.24;
    1931.11; 1935.2; 1936.12;
    1938.9; 1939.3; 1940.9;
    1941.7; 1949.7; 1953.18;
    1954.12; 1955.8; 1958.2, 11;
    1959.21; 1960.15; 1962.23;
    1969.13; 1971.18; 1977.20;
    1978.19
-Foreign, in England, 1912.19;

1920.14; 1921.3; 1929.15;
  1954.8; 1955.20
Adair, Edward Robert, 1924.1
Adams, Barry B., 1965.1
Adams, John Chester, 1904.1
Adams, John Cranford, 1935.1;
  1936.1-4, 10, 15, 20; 1938.1;
  1942.1; 1943.6; 1946.6;
  1947.5; 1949.3; 1950.2, 19;
  1951.1, 12, 28; 1953.1, 4, 9,
  27; 1954.17; 1956.1, 32;
  1957.9; 1958.18; 1960.11;
  1961.1, 25; 1963.12; 1964.1,
  22, 32; 1966.9; 1968.17;
  1970.18; 1972.17; 1976.3
Adams, Joseph Quincy, Jr., 1911.1;
  1912.1; 1917.1-3; 1919.1-2;
  1923.15; 1932.1; 1933.1;
  1935.6; 1940.1; 1946.1;
  1961.25; 1968.2
Adams, Victor J., 1976.1; 1977.1
Albrecht, Alexander, 1883.1
Albright, Victor Emanuel, 1908.1;
  1909.1-2; 1911.1; 1913.1;
  1914.20; 1933.1; 1961.25;
  1972.17
Aldus, Paul John, 1951.2
Alleyn, Edward, 1841.1; 1843.1;
  1877.1; 1881.4; 1886.7;
  1889.7; 1904.9; 1907.15;
  1916.5; 1919.1; 1927.7, 17;
  1929.12; 1939.1, 6; 1950.5;
  1952.9; 1954.2; 1955.1;
  1958.5; 1959.10; 1963.6;
  1966.9, 27; 1968.26; 1973.4;
  1975.21
Alsop, J. D., 1979.1
Alternation Theory, 1900.2;
  1907.4; 1908.1; 1909.2;
  1910.16; 1913.17; 1914.20;
  1916.16; 1922.7; 1949.11;
  1950.18; 1955.4; 1963.12;
  1976.3
Alton, R. E., 1959.1
Amphitheatres, 1894.4; 1914.3-4;
  1949.8; 1964.7
Anglo, Sydney, 1964.2; 1968.1
Angus, William, 1965.2
Anikst, Aleksandr Abramovich,
  1965.3
Animals, 1927.20; 1932.8

Anon., 1870.1; 1887.1; 1902.1;
  1909.3-4; 1910.1-2;
  1911.2-3; 1914.1; 1938.2;
  1954.1; 1956.2; 1974.1
Archer, Thomas, 1893.1
Archer, William, 1888.1; 1907.1;
  1908.2-3; 1916.1; 1924.2;
  1950.1; 1961.25
Arkwright, Godfrey Edward Pellew,
  1909.6, 1914.2-4
Armin, Robert, 1927.6; 1952.12;
  1956.11; 1961.10; 1972.7
Armstrong, William A., 1954.2;
  1957.1; 1958.1; 1959.2;
  1961.2; 1963.6; 1964.3
Arnott, James Fullerton, 1970.1
Aronstein, Philip, 1910.3-4;
  1925.1
Ashbee, A., 1872.2
Ashe, Dora Jean, 1954.3
Astington, John Harold, 1974.2
Aubrey, John, 1911.6
Audience, 1885.10; 1886.10;
  1888.12; 1892.1, 3; 1904.9;
  1910.5; 1911.4; 1913.13;
  1914.6; 1916.8, 15; 1920.4;
  1921.15; 1923.17; 1927.4,
  15; 1930.6; 1934.14; 1935.4,
  18; 1936.8; 1941.5; 1944.3;
  1946.2; 1949.3; 1951.23;
  1953.15; 1954.16-17; 1955.12,
  28; 1957.2; 1958.14, 18;
  1959.2, 12; 1960.10; 1964.35;
  1967.3-4; 1968.21, 24, 32;
  1969.9; 1970.10, 17, 28;
  1973.28; 1974.1, 6; 1975.6,
  24, 28; 1976.6; 1977.30, 33;
  1978.20
Auerbach, Lawrence, 1960.1
Avery, Emmet Langdon, 1968.34
Azzi Visentini, Margherita, 1976.2

Bachrach, Alfred Gustav Herbert,
  1949.1
Baesecke, Anna, 1935.2
Baiting Rings, 1964.7-8, 17;
  1967.7; 1973.16; 1979.7
Baker, Henry Barton, 1878.1;
  1879.1; 1881.1. 1889.1;
  1904.2
Baker, Sir Richard, 1972.1

Balcony, See Upper Acting Area
Bald, Robert Cecil, 1943.2;
    1952.1; 1959.3; 1960.13
Baldwin, Thomas Whitfield,
    1926.1; 1927.1-2; 1930.8;
    1931.1, 8; 1961.6; 1970.18
Bale, John, 1972.2
Ball, Robert Hamilton, 1943.6;
    1958.15
Ball, Roma, 1962.1
Bang-Kaup, Willy, 1904.3, 8;
    1910.20
Banks, Howard Milton, 1963.1
Bankside, 1878.3; 1909.13;
    1924.7; 1948.11; 1950.12
Barbetti, Emilio, 1946.2
Barker, Kathleen M. D., 1975.1
Barker, Rennie, 1949.2
Barrell, Charles Wisner,
    1944.1-2
Barriers, 1956.5
Barry, Lodowick [Lordinge?],
    1912.1; 1917.8; 1922.3
Bartholomeusz, Dennis Stephen,
    1966.1; 1969.1; 1973.24;
    1978.1
Baskervile, Susan Brown Greene,
    1885.2-3; 1954.25
Baskervill, Charles Read, 1911.4;
    1929.2, 9
Bateson, Frederick Wilse, 1940.2
Baty, Gaston, 1933.1
Bauande, William, 1972.20
Baur-Heinhold, Margarete, 1966.2
Baxter, Richard, 1977.29
Bayley, Arthur Rutter, 1915.1;
    1917.4
Bear Garden, 1881.4; 1884.3;
    1885.8, 15; 1894.4; 1909.34;
    1920.24; 1950.12; 1955.1;
    1979.8. See also Hope
    Playhouse
Beaumont, Francis, 1974.15
Beckerman, Bernard, 1953.1;
    1956.3; 1962.2; 1966.3;
    1971.1; 1972.17
Beckwith, Ada, 1929.3
Beeston, Christopher, 1953.15;
    1973.28; 1977.25
Beeston, William, 1849.4; 1911.6;
    1925.16; 1977.3

Beeston's Boys, 1941.1
Bel Savage Inn, 1963.21; 1971.4
Bell, Charles Francis, 1924.10
Bell, Walter George, 1912.7;
    1956.6
Bendishe, Sir Thomas, 1951.14
Bennet, Agnes, 1951.27
Bennett, Henry Stanley, 1944.3;
    1949.3
Bentley, Gerald Eades, 1928.1-2;
    1929.4-7; 1930.1; 1938.3;
    1941.1; 1942.2; 1948.1;
    1951.30; 1954.23; 1955.27;
    1956.4; 1959.21; 1963.2;
    1964.23; 1965.4; 1968.2-3,
    32; 1970.10; 1971.2;
    1973.15; 1976.3; 1977.2;
    1978.2; 1979.23
Bereblock, John, 1905.1; 1914.6
Bergeron, David Moore, 1964.4;
    1968.4-7; 1970.2-3; 1971.3;
    1975.2; 1978.3
Bernheimer, Richard, 1958.2
Berry, Herbert, 1966.4; 1967.1;
    1970.4; 1972.29; 1973.1;
    1976.4; 1979.2-5, 8, 16-17,
    33
Best, Michael R., 1964.5, 1968.8
Bethel, Samuel Leslie, 1944.4;
    1948.2; 1950.2
Bibliographies, 1888.9; 1917.3;
    1923.8; 1929.12; 1931.6;
    1937.3; 1940.2; 1957.16;
    1961.20; 1962.16; 1963.14;
    1966.16; 1969.3, 11; 1970.1;
    1974.18, 25; 1976.14; 1978.9,
    22
Billington, Sandra, 1978.4
Binns, J. W., 1972.13, 23; 1974.3
Binz, Gustav, 1899.1
Blackfriars Playhouse, 1870.1;
    1874.2; 1882.2; 1886.2, 4-6;
    1888.5-7; 1889.3; 1904.9;
    1906.10; 1907.20; 1908.18;
    1909.24, 30; 1910.12, 24;
    1911.4; 1912.4; 1913.3, 21;
    1914.21; 1915.1, 13; 1917.1;
    1927.19; 1928.8, 15; 1933.4;
    1938.3; 1948.1; 1951.14;
    1953.28; 1954.17; 1955.11;
    1956.2; 1958.7, 14; 1964.32,

35; 1965.15; 1966.4, 9, 11,
20; 1967.16; 1968.2, 13, 24;
1969.9-10, 21; 1972.12, 25;
1973.31; 1974.2; 1976.23;
1977.14; 1978.24; 1979.17
-First, 1910.8; 1911.13; 1912.6,
17, 23; 1913.3; 1914.6;
1917.1; 1959.16; 1961.8, 22;
1964.30, 32; 1968.8
-Reconstructions, 1921.5,
1954.17; 1964.32; 1970.13;
1975.15
Blackstone, Mary Anna, 1978.5
Blagrave, Sir William, 1929.16
Blanch, William Harnett, 1877.1
Bland, D. S., 1956.5
Blissett, William, 1974.4
Boar's Head Playhouse, 1888.11;
1936.21; 1966.9; 1970.5,
14; 1971.4; 1972.29; 1973.1;
1978.16; 1979.5
Boas, Frederick S., 1907.2;
1909.7; 1914.5; 1925.2;
1933.2
Boas, Guy, 1937.1
Boddy, G.W., 1976.5
Bolte, Johannes, 1888.2; 1893.2;
1895.1; 1900.1
Bolton, Janet, 1958.3
Booth, Stephen, 1979.6
Borcherdt, Hans Heinrich, 1926.2
Bordinat, Philip, 1952.2; 1956.6
Boswell, Eleanore, 1928.8; 1931.2
Boswell, James, 1821.1
Bourgy, Victor, 1969.2; 1975.3
Bowers, Robert H., 1948.3
Boyle, Robert Raymond, 1979.7
Bradbrook, Muriel Clara, 1932.2;
1906.2; 1961.3-4; 1962.3-5;
1964.6; 1968.9; 1975.4;
1976.6; 1978.6-7
Bradner, Leicester, 1925.3
Braines, William Westmoreland,
1915.2; 1917.5; 1921.1;
1923.11; 1924.3; 1948.11
Brandl, Alois, 1904.4; 1936.5
Brawner, James Paul, 1942.3;
1943.3
Brayley, Edward Wedlake, 1826.1;
1833.1
Brendon, Henry S., 1870.2

Brereton, John Le Gay, 1912.3;
1916.2; 1920.1; 1948.4-5
Brett-Evans, David, 1958.4
Brettle, Robert Edward, 1927.3
Bridges-Adams, William, 1957.2
Briley, John, 1955.1; 1958.5
Bristol, 1847.3; 1936.7; 1975.1
Brock, James Wilson, 1950.3
Brodmeier, Cecil, 1904.3, 5, 8;
1907.4; 1961.25
Bromberg, Murray, 1950.4; 1951.3
Brome, Richard, 1921.17; 1941.10;
1950.6; 1968.12, 15
Brook, Donald, 1950.5
Brotanek, Rudolk, 1902.2
Browker, Hugh, 1972.15
Brown, Arthur, 1951.4; 1952.3
Brown, Ivor, 1936.6
Brown, John Russell, 1953.2
Browne, Robert, 1936.21; 1954.25;
1970.4
Brownstein, Oscar Lee, 1964.7,
17; 1971.4-5; 1976.4; 1977.3;
1979.8
Bruce, John, 1844.1; 1868.1
Bryant, Joseph Allen, Jr., 1954.4
Buc, Sir George, 1849.3; 1930.9;
1933.3; 1957.3-4; 1972.16
Buchler, Klaus, 1970.5
Buck, Paul, 1975.5
Budde, Fritz, 1951.5
Bülow, Gottfried von, 1892.2
Burbage, Cuthbert, 1909.25;
1913.15; 1914.21; 1968.24
Burbage, James, 1849.1; 1886.4;
1887.1; 1909.26-27; 1910.19;
1913.15, 19; 1914.21; 1915.5;
1979.8, 17
Burbage, Richard, 1846.1; 1868.1;
1904.9; 1909.25; 1913.15, 18;
1914.21; 1916.5; 1927.9;
1929.12; 1939.1, 6; 1946.3;
1949.5; 1950.5; 1954.2;
1959.10; 1966.9; 1968.24;
1975.21
Burrell, John, 1947.1
Burton, E. J., 1960.3
Byrne, Muriel St. Clare, 1927.4,
1955.2

Cairncross, A. S., 1960.4

Calmour, Alfred Cecil, 1894.1
Cambridge University, 1923.20;
    1948.13; 1959.17; 1970.21;
    1978.4
Campbell, Lily Bess, 1921.2;
    1923.1; 1933.1; 1941.2
Campion, Thomas, 1977.24
Canopy, 1957.1; 1964.3; 1969.15
Capocci, Valentina, 1951.6
Cargill, Alexander, 1891.1;
    1916.3-4
Cargill, Oscar, 1959.17
Carrère, Félix, 1976.7
Carson, Neil, 1976.8-9; 1977.4;
    1979.9
Cartelli, Thomas Paul, 1979.10
Carter, Joel Jackson, 1956.7
Cartwright, William, 1929.8
Carwarden, Sir Thomas, 1836.1
Castle, Eduard, 1940.3
Cavano, Janet M. Jeffrey, 1974.5
Cecil, Sir Robert, 1971.9
Censorship, 1913.4; 1917.2;
    1922.1; 1971.2
Challen, W. H., 1957.3-4
Chalmers, George, 1797.1;
    1799.1; 1813.4; 1821.1;
    1917.2
Chambers, Sir Edmund Kircheven,
    1906.1-2; 1907.3-5; 1908.4;
    1909.8-9; 1911.5-9; 1920.22;
    1921.3; 1923.2-3; 1924.2;
    1925.1, 4-5, 8, 10; 1926.8;
    1931.2-3, 13; 1933.1;
    1934.16; 1935.6; 1940.4;
    1941.1; 1944.5-6; 1950.4;
    1951.30; 1954.23; 1955.27;
    1956.29; 1959.21; 1961.18,
    25; 1964.31; 1968.2, 32, 34;
    1970.10; 1972.17; 1973.3;
    1974.18; 1976.3
Chambrun, Clara Longworth, 1946.3
Chapel Royal, 1872.1; 1892.4;
    1900.3; 1905.9; 1908.18;
    1910.12, 20; 1911.5; 1914.2;
    1920.11; 1926.6; 1960.14;
    1967.16; 1968.21; 1971.8
Chapman, George, 1901.1; 1977.27;
    1979.30
Chapman, Raymond, 1951.7

Charney, Maurice, 1965.5; 1975.6;
    1979.11
Chettle, Henry, 1849.2; 1972.3
Child, Harold H., 1910.5; 1919.3;
    1932.3; 1934.1; 1949.4;
    1950.6
Children's Companies, 1883.1;
    1901.2; 1904.10; 1907.16;
    1908.18; 1914.2, 18;
    1916.14; 1923.2; 1926.6;
    1928.5; 1929.11; 1934.10;
    1941.9; 1943.3; 1956.14;
    1957.2; 1960.14; 1961.3, 8;
    1965.15; 1968.23; 1969.9, 12;
    1970.7; 1971.8, 15; 1972.6;
    1974.2, 7; 1975.6, 18, 21,
    28; 1976.14; 1977.2, 32;
    1978.24; 1979.30. See also
    the names of individual
    companies, such as Paul's
    Boys, King's Revels, etc.
Children of Paul's. See Paul's
    Boys
Children of the Chapel. See
    Chapel Royal
Childs, Herbert E., 1962.5
Chillington, Carol Anne, 1979.12
Cholmeley's Men, 1942.8
Christmas, Gerard, 1968.4
Clapham, Alfred W., 1912.4;
    1917.1
Clark, Andrew, 1907.6-9; 1909.10
Clark, Sandra, 1974.1
Clinton-Baddeley, V. C., 1953.3
Cochrane, Bruce B., 1968.32
Cockpit-in-Court Playhouse,
    1860.1; 1925.14; 1951.22;
    1966.9; 1967.15; 1970.21,
    25, 27; 1972.24, 30;
    1973.16, 18; 1974.23;
    1975.31; 1978.25
Cockpit Playhouse. See Phoenix
    Playhouse
Coghill, Nevill, 1975.7
Cohn, Albert, 1886.1
Coldewey, John C., 1975.8;
    1977.5-6
Collier, John Payne, 1831.1;
    1841.1; 1843.1; 1844.5;
    1846.1; 1848.1; 1849.1-2;

1861.1; 1875.1; 1879.2;
1886.8; 1887.7; 1889.7;
1891.2; 1904.7; 1912.2;
1917.3; 1924.8; 1928.16;
1929.6; 1950.15; 1958.17;
1959.19; 1962.7; 1978.17
Collins, Churton, 1911.10
Collins, Fletcher, Jr., 1931.4
Commedia dell'Arte, 1908.17;
    1912.19; 1920.7, 22; 1922.1;
    1926.13; 1928.11; 1929.15;
    1934.8; 1961.23
Commonwealth, 1888.3; 1921.13;
    1923.10, 19; 1928.7; 1936.10
Companies. See Acting--Companies
Company Licenses, 1909.9; 1917.2
Conrad, Hermann, 1910.6
Cook, Ann Jennalie, 1974.6
Cook, David, 1961.5
Cooper, Charles William, 1931.5
Cope, Jackson I., 1974.7
Corbin, John, 1906.3; 1911.11;
    1961.25
Costumes, 1903.2; 1911.22;
    1916.11; 1927.21; 1928.20;
    1933.2; 1936.17-18; 1938.6;
    1952.4; 1953.4, 15; 1954.17;
    1958.20; 1959.12; 1961.14;
    1962.6, 8, 18; 1964.26;
    1965.3, 5; 1966.10; 1968.26;
    1972.27; 1973.4, 28; 1974.12;
    1976.22
Court Performances, 1906.1;
    1909.8, 12; 1910.10-11;
    1912.24; 1913.6; 1916.15;
    1917.2; 1920.17, 29; 1923.2;
    1924.10; 1925.3, 17; 1926.10;
    1928.1; 1934.10; 1937.8;
    1941.1; 1945.2; 1950.7;
    1952.19; 1953.20; 1954.14;
    1955.27; 1956.26; 1961.24;
    1968.8; 1970.31; 1974.4;
    1975.31; 1976.18; 1977.32;
    1979.1, 23-24, 26
Cowling, George Herbert, 1913.2;
    1927.5
Craik, T. W., 1975.9, 15
Crane, Ralph, 1926.12
Crashaw, William, 1972.4
Creizenach, Wilhelm Michael Anton

1889.2; 1903.1; 1916.5;
    1923.4
Crosfield, Thomas, 1925.2
Cross Keys Inn, 1971.4; 1979.22
Crossley, D. W., 1974.8
Crouch, Jack Herbert, 1952.4
Crüger, Johannes, 1887.2
Crundell, H. W., 1936.7; 1937.2;
    1941.3
Cullen, Charles, 1912.5
Cummings, L. A., 1977.7
Cunliffe, John William, 1911.2
Cunningham, Peter, 1842.11;
    1845.1; 1848.1; 1849.3-4;
    1911.15-18, 26-28;
    1912.13-14, 20; 1913.8;
    1920.12-13, 26; 1922.8;
    1924.9; 1928.16
Curtain Playhouse, 1798.1;
    1844.5; 1885.6; 1894.4;
    1904.9; 1928.10; 1944.3;
    1954.11, 15; 1959.9; 1962.7;
    1964.11; 1966.9; 1977.16;
    1979.17
Cutts, John P., 1920.20; 1954.5;
    1955.3; 1956.8-9; 1957.5;
    1958.6; 1959.4; 1960.7;
    1966.5; 1973.2; 1974.9

Dance, 1927.24; 1951.26; 1953.4;
    1954.17; 1955.11; 1963.11;
    1979.21
Daniel, Samuel, 1927.3; 1958.23
Danzig, 1895.1. See also Gdansk
Darlington, William Aubrey,
    1949.5
Davenant, Sir William, 1923.10;
    1925.16; 1968.12; 1979.27
David, Richard, 1961.6
Davies, William Robertson, 1938.4
Davis, John Lee, 1943.4
Davison, Peter, 1972.1-5, 8-10,
    20-22, 27, 31, 33
Dawson, Giles E., 1947.2; 1961.7;
    1964.8; 1965.6
DeBanke, Cécile, 1953.4; 1954.6
Dee, John, 1969.23
Dekker, Thomas, 1920.14
DeMolen, Richard Lee, 1970.5;
    1972.6; 1974.10

Denkinger, Emma Marshall, 1926.3
Denmark House, 1977.31
Dessen, Alan C., 1975.10; 1978.8
de Vere, Edward, Earl of Oxford, 1944.1-2; 1961.8
Dewey, Nicholas, 1969.3
DeWitt, Johannes. See Swan Playhouse--DeWitt Sketch
Dickinson, Thomas H., 1916.6
Dickson, M. J., 1930.2
Discovery Space, 1891.2; 1903.6; 1904.3, 5, 8; 1907.4, 20; 1908.10; 1913.6; 1916.1, 5, 13, 16; 1918.1; 1921.5, 13; 1924.2, 12; 1927.5, 8, 13; 1928.6, 12; 1929.3; 1933.4; 1936.1; 1940.6, 10-11; 1942.1; 1945.1; 1948.6-7; 1949.3, 11; 1950.18; 1952.2, 11; 1953.8-9, 15, 23; 1954.14, 17; 1955.4; 1956.27, 31; 1957.1; 1958.1, 11, 14; 1959.8, 25; 1960.16; 1961.2, 21, 27; 1962.2, 15; 1963.1, 8, 11; 1964.20, 32-33; 1965.12; 1966.10-11; 1967.8-9; 1968.17; 1970.13; 1971.10; 1972.18; 1973.11, 15, 28; 1975.15; 1976.21; 1978.29; 1979.32
Disguises, 1902.2; 1916.15
Dobell, Bertram, 1901.1
Dodd, Kenneth M., 1970.6
Dodds, Madelain Hope, 1956.10
Dodsley, Robert, 1874.3; 1876.2
Doebler, John, 1973.3; 1974.11
Dolan de Avila, Wanda, 1965.7
Dollerup, Cay, 1974.11
Dolman, Robert Christopher Sibson, 1974.13
Dorset, 1977.18
Dowling, Margaret, 1930.3
Downer, Alan S., 1951.8; 1964.9
Downton, Thomas, 1977.4
Dramatic Criticism, 1903.7
Dramaticus, 1844.2; 1849.5
Drayton, Michael, 1922.3
Dryden, John, 1936.19
Duckles, Vincent, 1968.11
Duke of Devonshire, 1924.10

Duke of York's Men, 1849.9
Dukes of Wurtemberg, Visits of, 1865.2
Dulwich College, 1841.1; 1877.1; 1881.4; 1889.7; 1904.6; 1907.15; 1927.7; 1952.9; 1957.13; 1966.27; 1977.8
Dumb Show, 1919.4; 1951.11, 24, 31; 1964.29; 1966.13
Dunmow, 1951.14
Dunwich, 1921.4
Durand, Walter Yale, 1902.3; 1905.1; 1908.5
Durry, Marie-Jeanne, 1976.7
Dwarf Bob, 1972.16

Ebisch, Walther, 1931.6; 1937.3
Eccles, Mark, 1933.3; 1958.7
Edinborough, Arnold, 1951.9
Edmond, Mary, 1974.14
Edwards, H. R. L., 1960.6
Edwards, Richard, 1902.3; 1908.5
Eggar, Katharine E., 1961.8
Ehrstine, John W., 1968.34
Eich, Louis M., 1939.1
Eliot, Samuel A., Jr., 1939.2
Ellis, George, 1874.1
Ellis, Henry, 1798.1
Ellis-Fermor, Una M., 1936.8; 1947.3; 1953.5; 1958.8; 1961.9; 1964.10; 1965.8; 1969.4
Emmeroã, Jamelia, 1966.12
Empson, William, 1951.10; 1954.7; 1955.4
Engelen, Johannes, 1926.4
Errington, Richard, 1977.11
Essex, 1934.8-9; 1937.6; 1975.8; 1977.6, 21
Etheridge, Charles Larimore, Sr., 1975.11
Eutheo, 1972.27
Evans, G. Blakemore, 1973.4
Evans, Henry, 1961.8; 1968.24
Evans, M. Blakemore, 1923.5
Ewbank, Inga-Stina, 1975.12
Ewouts, Hans, 1950.7

Fairholt, Frederich William, 1843.2; 1845.4

Farrant, Richard, 1910.8; 1912.6; 1913.3; 1921.9; 1961.8
Farrar, J. H., 1924.6
Feather, John, 1972.7
Feil, J. P., 1958.9
Feilde, John, 1972.9
Feldman, Abraham Bronson, 1950.7; 1952.5; 1953.6
Felver, Charles Stanley, 1956.11; 1961.10
Fencing, 1974.20
Fenton, George, 1972.9
Ferrabosco, Alfonso, 1935.12; 1956.9
Feuillerat, Albert, 1908.6; 1910.7–8; 1911.13; 1912.6, 17; 1913.3; 1925.1; 1961.18, 22
Field, Nathaniel, 1849.2; 1904.9; 1914.19; 1926.1; 1933.5; 1965.15; 1968.26
Finance, 1886.6; 1904.9; 1907.14; 1909.30–32; 1910.4–5, 25; 1911.20; 1918.2–3; 1919.2, 19; 1920.27–30; 1921.8; 1927.2; 1934.6; 1935.4; 1942.7; 1952.7; 1955.1; 1957.2; 1959.1; 1961.5; 1971.1–2; 1979.3, 9
Firth, Sir Charles Harding, 1888.3
Fischer, Walther, 1950.5
Fisher, Sidney, 1964.11
Fitzgibbon, H. Macauley, 1931.7
Flatter, Richard, 1920.20; 1951.11–12; 1953.7; 1957.6; 1958.6; 1959.5; 1960.5, 7
Fleay, Frederick Gard, 1881.2; 1882.1; 1884.1; 1887.7; 1890.1; 1908.16; 1912.2; 1929.6; 1950.4
Flecknoe, Richard, 1664.1; 1909.11; 1931.19; 1957.7; 1963.3; 1972.33; 1973.5
Fletcher, Ifan Kyrle, 1954.8
Fletcher, John, 1974.15
Flood, William Henry Grattan, 1912.17; 1921.4
Fludd, Robert, 1958.2; 1966.20, 28; 1967.1, 17

Foakes, R. A., 1954.9; 1960.8; 1961.11–13; 1963.4; 1970.7; 1977.8; 1978.17
Ford, Boris, 1955.12; 1956.19; 1961.15; 1962.10; 1975.19
Fordyce, Rachel, 1978.9
Forestier, Amédée, 1910.9; 1911.14
Forman, Simon, 1849.6; 1876.1; 1907.18; 1919.8; 1947.11; 1958.17; 1959.19; 1973.24
Forrest, G. Topham, 1921.1, 5; 1961.25
Fortune Playhouse, 1813.1; 1870.2, 4; 1882.2; 1886.7; 1889.7; 1904.6, 9; 1906.8; 1907.1; 1908.2–3, 10–11; 1909.34; 1914.20; 1916.10; 1917.4, 7, 10; 1919.11; 1929.6; 1959.9, 15; 1966.9; 1971.12; 1977.15, 19; 1979.19, 25
–Contract, 1874.2; 1885.9; 1902.1; 1906.6; 1907.4; 1908.10; 1909.3; 1916.11; 1914.7; 1924.12; 1935.17; 1949.2; 1959.9; 1959.25; 1970.13; 1971.12; 1973.11; 1975.15, 20; 1976.9; 1976.24
–Reconstructions, 1908.10; 1911.2–3, 14; 1912.8; 1916.1; 1934.14; 1959.7; 1961.24; 1963.7; 1978.13
–Second, 1968.2
Fowell, Frank, 1913.4
Fredén, Gustav, 1928.4; 1939.3
Freehafer, John, 1968.12–13; 1971.6; 1972.30; 1973.6; 1975.17
Freeman, Arthur, 1973.5
Freeman, Sidney Lee, 1951.13
French, Joseph Nathan, 1964.12
Fronius, Hans, 1950.8
Fulman, William, 1933.8
Furniss, Warren Todd, 1952.6
Furnivall, Frederick J., 1878.2; 1882.2; 1904.6
Fusillo, Robert James, 1955.5; 1956.16, 22; 1966.6

G., G. M., 1908.7
Gabaleone, Giovanni Battiste, 1979.26
Gaedertz, Karl Theodor, 1888.1, 4, 10, 12
Gager, William, 1907.2; 1916.17-18; 1972.18; 1974.3
Gair, W. Reavley, 1968.14; 1978.10-11
Galloway, David, 1970.4, 7-9, 13 18-20, 25, 27, 29, 31; 1973.1, 7, 14-15; 1977.9
Gaw, Allison, 1925.6-7; 1936.9
Gayton, Edmund, 1941.4
Gdansk, 1979.19. See also Danzig
Gentili, Alberico, 1974.3
George Inn, 1972.29
George, David, 1974.15; 1977.10; 1978.12; 1979.13
Gerstner-Hirzel, Arthur, 1955.6-7
Gildersleeve, Virginia Crocheron, 1908.8-9; 1943.5
Giles, Nathaniel, 1911.5; 1961.8
Gilson, Julius Parnell, 1925.15
Glenn, Susan Macdonald, 1979.14
Globe Playhouse, 1849.1; 1858.1; 1870.1; 1874.2; 1878.3; 1882.2; 1884.3; 1885.9, 12; 1888.11; 1903.10; 1904.9; 1907.4, 20; 1909.30, 32; 1910.25; 1914.20-21; 1915.22; 1916.3, 10; 1921.1; 1928.8; 1935.1; 1938.3; 1942.1; 1944.3; 1948.6, 11; 1949.2, 15; 1950.7, 15; 1951.16, 29; 1952.18; 1955.11, 18; 1956.3, 14, 27; 1958.14; 1959.8-9; 1960.11, 16; 1961.2; 1963.1; 1964.15, 32, 35; 1965.13; 1966.9, 20, 28; 1968.16, 33; 1969.23; 1970.16; 1971.13; 1973.31; 1975.7, 15; 1976.9; 1978.12; 1979.16, 22, 25, 28
-Reconstructions, 1902.1; 1936.1-3; 1942.1; 1943.6; 1946.6; 1947.6; 1948.6; 1950.12; 1951.1, 16, 25, 28; 1953.1, 9, 27; 1956.32; 1961.1, 24; 1962.2; 1968.16; 1975.15
-Second, 1933.11; 1952.14; 1959.15; 1964.11; 1968.2; 1973.11, 16; 1975.16; 1979.5, 16
-Site of, 1909.3-5, 13-14, 19-21, 32; 1910.2, 13; 1912.12-15, 17, 24-25; 1915.6-12, 14, 16-19, 23; 1921.1; 1923.11; 1924.3; 1948.11; 1950.15
Godfrey, Walter H., 1908.10; 1911.2-3; 1912.8; 1913.5; 1916.1; 1920.24; 1934.14; 1950.15; 1959.7; 1961.25
Goldstein, Leonard, 1958.10
Gollancz, Israel, 1916.2, 9
Gordon, D. J., 1954.20; 1956.12; 1973.8
Gorelik, Mordechai, 1940.5; 1947.4
Gossett, Suzanne, 1973.9
Gosson, Stephen, 1908.19; 1910.26; 1942.6; 1954.27; 1972.10
Gousseff, James William, 1962.6
Government Regulation, 1908.7-9; 1910.3; 1916.15; 1923.2; 1939.5; 1943.5; 1953.17; 1959.12; 1963.20; 1965.3; 1971.2; 1973.27
Grabau, Carl, 1902.4
Grabo, Carl H., 1906.4-7; 1907.10-11
Granville-Barker, Harley, 1925.8; 1926.5; 1934.14; 1936.4-5, 10; 1960.19
Graves, Robert Bruce, 1976.10; 1978.13
Graves, Thornton Shirley, 1912.9-11; 1913.6-7; 1914.6-8; 1915.3-4, 15; 1916.7; 1917.6; 1920.2-6; 1921.6-7; 1922.1-2; 1925.9
Gray, Austin K., 1927.6
Gray, Cecil G., 1951.14-15
Gray, Henry David, 1919.4; 1920.7, 14; 1930.4; 1931.1, 8
Gray, Margaret Muriel, 1939.4
Great Yarmouth, 1977.9
Grebanier, Bernard, 1975.13
Green, Thomas, 1933.5
Greene, John, 1928.15; 1972.13

Greene, Thomas, 1885.2–3;
　1924.25
Greenslade, S. L., 1952.7
Greenstreet, James, 1885.1–4;
　1886.2, 8; 1888.5–8; 1889.3
Greg, Sir Walter Wilson, 1900.2;
　1904.7; 1907.15; 1908.4, 11;
　1909.7, 9; 1911.9; 1919.5–6,
　10; 1920.8–10, 15, 23;
　1921.8; 1923.6; 1924.4;
　1925.1, 10–12; 1927.7;
　1928.5; 1929.3; 1931.9;
　1932.4; 1938.5; 1940.1, 6;
　1954.3, 10; 1956.13; 1959.6;
　1963.4; 1966.7; 1969.5;
　1972.17; 1978.17
Griffin, William James, 1939.5;
　1943.5
Gurr, Andrew J., 1960.9; 1963.5–
　6; 1966.8; 1970.10; 1972.17

Haaker, Ann, 1968.15
Habicht, Werner, 1972.11
Haines, C. M., 1925.13; 1927.8;
　1928.6, 12
Hale, Edward Everett, Jr., 1903.2
Hall Screen, 1931.4; 1952.4;
　1963.15; 1964.17, 34; 1970.13;
　1973.12, 26; 1976.22
Hall, Samuel Carter, and Hall,
　Mrs. Samuel Carter, 1858.1;
　1859.1; 1867.1; 1869.1;
　1877.2
Hall, Vernon, Jr., 1959.7
Halliwell-Phillipps, James
　Orchard, 1843.1; 1844.3;
　1849.6–7; 1870.1, 3; 1874.2;
　1881.3; 1882.3; 1884.2–3;
　1885.5; 1886.3; 1887.3–4;
　1889.4, 6; 1890.2; 1891.2;
　1898.1; 1907.12; 1917.3;
　1943.2; 1957.10; 1974.15;
　1978.12
Hammer, Gael Warren, 1972.12
Hammerton, Stephen, 1977.2
Harbage, Alfred, 1936.11; 1939.6;
　1940.7; 1941.4; 1948.3;
　1951.23; 1952.8; 1953.8;
　1964.13–14; 1968.32; 1970.7;
　1972.17; 1974.6; 1976.11

Harris, Arthur J., 1963.7
Harris, Charles, 1907.13–14
Harris, John, 1973.10; 1977.25
Harrison, George Bagshawe,
　1923.7, 14; 1927.9; 1934.14;
　1956.14; 1960.19
Harrison, Gerald, 1968.32
Hart, Alfred, 1932.5–6; 1934.2–3;
　1962.11; 1967.5; 1970.11
Hartleb, Hans, 1934.4; 1936.12
Hasler, Jörg, 1979.15
Haslewood, Joseph, 1813.1–3;
　1814.1; 1837.1; 1845.2
Hawley, James Abgriffith, 1967.2
Hayward, Wayne Clinton, 1951.16
Hazlitt, William Carew, 1869.2;
　1874.3
Hecht, Hans, 1929.13
Helmholtz-Phelan, Anna Augusta,
　1909.12
Heming's Players, 1847.3
Henning, Standish, 1976.11, 13
Henslowe, Philip, 1841.1;
　1890.3; 1904.7; 1907.15;
　1908.11; 1927.7; 1929.8, 14;
　1950.4; 1952.9; 1957.13;
　1958.5; 1961.12; 1963.4;
　1964.31; 1966.9; 1970.15;
　1971.1; 1973.20; 1976.21;
　1977.4, 8; 1978.17; 1979.12,
　33
–Diary, 1845.3; 1881.4; 1885.7;
　1904.7, 11; 1906.3, 7, 15;
　1908.11; 1921.8, 16; 1927.2;
　1938.5; 1940.1; 1957.13;
　1960.8; 1961.13; 1962.9;
　1963.4; 1968.27; 1973.20;
　1974.8; 1976.9, 21; 1977.4,
　8; 1978.17; 1979.9, 12
Herbert, J. F., 1844.4
Herbert, Sir Henry, 1885.3;
　1913.4; 1917.2; 1923.15
Herbert, William, Third Earl of
　Pembroke, 1958.23
Hercules, 1977.27
Hereford, 1958.9
Herford, Charles Harold, 1923.8
Herz, Emil, 1903.3
Heywood, Thomas, 1972.13; 1977.31
Hibbard, George R., 1974.4, 16;
　1975.9, 12, 14, 26; 1978.6,
　11, 14–15

Hill, R. F., 1975.31
Hillebrand, Harold Newcombe,
    1914.9; 1915.5; 1920.11;
    1922.3; 1926.6; 1927.3;
    1961.22; 1976.14
Hind, Arthur Maygar, 1922.4
Hipwell, Daniel, 1892.1
Hodges, Cyril Walter, 1947.5;
    1948.6; 1949.6; 1950.9;
    1951.17; 1952.20; 1953.9-10;
    1954.11; 1955.26; 1959.15;
    1961.25; 1964.15; 1966.9;
    1968.16; 1970.12; 1971.13;
    1972.17; 1973.11; 1975.16;
    1979.5
Hogge, Ralph, 1974.8
Hollar, Wenceslaus, 1922.4;
    1933.11; 1948.11; 1949.15;
    1952.1; 1964.11; 1972.14;
    1973.11; 1978.21
Holmes, Martin R., 1956.15;
    1960.10; 1964.16
Holzknecht, Karl J., 1923.9
Honeyman, John, 1927.12
Honigman, E. A. J., 1976.12
Hood, Eu. See Haslewood, Joseph
Hook, Lucyle, 1962.7
Hope Playhouse, 1813.3; 1882.2;
    1885.8, 15; 1894.4; 1904.9;
    1908.11; 1929.9; 1962.21;
    1966.9; 1971.1
-Contract, 1920.24; 1959.25;
    1975.20
Hoppe, Harry R., 1949.7;
    1954.12; 1955.8
Hort, Patrick, 1971.18
Hosking, George Llewellyn, 1952.9
Hosley, Richard, 1952.10;
    1954.13; 1956.1, 16;
    1957.8-9; 1958.11; 1959.8;
    1960.11, 20; 1962.22;
    1963.2, 8-9, 12, 15; 1964.11,
    17-22; 1967.3; 1968.17-18;
    1969.8, 10; 1970.13, 18;
    1971.7; 1972.14, 17, 25;
    1973.12, 31; 1975.15; 1976.4;
    1978.15; 1979.5, 16
Hotson, John Leslie, 1923.10;
    1928.7; 1949.8; 1951.30;
    1952.11-12, 15; 1953.10-13;

1954.7, 10-11, 14-15;
    1955.2, 9-10, 14, 19,
    21-22; 1956.10, 25; 1959.9;
    1960.6, 12, 20; 1961.17, 25;
    1964.30; 1966.9; 1970.4;
    1972.17; 1977.16
Howarth, Robert Guy, 1948.4-5
Hubbard, Barbara, 1970.14
Hubbard, George, 1909.4, 13;
    1912.12; 1915.6-12, 14, 17;
    1923.11; 1924.3
Hudson, Katherine, 1971.8
Huffman, Clifford Chalmers,
    1978.22
Hugon, Cecile, 1916.5
Huminghorn, Peter, 1970.15
Hunnis, William, 1892.4; 1900.3;
    1910.8, 20; 1961.8
Hunt, J. A., 1966.10
Hunt, Richard William, 1947.11
Hunt, Theodore B., 1935.3
Hunter, George K., 1976.13
Hunter, Sir Mark, 1926.7;
    1927.19; 1928.8, 18

Immroth, John Phillip, 1974.19
Improvisation, 1903.2; 1908.17;
    1922.1; 1951.6
Ingleby, Clement Mansfield,
    1861.1
Ingram, Reginald William,
    1955.11; 1968.19; 1970.15;
    1971.9; 1972.15; 1976.4;
    1978.16; 1979.17
Inner Stage. See Discovery Space
Inns of Court, 1977.23; 1979.18
Innyards, 1905.1; 1906.5;
    1913.6; 1925.8; 1927.14;
    1931.4; 1967.7; 1968.34;
    1969.9; 1971.4-5; 1972.29, 32
Ipswich, 1931.3
Isaacs, Jacob, 1927.10-11;
    1933.4; 1958.1
Ives, E. W., 1961.14

Jackson, Henry, 1933.8
Jackson, Richard C., 1909.14;
    1914.14
Jacquot, Jean, 1956.9, 12, 17,
    28, 33-34; 1964.2, 18, 22,

34, 37; 1966.17; 1968.1, 10,
14, 18, 20–22, 24, 32, 37–38;
1973.13
Jamieson, Michael, 1964.23
Jarvis, Royal Preston, 1908.12–13
Jenkin, Bernard, 1945.1
Jenkinson, Wilberforce, 1914.10
Jensen, Ejner J., 1968.23;
1970.16; 1975.17
Jewell, Simon, 1974.14; 1976.16
Jewkes, Wilfred Thomas, 1956.18;
1958.12
Jigs, 1908.12–13; 1919.7;
1927.14; 1929.2, 9; 1952.22;
1977.22
Johnson, John, 1974.9
Johnson, Robert Carl, 1970.17
Johnson, William, 1976.16
Johnston, Elizabeth Carrington,
1964.24
Jonas, Maurice, 1914.11; 1915.13;
1917.7
Jones, Eldred D., 1962.8
Jones, Inigo, 1848.1; 1903.5;
1914.16; 1916.15; 1924.4, 6,
10; 1925.5, 14; 1937.7;
1946.4; 1952.19, 21;
1953.24–26; 1958.23;
1959.12, 14;
1966.15; 1967.2, 15;
1968.26, 28; 1969.10;
1971.6; 1972.24; 1973.10,
16, 18, 21, 30; 1974.23;
1975.24, 31; 1976.2, 17;
1977.25, 31; 1978.25
Jones, Marion, 1962.9
Jones, Tom, 1914.12
Jonson, Ben, 1848.1; 1901.1;
1902.5; 1921.8, 16–17;
1932.7; 1933.8; 1934.5;
1941.10; 1942.2; 1951.6;
1952.6; 1956.9; 1958.23;
1966.15; 1968.26, 28;
1973.2, 30; 1974.14, 16;
1977.27; 1978.28, 30
Joseph, Bertram L., 1949.1;
1950.10; 1951.18; 1954.18;
1955.12–13; 1956.19;
1959.10; 1961.6, 15–16;
1962.10; 1964.25; 1970.18;
1975.18

Joseph, Stephen, 1963.10
Jouvet, Louis, 1936.13
Junius, Archduke Philip, 1892.2;
1902.6

K., L. L., 1914.13; 1914.14–15,
17; 1915.12, 14
Kahrl, Stanley J., 1969.6
Keith, William Grant, 1914.16;
1925.14
Keller, Wolfgang, 1904.8
Kelly, Francis Michael, 1938.6
Kelly, William, 1855.1; 1865.1
Kempe, Alfred John, 1836.1
Kempe, Will, 1844.1; 1882.4;
1904.9; 1906.9; 1926.13;
1927.6, 9; 1930.4; 1931.1,
8; 1946.3; 1950.5; 1958.13;
1959.3; 1960.13; 1975.21
Kendall, Richard, 1925.2
Kent, 1961.7; 1965.6; 1977.6
Kernan, A. B., 1974.17
Kernodle, George Riley, 1937.4;
1944.7; 1959.11; 1961.25;
1972.17
Kerr, S. Parnell, 1957.10
Killigrew, Thomas, 1925.16;
1929.8; 1978.29
Kimbrough, Robert, 1976.11, 13
Kincaid, A. N., 1972.16
Kindermann, Heniz, 1959.12
King James I, 1828.1
King, Thomas James, 1963.11;
1965.9; 1966.11; 1971.10–11;
1972.17; 1973.14; 1975.19,
30, 1977.11, 34; 1979.5
King's Company (Restoration),
1929.8
King's Men, 1886.5; 1909.15, 31;
1911.7; 1920.17; 1921.4;
1926.12; 1927.12, 19;
1928.1, 8; 1941.1; 1946.3;
1951.22; 1954.17; 1955.18;
1957.5, 10; 1958.18, 1959.4,
8; 1961.6; 1963.5; 1968.13;
1973.20; 1974.2, 5; 1975.13;
1976.15; 1977.2, 10–11;
1978.7
King's Revels, 1912.1; 1919.9;
1922.3; 1926.6; 1958.7;
1977.2

King's Theatre (Restoration),
   1924.8
Kingland, Gertrude Southwick,
   1923.12-13
Kingsley, Charles, 1873.1;
   1889.5
Kipling, Gordon, 1977.12
Kirke, John, 1924.7
Kirsch, Arthur C., 1967.4;
   1969.8
Kirschbaum, Leo. 1949.9; 1959.13
Klein, David, 1956.20; 1962.11;
   1967.5
Knight, W. Nicholas, 1979.18
Knowles, Richard, 1976.11, 13
Kohler, Richard Charles, 1971.12
Kolin, Philip C., 1974.18;
   1976.14
Kopecký, Jan, 1966.12
Krempel, Daniel Spartakus,
   1953.14
Kyd, Thomas, 1977.27; 1979.31

L., H., 1854.1
Lacy, John, 1931.5
Lacy, Robin Thurlow, 1959.14
Laird, David Connor, 1956.21
Lamb, Margaret A., 1976.15
Lamborne, Edmund Arnold Greening,
   1923.14
Lancashire, 1931.16; 1979.13
Lancashire, Ian, 1977.13
Landsdowne Manuscripts, 1908.4;
   1947.8
Lane, Robert Phillips, 1956.22
Langhans, Edward A., 1965.10
Langner, Lawrence, 1955.15
Langley, Frances, 1970.4; 1971.9;
   1972.25; 1978.16
Lanier, Nicholas, 1959.14
Lanman, Henry, 1979.17
Latter, D. A., 1975.20
Laver, James, 1964.26
Lavin, J.A., 1970.18; 1973.15
Law, Ernest Philip Alphonse,
   1909.15; 1910.10-11;
   1911.15-18, 26-28; 1912.13-
   14, 20; 1913.8; 1920.12-13,
   26

Lawrence, William John, 1902.5;
   1903.4-6; 1905.2; 1908.14;
   1909.16-17; 1910.6; 1911.19-
   20; 1912.15-18; 1913.7, 9-12;
   1914.11; 1915.15; 1916.1,
   8-10; 1917.4, 6, 8; 1918.1;
   1919.6-11, 13, 19; 1920.8-10,
   14-24; 1921.3, 9-11;
   1922.5-6; 1923.15-17;
   1924.4-9; 1927.12-14;
   1928.8-10, 19; 1929.9;
   1930.5-7; 1931.10; 1932.7-9;
   1933.5; 1934.5-7; 1935.5, 7,
   13; 1936.3-4, 10, 14-15;
   1937.5; 1950.1; 1952.19;
   1954.5; 1958.6; 1960.20;
   1972.17
Lea, Kathleen Margarite, 1931.11;
   1934.8
Leacroft, Richard, 1973.16
Lecoq, Louis, 1968.24
Lee, Sidney, 1909.15, 18; 1916.1,
   14-15; 1950.1, 16-17
Leech, Clifford E. J., 1934.9;
   1935.8-9; 1941.5; 1950.11;
   1964.27; 1975.15, 21
Legerdemain, 1949.12; 1956.30.
   See also Magic
Leggett, Alexander, 1975.21
Leicester's Men, 1844.1; 1906.9;
   1911.8; 1943.2; 1962.4
Lell, Gordon, 1973.17
Lennam, Trevor N. S., 1970.19;
   1975.22
Lennep, William Van, 1962.12
Levin, Martha Wasko, 1977.14
Levyveld, Toby Bookholz, 1951.19
Lewes, George Henry, 1936.16
Lewis, John Colby, 1940.8
Liebscher, Frieda Margot, 1920.25
Lighting, 1952.21; 1954.17;
   1972.27; 1976.10; 1978.13
Limon, Jerzy, 1977.15; 1979.5, 19
Lincolnshire, 1969.6
Lindley, David, 1979.20
Linn, John Gaywood, 1951.20
Linnell, Rosemary, 1977.16
Linthicum, Marie Channing,
   1936.17-18
Livery Companies, 1954.20; 1959.22

Livy, 1975.19
Lodge, Thomas, 1908.19; 1910.25;
    1931.14; 1933.7, 9; 1934.15;
    1972.2
Logeman, H., 1897.1
London, City of, 1931.13
Long, John H., 1951.21; 1968.11,
    19, 25
Lord Admiral's Men, 1921.8;
    1923.6-7; 1925.11; 1927.1-
    2, 7; 1928.14; 1935.16;
    1956.14; 1961.26; 1964.31;
    1971.17; 1973.20; 1975.21;
    1977.4
Lord Chamberlain, Office of,
    1907.3; 1911.7; 1931.2;
    1951.22; 1958.23
Lord Chamberlain's Men, 1887.4;
    1907.3; 1910.17; 1919.14;
    1923.7; 1928.14; 1930.6;
    1933.10; 1935.16; 1939.2;
    1944.2; 1946.3; 1955.18;
    1956.14; 1961.26; 1963.5;
    1964.31; 1968.31; 1970.23;
    1972.7; 1975.13, 21; 1978.7;
    1979.22, 28
Lord Chando's Men, 1972.7
Lord Mayor's Pageants, 1837.2;
    1843.2; 1845.4; 1848.2;
    1909.29; 1913.18; 1920.32;
    1935.9; 1951.33; 1954.20;
    1956.28; 1957.17; 1964.4;
    1968.4-5, 7; 1970.3; 1971.3;
    1973.19; 1974.10; 1975.2
Lord Mounteagle's Men, 1977.26
Lord Stafford's Men, 1977.26
Lord Strange's Men, 1925.11;
    1931.16; 1946.3
Lord's Room, 1908.15; 1957.8-9,
    11. See also Upper Acting
    Area
Losely Manuscripts, 1836.1;
    1911.13; 1912.6; 1917.1
Lounsbury, Thomas R., 1923.18
Lowe, Robert W., 1888.9; 1970.1
Lower, Charles Bruce, 1965.11
Lowin, John, 1946.3
Lüdeke, Henry, 1917.9; 1950.12
Lyly, John, 1929.16; 1964.5;
    1968.8; 1974.9; 1979.11

Lyons, Clifford P. 1964.28
Lyzarde, William, 1939.7; 1959.14

Maas, Hermann, 1901.2; 1907.16
McCabe, John Charles, 1954.17
McCalmon, George, 1946.4
McCullen, Joseph T., Jr., 1953.16
McDonnell, Michael F. J., 1909.22
McDowell, John H., 1945.2;
    1948.7; 1949.11
McGuire, Philip C., 1979.6
Machyn, Henry, 1848.2
MacKenzie, D. F., 1970.21
McKerrow, Ronald B., 1931.12;
    1935.10; 1974.19
MacKichan, L. A. L., 1961.17
Mackintosh, Iain, 1973.18
McManaway, James G., 1951.22;
    1962.13; 1969.8
McMillin, Harvey Scott, Jr.,
    1965.12; 1968.26; 1972.19;
    1976.16
McNeir, Waldo F., 1941.4; 1962.14
Magic, 1927.22, 24; 1949.12;
    1956.30; 1964.12
Maginnis, James P., 1911.2
Mags, John, 1970.4
Maguo, Alessandro, 1964.8
Main, William W., 1957.11
Maldon, 1907.6-9
Malone, Edmond, 1790.1-2; 1794.1;
    1799.2; 1800.1; 1813.4;
    1821.1; 1839.1; 1875.1;
    1901.3; 1917.2-3; 1925.1, 18;
    1950.15; 1968.33; 1978.17
Manifold, John Streeter, 1956.23
Manly, John Matthews, 1910.12;
    1919.12; 1932.10; 1934.10;
    1949.10; 1950.13
Manning, Thomas John, 1972.18
Manningham, John, 1868.1
Mantzius, Karl, 1901.4; 1904.9;
    1937.6
Marcham, Frank, 1925.15; 1926.8
Marder, Louis, 1960.12; 1978.17
Marker, Lisa-Lone, 1970.20
Markham, Gervase, 1910.21
Markland, Murray F., 1969.7
Markward, William Bradley
    1953.15

Marlowe, Christopher, 1951.6;
    1964.27, 38; 1969.18, 39;
    1972.28, 35; 1974.7;
    1977.27; 1979.10, 31
Marshall, Wilhelm, 1928.11
Marston, John, 1977.27;
    1979.21, 30
Martin, R. L., 1921.5
Martin, William, 1909.4, 19–21,
    28; 1910.13–14, 17; 1915.9,
    16–19, 23
Martinelli, Drusiano, 1929.15
Masques, 1848.1; 1902.2;
    1903.5; 1904.1; 1909.23;
    1912.22–23; 1913.16;
    1916.15; 1920.18; 1921.9;
    1922.5; 1923.1; 1924.4,
    10–11; 1925.17; 1926.10;
    1934.14; 1935.9, 11–12;
    1936.9; 1937.7–8; 1940.8;
    1947.7–8; 1950.17; 1951.20;
    1952.6, 19, 21; 1953.24,
    28; 1954.5; 1956.12, 21,
    33; 1957.2; 1958.9, 20–21,
    23; 1959.12; 1962.13;
    1964.6, 24; 1967.2; 1968.28;
    1969.20; 1970.22; 1973.2,
    16, 21, 30; 1975.31; 1976.6,
    17, 18; 1977.24, 28; 1978.6;
    1979.20, 29
Massinger, Philip, 1927.18
Master of the Revels, 1836.1;
    1847.2; 1849.3; 1870.3;
    1886.2; 1906.2; 1908.6, 9;
    1910.7; 1913.4; 1916.15;
    1917.2; 1919.9, 1925.15;
    1926.8, 10; 1929.16;
    1933.3; 1947.2; 1951.9;
    1957.2–4; 1961.18; 1966.9;
    1972.16; 1973.3; 1974.11;
    1977.7; 1978.27
Matson, Marshall Y., 1967.6
Mattingly, Althea Smith,
    1954.16
Mead, Robert Smith, 1952.13
Meadley, T. D., 1953.17
Meagher, John C., 1973.19
Medici, Guilio de, 1969.7

Mehl, Dieter, 1964.29; 1966.13
Meissner, Johannes, 1884.4–5
Menius, Freidrich, 1939.3;
    1941.7
Mepham, William A., 1934.11–13;
    1937.6
Merchant, William Moelwyn,
    1956.24; 1959.15
Merzlak, Anthony George,
    1975.23
Messalina Print, 1908.1;
    1909.24; 1911.1; 1948.4
Metz, G. Harold, 1977.17
Meyer, C. F., 1902.6
Meymott, Joseph, 1887.8
Middle Temple, 1868.1; 1971.10
Middleton, Thomas, 1920.20
Mildmay, Sir Humphrey, 1938.3
Miles, Bernard, 1954.18
Miles, Theodore, 1942.4
Mill, Anna Jean, 1931.13
Miller, William E., 1959.16;
    1964.30
Mills, A. D., 1977.18
Mills, L. J., 1959.17
Milton, John, 1961.17
Mirabella, Bella Maryanne,
    1979.21
Mitchell, Lee, 1937.7; 1941.6;
    1947.6; 1948.8; 1949.12
Mithal, H. S. D., 1958.13;
    1959.3; 1960.13
Möhring, Hans, 1953.18
Mönkemeyer, Paul, 1905.3;
    1933.1
Montanus, Joannes Ferrarius,
    1972.20
Montgomery, Roy F., 1954.19
Moody, Dorothy Belle, 1938.7
Moore, John Robert, 1929.10
Morgan, Edmund S., 1966.14
Moritz, Landgraf, 1936.12
Morseberger, Robert E.,
    1974.20
Moryson, Fynes, 1904.4; 1907.14
Motter, Thomas Hubbard Vail,
    1929.11
Moynes, Jon Craig, 1978.18

Mulcaster, Richard, 1909.22; 1943.3; 1970.5; 1972.6; 1974.10
Mulholland, P. A., 1977.19
Müller, C., 1910.14
Müller-Bellinghausen, Anton, 1955.15-16
Mullin, Donald C., 1967.7; 1970.22
Mumming, 1916.15
Munday, Anthony, 1849.2; 1928.17
Mundy, John, 1961.8
Murad, Orlene, 1977.20; 1978.18
Murphy, J. L., 1977.21
Murray, John Tucker, 1905.4; 1910.15; 1912.2; 1920.30; 1929.6; 1936.7; 1954.23; 1968.32
Musgrave, Sir William, 1925.19-20
Music, 1845.4; 1886.6; 1908.14; 1909.6; 1910.14; 1913.2; 1914.2; 1920.19; 1922.5; 1923.16; 1927.15, 24; 1929.10; 1931.7; 1933.4; 1935.4; 1947.7; 1950.3; 1951.21; 1952.22; 1953.29; 1954.5, 17; 1955.3, 11; 1956.7-9, 23, 33; 1957.5; 1958.7; 1959.4; 1960.11; 1961.8, 24; 1963.11; 1965.3, 5, 10; 1967.3, 6; 1968.11, 19, 25, 35; 1972.27; 1973.2, 28; 1974.9; 1976.14; 1978.5
Mutschmann, Heinrich, 1950.5

Nabbes, Thomas, 1975.19
Nagler, Alois M., 1956.25; 1958.14; 1972.17
Nairn, J. Arbuthnot, 1914.18
Naogeorgus, Thomas, 1972.21
Nashe, Thomas, 1968.10
Neill, Michael, 1978.20
Neundorff, Bernard, 1910.16
Newington Butts Playhouse, 1888.11; 1894.4; 1904.9; 1970.15; 1971.4; 1979.22
Newman, Philip P., 1888.11
Newport, Edward, 1951.14

Nichols, John Gough, 1788.1; 1805.1; 1823.1; 1828.1; 1837.2; 1848.2; 1918.4
Nicholson, Brinsley, 1882.4; 1892.3
Nicolini, Francis, 1954.8
Nicoll, Allardyce, 1925.16; 1935.11; 1936.19; 1937.8; 1948.9-10; 1959.18; 1961.24
Niemeyer, Christian Bernard, 1979.22
Noble, Richard, 1927.15; 1928.6, 12
Noh, 1961.23
Norberg, Lars, 1955.17
Norman, William, 1914.19
Nosworthy, J. M., 1968.27; 1977.22
Nungezer, Edwin, 1927.16; 1929.12; 1959.21

O'Donnell, C. Patrick, Jr., 1973.20
Office of Works, 1975.31
Onions, Charles Talbut, 1916.1, 14-15; 1950.1, 16-17
Orbison, Tucker, 1977.21
Ordish, T. Fairman, 1885.6-10; 1886.4-8; 1887.5-7; 1894.2; 1899.2; 1908.16; 1971.13
Orgel, Stephen, 1968.28; 1973.10, 21; 1975.24
Orrell, John, 1976.17-18; 1977.24-25; 1979.23-26
Orsini, Napoleone, 1946.5
Ostler, William, 1933.5
Overall, H. C., 1878.2
Overall, William Henry, 1878.2
Oxford, Earl of. See de Vere, Edward, Earl of Oxford
Oxford University, 1907.2; 1909.7; 1933.8; 1948.13; 1959.1, 17; 1972.18; 1974.3
Oxford's Men, 1970.15
Ozaki, Makoto, 1975.25

Pafford, J. H. P., 1959.19; 1977.26
Paget, Alfred Henry, 1891.2-3

Palme, Per, 1956.26, 1957.12
Palmer, Frank, 1913.4
Palumbo, Ronald J., 1976.19
Paradise, N. Burton, 1931.14; 1933.9
Paris Garden. See Swan Playhouse
Parrott, Thomas Marc, 1943.6; 1958.15
Parry, Graham, 1978.21
Pascal, Roy, 1940.9; 1941.7
Patent Rolls, 1909.9
Paterson, Morton, 1961.18
Patterson, Remington Perrigo, 1957.13
Paul's Boys, 1814.1; 1889.6; 1912.7; 1914.2; 1915.5; 1926.6; 1943.7; 1951.4; 1952.3; 1960.4; 1962.1, 20; 1966.10; 1967.6, 10; 1968.14, 21; 1970.10, 19; 1971.8, 14; 1972.6; 1975.22; 1977.14; 1978.10
Pavy, Salathiel [Salmon?], 1914.18; 1942.2
Peake, Robert, 1959.14
Peckham, Morse, 1968.34
Peele, George, 1961.8
Peerson, Martin, 1958.7
Peet, Alice Lida, 1961.19
Pembroke's Men, 1911.28; 1921.8; 1950.20; 1960.4; 1972.19; 1974.14, 21; 1976.16
Penshurst, 1979.27
Penniman, Josiah Harmar, 1895.2; 1897.2
Penninger, Frieda Elaine, 1976.20
Percy, Eustace, 1907.17
Percy, William, 1913.1; 1914.20
Periaktoi, 1959.16; 1964.30
Petit, J. B., 1968.29
Phelps, Wayne H., 1979.27
Phillips, Augustine, 1951.27
Phoenix Playhouse, 1860.1; 1882.2; 1885.1-3; 1887.5; 1904.9; 1905.2; 1921.14; 1928.15; 1938.3; 1953.15; 1963.11; 1965.9; 1966.9; 1968.2; 1972.12; 1973.18, 28; 1977.25, 31, 34

Pilch, Leo, 1911.21
Pinciss, G. M., 1970.23; 1974.21
Planche, James Robinson, 1848.1
Platter, Thomas, 1899.1; 1929.13, 1937.9; 1956.29; 1962.18
Plomer, Henry R., 1906.8
Poel, William, 1913.14; 1916.11; 1963.7; 1966.23
Pokorný, Jaroslav, 1955.18
Pollard, Alfred W., 1919.10, 13-16, 18, 21-22
Pollock, Arthur, 1915.20; 1916.12
Porter, Charlotte, 1915.21-22; 1916.13
Powell, Wilford, 1892.2
Presley, Horton Edward, 1966.15
Price, Joseph G., 1975.4, 7
Prince Charles's Men, 1849.9; 1978.2
Prindle, Roderic Marvin, 1977.27
Prior, Moody E., 1951.23
Private Playhouses, 1874.1; 1875.1; 1908.14; 1912.17; 1916.10; 1920.19; 1921.9, 15; 1923.2; 1930.5; 1934.10; 1942.4; 1952.8; 1953.20; 1955.23; 1958.12; 1959.2; 1964.6; 1965.13; 1967.3-4; 1968.2, 30; 1972.24, 32; 1978.29. See also the names of individual playhouses, such as Blackfriars, Phoenix, Salisbury Court, Whitefriars
Privy Council, 1907.17; 1911.9; 1912.21; 1924.1; 1970.31; 1971.9
Proudfoot, G. R., 1977.7, 28
Prouty, Charles Tyler, 1961.18, 20, 22, 25
Provincial Companies, 1905.4; 1910.15; 1920.20; 1922.11; 1941.13; 1942.8; 1953.19; 1959.27; 1961.7; 1965.6; 1975.1; 1977.4, 11, 13, 21, 26
Provincial Tours, 1887.4; 1905.4; 1909.10; 1919.10, 13-16, 21-22; 1920.16, 30-31; 1922.11; 1927.7, 24; 1931.15; 1933.10; 1936.7; 1937.6; 1941.11, 13; 1953.3; 1954.23;

1959.27; 1961.7; 1965.6;
1973.4; 1976.11; 1977.6;
1979.22
Prynne, William, 1910.26; 1912.5;
1917.10; 1920.6; 1923.18;
1928.8; 1928.19; 1943.4;
1972.22
Public Record Office, 1889.3;
1909.16, 18, 34; 1910.21-25;
1911.7, 29; 1925.20; 1928.3,
7; 1929.14; 1930.2; 1931.2;
1942.8; 1943.7; 1954.18;
1958.7; 1966.4; 1971.9;
1972.29; 1978.2; 1979.2
Purdom, C. B., 1950.14; 1951.24
Puritan Opposition to the Stage,
1873.1; 1886.10; 1889.5;
1903.8-9; 1907.2; 1908.9;
1910.26; 1912.5; 1916.14, 17-
18; 1920.6; 1921.6; 1923.18;
1930.10; 1931.14; 1934.14;
1942.5-6; 1953.17; 1954.27;
1957.2; 1965.3; 1966.14;
1972.1-5, 8-10, 13, 20-23, 26,
31; 1975.8, 25
Putzel, Rosamund. 1960.14

Queen Anne's Men, 1849.9; 1947.9;
1954.25
Queen Elizabeth, 1788.1; 1805.1;
1838.1; 1912.22; 1974.8
Queen Elizabeth's Men, 1911.8;
1926.1; 1939.4; 1956.22;
1970.23; 1974.21; 1976.16
Queen Henrietta's Men, 1968.15
Queen Jane's Men, 1914.22
Queen Mary, 1905.9
Queen's Revels, 1912.2; 1926.6;
1927.3; 1968.24
Quinn, Seabury Grandin, Jr.,
1958.16

R., 1938.8
Race, Sydney, 1955.19; 1958.17
Rainolds, John, 1907.2; 1910.26;
1916.17-18; 1954.27; 1972.23;
1974.3
Raleigh, Walter A., 1916.1, 14-15;
1950.1, 16-17
Rankin, George, 1870.4

Rankins, William, 1910.26; 1972.3
Rannie, David Watson, 1926.9
Ravn, Vilhelm Carl, 1906.9
Rawlidge, Richard, 1920.6
Rear Stage. See Discovery Space
Reardon, James Purcell, 1847.1;
1849.8
Red Bull Playhouse, 1885.1-4;
1886.8; 1904.9; 1909.34;
1914.12, 19; 1916.10; 1921.14;
1933.6; 1940.10; 1942.7;
1954.25; 1962.12; 1963.6;
1966.9
Reese, Georg Hermann, 1911.22
Reese, M. M., 1958.18; 1965.13
Remembrancia, 1878.2; 1907.5;
1956.35
Rendle, William, 1878.3-4; 1885.9,
12-15; 1887.8; 1888.10-11;
1890.3; 1909.3; 1910.13
Renwick, William Lindsay, 1935.12
Revels Accounts, 1842.1; 1909.12;
1911.15-18, 26-28; 1912.13-
14, 20; 1913.8; 1920.12-13,
26; 1922.8; 1924.9; 1925.20;
1930.9; 1964.21; 1966.9
Revels Office. See Master of the
Revels
Reyher, Paul, 1909.23
Reynolds, George Fullmer, 1905.5-
8; 1906.7; 1907.4, 18;
1908.16; 1911.23; 1914.20;
1919.17; 1920.1; 1930.8;
1933.6; 1940.10; 1941.8;
1949.13-14; 1951.25; 1953.9;
1956.27; 1962.15; 1963.12;
1964.27; 1967.8; 1972.17;
1975.30; 1977.14
Rhenanus, Johannes, 1931.10
Rhodes, Ernest Lloyd, 1959.20;
1976.21
Rhodes, R. Crompton, 1921.12-13;
1922.7
Ribner, Irving, 1966.16; 1969.9;
1978.22
Rice, John, 1913.18
Richards, Kenneth R., 1968.30;
1977.29-30
Richey, Dorothy, 1951.26
Richter, Bodo L. O., 1966.17

Rickert, Robert Turnham, 1958.19;
    1961.12-13; 1964.31; 1978.17
Riddell, James A., 1970.24
Riewald, J. G., 1959.21; 1960.15
Riffe, Nancy Lee, 1962.16
Rimbault, Edward Francis, 1846.2;
    1872.1; 1920.11
Ringler, William A., 1942.5-6;
    1968.31
Roberts, J. R. H., 1950.15
Robertson, Jean, 1954.20; 1956.28;
    1959.22; 1973.22
Robinson, Richard, 1845.1
Rollins, Hyder E., 1921.14;
    1923.19
Rose Playhouse, 1813.3; 1885.7,
    15; 1888.11; 1894.4; 1903.10;
    1904.9; 1908.11; 1910.17;
    1914.20; 1924.8; 1950.15;
    1957.13; 1959.20; 1964.21;
    1965.12; 1971.1, 12; 1974.13;
    1976.21; 1979.9, 33
Rosenberg, Marvin, 1954.21-22
Rosenfeld, Sybil M., 1954.23;
    1955.20; 1957.14; 1962.17
Ross, Lawrence J., 1961.21; 1963.9
Rosseter's Porter's Hall, 1956.35
Rothwell, William Francis, Jr.,
    1953.20; 1955.21; 1959.23
Rowan, D. F., 1967.9-10; 1970.25-
    27; 1972.24-25; 1975.26
Rowley, Samuel, 1966.23; 1977.4
Roxana Print, 1911.1; 1948.4
Royal Entries, 1902.5; 1918.4;
    1951.33; 1956.34; 1968.6-7;
    1970.2; 1971.3; 1973.23, 25;
    1974.10; 1975.24; 1978.3, 18
Royal Processions. 1788.1;
    1805.1; 1828.1; 1837.2;
    1951.33; 1971.3; 1973.25;
    1975.24
Royal Progresses, 1788.1; 1805.1;
    1828.1; 1855.1; 1910.14;
    1911.12; 1924.6; 1934.6;
    1951.33; 1953.12; 1960.2;
    1971.3; 1973.25; 1974.9;
    1975.24; 1978.18
Russell, Douglas A., 1958.20
Rye, William Brenchley, 1865.2

Sabol, Andrew Joseph. 1947.7
Sack, Marie, 1928.13
St. Giles, Cripplegate, 1929.6
St. Paul's, Playhouse at, 1902.4;
    1909.17; 1915.5; 1962.20;
    1966.10; 1968.8, 14; 1970.19,
    28; 1971.13; 1978.11
Salgado, Gamini, 1975.27
Salingar, L. G., 1968.32
Salisbury, Earl of, 1969.21
Salisbury Court Playhouse, 1813.2;
    1849.4; 1882.2; 1887.6;
    1904.9; 1912.2; 1916.1;
    1925.2; 1928.7; 1929.8;
    1952.2; 1956.12; 1957.14;
    1965.10; 1966.9; 1968.2, 15;
    1972.12; 1977.2-3; 1979.32
Salomon, Brownell, 1972.26
Salvetti, Amerigo, 1976.17; 1979.23
Salvianus, 1972.27
Sampson, George, 1935.13;
    1936.3, 20
Samuelson, David A., 1979.6
Samwell, Richard, 1970.4
Sanders, Norman, 1964.28
Sands, William, 1977.1
Sanvic, Romain. See Smet, Robert
    de
Saracen's Head Inn, 1971.5
Sarlos, Robert K., 1961.22
Saunders, F. R., 1952.14
Saunders, J. W., 1954.24; 1955.22;
    1960.16; 1974.26
Savage, Jerome, 1970.15
Savoy, Agent of, 1972.24; 1979.26
Schaar, Claes, 1966.18, 21
Schanzer, Ernest, 1956.29;
    1968.33
Schelling, Felix E., 1902.7;
    1904.10-11; 1908.16; 1911.24;
    1935.14
Schless, Howard H., 1952.15
Schneiderman, Robert Ivan, 1956.30
Schoenbaum, Samuel, 1964.13;
    1979.28
Schoenherr, Douglas Edgar, 1973.23
Schücking, Levin L., 1931.6;
    1937.3; 1941.9
Schuman, Samuel, 1969.11

Scouten, E. H., 1968.34
Scragg, Leah, 1973.24
Seh, L. H., 1935.15
Seltzer, Daniel, 1959.24;
    1966.19
Semper, I. J., 1952.16-17
Shady, Raymond C., 1977.31.
Shakespeare Association, 1927.17
Shakespeare, William, 1868.1;
    1891.1; 1902.3; 1909.32;
    1910.20-25; 1911.21; 1912.22;
    1915.1, 13; 1916.11, 13-14;
    1918.3; 1919.13-16, 21-22;
    1920.18, 20, 22, 25, 28, 30-
    31; 1921.12-13; 1925.21;
    1927.4-5, 8-11, 14-15, 17, 19;
    1929.10; 1930.7-8; 1931.15-
    16; 1932.8; 1933.8; 1934.7,
    14; 1936.9-10, 14-20; 1940.3,
    5-6; 1946.3; 1950.19-20;
    1951.6, 14; 1953.7; 1961.11,
    21, 26; 1964.6, 17, 19, 23,
    26-28, 35-36; 1974.21-22, 25;
    1977.27; 1978.7; 1979.6, 15,
    21-22, 28
Shapiro, I. A., 1948.11; 1949.15;
    1966.20; 1967.1, 17
Shapiro, Michael, 1967.10;
    1968.35; 1969.12; 1970.28;
    1971.14-15; 1975.28; 1977.32
Sharpe, Robert Boies, 1928.14;
    1935.16
Sharpham, Edward, 1935.8
Shaw, Catherine M., 1979.29
Shaw, John, 1967.11; 1974.22
Shaw, Robert, 1977.4
Sherborne, 1953.3; 1977.18
Shibata, Toshihiko, 1977.33
Shield, H. A., 1951.27
Shirley, Frances Ann, 1960.17;
    1963.13
Shirley, Henry, 1928.1; 1929.4
Shirley, James, 1944.8; 1973.30;
    1977.34
Shoap, Jeffrey, 1979.30
Shoreditch, 1978.1; 1979.2-4, 8,
    16-17, 33
Sidney, Sir Philip, 1844.1;
    1958.13; 1959.3; 1979.27
Simmons, J. L., 1972.28
Simpson, Percy, 1916.14-15;
    1924.10; 1950.16-17

Simpson, William Sparrow, 1889.6
Simpson's Men, 1942.8
Sincklo, John, 1925.7
Sisson, Charles Jasper, 1921.15;
    1927.18; 1929.14; 1933.7, 9;
    1934.14; 1936.21; 1940.11;
    1942.7-8; 1943.7; 1954.25;
    1960.18-19; 1970.4; 1972.29
Sjögren, Gunnar, 1969.13
Skelton, Tom, 1961.14
Skemp, Arthur R., 1909.24
Skopnik, Günter, 1938.9
Skura, Meridith Anne, 1971.17
Slover, George W., 1968.36
Sly, William, 1946.3
Small, George Wilson, 1935.17
Smeath, Frances Ann, 1979.31
Smet, Robert de, 1955.23
Smith, Duncan Bruce, 1978.23
Smith, G. C. Moore, 1923.20
Smith, Gordon Ross, 1963.14
Smith, Hal H., 1962.18
Smith, Irwin, 1951.28; 1952.18;
    1956.31-32; 1958.21; 1961.25;
    1964.22, 32; 1966.11; 1967.12;
    1970.18; 1972.17; 1973.31
Smith, James L., 1966.21
Smith, Mary E., 1976.22; 1978.24
Smith, Milton, 1931.15
Smith, Warren D., 1948.12;
    1951.29; 1953.21-22; 1975.29
Smith, William Henry, 1857.1
Smith, Winifred, 1908.17; 1912.19;
    1929.15
Snyder, Frederick E., 1973.25
Soens, Adolph E., 1969.14
Solem, Delmar E., 1953.23
Somerset House. See Court Per-
    formances
Somerset, John Alan Beaufort,
    1966.22-23
Sound Effects, 1924.5; 1927.14;
    1945.3; 1947.6; 1950.3;
    1953.15; 1960.17; 1963.13;
    1965.5; 1972.27
Southern, Richard, 1939.7;
    1947.8; 1952.19-20; 1953.24;
    1954.1, 11, 15, 26; 1958.11;
    1959.25; 1960.20; 1961.23,
    25; 1963.15; 1964.22, 33-34;
    1968.37; 1970.13; 1972.17;
    1973.20

Southwark, 1878.3-4; 1903.10;
  1933.11
Spencer, M. Lyle, 1911.25
Spencer, T. J. B., 1970.29
Spens, J., 1919.5, 18
Spinchorn, Evert, 1969.15
Spingarn, Joel Elias, 1909.11;
  1957.7; 1963.3
Spinucci, Pietro, 1973.27
Sprague, Arthur Colby, 1935.18;
  1945.3; 1953.25; 1966.24
Stage Directions, 1904.5; 1905.3;
  1907.10, 20; 1910.16; 1911.20-
  21; 1916.13; 1920.18, 25;
  1921.12-13; 1927.13, 18;
  1930.7; 1935.10; 1938.1, 7;
  1940.5; 1947.6; 1952.10;
  1953.22; 1959.26; 1962.22;
  1964.28, 38; 1965.5, 11;
  1966.18, 21; 1971.10; 1974.5,
  22; 1975.5, 9, 15; 1976.12
Staging, 1885.10; 1903.2; 1905.8;
  1906.3; 1907.18-20; 1909.12;
  1910.5; 1911.23; 1912.3, 16;
  1913.1; 1914.20; 1916.1, 6,
  13, 16; 1919.17; 1921.13;
  1923.2; 1927.1, 5, 8, 13-14,
  21-22; 1934.14; 1935.13;
  1936.1, 9-10, 15; 1938.1;
  1940.6, 9-10; 1941.6-7;
  1942.3; 1943.1; 1945.2;
  1947.8; 1948.6-7; 1950.18-19;
  1951.5, 10; 1952.2; 1953.4,
  11, 15, 28; 1954.17, 24;
  1955.5, 28; 1956.27, 30-31;
  1957.8, 14, 16; 1959.8-9,
  18, 20, 23, 26, 28; 1960.16;
  1961.1-2, 21, 27; 1962.2,
  5-6, 9, 14-15, 19, 21-22;
  1963.9, 11; 1964.12, 14, 21,
  28, 32, 38; 1965.3, 9, 11-12,
  15; 1966.6, 10-11, 19;
  1967.6, 9, 11, 16; 1968.8,
  26; 1969.9, 14; 1970.10, 13,
  22, 25; 1971.10; 1972.12, 18,
  28-29; 1972.30; 1973.25, 28;
  1974.1, 13, 22-24, 26; 1975.7,
  9-10, 15, 26, 29-30; 1976.22,
  25; 1977.14, 34; 1978.8, 11,
  28-29; 1979.32

Stamm, Rudolf, 1951.30; 1955.24;
  1959.26; 1962.19
Stamps, Alfred Edward, 1930.9
Star, Leonie Rachel, 1972.30;
  1974.21; 1975.30; 1976.23-24;
  1978.25
Steele, Mary Susan, 1924.11;
  1926.10-11
Steevens, George, 1968.33
Stevens, David, 1973.28; 1977.34;
  1979.32
Stevens, Denis, 1956.33, 1973.29
Stevens, John E., 1961.24
Stevenson, Allen H., 1944.8
Stewart, Alan, 1917.10
Stinson, James, 1961.25
Stolzenbach, Conrad, 1962.20
Stone, Lawrence, 1959.27
Stopes, Charlotte Carmichael,
  1892.4; 1900.3; 1905.9;
  1907.19, 25-27; 1910.17-20;
  1911.26-28; 1912.20-21;
  1913.8, 15; 1914.13, 21-23;
  1915.6, 16, 23; 1920.12-13,
  26; 1924.9; 1925.1; 1931.12;
  1979.2
Stratman, Carl J., 1948.13
Street, Peter, 1952.5, 18;
  1979.25
Streitberger, W. R., 1978.27
Stribrný, Zdenek, 1966.12
Strong, Roy, 1973.10, 21
Strunk, William, Jr., 1917.11;
  1920.3
Stubbes, Philip, 1847.1; 1849.8;
  1910.26; 1912.5; 1928.10;
  1954.27; 1972.31
Stunz, Arthur Nesbitt, 1939.8
Sturman, Betta, 1947.9
Styan, J. L., 1959.28; 1967.13
Suffolk, 1970.6; 1977.6
Suga, Yasuo, 1963.16-17
Sullivan, Mary, 1912.22; 1913.16
Summerson, Sir John Newenham,
  1953.26; 1955.25; 1958.22;
  1963.18; 1969.16; 1970.30;
  1977.35
Swan Playhouse, 1813.3; 1858.1;
  1885.11, 13-14; 1894.4;
  1910.17; 1911.29; 1912.10;

1913.13; 1950.15; 1951.7;
1952.20; 1962.21; 1963.20;
1964.18, 31; 1966.9, 25;
1967.9; 1968.18; 1971.4, 12;
1972.15; 1973.16; 1974.13;
1975.15; 1978.16; 1979.5, 22
-DeWitt Sketch, 1881.1, 4, 10,
12; 1897.1; 1902.1; 1903.6;
1904.9; 1906.6; 1907.20;
1908.1, 3, 10; 1909.3; 1911.1;
1916.1-2; 1920.1; 1922.7;
1924.2; 1931.4; 1935.17;
1940.9; 1944.1; 1948.4, 9;
1950.9, 18; 1951.7; 1952.1;
1954.1, 15, 26; 1955.4;
1956.15; 1957.8-9; 1959.25;
1960.9; 1961.27; 1964.14, 18,
33; 1965.12; 1967.9, 14, 19;
1970.21, 27; 1972.14, 24;
1975.15
Swinney, Donald H., 1953.27
Symmes, Harold S., 1903.7
Symonds, E. M., 1928.15

T., S. A., 1921.11
T., S. W., 1870.5
T.-D., G., 1925.17
Tannenbaum, Samuel A., 1928.16;
1929.3
Tarlton, Richard, 1844.3; 1882.2;
1904.9; 1920.21; 1937.5;
1938.2; 1941.2; 1950.5;
1954.4; 1969.2; 1975.21
Tarras. See Upper Acting Area
Tatarkiewicz, W., 1965.14
Tathum, John, 1977.21
Taylor, Alison, 1967.14
Taylor, Dick Jr., 1958.23
Taylor, George C., 1930.10
Teagarden, Jack E., 1957.15
Teague, Frances, 1978.27
Teatro Olimpico, 1961.23
Thaler, Alwin, 1918.2-3; 1919.19;
1920.27-30; 1921.8, 16-17;
1922.9-11; 1931.16; 1932.11;
1941.10-13; 1964.28
Theatre Playhouse, 1798.1; 1849.1;
1885.6, 11; 1887.1; 1894.4;
1904.9; 1909.25-27; 1910.19;
1913.15, 19; 1914.18, 21, 23;
1915.2; 1916.1; 1917.5;

1928.10; 1944.3; 1952.18;
1954.19; 1956.14; 1959.15;
1963.21; 1964.7, 11; 1966.9;
1971.4; 1973.26; 1979.2-4,
8, 16, 22, 33
Thompson, Elbert Nevius Sebring,
1903.8-9
Thoresbie, William, 1951.14
Thornberry, Richard Thayer,
1964.35
Thorndike, Ashley Horace,
1913.17; 1916.16; 1972.17
Tieck, Ludwig, 1917.9; 1959.7;
1961.25
Tillotson, Geoffrey, 1933.8
Tilting, 1958.23
Tittman, Julius, 1880.1
Tomlins, Thomas Edlyne, 1844.5;
1847.2; 1849.9
Trace, Arthur Storrey, Jr.,
1954.27
Trafford, Sir Edmund, 1931.16
Trautmann, Karl, 1886.9; 1887.11-
12
Tree, Herbert Beerbohm, 1909.19,
28
Trevell, William, 1930.2-3
Triebel, L. A., 1950.18
Turner, Celeste, 1928.17
Turner, Olga, 1949.16
Turner, Robert Y., 1964.36
Tweedie, Eleanor M., 1976.25
Tylney, Edmund, 1847.2
Tyson, William, 1847.3

Ungerer, Gustav, 1961.26
Unwin, George, 1909.29; 1925.18;
1938.10; 1963.19
Upper Acting Area, 1903.2;
1907.4, 20; 1908.10, 15, 24;
1912.18; 1916.1, 5, 13;
1921.5; 1922.7; 1924.2, 12;
1927.5, 8; 1929.3; 1933.4;
1935.5; 1936.1, 3, 5, 10, 15;
1940.6; 1942.1; 1944.7;
1948.6; 1949.3; 1951.10, 25;
1952.2; 1953.9, 15; 1954.13-
14, 17; 1955.4; 1956.1, 15;
1957.8; 1958.1, 14; 1959.25;
1960.16; 1961.27; 1962.2, 14;
1963.1, 11; 1964.32, 38;

1965.12; 1966.10-11; 1968.17;
1970.13; 1971.10; 1972.18;
1973.11, 16, 28; 1975.15;
1976.21; 1978.29; 1979.32
Upper Stage. See Upper Acting
Area
Ure, Peter, 1951.31

Variety Entertainments, 1927.20,
22-24; 1928.21-22; 1931.17
Vatke, Theodor, 1886.10
Velz, John W., 1969.8
Venezky, Alice S., 1951.32-33
Vestiarian Controversy, 1975.8
Views of London, 1884.3; 1902.1;
1922.4; 1924.3; 1933.10;
1948.11; 1949.15; 1952.1;
1954.15; 1961.25; 1964.10;
1972.14; 1973.11; 1978.21
Visser, Colin, 1978.29
Viswanathan, S., 1974.24

W., T., 1972.8
Waith, Eugene M., 1962.2
Walker, Alice, 1933.9; 1934.15
Walker, John Anthony, 1952.21
Wallace, Charles William,
1906.10-11; 1908.18; 1909.5,
14, 18-19, 21, 28, 30-34;
1910.1, 21-25; 1911.4, 29;
1912.23; 1913.15, 18-19;
1914.1, 8, 13, 17, 24-25;
1915.14; 1925.1; 1961.22;
1968.15; 1977.2; 1978.2;
1979.2
Waller, W. R., 1910.5, 12, 26;
1919.3, 12, 20; 1932.3, 10,
12; 1934.1, 10, 20; 1949.4,
10, 17; 1950.6, 13, 21
Walton, Charles E., 1953.28
War of the Theatres, 1896.2;
1897.2; 1923.7; 1928.14;
1935.16; 1952.8; 1956.14;
1968.14
Ward, A. W., 1910.5, 12, 26;
1919.3, 12, 20; 1932.3, 10,
12; 1934.1, 10, 20; 1949.4,
10, 17; 1950.6, 13, 21
Ward, Bernard Mordaunt, 1929.16;
1933.10

Warner, Sir George Frederic,
1881.4
Watkins, Ronald, 1946.6; 1947.10;
1950.19
Watson, George, 1957.16; 1964.25
Webb, John, 1925.14; 1959.14;
1969.10
Wegener, Richard, 1907.20;
1909.24
Weiner, Albert B., 1961.27;
1962.22
Weixlman, Joseph, 1974.26
Wells, Stanley, 1972.29
Wentersdorf, Karl, 1950.5, 20
Wertheim, Albert, 1973.30
Westcott, Sebastian, 1912.7;
1915.5; 1943.3, 7; 1951.4;
1952.3; 1961.8; 1970.19;
1975.22
Whalley, Joyce I., 1966.25
Whanslaw, Harry William, 1924.12
Wheatley, Henry B., 1888.12
White, Anne Terry, 1955.26
White, Beatrice, 1934.16
White, Eric Walter, 1952.22
Whitefriars Playhouse, 1813.2;
1849.4; 1887.7; 1888.8;
1912.1-2; 1922.3; 1930.2-3;
1935.6; 1956.35
Whitehall. See Court Performances
Whitmarsh-Knight, David, 1973.31
Whitty, John Christopher, 1971.17
Wickham, Glynne, 1956.34; 1959.29;
1962.9; 1963.20; 1964.14, 37-
38; 1967.15; 1968.32, 38;
1969.17-20; 1970.31; 1972.17,
32; 1973.32; 1976.4; 1978.28;
1979.33
Wikland, Eric, 1962.23; 1971.18
Wilkinson, Robert, 1825.1;
1919.11
Williams, Clare, 1937.9
Williams, Iolo A., 1933.11
Williams, Patrick R., 1978.30
Williams, S. H., 1957.17
Willoughby, Edwin Elliot, 1928.18
Wilson, Edward M., 1949.16
Wilson, Frank Percy, 1926.12;
1955.27-29; 1956.35; 1963.21;
1975.31
Wilson, Jack, 1846.2

Wilson, John Dover, 1908.19;
1910.26; 1919.10, 14–16, 20–
22; 1920.16, 31; 1927.19;
1928.8, 19; 1932.12; 1934.17;
1947.11; 1948.14; 1949.17;
1950.21
Wilson, Robert, 1926.1; 1958.13;
1959.3
Wilson, William, 1919.1
Winninghof, Elisabeth, 1928.20
Withington, Robert, 1913.20;
1918.4; 1920.32
Wits Frontispiece, 1911.1; 1973.12
Wood, D. T. B., 1925.19–20
Woodfill, Walter L., 1953.29
Woodford, Thomas, 1922.3
Woodliffe, Oliver, 1970.4
Woolf, Arthur H., 1903.10
Worcester's Men, 1849.7
Wren, Robert Meriwether, 1965.15;
1967.16; 1969.21
Wright, George R., 1860.1; 1887.13
Wright, James, 1699.1; 1845.1;
1872.2; 1874.3; 1876.2;
1972.33

Wright, Louis Booker, 1926.13;
1927.20–24; 1928.20–21;
1931.17; 1958.24; 1961.28;
1963.22; 1966.26; 1969.22;
1922.34; 1979.34
Wright, Thomas, 1838.1
Wright, W. S., 1966.27
Wyatt, R. O., II, 1974.18
Wylie, Charles, 1875.1

Yarrow, David Alexander, 1973.33
Yates, Frances A., 1925.21;
1956.28; 1958.2; 1966.20, 28;
1967.1, 17; 1969.23; 1971.12;
1972.17; 1974.24; 1976.21
Yoh, Suk-Kee, 1969.24
Yorkshire, 1942.8
Young, Alan R., 1979.5, 35
Young, Karl, 1916.17–18
Young, William, 1889.7

Zucker, David Hard, 1968.39,
1972.35